PETER JACKSON

A Film-maker's Journey

PETER JACKSON
A Film-maker's Journey

* * *

Brian Sibley

HarperCollins*Entertainment*
An Imprint of HarperCollins*Publishers*

HarperCollins*Entertainment*
An Imprint of HarperCollins*Publishers*
77–85 Fulham Palace Road,
Hammersmith, London W6 8JB
www.harpercollins.co.uk

Published by HarperCollins*Entertainment* 2006
1 3 5 7 9 8 6 4 2

A catalogue record for this book is
available from the British Library

ISBN-13 978-0-00-717558-1
ISBN-10 0-00-717558-2

Set in Minion

Printed and bound in Italy by Lego SpA

CONTENTS

PICTURE CREDITS

HarperCollins*Publishers* would like to thank the following for providing photographs and for permission to reproduce copyright material.

While every effort has been made to trace the owners of copyright material reproduced herein, the publishers would like to apologise for any omissions and will be pleased to incorporate missing acknowledgements in any future correspondence.

Andrew Lesnie pages 525, 527, 538, 547; plate section two, page 6 (top): **Berliner Images** page 500; plate section two, page 5 (second from the bottom), 7 (top): *The Dominion Post* page 209: **Getty Images** page 518; plate section one, page 8 (bottom): **Jim Rygiel** page 517: **Newline Cinema** page 472; plate section two, page 5 (second from the top): **Pierre Vinet** page 411, 447, 470, 509, 536 (bottom); plate section one, page 7 (top), 8 top; plate section two, page 1, 3 (bottom): **Randall William Cook** page 523: **Rick McKay** page 532: **Trae Patton/*TV Guide*** plate section two, page 7 (bottom): **Victoria Sullivan** pages 420, 534, 536 (top), 539, 543, 550; plate section two, page 6 (bottom): **Wingnut Films Collection** pages 70, 71, 74, 82, 77, 75, 89, 80, 96, 79, 100, 125, 110, 113, 120, 116, 112, 122, 117, 118, 128, 137, 137, 132, 132, 132, 139, 144, 144, 147, 148, 148, 150; plate section one, page 3 (bottom)

All other photographs are from the author's personal collection.

PREFACE

'How on earth did this guy ever come to be making *The Lord of the Rings*?'

That is a question that has been asked many times over the past few years. The person asking it, on this occasion, is the person about whom it is *asked* – Peter Jackson…

'Most fans of *The Lord of the Rings*,' he says, 'are probably not that familiar with my earlier films, so they may have the impression that I popped up out of nowhere and was suddenly directing this huge movie-project. But, from my perspective, I certainly didn't pop up out of nowhere. If I had, I never would have been equipped to direct *The Lord of the Rings*!'

Peter Jackson is about to give me another interview for this book. Our conversations – scattered across five years – have taken place on movie-sets, in editing suites, via telephone from opposite ends of the earth and at opposite ends of the day, in his home in New Zealand and in various hotels during moments snatched between attending scoring sessions, giving media interviews and going to (or coming from) award ceremonies…

For this interview we are in London's Dorchester Hotel and Peter and his partner Fran Walsh are *en route* to what will turn out to be their grand-slam night at the Oscars.

We are having another conversation about this book and, specifically, how it should be described. Is it, for example, a 'biography'? Frankly, that is not a definition with which Peter is altogether easy: it smacks, perhaps, too much of ego, suggests a sense of self-importance that is not quite to his taste…

Certainly there must be biographical elements, but they ought to serve a specific end, which is to answer that question: 'How did this relatively unknown guy from New Zealand, whose previous career seems to have been predominantly concerned with making splatter-movies, end up directing a literary 'Holy Grail' like *The Lord of the Rings?*'

The short answer – the longer version will be found in the pages which follow – is that, throughout his childhood and adolescence, Peter Jackson was unwittingly auditioning to make *The Lord of the Rings*. His hobbies and interests – passionately, even obsessively, pursued – were consistently preparing the man for the task. And those preparations were to continue when he began his professional film-making career.

'It was,' he says, 'a hard slog to get as far as making *The Lord of the Rings* and it only happened because, for the ten years before, I had made movies and learnt enough about film politics to give me the skill base I needed to tackle this particular project. Ten years of film-making – if you count the little amateur ones I made as a child, *thirty years* of film-making. People may or may not have seen, or even *know* of, those films, but that is almost beside the point, because it was the experience of facing the often seemingly overwhelming odds involved in making them – creatively, technically, politically – that really equipped me to face the enormous challenges that were involved in filming *The Lord of the Rings*.'

Once that has been understood, the tale of the Kiwi who got to make a movie based on one of the most popular books in the world is less fluke than inevitability.

True, for every ambition there was a disappointment, for every dream, a nightmare. But one of Peter Jackson's commonly underestimated attributes is his pragmatism. Yes, he is a perfectionist, an idealist; but he is also a down-to-earth realist: someone who – for better or worse, and regardless of accolades or criticisms – sees life as it is and then does his level best to handle it in whatever way seems most desirable – but always with the proviso that if it doesn't work out, then it is time to re-think, to adapt and survive…

A combination of vision, talent, confidence, boundless enthusiasm and unswerving tenacity – together with a reasonable helping of sheer, unadulterated good luck – brought Peter Jackson to a point where he was directing the biggest, most ambitious film project in the history of cinema. And this then sustained him through the fourteen months of principal photography, during which that project – one film but at the same time *three* films – was brought to the screen.

'This book,' Peter said in one of our earliest conversations, 'should not be a mere re-run of the story people have read in the magazines and newspapers. Nor should it be just a "nuts-and-bolts" account of making three complex films. It must be a frank "insider" look into the workings and politics of film-making – both independently and within the Hollywood system.'

And, of course, to answer that question 'Why Peter Jackson?' along with other intriguing questions, not least among them: 'Why, having made the phenominally successful *The Lord of the Rings*, did he then decide to devote his energy to a remake of a 1930s movie about a giant gorilla?' and 'Why did it take him quite so long to get around to doing it?'

But that's more than enough about questions. Time for some answers...

Brian Sibley

PROLOGUE

Where is Peter Jackson?

'*Where is Peter Jackson?* That's what people are asking. It is 25 November 2003, and the Embassy Theatre in Wellington is re-opening its doors for the first time after a $4.66 million refurbishment that has been the price demanded by civic pride since New Zealand is to host the World Premiere of *The Return of the King*, the third and final part of the phenomenally successful movie trilogy, *The Lord of the Rings*.

That premiere is to take place at the Embassy in a week's time and a gigantic figure of the Witch-king astride his Nazgûl steed is perched on the roof in readiness to welcome a deputation of hobbits, dwarves, elves, warriors and wizards, not to mention the world's media and thousands of devoted *Rings* fans who are already converging on the city.

Wellington is gearing itself up for a celebration that will be unlike any other movie opening in the history of cinema. It is about a great deal more than just the picture that will be screened on the night of 1 December 2003. It is about a new sense of national identity, about a Kiwi – an idiosyncratic little fellow lacking the facile suavity usually associated with moviedom – who has taken on Hollywood at its own game, produced a cinematic phenomenon and, at the same time, made the world aware of New Zealand as somewhere more than just a place that has a famous rugby team and which exports quantities of butter and lamb.

On this particular night, the great and the good of Wellington are gathering at the Embassy in order to witness the rebirth of a movie palace that, when it had originally opened – in 1924, under the name of the 'de Luxe' – was hailed as one of the finest theatres 'south of the line'. Now, after its costly facelift, it is ranked as being worthy of hosting a movie premiere which in Hollywood may be ten-a-cent any night of the week, but which *here* will be a historic event.

The film that is to be shown to the audience privileged to have a sneak peak at the Embassy's revitalised Twenties opulence is a tale of two girls who retreat into a shared world of fantasy and then commit a shockingly violent crime. Made in 1994, *Heavenly Creatures* was based on the true story of the Parker/Hulme murder case that, forty years earlier, had rocked New Zealand society. *Heavenly Creatures* was Kate Winslet's movie debut and the fourth feature film to be directed by Peter Jackson.

Some of the guests drinking champagne and nibbling canapés are wondering whether the acclaimed director is going to turn up to the event; those aware of Peter's well-documented reputation for avoiding public appearances will be very surprised if he does. But the truth about what Peter is actually doing on this evening, instead of attending the bash at the Embassy, provides a pin-sharp focus on the Jackson character.

So, where *is* Peter Jackson? Peter Jackson is watching a movie; it's not one of his own, but an *old* movie: in fact, *70 years* old.

Peter is screening this old movie for an audience that includes animators, model-makers, visual-effects artists and a group of Hollywood executives with whom Peter will be working on his next film.

The screening is being held this evening because the print of this old movie has been flown in from Los Angeles and is only available for the next twenty-four hours…

The cinema where it is being shown makes the art deco Embassy look positively dull. Wall-sconces in the shape of torch-bearing rat-monkeys from *Braindead* and bronze decorations of assorted grotesques from *Meet the Feebles* are typical features of the viewing theatre at Weta Workshop. The ceiling is a night-sky of electric 'stars', while 'windows' on either side open on to sunlit vistas of a Tolkienesque landscape: murals of towers and turrets against a range of blue snow-capped mountains.

The lights go down, the curtains open and the titles roll: a radio mast on top of a turning globe, the dot-dot-dash-dot Morse-code signifying 'A Radio Pictures', a swell of dramatic movie music (the work of the great Max Steiner) and the black-and-white block-capital letters of the title:

KING KONG

Made in 1933 by Merian C. Cooper and Ernest B. Schoedsack, the film gives first credit not to the stars Fay Wray, Robert Armstrong and Bruce Cabot, but to Chief Technician, Willis H. O'Brien, and his team of special-effects artists who aided him in the creation of Kong and the prehistoric realm of which Kong is king.

The film begins: a New York quayside at night, snow and fog and the looming hulk of the SS *Venture*. On board, Captain Englehorn turns to world-renowned explorer and film-maker, Carl Denham, and asks what the authorities would be likely to make of 'these new gas bombs of yours'. Opening a box, the captain takes one out – a hand-grenade the size of a small football. 'According to you,' continues the captain, 'one of them is enough to knock out an elephant.'

Two rows in front of me, Peter Jackson holds up an identical gas-bomb. 'This is it!' he calls out over the soundtrack. 'This is one of the original props!'

This is Peter Jackson's favourite film. He has more posters and memorabilia connected with *King Kong* than any of the other films and vintage TV shows that he has adored since boyhood. However, he has never seen the film projected onto a cinema screen. Until now...

No wonder then that having this rare chance to see the picture again – not on TV or video, but up there on the big screen where a star as big as Kong truly belongs – *and* to watch it holding an actual artefact that was used in the film is, in comparison with viewing *Heavenly Creatures* at the Embassy, a simply unmissable opportunity.

This is the film that made Peter Jackson want to make movies.

Savouring the pleasure of this evening: watching, once more, as the great ape rampages through the tropical jungle of Skull Island and the concrete jungle of New York City, Peter knows that – after the hoopla and circus of that imminent world premiere – he too will be setting out in pursuit of that monstrous, heroic, romantic creature known as 'Kong: the Eighth Wonder of the World…'

MODEL BEGINNINGS

The date: Sunday 2 March 2003. The Place: Universal Studios, Los Angeles.

Peter Jackson and his partner, Fran Walsh, are in town for the Directors Guild Awards. While in the City of Angels, they are due to meet with Stacey Snider, President of Universal Pictures, and assorted movie executives in order to reach a decision on whether or not they will be signing to make *King Kong*. The Fates, perhaps, have already decided the outcome of this meeting since Peter's opening remark is, quite simply, that of a passionately devoted film fan: 'This may not mean anything to you,' he tells those present, 'but today, 2 March, is the seventieth anniversary of the opening of the original 1933 film, *King Kong*. Our meeting is taking place, seventy years since *King Kong* opened – *to the day!*'

*   *   *

The date: Sometime in 1971. The Place: Pukerua Bay, an idyllic seaside community on the Kapiti Coast, just over 18 miles north of the New Zealand capital, Wellington.

The 9-year-old Peter Jackson is watching a movie on television. It doesn't matter that the family only has a black-and-white TV set because the film is in black-and-white and old. It had been made in the golden age of Hollywood when film-publicist's hyperbole knew no bounds. It was, moviegoers in 1933 were told, the 'Strangest Story

Pukerua Bay – my parents bought a tiny cottage there after their wedding, and that's where I lived for my first twenty-six years. Our house was perched on the top of cliff above the sea. A great place to grow up.

Ever Conceived by Man! Out-thrilling the Wildest Thrills! Out-leaping the Maddest Imaginings!'

Cavalier film-maker Carl Denham picks up pretty blonde Ann Darrow, down on her luck on the streets of depression-racked New York, and whisks her off to an exotic, dangerous world of primal fantasies. 'It's money and adventure and fame,' Denham promises her. 'It's the thrill of a lifetime and a long sea voyage that starts at six o'clock tomorrow morning…'

It was also, if she had but known it, an excuse to re-live, with variations, a scenario borrowed from an old fairy-tale: 'It's the idea of my picture,' Denham confides to first mate Jack Driscoll. 'The Beast was the tough guy. He could lick the world. But when he saw Beauty, she got him. He went soft. He forgot his wisdom and the little fellas licked him…'

Ann Darrow and Kong re-enact an eighteenth-century fable in a contemporary twentieth-century setting, featuring, in its climactic sequence, what was, at the time, the newest icon of human endeavour and achievement: the 102-storey-high Empire State Building, completed only two years before *King Kong* was made.

But the appeal of *King Kong* – in 1933 or 1969 – is that its heroes and heroine forsake the world of today to go in search of a place where mysteries and wonders can exist without explanation or rationalisation. The SS *Venture* steams away from the steel-and-concrete civilisation of New York City and heads for a location not found on any map or chart: a land that time forgot filled with palaeontological nightmares; a carnival freak-show of savages and monsters; Skull Island…

And what did it mean to the young boy watching this story unfold to the orchestrated snarl and gnash of dinosaurs, the enraged bellowings of a great ape and the endless, ear-piercing screams of a woman in peril? Peter recalls…

It was around nine o'clock, one Friday night when I first saw *King Kong*. I remember being totally swept away on this great adventure! The ingredients of this film were everything that I *loved*! Like any kid, I was intrigued by the notion of lost places, uncharted islands – *King Solomon's Mines*, *The Lost World* – and the idea that, on such an island, there might exist some colossal, unknown beast.

And what absolutely *made* it for me wasn't just that there was a huge, terrifying gorilla that carried the girl away in his hand: it was that when the guys go after them into the jungle, they find *what*? *Dinosaurs!* It was just so great!

It is a very simple story, but one that is loaded with strong, potent, poetic themes: beauty and the beast, love and death – 'It wasn't the airplanes. It was Beauty killed the Beast.' Even today I am moved – often to tears – by the end of the film; but the *real* moment of emotion is not actually Kong falling off the Empire State Building and crashing to his death on the sidewalk below, it is the moment where, knowing that he is going to die, he carefully puts Ann down, makes sure that *she* is safe, regardless of what happens to him.

Ask me today what I think of *King Kong* and I will tell you that it is one of the most perfect pieces of cinematic escapism. If you had asked me as a child, I would have said that it was everything that I imagined an adventure story should be. *Kong* was, quite simply, a ripping yarn! More than that, it created a totally believable fusion between the real and the fantastic. The story is set in *this* world, not in some outrageous, outlandish Other Place. Then, in introducing a giant gorilla and dinosaurs you make that leap from the real to the fantastical.

That has always been my aim as a film-maker: you have to *believe* in order to become involved with the story and to care about its protagonists. That is why, when we approached the filming of *The Lord of the Rings*, I was determined – no matter how many trolls, balrogs and fell-beasts we might encounter – that the world in which they exist would be real – just as I'm sure it was real for J. R. R. Tolkien.

King Kong was important because it showed me the power of movies to make you experience things that are outside what you could ever experience in your daily life. I came to love the fact that film had that potential; and, in a way, it has been what has defined every film that I've ever made.

That is the legacy I owe to *King Kong* and it is one of the reasons why I have so long wanted to make my own film version of the story. I want to re-tell that tale for a modern movie audience. I want them to discover the excitement of travelling to Skull Island…

Skull Island…

It was right there, just across the water from where Peter Jackson grew up. He saw it every day from the living-room window in his parents' home at Pukerua Bay.

The local name for the long grey misty hump of an island that rose out of the sea was Kapiti Island but, as Peter's childhood friend Pete O'Herne remembers, even if it were not *the* Skull Island, then at least it might be a place of potential adventures of the kind offered by *Kong* and other legendary movies: 'We always thought it was possible; that maybe, if we could only get over there, get past the krakens that were probably living in the waters around its shores, that we'd find a fantasy island inhabited by monster crabs and other strange creatures.' Peter Jackson also recalls the lure of the island:

I remember a lot of fun things from my childhood. Pukerua Bay was a great place to grow up because it was a very small town but it was also surrounded by bush and forests; there were steep hills and deep gullies;

there were the beaches and the rocks and the ocean and, only five miles away – but totally inaccessible – a mysterious, fantasy island...

We would always wonder what was on that island. It wasn't simply down to juvenile fancy, because there were many stories and legends about Kapiti: tales of the Maori chieftain, Te Rauparaha, leader of the Ngati-Toa tribe in the 1800s, who had established a 'pa' – a fortified Maori settlement – on the island.

There were melodramatic, bloodthirsty rumours of cannibalistic rituals and secret tunnels and caves filled with the skeletal remains of Maori warriors. As kids we never bothered about what was true and what wasn't, we believed it all! And we dreamed of, one day, getting a boat and going over there and exploring. How bizarre that, years later, when the ship we were using to film *King Kong* started taking on water and beginning to sink, we ended up having to land on Kapiti Island, the Skull Island of our young fantasies.

Peter Robert Jackson was born in Wellington hospital on 31 October 1961. It was Halloween: although, at the time and for many years after, that appellation had little significance in a British Commonwealth country. Halloween was, after all, a strange, sinister, American festival...

Many New Zealanders celebrated, instead, Guy Fawkes Day, 5 November in commemoration of the thwarting of the Gunpowder Plot of 1605. Although popularly known as 'Firework' or 'Bonfire' Night it occasionally took on other names – 'Mischief Night' or 'Danger Night' – that hinted at links to that other holiday with its spooks and masks and trick-or-treating...

But, as it happened, Halloween wasn't a wildly inappropriate date on which to be born. For Peter Jackson would not only fall under the spell of the fiends, monsters and extra-terrestrials of Hollywood and the comic-books, but would, eventually make his name and his reputation as a film-maker with movies about aliens, zombies and vampires – a true child of Halloween, Walpurgisnacht, the Day of the Dead...

Peter is a first-generation 'pakeha', a New Zealander of European descent; his parents, Joan and Bill, having met in New Zealand after separately emigrating there in the early 1950s.

My dad is the first child on the left, with two of his four brothers. Both my parents came from five-child households, yet I was an only child. My dad loved Charlie Chaplin movies and encouraged my love of silent comedy. He always said his father looked like Chaplin and would get people yelling 'Hi Charlie' at him. I can see why in this photo from the early Twenties. My granddad died at a comparably young age in 1940 – my dad always said it was due to his war injuries.

William Jackson had been born in 1920 in Brixton, South London; Joan Ruck, his wife to be, was also born in 1920 near the Hertfordshire village of Shenley; both of them were drawn to New Zealand – as were many others in the years immediately following the Second World War – in response to a tantalizing scheme in which the New Zealand Government offered free or assisted passage to single men and women, under the age of 36, looking to make a fresh start.

'Emigrate to New Zealand for a NEW way of life,' read a typical advertisement in a London newspaper of 1949. 'Good Jobs... Good Pay... Good Living... New Zealand has a place for YOU in her future development.'

When Bill Jackson set sail on the *Atlantis* in 1950, his motivation for leaving home and family was less to do with good jobs and good pay as with his affection for a girl who wanted to emigrate from Britain. Bill, who had been working with a division of the travel agency, Thomas Cook, organised the girl's passage and decided to go along too. The romance ended before ever the ship docked in Wellington, but Bill never regretted his journey to the other side of the world.

Bill became a government employee working for the post office – the deal on assisted passages required the émigré to sign a two-year work contract – found accommodation in Johnsonville, a few miles out of Wellington, and joined the Johnsonville Football Club, into which he later enlisted two other British lads who had recently arrived in New Zealand: Frank and Bob Ruck.

In 1951, the Ruck brothers' sister, Joan, came to Wellington,

---

The only hint of any film or theatrics in my family's background came through my mother, who was a member of the local amateur dramatics club in her home village of Shenley in Hertfordshire, England. Here's Mum in some melodrama from what looks like the late 1940s.

together with their mother, for what was originally intended to be a six-month visit. After years of war-time rationing and post-war privations, the 'good living' promised in those immigration advertisements ensured that an eventual return to Shenley soon ceased to be an option for the future.

Joan got a job at a hosiery factory in the city and whilst attending Saturday matches at the Johnsonville Football Club where her brothers played, met and struck up an acquaintanceship with one of their British mates – Bill Jackson.

Bill and Joan's friendship blossomed and two years later, in November 1953, they were married and moved to Pukerua Bay, purchasing a small holiday home. The single-storey, two-bedroom house was small, but had a wide uninterrupted view overlooking the ocean and the rugged splendour of the Kapiti coastline.

Taking its name from the Maori word for 'hill', Pukerua was founded on the site of a Maori community. Along the side of the hills, which drop sharply to the sea, snakes the precarious track of the Paraparaumu railway line out of Wellington. The area is virtually as unspoilt today as it was fifty years ago, with its wooded and heather-covered slopes; its equitable climate, facing north and protected from the cold south winds by the hills of the Taraura Ranges; and its glorious sunsets that, in the late afternoon, turn sea and sand to gold.

The year after their marriage, Bill Jackson got a job as a wages clerk with Wellington City Council. Loyal, dedicated and hardworking, he remained an employee of the Council until his retirement, by which time he had risen to the position of paymaster.

Mum and Dad both emigrated to New Zealand separately and met in Johnsonville.

After years of my parents trying to have a baby, I finally turned up in 1961. For whatever reason, Mum and Dad couldn't produce a brother or sister for me.

Born in 1961, Peter was a late child of Joan and Bill's marriage, and complications during the confinement meant that he was destined to be an only child.

Being an only child and not having anyone else to bounce ideas off, you have to create your own games with whatever props come to hand. You find that you create your fun and entertainment in your own head, which helps to exercise the mind and trains you to be more imaginative…

As an only child – as well as being long-awaited and, therefore, much treasured – Peter was also the sole focus of his parents' love, care, attention and encouragement. Without sibling companionship or competitiveness, Peter instinctively related to an older generation and, in particular, one that mostly comprised veterans of the 1939–45 war. Peter's youthful imagination was excited by the overheard reminiscences of his elders and the stories that they told a youngster eager for tales of dangers and heroisms.

The Second World War was the dominant part of their most recent lives. Mum would tell me lots of stories about her life: the air-raids and doodlebugs and her experiences working as a foreman in a De Havilland aircraft factory where they built the Mosquito bomber which was largely made out of wood and was known as the 'Timber Terror'.

My father didn't talk as much about his wartime experiences, as I

I grew up with Grandma Emma as the matriarch of the family. She taught me to love card games and was a wonderful cook. In her younger years, she was a cook for an upper-class family in London. Upstairs, Downstairs *was her favourite show – it was the world she came from. Here she is holding me as a baby. She lived to be 98 and died just as I was making* Bad Taste.

would now have liked... He had served with the Royal Ordnance Corps in Italy and, before that, on the island of Malta. This was during the grim years of 1940–43 when German and Italian forces lay siege to the British colony that was of such crucial importance to the war in the Mediterranean and which, as a result, suffered terrible hardships.

Dad spoke about some of what he had seen, but he never really dwelt on the bad things; although he did talk about his time on Malta when, due to enemy blockades and the bombing of supply-ships, the entire island was starving for a period of months and his body-weight dramatically dropped to around seven stone.

He told me the story of the SS *Ohio*, the American tanker that, in August 1942, was carrying vital fuel to Malta for the British planes when it was attacked by German bombers and torpedoes. Without a rudder, with a hole in the stern, its decks awash and in imminent danger of splitting in two, the tanker was eventually strapped between two destroyers and towed towards the island. Dad was one of the soldiers on the fortress ramparts of the capital, Valetta, when – at 9.30 on the morning of 15 August 1942 – the *Ohio* finally, and heroically, limped into Malta's Grand Harbour.

I also heard about the arrival by aircraft-carrier of the first Spitfires in October 1942 and how the 400 planes based at Malta's three bomb-savaged airfields, instantly began an air-defence of the island, flying daily sorties to repel attacks from the German Luftwaffe and the Italian Regia Aeronatica that were based in Sicily.

Enemy aircraft, which were not used to being opposed, were in the regular habit of flying in and beating the hell out of the island – they made some 3,000 air-raids in just two years. On the first raid after the Spitfires had arrived, Dad remembered how he and many others had chosen not to go into the shelters but to stay outside and watch as the bombers roared in across the sea to be greeted by a swarm of Spitfires and the cheers of an island full of people who could, at last, fight back.

But the stories that most excited me – and which led to what has been a life-long interest in the First World War – were those my father would relate about *his* father, William Jackson Senior. My grandfather joined the British army in 1912 and, when war broke out two years later, was one of the comparatively few *professional* soldiers amongst the legions of raw conscripts. He went through many of the major engagements of WWI: on the Western Front at the Battle of the Somme; at Tsingtao in China and at Gallipoli, where he was decorated with the DCM (Distinguished Conduct Medal), the oldest British award for gallantry and second only to the Victoria Cross.

The story of the heroic, but ill-fated, struggle on the beaches of the Turkish peninsula of Gallipoli is one of the most dramatic conflicts of the First World War. The combined Allied operation to seize the Ottoman capital of Constantinople, staged in 1915, was a tactical disaster and the price paid by both sides in terms of lives lost and injured was disastrous: more than 140,000 Allies and over 250,000 Turks killed and wounded.

My grandfather served in the British Army, in the South Wales

My dad in Malta, 1941. He served in the British Army during the Siege of Malta, suffering the constant bombing and starvation along with the rest of the population. My mother worked at DeHavilland's aircraft factory, building the Mosquito fighter bombers. I was in the generation who grew up with 'the War' a constant undercurrent in our household.

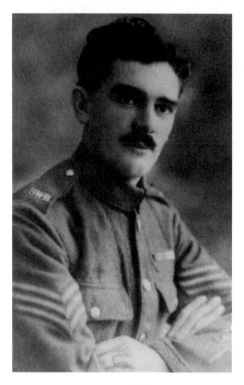

My dad's father, William Jackson. He was a professional soldier and served in the South Wales Borderers from 1912 to 1919. He went through just about every major battle of the First World War, was mentioned in dispatches for bravery several times, and won the second highest medal, the DCM, at Gallipoli.

Borderers, but I now live in a country where the bravery and tragic losses of the Anzac forces (over 7,500 New Zealand deaths and casualties) are still remembered and annually commemorated. One day, that story should be told on film.

Of course, Peter Weir made a film in 1981 that was set in Gallipoli and starred Mel Gibson; but it was essentially an Australian view of the conflict. In New Zealand, memories and stories of Gallipoli still hold such a potent place in the history of our country that they deserve to have a good movie made about them. It is not a project that I am pursuing at the moment, but, maybe, one day…

Peter Jackson may well, one day, make a war film – perhaps even one about Gallipoli… In 2003, wandering around Peter Jackson's Stone Street studios, I came across an extensive scale model of a beach with rising hills. This might easily represent the tortuous terrain of ravines, spurs and ridges that confronted the Australian and New Zealand troops that landed at what is now known as Anzac Cove on 25 April 1915, and where, within the first day's engagement with the Turks, one in five New Zealanders became casualties of war.

In the same building as the scale model of the beach, sculptors from Weta Workshop were carving the enormous wings, tails and assorted body parts that would eventually be assembled into the huge sculptures of the Nazgûl fell-beasts destined to decorate Wellington's Embassy and Reading theatres for the premiere of *The Return of the King*: a reminder that J.R.R. Tolkien, himself a veteran of the Somme, had originally suggested that a suitable title for the third part of *The Lord of the Rings* would be 'The War of the Ring'. So, in a sense, Peter Jackson has *already* made a war-movie, albeit set in the fantasy realm of Tolkien's Middle-earth.

If and when Peter makes a film based on some twentieth-century wartime event (and it seems inconceivable that he won't) it will simply be a fulfilment of an ambition that dates back to his debut film, made in 1971 – when he was 8 years old!

> The first movie I ever made, which I acted in and directed, was shot on my parents' Super 8 Movie Camera. I dug a trench in the back garden, made wooden guns and borrowed some old army uniforms from relatives. Then I enlisted the help of a couple of schoolmates and we ran around fighting and acting out this war-movie – or, more accurately, something out of a war-comic – full of action and high drama! In order to simulate gun-fire from my homemade machine-gun, I used a pin to poke holes through the celluloid – frame by frame – on to the barrel of the gun in order to create a burst of whiteness when the film was projected. My first special-effect – and without the aid of digital graphics!

Peter's earliest recollection of going to the movies was a visit, several years before, to one of Wellington's cinemas to see a film now long forgotten – and, frankly, deservedly so: *Noddy in Toyland*. Made in 1957, four years before Peter was born, it had obviously taken its time in reaching the cinemas of New Zealand!

Directed by MacLean Rogers, whose filmography of over eighty titles included many pictures featuring popular radio and music-hall stars including the famous 'The Goons', *Noddy in Toyland* was simply a filmed performance of a musical play for children by Enid Blyton.

Based on Blyton's popular children's books about Noddy and his friend Big Ears, the author had constructed a rambling and tortuously complicated plot featuring, in addition to the denizens of Toyland,

I remember my childhood as being reasonably idyllic, with lots of family vacations in our Morris Minor. Although I was an only child, I was never lonely – we had a wonderful extended family of uncles, aunts and cousins, most of whom had followed the family migration to New Zealand.

characters from her other books, including *The Magic Faraway Tree* and *Mr Pinkwhistle*.

The photography was pedestrian, the stage business dull and laboured – especially without the enthusiastic audience of cheering kids that it doubtless enjoyed in theatres – and the only tenuous link between Noddy's exploits and the films of Peter Jackson is an encounter with some 'naughty goblins' but who, in their baggy tights, were a far cry from the malevolent, scuttling creatures that swarm through the Mines of Moria. Nevertheless, to the young Peter, it was a remarkable film.

I was highly entertained by *Noddy in Toyland*; it was the first movie that I ever saw and, although I've never seen it since, I remember thinking it was pretty amazing!

Seeing a film when I was very young was a big event: we didn't have a cinema in Pukerua so a trip to 'the pictures' meant a car or train journey into Wellington. My parents seldom took me into the city, so the occasional visits to the cinema were rare and special treats and the few films that I saw at this stage of my life tended to make a big impact on my youthful imagination – even if they really weren't very good!

One such was *Batman: The Movie*, the 1966 spin-off of the high-camp TV series starring Adam West and Burt Ward, which I saw with my cousins, Alan and David Ruck. I remember being fascinated by the scenes where Bruce Wayne and Dick Grayson leapt on to the 'bat-poles' behind the secret panel in Wayne Manor in order to reach the Bat-cave. They started their descent wearing 'civilian' clothes but, by the time they'd reached the Bat-cave, they were miraculously kitted out in their Batman and Robin outfits.

My cousins were a few years older than me and therefore less impressionable, but I thought that it was just about the most astonishing thing I had ever seen. After the screening, we went back to Alan and David's house in Johnsonville and I can still remember standing in their dining room and asking, 'How did they *do* that? How could they have changed their clothes so *fast*?' and my cousin David turning to me and saying, 'Oh, that's just special-effects.'

That was the first time in my life I had ever heard the term 'special-effects' and I've never forgotten the moment that I heard it or who said the words to me. I was 6.

Another early memory of going to the movies was having to stand up while they played 'God Save the Queen', which was accompanied by a film of the Changing of the Guard, the Trooping of the Colour or some such ceremony. I've never forgotten my cousin Alan winding me up by telling me that if I *didn't* stand up, one of the guardsmen would come down and arrest me!

Years later, when I made *Braindead*, I decided to pay tribute to that vivid memory by beginning the film with the National Anthem and footage of Her Majesty. We had to go through a great deal of red tape to get approval and I can only assume that, somewhere along the line, we must have failed to give them a synopsis of the movie!

Apart from these odd excursions, cinema-going wasn't a huge part of Peter's first seven or eight years. The major influences that were to fire his interests and transform them into the passions that would play a part in shaping his future career came, in the first instance, not from the movies, but from television.

It was 1965 and I was 4 years old when television entered my life. We had been on holiday, and while we were away the TV had been delivered. We returned to find a huge cardboard box in the lounge, and I recall Dad unpacking it and lifting out what would now seem a terribly old-fashioned Philips black-and-white, single-channel television and a set of four legs that had to be screwed on underneath.

It's difficult for today's generation to realise just what an impact television had on our lives when we were first exposed to it. I

The arrival of our first television set was my first exposure to escapism – Thunderbirds *was screening and I fell in love with model-making, storytelling and fantasy.*

initially encountered almost all my adult enthusiasms through 'the box'.

We used to get all those great old British Fifties black-and-white war movies that my father and I really loved such as *Ice-Cold in Alex*, *Sink the Bismarck*, and *The Wooden Horse*. Dad also loved old silent comedies: I can remember him roaring with laughter at Charlie Chaplin movies, till tears were streaming down his face.

I enjoyed Chaplin, although I wouldn't describe myself as a *fan*, but watching his films and those of Laurel and Hardy led me to Buster Keaton and I am most certainly a Keaton fan: I love the dead-pan sense of humour that earned him the nickname 'Stone Face', and I really admire his eye for sight-gags and his immaculate sense of timing, particularly the split-second perfection of his stunt-work. I've seen all of Keaton's movies and consider his 1927 picture, *The General*, to be a work of pure genius. Along with *King Kong*, *The General* is among my all-time favourite movies.

Set during the American Civil War, Keaton plays a brave but fool-hardy train engineer in the Confederate South, whose beloved locomotive – *The General* of the title – is hijacked by Yankee troops from the North. Although Keaton was making a comedy-chase movie, it is completely authentic in terms of its period setting. The texture of the world Keaton creates in the film is detailed and realistic and that is something that I always strive to do with my movies.

Keaton was doing comedy while we – with *Rings* and *Kong* – have been doing a fantasy; but I honestly believe that even if you are showing outrageous things on the screen – in our case giant spiders, walking trees and huge gorillas or, in Keaton's case, incredible routines with runaway steam-trains – as long as everything is grounded in a believable environment then it will have greater intensity and more poignancy.

When, years after first seeing *The General*, I was making *Braindead*, I'd often try to imagine what sort of gags Buster Keaton would have come up with if – bizarre concept though it is – he had ever made a splatter movie! There's one particular scene in *Braindead* that illustrates this perfectly: the hero, Lionel Cosgrove is desperately trying to escape from the zombies; he's running like crazy and he suddenly realises that he hasn't actually gone anywhere because the floor is so slippery with zombie-blood that he is just running on the spot! That's a Keatonish kind of gag.

Old movies aside, the most memorable and influential programme that I remember watching on TV, was undoubtedly *Thunderbirds*. I loved it! I was a complete, total and absolute fan!

For a generation of youngsters in the Sixties the clarion call: '5… 4… 3… 2… 1… Thunderbirds are *GO!*' was a weekly prelude to fifty minutes of thrill-laden adventures. First aired in 1965, *Thunderbirds* was the work of pioneering British puppet film-maker, Gerry Anderson, who had already excited young television viewers with such futuristic series as *Fireball XL5* and *Stingray*.

Set in the year 2026, *Thunderbirds* featured the heroic deeds of International Rescue, a family of fearless action heroes located on a secret island in the Southern Pacific and headed by former moon-pilot, Jeff Tracy. The Tracy boys – Scott, John, Virgil, Gordon and Alan – tackled dangerously impossible missions, often pitting their wits against arch-villain and master of disguises, The Hood.

International Rescue had a fleet of fantastic vehicles – rockets, supersonic planes and submersibles – and were aided by the bespectacled boffin, Brains; the chicest of secret agents, Lady Penelope Creighton-Ward and Parker, a former safe-cracker who gave up a life of crime to become Lady Penelope's butler and chauffeur of her pink Rolls Royce, FAB 1.

The puppets, operated by near-to-imperceptible strings, were given verisimilitude by the use of a technique called 'Supermarionation' which used electrical pulses to create convincingly synchronised lip-movements. *Thunderbirds* married a centuries-old entertainment – the puppet show – with Sixties, state-of-the-art technology; the results were impressive and made compelling viewing.

Many years later, Peter would have the opportunity to meet puppet-master Gerry Anderson, and in 1997 made an unsuccessful bid to direct a live-action movie version of *Thunderbirds* (a project that eventually went elsewhere and made a poor critical showing). But in 1965, he was – like millions of other kids – just another devoted young fan…

I loved the big spaceships and was excited by the rescues and the dramatic storylines that now seem incredibly melodramatic! Of course, I knew it wasn't real; I knew they were puppets and that fascinated me: I wanted to know how they were made and operated.

I remember wanting to make models of the Thunderbirds crafts and buying plastic clip-together model-kits that were around at the time and which I incorporated into my games. Like lots of kids, I had Matchbox toys of various vehicles and I created International Rescue-style scenarios in the garden: cutting a road in the side of a dirt bank that was just big enough for some truck to fit on and then it would be half-hanging over the edge and Thunderbirds would have to come to the rescue!

Setting-up those little backyard dramas with my toys was when 'special-effects' really entered my awareness: I knew that was what I'd seen done in *Batman: The Movie* and that it was what Gerry Anderson was now doing in *Thunderbirds*; from that point on, I started to have a real interest in special-effects.

It was only when I started discovering what could be done with a camera that I began to think that I might be able to create my *own*.

The first movie camera I ever saw was a Super 8 camera belonging to my Uncle Ron, Dad's brother, who would show up at family outings and get-togethers with his camera and shoot movies of us. The earliest movie image of me, shot when I was about 6 years old, shows me walking along a beach with some ice-creams.

Then, happily, my parents acquired a Super 8 Movie Camera! It had come from a neighbour and family friend, Jean Watson, who worked at the Kodak processing lab in nearby Porirua. One year, about 1969, Kodak brought out a really compact movie camera – it was about as simple as it got: just point-and-shoot – and gave their staff the opportunity to buy the cameras at discount. Jean decided to get a camera for my mum and dad, not because at that time I had exhibited any interest in movie-making, but because she thought that my parents might find it fun to be able to capture something of their son's childhood on film. However, it didn't take me long to commandeer the camera and, instead of acting out dramas with Matchbox cars and trucks, I was marshalling my friends and filming the Second World War in the back garden!

A few years later, in 1973, Peter made a more ambitious war-movie, featuring some of the same troops as had appeared in his earlier film. One volunteer (or conscript!) was fellow pupil at Pukerua Bay School, Pete O'Herne: 'I remember running around wearing a German helmet

Pukerua Bay Primary School. I was always a very well behaved child, terrified of authority. I'm the fourth boy from the left on the second to highest row. On the top row, third from the right, is a friend who went on to help me with all my childhood films and starred in Bad Taste *under the name Pete O'Herne.*

and there being quite a few effects-shots because part of the action took place on a mine-field – we had a warning notice with a skull-and-crossbones on it and the words "ACHTUNG – MINE!" – all of which required a setting bigger than Mr and Mrs Jackson's garden, so we went on to location to Porirua and filmed some of the sequences on the council rubbish-tip!'

Pete O'Herne had a really good sense of humour and we both liked movies – and the same type of movies! Pete was always one of those friends at school who was really happy to help and when you're trying to make films as a kid that's a real bonus!

Obviously there's a limit to what you can do as a moviemaker if you're on your own and I didn't have brothers and sisters that I could stick in front of a camera. So I was always trying to hook up with people who would be interested in film-making and in helping me try to make them. Pete was not only into films he was also nearly always available at weekends. Like me, Pete wasn't exactly the sporting-type, which was a really good thing because when you're trying to get kids to help you make a film, Sport is Enemy Number One! You're in school all week, so you want to shoot on Saturday and that is the one day on which the guys in the rugby and soccer teams are going to be far too busy to be messing about with films!

Most of Peter's early experiments with film were attempts at creating effects, rather than in demonstrating any embryonic talent as a director. Pete O'Herne recalls: 'I'd often ring Peter up on a Friday night and say, "What are you doing, tomorrow?" and he'd always be up to something or other and would ask if I wanted to go down the valley with him and try out this or that special-effect that he was working on. Every weekend, more or less, we were in and out of each other's homes, doing crazy things together. I always think of Peter as wearing an old duffle coat that would eventually become a kind of trademark that folk would rib him about. And the pockets of this coat were always bulging with heaps of stuff for his various experiments.'

Like virtually everyone who has operated a camera since the invention of cinematography, Peter Jackson particularly enjoyed playing with the simple effect created by time-lapse photography: shoot; stop; change something in front of the camera and shoot again. Hey presto! You have an appearance, a disappearance or some magical transformation. Although Peter was yet to make the discovery, time-lapse – using a camera to trick the eye into seeing the impossible – is also the basic principle behind the stop-motion animation that had enabled King Kong to grapple with the prehistoric creatures on Skull Island. Initially, however, Peter's films were confined to live-action subjects that, whilst simple in their approach, were inevitably time-consuming for participants…

Most of what I shot didn't amount to more than odd little test films, like a time-lapse record of a longish car journey; there were no sophisticated structures or stories. But then, within a year, I saw *King Kong* and the gorilla really sealed my destiny. I knew nothing about stop-motion animation: I'd never heard of Willis O'Brien before I saw *King Kong* and I had yet to see any of Ray Harryhausen's films, but I began finding out how it was done and started experimenting…

I was in the Boy Scouts and, on the morning after I'd seen *King Kong*, we went on a hike through the bush and I took the camera and got the Scout troop to do this thing where I would get them to stand still, shoot a few frames, then get them to move and stand still again and shoot a few more frames, so that it looked as if they were sliding along the ground. I remember being a real pain because, instead of hiking, I had them acting in stop-motion all the way to the camp!

Perhaps I was drawn to stop-frame animation because I realised that it was one way in which I could attempt to make movies on my own. So I made little Plasticine models of dinosaurs and filmed them as best I could, achieving one or two rather crude animation effects.

The chief problem was that stop-motion is achieved by filming a single frame of film, adjusting the puppet or model, taking another single frame and so on until the finished footage, when shown, creates the illusion that something inanimate is moving.

Unfortunately, the Super 8 Movie Camera I had didn't have a facility to allow you to shoot a single frame of film at a time. The best that I could do was to squeeze the trigger for the shortest possible interval and hope for the best. Inevitably, the camera would fire off at least two or three frames of film, which meant that the movements of my dinosaurs were always jerky and unconvincing.

The camera was incredibly crude and the focus was bad, but I think of all my early attempts at filming as being – if nothing else – valuable experiments…

Pete O'Herne recalls those experiments: 'We were in our last year at primary school when Peter embarked on another zany film project. He got some of the kids involved and they'd all have little bits to do on the film and he even persuaded one of the teachers, Mr Trevor Shoesmith, to take part. Peter was such an enthusiast and his enthusiasm was infectious: he had a great deal of self-motivation and he passed that motivation on to others. He was also persuasive: he'd come up with some mad idea and we'd all find ourselves pitching in and taking part because we knew it would be fun. This particular epic was entitled *Ponty Mython* and was Peter's ode to what,

As I became interested in stop-motion following the screening of King Kong, *I tried building puppet animators. Here is a stop of Kong and a Triceratops, filmed on a table top in the living room. I had no lights, so the sun would drift around over time, creating time lapse shadows during the hours it would take me to animate.*

by then, was his favourite television show.'

Monty Python's Flying Circus landed on the unsuspecting viewers of BBC television in October 1969 to the accompaniment of a strident blare of brass-band music, the crushing descent of an animated foot and irreverent blowing of what in English slang is referred to as 'a raspberry'. The circus troupe were five young writers and performers – John Cleese, Eric Idle, Terry Jones, Michael Palin and the late Graham Chapman – who set about revolutionising British comedy with the help of ingeniously quirky animations by American cartoonist, Terry Gilliam.

Over a period of five years *Monty Python* developed from an alternative (and decidedly subversive) late-night show that outraged and offended the easily-shocked into, firstly, an essential cult-classic and then, eventually, into a much-loved British institution. As a result of the Flying Circus, an entire generation grew up for whom comedy was defined by such phrases as, 'Is this the right room for an argument?', 'Nudge, nudge, know what I mean, know what I mean!' and the all-purpose, sketch-changing 'And now for something completely different' along with spam, flying sheep, silly walks, lumberjacks and a dead parrot.

What surprises Peter Jackson is not that *Monty Python's Flying Circus* should have left its mark on his nascent creativity, but that he ever got to see it in the first place...

The one thing that, to this day, I've never quite fathomed out is how I was ever allowed to stay up late on a Sunday night and watch a programme like *Monty Python's Flying Circus!* Although Dad loved comedy and had a great sense of humour, when it came to *Python*, he would sit through an entire show and never laugh.

I was not sure, initially, that *I* ever laughed out loud – partly because there were all kinds of innuendos that I probably didn't pick up on, but also because it was so bizarre and off-beat: it was the weirdest comedy show ever and I had never seen anything like it in my life.

Because I saw the *Flying Circus* at just the right age – I was 11 or 12 years old and just starting to form adult sensibilities – it had a profound influence on the way in which my sense of humour developed. *Monty Python* taught me to love the ludicrous and love the extreme.

When, during my last year at primary school, we had to do a school project with our friends I decided that I was going to make a film. Getting together with some of my chums we put together a script. It was entitled, somewhat derivatively, *Ponty Mython!*

Heavily influenced – pretty much *totally* influenced – by *Flying Circus* it comprised skits from the TV series along with some of our own. I even tried to create some Terry Gilliam-style animations using cut-out pictures from magazines.

Ponty Mython ran for about twelve minutes and contained a sequence in which one of our teachers, Mr Shoesmith, was shown walking along with an umbrella and then suddenly exploding.

I had cut the film, substituted Mr Shoesmith with a homemade bomb – made from firecrackers and flour – which I then detonated so that it looked like he had blown up!

I even remember details of my first-ever movie budget: four rolls of Super 8 film at $3 NZ a roll to buy and process; total cost $12 NZ. We screened it at school over several lunch times – it always got a big cheer when Mr Shoesmith exploded! – and we charged 10 cents admission. We made exactly $12! No going over-budget, but no profit either! But at least we broke even…

Monty Python would continue to be a powerful influence on Peter and his love of 'splatter that would eventually inspire his first commercial movies, was really borne out of a sketch from the third season of *Flying Circus*. Called 'Sam Peckinpah's "Salad Days"', it imagined what might have happened if the American director of such uncompromising movies as *The Wild Bunch* and the then recently-released *Straw Dogs* had made a film of Julian Slade's Fifties musical *Salad Days*.

The result is an English country house-party that unexpectedly turns into a fevered gore-fest. Beginning innocently enough with someone playing a piano on a lawn and lads in blazers and flannels and girls in pretty frocks frolicking about to the music, things start going wrong when the bright young things embark on a game of tennis: someone is hit in the eye with a tennis-ball; a girl gets a racquet embedded in her stomach; another person's arm is ripped off; the piano-lid drops, severing the pianist's hands and causing fountains of blood to erupt from the stumps. Finally, the piano collapses in slow-motion, crushing everyone to death and the grisly debacle concludes with a shot in which, as the script tastefully puts it, 'a volcanic quantity of blood geysers upwards.'

It was Python at its most outrageous: defiantly unapologetic, even down to the on-screen 'Apology': THE BBC WOULD LIKE TO APOLOGISE TO EVERYONE IN THE WORLD FOR THE LAST ITEM. IT WAS DISGUSTING AND BAD AND THOROUGHLY DISOBEDIENT AND PLEASE DON'T BOTHER TO PHONE UP BECAUSE WE KNOW IT WAS VERY TASTELESS, BUT THEY DIDN'T REALLY MEAN IT AND THEY DO ALL COME FROM BROKEN HOMES AND HAVE VERY UNHAPPY PERSONAL LIVES…'

I remember watching that episode on TV and being absolutely gobsmacked. Quite simply, it was the most extraordinarily funny thing that I'd ever seen. That sketch did more to steer my sense of humour towards over-the-top bloodletting than any horror film ever did! My splatter-movies – *Bad Taste*, *Meet the Feebles* and *Braindead* – owe as much to Monty Python as they do to any other genre. It is about pushing humour to the limit of ludicrousness, the furthest and most absurd extreme imaginable – so extreme that the only possible response to it is to laugh because there is nothing else left to do!

In 1975, Peter moved on to secondary education, attending Kapiti College, located north of Pukerua Bay at Raumati Beach, where he demonstrated an exceptional aptitude for maths, a complete lack of skill (or interest) in sport and where he was variously perceived by his peers, some of whom have described him as being painfully shy with an awkward stammer, as a boy who was so retiring, remote and self-effacing that he went all but unnoticed by teachers and fellow pupils. Others, who shared his passionate excitement for movies, saw beyond the shyness and the occasional stutter and found him an entertaining, intriguing, slightly eccentric character.

'You would never have called Peter "a leader of men",' says one friend, 'and yet we all followed him around! He came up with ideas, schemes and enterprises and we went along with them, took part, got involved. People have said he was reserved and lacking in self-confidence and he could, sometimes, give that impression – he rarely made vocal contributions in class – but he had massive self-confidence in his ideas and abilities. In that sense, you would not describe Peter as modest. I believe he always knew that he was going to be special, that he would have a charmed life…'

To his close mates, Peter was often the joker: pulling stunts and gags. 'He was totally lunatic!' remembers Pete O'Herne. 'We went into town one day and we got off the bus in Wellington and, as soon as it had driven away, Peter suddenly said, "Oh my God, Pete, where's your bag?" I start panicking, thinking, 'I've lost my bag! I've left it on the bus…' And then I realised, for Christ's sakes, that I'm actually *holding* the bag in my hand! And there's Peter, laughing like hell!'

There were also occasional trips to see a live taping of a TV comedy show: 'Oh dear, oh dear,' laughs Pete, 'there we'd be in the audience – these guys from the loony-left, of the school of *Python* – watching some normal, mainstream comedy show that really just couldn't do it for us! So, Peter and I would start hee-hawing away, making up the loudest, silliest, high-pitched laughs and crazy demented sounds. Then we'd watch the show on transmission and spot ourselves on the soundtrack which was easy because we were always way over the top for the kind of jokes in the show.'

If the antics of the *Monty Python* team were shaping Peter's sense of humour, he was also still in the thrall of the film fantasists. He had already discovered the American publication, *Famous Monsters of Filmland* that had been founded in 1958, three years before he was born and which was generally regarded by sci-fi, fantasy and horror-geeks worldwide as being the bible on all forms of movie-monster-life.

In the pages of *Famous Monsters of Filmland*, Peter read about the work of veterans Boris Karloff, Bela Lugosi and Vincent Price as well as the Sixties stars of Hammer's House of Horror, Peter Cushing and the man who would one day play Saruman the White, Christopher Lee. Behind-the-scenes features on the making of some of the great monster classics, fuelled his interest in special-effects while revelations about the tricks-of-the-trade of stop-frame animation and, in particular, the work of Willis O'Brien and the team who created *King Kong* deepened his appreciation for the movie-magic behind the Eighth Wonder of the World.

In homage to *Kong*, Peter had toyed with attempting a possible ape movie of his own, building a gorilla puppet (using part of an old fur stole belonging to his mother), constructing a cardboard Empire State Building and painting a Manhattan skyscape for the backdrop.

Peter's first original monster was constructed around a 'skeleton' made from rolled-up newspapers and was what he describes as 'a crazy hunch-back rat' – a forerunner, perhaps, of the rabid rat-monkey that wreaks havoc in *Braindead*.

More simian life forms were to exert their influence when Peter saw the 1968 movie, *Planet of the Apes*. The first – and unarguably the best – of a series of ape pictures, *Planet* was no conventional monster-movie. Based on a novella by Pierre Boulle, it had a satiric script, a seminal Sixties 'message for mankind', a compelling central performance from Charlton Heston and – for the period in which it was made – cutting-edge make-up effects that convincingly turned Roddy McDowall and others into assorted chimps, gorillas and orang-utans.

> I saw *Planet of the Apes* on TV and was blown away by it. I loved the special make-up effects but I also loved the story. I was already a fan of *King Kong* – although my fascination is not really with apes and gorillas so much as with a couple of great movies that both happen to have apes in them!
>
> Nevertheless, both films, though they approach it in a very different way, have an intriguing theme in common: that the gap separating humans from apes is far less than we might like to suppose!

It wasn't long before Peter Jackson was sculpting and moulding ape-masks and involving his friend Pete O'Herne in the process. Pete, who still proudly owns and displays highly competent prototypes for their handiwork – albeit now incredibly fragile – recalls, 'Peter's imagination was such that if something impressed him, he had to try and do it for himself – filming, sculpting, whatever – and if Peter was doing it, you'd want to do it, too! We'd seen *Planet of the Apes* and I went round to his house the following week and he had a model head and was working on a face mask: sculpturing it in Plasticine, *free-hand* – not using drawings or photographs but creating this thing in three-dimensions, from his own mind. Of course, I'd think, "I'll give that a go as well…" So I did!'

The process, as Pete remembers was time-consuming and expensive on pocket-money budgets: 'Peter found this latex rubber in a hardware store; it came in little bottles that cost about $8 each. Once we'd sculpted the faces, we'd just get little paint brushes and paint it onto the Plasticine; then we'd have to leave it to dry and then paint on another coat and so on until you'd built it up layer by layer into a skin of a reasonable thickness to work as a mask. Then we'd paint them and stick on hair that we'd chop off old wigs! Peter's mother always helped out at school fetes and jumble sales and she'd always be on the look out for suitable stuff that we could use for costumes and

I enjoyed sculpting in plasticine, and this was an early goblin design.

make-up. The trouble with the latex was that it reeked of ammonia – a sickening, vomit-making smell!'

The *Planet of the Apes* style film for which these masks were made never progressed beyond some footage of Pete O'Herne in an even more elaborate full-head mask made with a foam-latex product, which Peter Jackson purchased from a supplier in Canada and which he would bake in his mother's oven. 'It rose like a cake,' says Pete, 'but it also stank to high heaven!' Existing photographs showing Pete wearing the gorilla head and a costume inspired by those worn by the ape soldiers in the film indicate a remarkable level of competence, although the setting – a domestic garden with a carousel clothes dryer – add a bizarre dimension!

Although the ape film project never got beyond the idea stage, who could have guessed that the young man who was so fired up by *Planet of the Apes* that he created his own gorilla masks, would years later, as a professional film-maker, come near to adding a new title to the *Apes* franchise? Instead, Tim Burton re-made the original, and cinema audiences were denied the opportunity of seeing what Peter Jackson would have done with the theme of ape superiority.

Now into his teens, Peter was broadening his knowledge of film with books about movies and moviemakers although, ironically, the students' Film Club at Kapiti College – which seems to have been run by a smug, self-perpetuating oligarchy – repeatedly declined to accept the young Peter Jackson into membership.

Undaunted, Peter pursued his interest in cinema alone or with friends like Ken Hammon, a fellow pupil at Kapiti College, who shared his love of movies, was a fan of *Famous Monsters of Filmland* and was, conveniently, another non-sportsman! Both boys had film projectors and were spending their pocket money buying 8mm copies of various movies.

One of the first films in Peter's collection was, unsurprisingly, *King Kong*, but he also owned prints of the original vampire movie *Nosferatu* and Lon Chaney's versions of *The Hunchback of Notre Dame* and *The Phantom of the Opera*. Ken broadened the repertoire with such titles as D.W. Griffith's silent epic, *Intolerance*, Chaplin's *The Gold Rush*, Howard Hawks' gangster movie, *Scarface* and the Hitchcock thriller, *The 39 Steps*.

Other 8mm films were hired from a low-profile, illegal operator in the Wellington suburb who was able to supply such assorted delights as *Dr Terror's House of Horrors* with Christopher Lee and Peter Cushing which, Ken recalls, 'freaked us out', and Tobe Hooper's 1974 seminal tale of murder and cannibalism, *The Texas Chain Saw Massacre*. Publicised in America with the poster slogan 'Who will survive – and what will be left of them?', *Chain Saw Massacre* was, for many years, banned in several countries including New Zealand so its illicit avail-ability on hire was especially irresistible to the young film fans.

'We humped four cans of film back home,' says Ken, 'watched the first reel, which was so psychologically unnerving that we were seri-ously rattled! I remember saying to Pete, "Are you really sure you want to watch the rest?" At the time we were hardly overexposed to such thrillers, so they inevitably made an impression.' It was an

My Uncle Bill visited us from England in 1976, and bought me my long-wished-for copy of King Kong *in Super 8. In the days before video, projecting in Super 8 was the only way to actually own a movie and watch it again and again.* Kong *got played a lot in my bedroom!*

impression that, for Peter Jackson, would endure, as is testified to by the gorier sequences in *Bad Taste* and *Braindead*.

In company with Ken and Pete O'Herne, or sometimes on his own, Peter was now regularly travelling into Wellington – or anywhere else that had a cinema and was within commuting distance – in order to catch the latest movie releases or fleeting screenings of vintage films.

I saw American World War II movies for the first time – *The Dirty Dozen* and *Kelly's Heroes* – and a film, made in 1970, about a much earlier war, *Waterloo*.

Waterloo was the work of Russian director, Sergei Bondarchuk, and starred Christopher Plummer as the Duke of Wellington and Rod Steiger as Napoleon Bonaparte. It inspired an interest in that period of time which has remained with me across the years. I collected – and still collect – toy-soldiers, including a number representing various Napoleonic troops.

What I loved about *Waterloo* were the uniforms and the big formations of soldiers. Filmed in the Soviet Union, Bondarchuk had used the Russian army as extras on the battlefield – *20,000 of them!* I was impressed at seeing such a huge number of people on screen, but was also frustrated because the real Battle of Waterloo involved almost 140,000 soldiers, so I remember watching these 20,000 extras and thinking, 'God! What would it be like to see the *real* battle?' That's why I wanted to create these formidable-looking armies in *The Lord of the Rings* which, with the aid of computers we were able to achieve.

Ken Hammon offers an interesting perspective on Jackson the young cineaste: 'People always talk about Pete's obsession with horror movies, his fascination with gore and splatter, but they overlook another of his early cinematic passions that would certainly inform much of his work on *The Lord of the Rings*. Pete adored the widescreen, three-hour historical epics that proliferated in the Fifties and early Sixties: *Quo Vadis, Spartacus, El Cid, The Fall of the Roman Empire* and the like. He loved these sprawling films with their great battles and thirty years later started making them himself, here in New Zealand!'

I first saw *Waterloo* on its original release at the Embassy Theatre in Wellington and then, later, I dragged some friends along to see it when it popped up on a Sunday afternoon screening at a flea-pit of a cinema on the outskirts of the city suburbs which involved us in a train journey followed by a half-hour bus ride.

I remember that particular day quite vividly because I had badly cut my thumb that morning. This is the sort of child I was... I had been reading WWII Prisoner of War books and I was intrigued by how, when they were planning an escape, they forged identity papers to show the various inspectors on the trains as they tried to make their way back across Germany to Switzerland. I was particularly fascinated by stories of how they would make fake rubber stamps with which to authorise the forged documents by carving them from the rubber soles of their boots.

On this day, I'd decided to try this myself and was busy in my father's shed in the back garden carving away at the rubber sole of an old shoe. The knife slipped and it nearly cut the top of my thumb off. It was a very deep cut, so bad that I still have the scar to this day. I should probably have gone to the hospital and had it stitched, but I wanted to go to the cinema to see *Waterloo*, which was only screening this one day. So I didn't tell my parents about the wound – I just put a plaster on it and headed out the door. I remember how it throbbed like hell all the way to this terrible little theatre in the back of beyond, but that once I was there watching the film, I became so utterly absorbed in the action that I completely forgot the pain. As for the friends I dragged along to see it, I'm not sure that they appreciated it quite as much as I did!

If *Waterloo* and other movie epics were to provide a long-term inspiration for the cinematic scope later achieved in *The Lord of the Rings*, the desire to capture on film the elusive magic of fantasy realms was reinforced by seeing the work of a master-moviemaker whose pictures became an inspiration and a touchstone for Peter Jackson. That man was Ray Harryhausen.

A veteran stop-frame animator, Harryhausen was – and still is – a link with some of the greatest names in twentieth-century fantasy writing and film-making. Harryhausen's friends include the legendary futurist Ray Bradbury and Forrest J. Ackerman, founding editor of *Famous Monsters of Filmland*. A writer, actor and collector, Ackerman, at one time, negotiated with J. R. R. Tolkien to make an animated film of *The Lord of the Rings* and, years later, would make a cameo appearance in Peter Jackson's *Braindead*.

Ray Harryhausen had worked on the early animated films of key fantasy film director George Pal (*The War of the Worlds*, *The Time Machine* and many others) and, most significantly, was a direct link to Willis O'Brien, the special-effects wizard who was 'father' to *King Kong*, having served as first technician to O'Brien in 1949 on another Merian C. Cooper–Ernest B. Schoedsack gorilla movie, *Mighty Joe Young*. In terms of consummate skill in stop-frame animation – the ability to endow a puppet with emotions – Harryhausen was O'Brien's unquestioned heir and his films made an immediate, and lasting, impression on the young Peter Jackson.

Some of cinema's most exciting and technically accomplished animated sequences appear in films to which Ray Harryhausen contributed as a producer, writer and/or visual effects creator. In titles such as *The Beast from 20,000 Fathoms*, *20 Million Miles to Earth*, *Mysterious Island*, *First Men on the Moon* and the incomparable *Jason and the Argonauts*, Harryhausen's fertile imagination conjured a cavalcade of dinosaurs, aliens and mythological creatures that entranced fantasy film fans over two and half decades.

Two films, that Peter saw around this time were *The Golden Voyage of Sinbad* and *Sinbad and the Eye of the Tiger*, but it was a 1975 re-release of the first of Harryhausen's Sinbad movies that proved a pivotal point in his movie-making aspirations. *The Seventh Voyage of Sinbad*, made in 1958, featured an amazing bestiary of inventive creatures, including a dragon, a goat-legged Cyclops, a two-headed Roc and a four-armed snake-woman!

As a 16 year old in 1977, I was the perfect age for Star Wars, *and it led to a flurry of model making and filming with my Super 8 camera. Here are several models I made from cardboard and model parts, a copy of Gerry Anderson's* Space 1999 Eagle *and a couple of original designs.*

There's something magical, captivating, about stop-motion animation that you can only really understand if you are… captivated by it! After being entranced by *King Kong*, *The Seventh Voyage of Sinbad* really confirmed my dream of becoming a professional stop-motion animator. I wanted to make the same types of films as Ray Harryhausen. I loved the way his monsters and images flowed from his imagination and I couldn't imagine a more enjoyable way to spend your life. *King Kong* was an old film, and Willis O'Brien was no longer alive, but for a wonderful period during my teenage years and beyond, these stop-motion artists like Harryhausen, Jim Danforth, Dave Allen and Randy Cook were my idols, doing exactly what I dreamed of doing as a career.

This was before video, so there was no way to own a copy of a movie. I remember smuggling a small cassette sound recorder into a screening of *The Seventh Voyage of Sinbad* in a bag, and I taped the entire film. I would lie in bed at night, listening to this echoey, fussy sound recording – complete with audience rustling chippie-wrappers and coughing – and relive the visual excitement of the film in my head.

Such was the impact of the *Sinbad* film that it inspired my next film project that, unlike some of my earlier efforts that were always hampered by waning enthusiasm or even downright loss of interest – eventually saw completion. The necessary incentive came in the form of a Sunday afternoon television programme called *Spot On* that, in 1978, ran a children's film-making contest for schools, so I teamed up with two school friends from Kapiti College, Ken Hammon and Andrew Neale, and another former cast member of my earlier films, Ian Middleton, and we started work on a short fantasy film.

As I now had a new camera which my parents had bought me for my previous birthday and as it had the much-desired facility for shooting single-frames, I was absolutely determined that our film would feature some elaborate sequences in stop-motion animation. Heavily indebted to the work of Ray Harryhausen, it was called *The Valley*.

Peter's determination to experiment with stop-frame animation meant that the storyline of *The Valley* was essentially little more than a means to that end. The action concerns the adventures of four gold-prospectors – although, since there always had to be someone operating the camera, only three of the four could be ever seen on screen at one time!

Whilst trekking through the bush, the intrepid group conveniently blunder into a 'space-time continuum': a special effect achieved by pulling a pantyhose over the lens of the camera in order to create a 'mist'. Undaunted at finding themselves in some, mythic 'other age', the foursome continue on their way only to encounter a couple of Harryhausen-inspired monsters, the first of which – a harpy-like creature – swoops down and carries off one of their number just as, years later, in *The Return of the King*, the Nazgûl fell-beasts would swoop down and snatch Gondorian soldiers from the battlements of Minas Tirith.

The winged assailant in *The Valley* (called a Trochoid, after a term used of a family of curves which they heard used in geometry class) solved a major problem facing the film-makers – namely their lack of acting ability! 'None of us were very good actors,' recalls Ken Hammon, 'but Ian Middleton was arguably worse than the rest of us which is why he was the first to get killed off!' As the Trochoid flew off with a puppet of Ian in its clutches, Ken demonstrated his own acting skills by providing a reaction shot on the demise of his comrade: though filmed

These are shots from The Valley, *a film I made with friends at Kapiti College in 1978. I shamelessly copied Ray Harryhausen's Cyclops for my villain.* The Valley *was shot in the rugged gorge that runs through the middle of Pukerua Bay. I think this shot of me and Ken Hammon is the first photo I have of me holding a movie camera. I met Ken at Kapiti and he became a good friend and one of the core members of the* Bad Taste *team.*

without sound, Ken could clearly be seen to mouth a four-letter word.

The problem of having Peter on screen and behind the camera, led to his character taking a convenient tumble off a cliff, leaving Andrew Neale and Ken to deal with an attack by a close relative of the Cyclops in *Seventh Voyage*. In what is a superbly choreographed moment in the film, cutting back and forth between live action and animation: Ken stumbles, falls and is grabbed by the Cyclops; Andrew, seeing his friend's plight – dangling by one leg from the monster's fist – grabs a large branch and hurls it, javelin-style, at the creature; next, cut to the Cyclops, as the well-aimed branch finds its mark and plunges into the creature's throat with an eruption of blood.

The scenario moves towards its climax with Andrew and Ken building a raft and taking to the water. Eventually, the travellers come in sight of 'the Beehive', Wellington's parliamentary cabinet offices, not as they are today, but ruined and overgrown with vegetation. In a *dénouement* borrowed from *Planet of the Apes* (in which Charlton Heston discovers the remains of the Statue of Liberty and

My bedroom, circa 1979. My trusted Eumig projector is there along with some of the models I'd built for my films. Kong atop the Empire State Building was from an attempt to remake the film in Super 8, along with a few stop-motion puppets and masks I'd made.

realises that the monkey planet on which he has landed is, in fact, the earth in a future age) the two survivors in *The Valley* reach the conclusion that they have travelled *forward* not back in time! 'Let's be honest,' says Ken Hammon, 'it wasn't anything to do with "homage" or "tribute" – we just *stole* stuff!'

With the live-action footage completed, the animation sequences were added and the film was edited by Peter and submitted to *Spot On* and, following a long wait, the programme began screening the winning films. Entries were supposed to run for three to five minutes but (like some of Peter Jackson's later movies!) *The Valley* ran somewhat longer than expected and its almost twenty-minute duration may have contributed to its not being placed among the winners. The makers were, however, commended on what one of the judges – New

Zealand film director, Sam Pillsbury – called 'a really impressive piece of work'. He added that the film-makers' storyline was 'almost non-existent', due to their being 'more interested in techniques', a somewhat grudging criticism that belied the fact that the film's technical achievements were of an exceptionally high order for an amateur film made by 15 and 16 year olds.

The stop-motion animated sequences alone were a triumph and demonstrated not just a high degree of skill but also a determination to master one of the most time-consuming, concentration-intensive of all the film arts. Peter's mother, recalling her son's dedication, commented that he had 'oodles of patience' and that acute singularity of focus would remain one of the qualities to mark out his later professional productions.

Years later and just days after the exhausting final haul of delivering the final cut of *The Return of the King*, Peter spoke of his belief that it was always possible to 'somehow figure something out'…

> If I say 'we'll figure it out', then I mean it; I've logged the problem in my mind and will take my share of responsibility. With each part of *The Lord of the Rings* there would always come a point in the year, usually the second half, when the studio began to think that they might possibly not have a movie to release. I always knew that such a situation would be a complete disaster and, therefore, could never happen.
>
> You may have problems to solve but for every problem there is always a solution. It's a positive-and-negative thing: you can't *have* a problem without there being a solution.
>
> There always is. Your job is to find it…

Despite not winning the *Spot On* competition, extracts from *The Valley* were screened on television – including the harpy carrying off Ian Middleton (complete with Ken Hammon's expletive) and the fight with the Cyclops – and earned the makers a degree of notoriety among their schoolfellows. After all, to have got a violent, bloody action sequence (albeit with a mythical creature) *and* a four-letter word (albeit silently spoken) screened on national television was no mean achievement!

The success of *The Valley* was endorsed when (with an added soundtrack borrowed from Max Steiner's score to *King Kong*) it went on to win a prize of $100 in a competition sponsored by the local newspaper, the *Kapiti Observer*.

For Peter Jackson, the real reward for having made *The Valley* would come many years later, when as an established film-maker he finally met his childhood hero, Ray Harryhausen, for the first time. There is an appropriate and satisfying synchronicity about a friendship between the man who worked with Willis O'Brien on a sequel to *King Kong* and the man who seems to have been destined to remake the original for a new generation of moviegoers.

> When we first met, I found myself saying, 'Ray, I want to thank you, because seeing *The Seventh Voyage of Sinbad* and *Jason and the Argonauts* when I was a kid inspired me to make films, to be a stop-motion animator, to keep making my little Super 8 experiments. So, thank you...'
>
> I sometimes think to myself how amazing it would be if, one day, somebody were to say something like that to me...
>
> Perhaps it is already happening and in twenty years time, when I'm a 60 year old, some young film-maker will come up to me and say, 'I saw *The Lord of the Rings* when I was 8 and it made me want to make films. Thank you...'
>
> To feel that what I had done had made a significant difference to somebody's life to the extent of inspiring that person to take up a career would really mean a lot to me...

For the 17-year-old Peter Jackson the thought of one day meeting his hero Ray Harryhausen, would have been a dream; the notion that he might eventually have a similarly inspiring influence on another generation of aspiring film-makers, unimaginable.

Nevertheless, in 1978, *The Valley* made an impact and not just among the pupils of Kapiti College but also with the principal. Towards the end of the school year, Peter Jackson and Ken Hammon were summoned to the principal's office and offered a potential film commission: if the boys decided to return for a further year, it was suggested, there might be an opportunity for them to make an official film about the school.

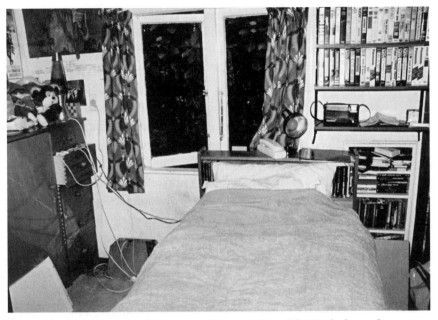

My bed, where I slept the first twenty-six years of my life. My bedroom become my workshop and model-making room. Most of the time it was a lot more untidy than this!

'The prospect really scared the hell out of us!' recalls Ken, who hated college, 'I felt it was like being asked to make a propaganda film about a concentration camp. So we just listened, said we'd give it our consideration and then got the hell out of there, as quick as we could!' Peter also recalls the proposition:

> On the one hand it was exciting, because someone was interested in our doing something as a result of seeing this film that had been on TV; on the other it didn't fit in with my plans as I had already decided to leave at the end of that year. I didn't want to be in school, I had passed my School Certificate and although I was University Entrance accredited, I had no interest in going to further education and, fortunately, my parents didn't try to force me into doing so.

Responding to this comment by Peter, Fran Walsh remarks, 'He says "fortunately" he didn't have to go to university. I think, in some ways, it's a shame he didn't go; he's very bright – one of the brightest people

I've ever met – and would have been good at university and, had he gone there, might well have loved what it had to offer. As it was, he took another road, another path... Pete went to his own university; he went to his own film school; taught himself everything. It's not everyone who can do that.'

It's a view shared by friend and colleague, Costa Botes (with whom Peter would later make *Forgotten Silver*): 'Peter would have done fine at university, but what he did, instead, was to immerse himself in his enthusiasms and, as a result, gave his talent a bit more of a run. Ultimately, if your destiny is to be a film-maker, then – regardless of your academic learning or your theoretical knowledge of film studies – you should always be trying to get in touch with your own innate talent and to follow that. It's possible that university might have helped Peter get to where he is now a bit quicker, but he would have lacked the wisdom and experience he gained from just getting on and doing it.'

Moreover, says Costa Botes, university might have changed Peter Jackson as a person: 'Intellectual success has made many a young man arrogant and insufferable. Instead, Peter has humbleness and a self-defensive sense of humour, which gives him more empathy, makes him a better human being. So I'm not going to argue with that one!'

Whilst Peter's parents may not have sought to exert any pressure over his career choices, they nevertheless still entertained ambitions for their son.

Mum and Dad always hoped that I might get a job as an architect: at school I had been top of my form at technical drawing, I was good at it and passed my exams in it, but it wasn't what I wanted to make my career. My parents probably hoped I'd pursue architecture as being something that I could fall back on if I didn't make it in the movie business. I think they always thought that's where I'd end up, but they never pushed me into it and always did everything that they could to support my film-making ambitions – it wasn't their world, but I think they felt that if somebody has a passion to do something, then you try to encourage them not dissuade them.

Ultimately, I knew that I wanted to try and get a job in the film industry – to be a film-maker – and since I had this feeling that I was going to go on making films, I wanted to be able to afford better film equipment – a 16 mm rather than a 8 mm camera – but that was going to cost a few thousand dollars and I wasn't going to be able to afford it unless I could start earning some money...

I was pretty much revved up and ready to get out in the world and move on, so I left school at the end of the sixth form and started the New Year in 1979 by looking for a job. However, since there had been no real film industry, as such, in New Zealand for many years, I knew that – regardless of my ambitions – I wasn't going to be able to leave school and walk into a job working on movies.

In fact, people had been making movies in New Zealand for sixty years, the first feature film being *Hinemoa*, a famous Maori legend brought to life, as the posters put it, 'in animated form and 2,500 Feet of Glorious Photography' and premiered in 1914. The same posters also declared that *Hinemoa* was part of 'A New Industry in New Zealand' and, indeed, during the silent era, a number of films were produced and distributed with considerable success: historical epics including *The Mutiny of the Bounty* and *The Birth of New Zealand*; knock-about, slapstick comedies and what Peter Jackson would call 'ripping yarns' such as the 1922 film *My Lady of the Cave*, a 'Rattling Tale of Adventure on the New Zealand Coast, with a Love Story that Steals into your Heart like some Weird and Beautiful Melody.'

New Zealand-produced films appeared intermittently over the next two decades with occasional pioneers emerging – like the revolutionary animator of abstract film, Len Lye – and one or two Kiwi film-makers achieving success in Hollywood. Indigenous productions, however, eventually all but died out and New Zealand film languished until the arrival of a new wave of directors in the 1970s.

Significantly, at the time when Peter Jackson was beginning his juvenile experiments, the concept of film as a 'New Zealand industry' was to re-emerge with the success of such films as Roger Donaldson's 1977 movie, *Sleeping Dogs* and *The Wildman* made in the same year, by Geoff Murphy, who over twenty years later would serve as Second Unit Director on *The Lord of the Rings*. Again in 1977, the New Zealand documentary *Off the Edge*, earned an Academy Award nomination.

The following year, in which Peter and his friends made *The Valley*, the New Zealand Film Commission was established, under Act of Parliament, with the remit 'to encourage and also to participate and assist in the making, promotion, distribution, and exhibition of films,' which made it an interesting time for an eager young film-maker to attempt to find a way into the business.

Peter's first port of call was the National Film Unit that had been founded in 1941, following a visit from John Grierson, the legendary documentary film-maker and influential head of the National Film Board of Canada. The aim of the National Film Unit – in addition to providing the country's only film processing laboratory and full post-production facilities – was the financing and production of travel-ogues and promotional films such as *Journey of Three*, a dramatised documentary aimed at encouraging immigration and which was released theatrically in Britain in 1950 and spurred many people of Peter's parents' generation to follow the example of the 'new settlers' which the picture depicted.

> My parents rang the Film Unit and said that their son was very inter-ested in film-making and might they have a position for him? Someone at the Unit offered to meet me and I took some of my models and went for an interview.
>
> As an only child there were times when I would get terribly nervous and I was so anxious at the thought of going for a job at this big film-making place that I had Dad come with me and sit in on the interview. It turned out that they had nothing suitable to offer me, so I took my models and went home again…
>
> Ironically, in 1990 the Film Unit was sold off to a subsidiary of New Zealand Television and when, ten years later, it came on the market, and would have otherwise passed to owners outside the country, I decided to buy and run the Film Unit. They knocked me back at my first job interview, and I ended up owning the place. Life is weird!

One or two of Peter's friends remember him talking about the possi-bility of going to Britain in the hopes of finding work in the film industry there. 'I don't recall thinking about going to England then,' says Peter, 'but maybe I did. My mum's brother, Uncle Bill, knew people who worked at Elstree Studios (just down the road from

Shenley); one chap had worked on *2001* and other films in the Wardrobe Department and, years later, after I had made *Bad Taste*, Uncle Bill took me to meet him.' It seems unlikely that a lad who needed his father to accompany him to an interview would have ever seriously contemplated travelling halfway round the world in search of a job. If he did, then it was probably no more than the fleeting thought of someone who desperately wanted to get into the film business but really didn't know how that ambition might be achieved.

In the event, Fate played a different card...

2

GETTING SERIOUS

The 'Situations Vacant' column of Wellington's *Evening Post* wasn't the most promising place for a would-be film-maker to be looking for an opening, but Peter Jackson needed a job...

On that evening, in 1978, when Peter and his father returned from the unsuccessful interview at the National Film Unit, the Jackson family went through the *Evening Post* newspaper to see what employment opportunities were on offer.

We found an advertisement for a vacancy at the newspaper itself – as an apprentice photoengraver. I didn't have a clue what a photoengraver was, but it had the word 'photo' in it and that was good enough for me. At this point, I wanted to take anything so I could, at least, start earning some money. I also think if I'd failed to get this job, my parents would have sent me to university, so a job interview was arranged. I was as nervous as all hell – it's weird the things you remember, but the night before my interview I saw *The Sound of Music* for the first time. In the movie, Maria sings a song about being confident – and I sat there in the dark, being totally inspired by this damn song. The next day, I walked into the interview carrying the sound of Julie Andrews' voice in my head! I also took Dad to this interview as well – and, thank God, I got the job!

I was amazed at what it felt like to be earning money: my first week's pay cheque was for NZ$77. I couldn't believe it: all I had to do was turn up there and every week somebody would give me $77! After sixteen years of pocket money, it opened up a lot of possibilities!

The apprenticeship required Peter to attend a twelve-week course at the Auckland Technical Institute (now the Auckland Institute of Technology), which had originally been founded in the 1890s by the local Working Men's Club to run evening classes in teaching various trades. By 1978, when Peter began his studies, the ATI was a full-time establishment running courses in engineering, commerce, fashion technology, printing, art and design.

At the concourse bookstall on Wellington railway station, the 17-year-old Peter Jackson decided to buy a chunky paperback to while away the twelve-hour rail journey to Auckland that lay ahead. The book was *The Lord of the Rings* by J. R. R. Tolkien.

He was prompted to buy this particular volume because the cover featured tie-in art from the first – and only – part of animator Ralph Bakshi's aborted attempt to bring Tolkien's epic to the screen. Years later, millions of people would start reading the same story because the book carried images from the Jackson film trilogy…

Peter had gone to see Bakshi's film with high expectations, having seen the director's earlier foray into the fantasy genre, *Wizards*, in company with Pete O'Herne and Ken Hammon. 'It was screened at a cinema in town,' recalls Ken, 'and, as soon as we got out of school, we had to run to catch the train into Wellington, run to the picture house to be in time for the screening and then, afterwards, run all the way back to the station to catch the train home. It was a typical Jackson expedition!'

Wizards was the latest animated film from the renegade director who had already outraged Seventies moviegoers with his adult-rated *Fritz the Cat*, *Heavy Traffic* and *Coonskin*. A bizarre post-apocalyptic vision set in a world of elves, dwarves and good-and-bad-wizards with strong parallels to Middle-earth, *Wizards* now seems like an audition for Bakshi's ill-fated attempt at *The Lord of the Rings*, which was yet to come.

I saw Bakshi's *Rings* when it first came out and, at the time, I hadn't read the book. As a result, I got pretty confused! I liked the early part – it had some quaint sequences in Hobbiton, a creepy encounter with the Black Rider on the road, and a few quite good battle scenes – but then, about

half way through, the storytelling became very disjointed and disorien-
tating and I really didn't understand *what* was going on.

However, what it did do was to make me want to read the book – if
only to find out what happened!

Sitting on the 'Silver Fern' train from Wellington to Auckland, he
began to do just that…

Being mad about movies and fascinated by the whole business of film-
making – especially special effects – I kept saying to myself, 'This book
could make a really great movie!' Of course, it never even occurred to
me that *I* could make it – I didn't even fantasise about making it! That
would have been ridiculous: after all, I was just a 17-year-old, apprentice
photoengraver, so there was no romantic moment that had me sitting
on the train thinking, 'One day, I will make a film of this book!' Such a
thought would have been totally crazy.

But I *did* think, 'I can't wait for somebody to make this movie! My
real fantasy would have been a Ray Harryhausen version of *The Lord of
the Rings* – because that's what I really want to see! Years later, a moment
came when it felt like, since nobody else seemed to be going to make it,
I would simply have to make it myself! But that was way off in the
future…

In fact, although people probably have this impression of me as having
been a geeky Tolkien-reader as a kid, the truth is I didn't read the book
again until the idea of making the film came up – eighteen years later.

Ken Hammon recalls that it took Peter some time to wade through the
full 1,000-plus pages of Tolkien's book: 'We ribbed Pete about it
so much that it became something of an on-going joke: 'Have you finished reading *The Lord of the Rings* yet?' we'd ask. Now, I guess the
joke's on us, because whenever I hear Pete talking about the film, he
clearly knows Tolkien's writings inside out and back to front. Not only
that, but I remember telling Pete that the "unreadable book" would
make an "unwatchable film", but he sure as hell disproved that theory!'

Meanwhile, back in 1978, Peter excelled at his studies at Auckland
Technical Institute. As he was to report in a funding application to
the New Zealand Film Commission, a few years later: 'I served my

three-year term, gaining the highest marks out of fifty students for both Trade Certificate and Advanced Trade Certificate.' To which he added, 'I mention this not to boast, but to show that I do try my best at anything I take on.'

Peter was to spend seven years working at the *Evening Post* and as he jokingly reflects:

> It's reassuring to know that I've always got a career in photoengraving to fall back on if I ever need it!

Photoengraving is the process by which images are engraved onto zinc or magnesium plates to be used on a press for printing photo-graphs and images in newspapers. The metal plate is coated with a substance called a 'photo-resist', which is both photosensitive and yet resistant to acids. Strong ultraviolet light is then shone through a photographic negative causing those parts of the image through which the light has passed to harden. The image is then developed, using a solvent to wash away the unhardened parts of the image on the photo-resist. The metal plate is next placed in a bath of acid that dissolves those areas of metal that have been exposed and creates a plate from which a positive image can then be printed.

> The process at the time was pretty primitive, and as the lowly appren-tice, it was my job to etch the magnesium plates in big sulphuric-acid baths that, afterwards, had to be drained and scrubbed-out by hand. There were no real safety precautions and I'd lose the skin off my fingers and have my T-shirts go into holes and fall apart from the effects of the acid!

About a year into Peter's apprenticeship, the *Evening Post* merged with Wellington's daily paper the *Dominion Post* and Rob Lewis ('Mr Lewis' to the apprentice lads) became manager of the process depart-ment for the combined papers. Peter Jackson was one of Mr Lewis's employees and he still has clear memories of the young man who was already trailing clouds of glory as 'Apprentice of the Year': 'Peter was a delight. He was a little shy or, more accurately, someone with a cer-

Rob Lewis, my boss in the Evening Post *process department, standing on the left. Mr. Lewis was a little fearsome at first, and certainly a boss who commanded respect – but looking back, his idea to feature my home-made gorilla suit in a newspaper story kicked off a series of incidents and meetings that changed my life. I love the way fate weaves its complex, unpredictable path.*

tain quietness about him; that said, he could also be full of fun and mischief. There was no question that he was good at his work – very good, although he clearly had his own agenda, his own road to run. With two daily papers and a Sunday edition to print each week, I always needed people to take on overtime and Peter was always the one person it was difficult to get to do overtime – not because he was a reluctant worker, but because he had other things to occupy his spare time – like making movies!'

> Mr Lewis is not entirely accurate – there were periods when I'd desperately do as much overtime as I could squeeze in, to pay for ever-growing film-making costs!

Indeed, despite the demands of the day-job, Peter still retained his filmic ambitions, one of which was to emulate a particular effect created by Ray Harryhausen in *The Seventh Voyage of Sinbad*, the film that had provided so much of the inspiration for *The Valley*. One of the most ingenious sequences in the film was that in which the actor playing Sinbad had a sword-fight with an animated skeletal warrior. It was a brilliant set-piece and the precursor to a *tour de force* scene in the later *Jason and the Argonauts* in which the crew of the Argos engage with an entire army of battling skeletons.

I really wanted to try and do the types of movie tricks Ray had done: I wanted to film a sword-fight, with a human (me!) sword-fighting an animated skeleton. You had to film the live-action human first – a shadow-sword-fighting – rear-project it on a small screen and shoot a stop-motion model in front of it.

I built a little skeleton in cardboard with a wire 'armature' – that's what animators call the poseable skeleton inside a stop-motion puppet, so this was a skeleton inside a skeleton! This figure was going to be my opponent in the scene I wanted to film.

Even though I didn't have any of the equipment which Ray Harryhausen would have used to create his effects, I was still determined to try and make this work using just my Super 8 camera, so I shot some animation tests with the skeleton, copying the moment when one of them breaks out of the ground in *Jason and the Argonauts*. I was then forever attempting to figure out a way of projecting an image of me onto a screen so that I could put the skeleton in front, animate it in synchronisation with the film and photograph the combined images. I tried various experiments, but the results were *terrible!*

While I was trying to solve the logistics, I carried on filming the live-action half of the sequence. I made myself a Sinbad costume, dressed up in it and went with Pete O'Herne down onto the Pukerua Bay beach to film the live-action side of the fight among the rock-pools.

I plotted a sword-fight routine where I was battling with this imaginary skeleton. There were to be several shots of me – as Sinbad – fighting desperately, swinging the sword round and then, at the end of the fight, the climactic moment was me being knocked backwards off the rock and falling into the sea with a splash!

At the beginning of the day, we looked around for a safe place where

I could fall back into the water, found one that was good and deep and started shooting…

Pete O'Herne recalls filming among the rocks, operating the camera to immortalise Peter's performance: 'I remember Peter saying that he wanted to do a skeleton sword-fight like the one in *Sinbad* or *Jason and the Argonauts*, so, of course, I went along to help out. That was how it was in those days; it was just what we did. We were always going to be there, hanging out, doing stuff… It never occurred to me to say, "Hey, Pete, hope you don't mind, but I really want to hang around with some other guys…" I didn't question it. It was, "OK, so what are we up to this weekend?" And it was fun, good fun.' Except, on this particular weekend, it was also *wet!* 'We shot versions of the sword fight for best part of a couple of hours, with me in the water almost up to my waist and pretty much drenched. Then the accident happened…'

Peter has his own painful memories of that day…

After several hours of shooting me sword-fighting with an invisible skeleton, we reached the point at which I had to hurl myself backwards, as if knocked into the water by the skeleton. I splashed into the water – and suddenly felt a sickening pain as something whacked against my spine.

Unfortunately, as we had been shooting for several hours, the tide had dropped a couple of feet – something that hadn't occurred to me – so when I took my spectacular stunt dive I crashed onto a sharp rock that was now just below the surface of the water. I was in instant agony, but somehow managed to get home. Some time later, however, I developed a pilonidal cyst, caused by the trauma to the lower vertebrae, and ended up being admitted to hospital for surgery.

After the operation, I was off work on convalescence for two or three weeks. This was valuable time, not to be wasted, so I started chopping up foam rubber and began work on building a full gorilla suit which would later play an unexpected, but life-changing role in my future career…

As for the skeleton fight, I never did manage to solve the technical problems involved and it remained a sadly unfulfilled ambition. But what

I just love about such things is that a few years ago, Ray Harryhausen visited our house in Wellington and he opened this little box, produced his original stop-motion skeleton puppet to show us… And I couldn't help thinking that there I'd been, as a kid, animating skeletons and falling off rocks because I'd seen Ray's movies and now here he was in my home with an original model from one of those films!

It is simply the greatest thing in the world when those kinds of circles turn and connect. Little moments that connect me to the kid I was, and remind me of the kid I still am.

The accident temporarily forestalled Peter's plans to make his Sinbad adventure and it was destined to be one of many juvenile projects that would never see completion.

I was always thinking of ideas that were ambitious, technically complex films and all I had was a little Super 8 camera that couldn't shoot sound. So I'd always be disappointed by the results and eventually abandon one project and start work on something else. This pattern of being unable to make something within my means – and most of all original – became something I was conscious of and which started to worry me.

Among the discarded Jackson ventures of the late Seventies was a short experiment loosely inspired by Stanley Kubrick's *A Clockwork Orange* and John Carpenter's *Halloween* in which an unseen intruder – the camera films from the intruder's point-of-view – enters a house and shoots a terrified old man. Filmed in the Jackson home (with Pete O'Herne in heavy make-up as the elderly victim) the exercise was shot in a single, continuous take.

Another uncompleted project later came to be referred to as *Coldfinger* although, at the time, it was known simply as 'The *James Bond* Thing'.

The first Bond movie I saw was Roger Moore in his debut performance, *Live and Let Die*, in 1973. Shortly afterwards, The Roxy cinema in Wellington ran interesting (if slightly unlikely) double-bill featuring the WWII movie, *The Dam Busters* along with the first-ever James Bond film, *Dr No*, starring Sean Connery. Then, in 1974, I saw the film that confirmed me as a huge *Bond* fan: *The Man with the Golden Gun* with Roger Moore in his second outing as Agent 007 and my favourite actor from the Hammer horror movies, Christopher Lee, as Francisco Scaramanga. A fabulous villain, Scaramanga had, supposedly, been born in a circus as the son of a Cuban ringmaster and a British snake-charmer and had, as a distinguishing feature, a third nipple or, as Bond refers to it, 'a superfluous papilla'!

I loved *The Man with the Golden Gun!* I just had to keep going back to the cinema to see it. It was the first film that I saw *four times in one week* (the next would be David Lean's *The Bridge on the River Kwai*), and it made such an impact that I even tried to take photos of it. I had a camera that used to take slides, so I smuggled it into the cinema and during some of my favourite moments in the film – like when the car jumps over the bridge – I'd whip out my camera and snap off some pictures.

It's hard for anyone to understand who wasn't living in the time before videos but, unlike now, we weren't able to watch just about any movie that's ever been made whenever we wished. Videos and DVDs have profoundly changed movie-watching: when I was young, a film came to the local cinema for one week only – it was on and then gone; only a handful of cinemas ever showed double-bill revivals and our single-channel TV station in New Zealand didn't get films for years and years. So, once a film had played, you were unlikely to see it again in under a decade.

Film fans had to content themselves with collecting images in magazines and books, buying soundtrack recordings of film scores (or illicitly record them yourself as I had done with *The Seventh Voyage of Sinbad*) collecting toys and merchandise – anything to keep hold of the memories. That's why I tried to grab a few souvenir photos of *The Man With the Golden Gun* but, needless to say, when I got them developed I found that they were all completely blank!

Catching old movies on sporadic re-release meant, in the case of Bond movies, seeing the films out of chronology and with a central character alternately played by Sean Connery and Roger Moore. Ken Hammon recalls going with Peter to a screening of Connery's 1971 final foray into the world of Bond, *Diamonds Are Forever*: 'It was also around this time that Pete hired a copy of the fourth movie in the series, *Thunderball* ("Here Comes the Biggest Bond of All!"), and screened it at school over two lunchtimes, advertised by a Jackson-drawn poster of Sean Connery who, by now, was probably Pete's favourite action hero.'

The dynamic, thrill-packed opening which became the hallmark of every Bond film was something that would inform Peter's later approach to *The Lord of the Rings* and in particular the prologue to *The Fellowship of the Ring*.

I've always been a believer in the *James Bond* approach, which is to blow people away in the first five minutes of the film, which buys you that little bit of story set-up time during your first act. You shift people from the state of mind they're in when they enter the cinema, and very quickly try to ensnare them into the world of your movie. The prologue in *Fellowship* served two functions: it got a lot of the back-story information out of the way at the beginning of the film, which would otherwise have had to explain by Gandalf in Bag End; but we also wanted the prologue to be more than just information and having the battle scenes – even though I now feel that they were rather rushed and not as good as they should have been – provided something spectacular and visceral to rip people out of whatever frame of mind they're in when they enter the cinema. If people sit there and their jaws drop open and they go 'Wow!' then you've got them, you're in control.

As for Peter's youthful attempt at filming something in the *Bond* style, all that ever made it onto celluloid were two fight-sequences with Peter playing his hero in his father's dinner-suit and with, says Ken Hammon, 'a ton of face make-up to make him look like Sean Connery – only ten inches shorter!' Bond's first fight, set amongst those perilous rocks at Pukerua Bay was with Ken playing a villain who almost succeeds in garrotting the special agent with a fishing line – until the ever-resourceful 007 removes his bow-tie which handily converts into a flick-knife.

The second fight with another baddie (played by Andrew Neale, another of those gold prospectors in *The Valley*) was shot on the Jackson balcony overlooking the Kapiti coast. The scene took up an entire day's shooting and yet not a frame of footage was ever to be seen: the film had been incorrectly loaded and although the camera was whirred away as if filming, it was, in fact, doing nothing of the sort. Before a re-shoot could be scheduled, Andrew Neale had left New Zealand and so the scene was later recreated with Pete O'Herne playing the villain.

The *Bond* project was another destined to remain unfinished, but Peter Jackson never lost his love of the film incarnations of Ian Fleming's special agent. A colleague on the *Evening Post*, Ray Battersby, has a photograph of Peter posing in his bedroom with a cinema foyer standee of *Bond* from the 1987 film *The Living Daylights*. Since the cardboard cut-out had a removable head, the photograph shows Peter Jackson substituting for the actor who had just taken on the role of Bond, Timothy Dalton.

As a child, Peter Jackson's bedroom was full of model cars and aircraft-kits. Today, he owns the real things – not just an Aston Martin, but also several vintage planes from the First World War. The toys it seems have just got bigger…

> My hobbies and interests are exactly the same now as they were when I was 12 – they are essentially no different. Most people develop their hobbies when they're young; certainly I don't have any hobbies that I've taken up as an adult. For me, everything is an extension to what has gone before. Owning a WWI airplane is just a continuation from buying and building Airfix plastic kits when I was a kid; I've just been lucky enough now to have earned sufficient money to move on to full-sized planes. It's really just the same old hobbies! I still have Super 8 footage of WWI dogfights I shot when I was about 10 years old.

As Peter's childhood friend, Pete O'Herne remarks: 'Peter hasn't changed one bit. If he had $10 he'd go and buy himself a model of a Spitfire. If he's got a million dollars, he'll just go buy the bigger version. Why not? That's exactly what any of us would do!'

Maybe so, but all of these things – becoming a professional film-maker or owning an Aston Martin – were distant, if not impossible, dreams for the young Peter Jackson in 1979. However, it wasn't long before Peter was demonstrating his technical ambitions by not only upgrading his movie equipment to a Super 8 camera – with *sound* –

This shot really captures the spirit and feel of The Curse of the Gravewalker, *filmed amongst the old graves at a local cemetery. I'm playing the swash-buckling zombie-hunting hero, as Pete O'Herne goes for my jugular. Pete's make-up would be done in my bedroom and then Mum or Dad would drive us to the cemetery and leave us there most of the day.*

but also by aspiring to produce wide-screen images by shooting in CinemaScope.

CinemaScope had come hot on the heels of various movie innovations in the early Fifties – including 3-D and Cinerama – aimed at wooing American TV audiences back into the picture-houses. The system debuted with the 1953 religious epic, *The Robe*, advertised as 'The Modern Miracle You See Without Glasses', and CinemaScope (along with such successors as VistaVision, *Super*scope, Todd-AO and Technirama) quickly became *the* way to view movies, especially big-budget musicals, westerns, war movies and costume dramas.

In 1953 a mere five CinemaScope titles were released, during the following year, that figure rose to thirty-seven films including *20,000*

LEFT: *The smallest stage I've ever used. Dad's first car was a Morris Minor and he carefully built the garage with just enough space to squeeze in and out of the drivers' door. Here, Pete and I are shooting a scene with Clive Haywood, another of my pro-duction stalwarts from the* Evening Post *process department. In those days, photo-litho plates came in wide flat cardboard boxes, and I used to lug piles of these home each week. Cardboard was my main building material for everything – here the boxes have been painted grey, sprinkled with beach sand and used to line the garage.*

Leagues Under the Sea, Demetrius and the Gladiators, Prince Valiant, Bad Day at Black Rock, Seven Brides for Seven Brothers and *Three Coins in the Fountain*. Within a decade, wide-screen movies were less a novelty, more the norm and, for a young man with a taste for cinematic spectacle, what he calls 'the huge letterbox-shaped CinemaScope image' couldn't fail to appeal.

Peter sent to a supplier in England for an anamorphic lens of the kind used for filming in CinemaScope. Based upon a technique pioneered in France in the late Twenties by the inventor Henri Chrétien, the lens worked using an optical trick called 'anamorphosis' which allowed an image twice the width of that captured by a conventional lens to be horizontally 'squeezed' onto film. When projected onto a screen using a similar lens, the image was 'unsqueezed' to provide dramatic, eye-stretching, cinematic experience. With his new camera and his anamorphic lens, Peter embarked on another movie project with Pete O'Herne and veterans from *The Valley*, Ken Hammon and, temporarily back in New Zealand, Andrew Neal.

> We started work on what is sometimes referred now to as *The Curse of the Gravewalker*, although – like all my early experiments – it never really had a title. The film was shamelessly spawned by my adolescent love of the blood-spattered, over-the-top Gothic horrors from Hammer films which I started going to see on double-bills when I was in my late teens and one in particular, *Captain Kronos – Vampire Hunter*, which I thought was really cool!

Unlike many pictures to emerge from what has been called 'the studio that dripped blood', *Captain Kronos – Vampire Hunter*, made in 1974, did not star either of Hammer's legendary stalwarts Peter Cushing or Christopher Lee, nor even the seductive Ingrid Pitt, who had sucked the blood of young heroes and quickened the pulse of young movie-goers in such pictures as *The Vampire Lovers* and *Countess Dracula*. *Captain Kronos* – billed as 'The Only Man Alive Feared by the Walking Dead' – was an ingenious attempt at combining the vampiric myth with the dash and derring-do of the swashbuckler.

Captain Kronos, played by German actor Horst Janson, is a master swordsman, late of the Imperial Guard (but flashing a blade forged from the metal of a crucifix), who seeks out and destroys the usual plague of 'blood-thirsty' vampires.

The film had a significantly open-ended conclusion, clearly paving the way for a possible series. However, Hammer never accorded Captain Kronos the opportunity for a hoped-for encore and it was left to a young man in Wellington, New Zealand, to take up the theme with his *Grave Walker* project.

Ken Hammon and Andrew Neal, played assorted vampires and met repeated deaths while Pete O'Herne portrayed their leader, 'Count Murnau', named after W. F. Murnau, the German director of the first 'Dracula' movie, *Nosferatu*. Not surprisingly, Peter Jackson cast himself as the hero, a fearless vampire-slayer going by the name of 'Captain Eumig' – a film-maker's joke on the name of a well-known Austrian make of cameras and projectors.

> As well as acting and directing, I created the make-up effects for the zombie-kind-of-undead-creatures. I was continually coming up with story ideas and shooting endless bits and pieces in the hope that I'd eventually end up with a feature-length film! The results still exist, albeit as a rather fragmentary thing running probably forty-five minutes to an hour and very roughly cut and glued together.

'My strongest memory of the film,' says Ken Hammon, 'is of *digging!* We dug for corpses of the undead in an overgrown graveyard, in the woods around Pukerua Bay, in the Jackson's backyard. The joke was, "OK, guys we need some more digging!" If Peter knew what the final outcome was supposed to be, I never heard it! Shot over a period of

When it came to needing actual graves, we wisely abandoned the cemetery and my parents found me a tiny spot in the middle of their carefully tended garden. Here, amongst the rows of carrots and spuds, I am happily going about my grave robbing duties. From the first trenches I dug when I was about 8 years old, I was constantly digging holes – either graves or trenches – in my parents' garden.

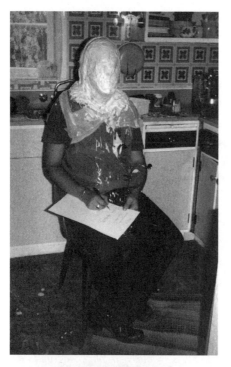

Pete O'Herne under a headful of Plaster of Paris in my mum's kitchen. Pete was playing a zombie in my Super 8mm epic Curse of the Gravewalker. *A much softer material, alginate, is used by the professionals to make head casts. I didn't know that then, and we all suffered through the hot, stifling, direct plaster moulding process. The pad in Pete's hand is a safety measure, so that he can scribble a warning if he can't breathe!*

The result of the head cast, the severed head, is sitting on the cabinet behind Pete as I make him up for a day's shooting on Gravewalker. *The look of the zombies is very much inspired by the Hammer horror* Plague of Zombies.

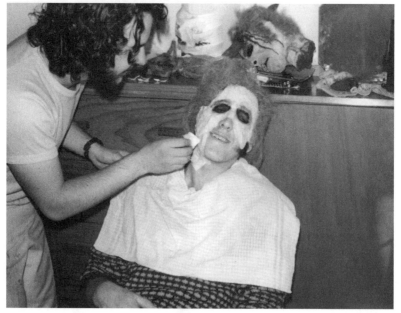

perhaps two years, it was, without doubt, the maddest project of them all! Pete's homage to Hammer, filmed with an anamorphic lens gaffer-taped onto camera and then shown with the lens gaffer-taped onto the projector, but throwing this amazing great image that filled the entire wall of the Jackson living-room.'

Peter's ambition was still that of an aspiring special-effects man as opposed to a director, and he was already devising ideas for using forced-perspective in a way not unlike that in which it would later be used in *The Lord of the Rings*. Ken remembers Peter plotting a scene that would feature adults in the foreground and school children (as adults) in the background in order to create an illusion of distance. Make-up experiments were, on an amateur scale, as ambitious as some of those that would be eventually created for the occupants of Isengard and Mordor – with as much discomfort for those involved! Pete O'Herne recalls: 'Do you know how I'd spend my Saturdays and Sundays back then? I'd go round to Peter's house and he'd say, "OK, mate, I'm going to put Plaster of Paris over your head today, and you're going to have to breathe through drinking straws up your nostrils until it sets!" God knows how many nights I'd be coming home tearing bloody tissue-paper off my face; or, worst of all, trying to get latex rubber out of my eyebrows!'

Peter shot 'day-for-night' using a blue filter on the camera lens to give the impression that the film had been shot by the light of the moon when vampires might be expected to prowl. He also experimented with dry ice in order to create the obligatory misty atmosphere typically found in woods frequented by zombies. 'We went down into the forest,' recalls Pete O'Herne, 'dug a pit and filled it up with dry ice so that I could lie in it and rise up out of the grave in a spooky way. The problem is that dry ice is comprised of CO_2, and if you're going to be stupid enough to lie in a lot of it, you have to be very careful not to inhale! My only consolation was that Peter had already discovered the dangers through experimenting with dry ice in the bathtub at home!'

The making of *Gravewalker* was clearly an ad-hoc process and Peter was undoubtedly the engine driving the project; nevertheless, his approach was also – as it would often be on *Rings* – collaborative.

LEFT: *Occasionally the holes were faked, as this interesting pair of shots reveal. I'm firing my zombie-killing crossbow into the bottom of a grave, and this was the way we faked it in our garage, which also doubled as a sound-stage on a number of occasions.*

Ken Hammon recalls: 'Peter was a spontaneous film-maker: open to other people's ideas and not in the least protective of his own ideas – which probably sometimes accounts for the jagged rhythms of his first experiments.' Despite all the work that went into the film, the results were, for Peter, disappointing...

> Towards the end, I was getting kind of dispirited, because I was pouring a huge amount of effort into the project – making stuff for it, shooting it at the weekends – but, however much work I did, it never seemed to look quite how I saw it in my mind's eye...

Pete O'Herne understands Peter's frustration: 'The problem was that the limited equipment available to us for effects meant that whatever we achieved fell short of what was going in Peter's head. With *The Curse of the Gravewalker* he probably would have liked to have seen all those things he loved in the movies – the horse-drawn carriage galloping along in the dark, down an old road in a dense forest – and of course he had to make do with us guys, doubling up and playing all the parts and not being particularly good at it either. We couldn't even manage decent fight sequences because there weren't enough of us. With someone always having to operate the camera, just about every encounter was inevitably limited to one-on-one. So, I think Peter began to get bored by just how frustrating it was.'

Eventually, Peter reached the conclusion that, in their current form, his film experiments were going nowhere.

> I realised that nobody was ever going to see the vampire film since Super 8 was a format that had no ability to be copied and no means of ever being professionally screened anywhere... What, I asked myself, am I ultimately doing all this for? I knew it was time to move on – to put the 8mm camera away and start filming on 16mm. I was going to have to figure out how to make films in a more professional format.

My twenty-first birthday cake, decorated by my mum.

In 1982, around the time that Peter's ambitions were focusing on pursuing a more professional approach to film-making, he and Ken Hammon took a three-week trip to Los Angeles, his first close-up experience of the movie-Mecca – Hollywood.

The lads packed a lot into their time in 'tinsel town': going to horror and sci-fi conventions (at one of which they met Dave Prowse, the man under the Darth Vader mask in *Star Wars*) and attending a talk by Frank Marshall, an associate of Stephen Spielberg who had recently served as a producer on *Raiders of the Lost Ark* and *Poltergeist* and whose next few films would include *The Goonies* (the cast of which included the young Sean Astin), two more Indiana Jones titles and three *Back to the Future* movies.

Peter and Ken watched a taping of the then-popular TV comedy, *The Dukes of Hazard*. Although an interesting experience, it was a series that neither of them followed or particularly liked and Ken remembers their disappointment that the recording had not been of the contemporary show, *Fantasy Island*. Set on a mysterious island resort where any fantasy requested could be fulfilled, the show starred Ricardo Montalban as Mr Roarke, the island's urbane, white-suited host, and Hervé Villechaize as Roarke's diminutive assistant, Tattoo.

'We visited the set of *Fantasy Island*,' says Ken, 'but we were really frustrated that we weren't able to see the show being recorded because it was unique in that it not only featured a former *Star Trek* villain – Montalban was Khan Noonian Singh in *The Wrath of Khan* – but *also* an ex-*James Bond* villain, since Villechaize had been Nick Nack, Christopher Lee's side-kick in *The Man with the Golden Gun*. You have to remember that we were real movie-buffs!'

Neither Ken nor I had our driver's licence – that's a kind of necessity to be a real geek – and we somehow thought that everything in LA was

After my twenty-first birthday, Ken and I travelled to LA to attend a sci-fi convention. Getting an autograph from Dave 'Darth Vader' Prowse was a thrill, especially since he was also in some of my beloved Hammer horror movies.

within walking distance! We discovered that was not quite the case. We had absolutely no money to hire taxis or drivers.

They visited all the Hollywood tourists sites and several less well-known ones: 'We took long foot tours,' recalls Ken. 'We walked miles and Peter never got lost, though he'd never tell me where we were going until we got there! One route march ended outside St Joseph's Hospital in Burbank with Peter announcing, "That's where Walt Disney died"!'

They went to the rather better known Disney memorial, the Disneyland theme park in Anaheim where Peter was sufficiently delighted by the mix of fantasy and futurism to immediately decide to make a return visit on the following day, while the less-enamoured Ken opted, instead, for a day by the swimming pool.

The Hollywood trip was perhaps the final spur needed to goad Peter Jackson onto the course that would eventually determine his career. The dream factories that produced the films and television shows that he loved were now real places as opposed to being part of some remote other world on the other side of the globe. He returned to Wellington and his photoengraving job with his film-making ambitions strengthened.

One lunch break I happened to be walking past a photo-shop, next to the old Regent Theatre in town. The shop sold various second-hand movie-gear and I always stopped and looked in the window. On this particular day, I saw a Bolex 16mm camera with a big zoom lens. I'd read about them in magazines, but I'd never seen one before and now, suddenly, here *was* one sitting in the window of a Wellington shop. I was virtually trembling with excitement.

The Bolex camera was light and easy to handle. It was spring loaded so all you had to do was wind it up and you were then ready to shoot up to thirty seconds of 16mm footage. A second-hand Bolex was a rare find in New Zealand and it was exactly what I needed if I was to make real progress with my film-making. I could abandon the Super 8 footage we'd shot on *Gravewalker* and start something new. There was only one problem: the price ticket on the Bolex was for $2,500 NZ, not a small sum today and, in 1982, a fortune. *Two-and-a-half grand!* There was no way that I could have saved that kind of money from my job on the paper.

I raced home and I begged my parents if they could possibly lend me the money. They gave me a loan – which I don't think I ever repaid! – and I rushed back to the shop and bought the camera. The feeling of holding it – *owning* it – was incredibly, unbelievably exciting! That kind of support from your parents is so important, and that loan was the most significant thing my mum and dad did to help me become a film-maker. When I won the Oscar for Best Director, I did what has become almost a joke – thank my parents. But for me, just saying their names – Joan and Bill Jackson – on Oscar night had a personal meaning to me that nobody could ever really understand.

It wasn't long, however, before Peter realised that using a 16mm camera would necessarily involve serious on-going financial commitments. One reason for the initial popularity of 8mm film was that developing the film stock, using what is called a 'reversal' process, gave a positive print (rather than a negative) that could be immediately projected and viewed – which was ideal for the home-movie enthusiast. The drawbacks for anyone with serious film-making ambitions were that, without a negative, any attempt at editing film was fairly irrevocable and, whilst a negative could be made from the print, doing so involved serious loss of quality.

In comparison, film shot on a 16mm camera could either use film-stock that employed a similar 'reversal' process to 8mm or film that could be developed using a 'negative/positive' process resulting in a 'master' negative from which a print could be struck in order for the film to be edited. Then, once the edit had been complete, the negative itself would be cut to match and prints of the finished film would be struck.

Super 8 cartridges, giving you three minutes of film each cost three to four dollars. To get the equivalent three minutes on 16mm, I discovered, would cost twenty times as much! It was a painful realisation that every time I loaded a 100-foot roll of film it was going to cost $100 to buy the negative and make a print. This was serious money: I couldn't just muck around with this camera, popping-off shots without thinking. From the get-go I really had to have a plan!

So I bought one roll of film and shot some trial footage in order to learn how the camera worked: finding out about speed controls and how to read light-metres and set exposures. There was a lot to learn – all the things that I'd not had to even think about with the Super 8 cameras. That was a $70 experiment, but I was determined that when I bought the next roll of film, I wasn't going to waste more money on ideas that didn't lead anywhere. I decided I was going to make a little ten-minute film: something short and entertaining that I could hopefully enter into festivals.

That, however, wasn't quite how it would work out...

Roast of the Day is what it was going to be called and it was a nice little Jacksonish joke: Giles Copeland, a young man employed by a food-processing company, drives into a sleepy little New Zealand town and begins a door-to-door collection of envelopes for an annual charity-appeal organised by his employers.

Giles' firm uses its sponsorship of the nationwide famine-relief appeal as a blatant public relations exercise and employees are promoted or demoted depending upon the amount they manage to solicit from the public.

Giles, a formerly not-too-successful collector, has been given the 'wop-wops' run of small coastal towns miles from anywhere and it his last chance to show what he can do… It just so happens that collection-day is 31 October – Peter Jackson's birthday but, more to the point, *Halloween!*

Although Giles manages to collect a number of envelopes pinned to the doorframes of the houses, the town seems unaccountably – even eerily – deserted. Then he notices 'a scruffy, bearded, tramp-like character' eating a squashed possum off the road. On spotting Giles, this unsavoury character becomes a homicidal lunatic, producing a bayonet and lurching menacingly towards him. Only just succeeding in making a getaway in his car, Giles stops at a large mansion – hoping to pick up an envelope 'bulging with green ones' – only to find that he has stumbled into the den of cannibal-aliens-in-human-form for whom he is destined to provide first-hand famine-relief as their 'roast of the day'.

The services of Ken Hammon were once again enlisted and Ken, who at this time was working for a housing association in Porirua, inducted a work-colleague, Craig Smith, into the project to play Giles. In fact, Craig was another former Kapiti College student, although in

Bad Taste *shoot – Day One, 27 October 1983. At this point in time I thought we would be shooting for a few weeks to make a ten-minute short called* Roast of the Day. *One of my photoengraving mates, Phil Lamey, was there helping with the camera, along with Craig Smith and Ken Hammon.*

a different year to Ken and Peter. 'My only memory of Peter at school,' recalls Craig, 'was when the television programme, *Spot On*, launched its contest for young film-makers and I went to one of the classrooms where you could pick up a leaflet and entry-form. Peter happened to be there and when he heard me ask for the form, he said, "Ah-ha! *Competition!*" That's the last we saw of each other until I got involved in *Roast of the Day*.'

Craig was deemed a positive asset to the production by virtue of the fact that, unlike most of the cast-members of Peter's earlier films, he was an accomplished amateur actor with aspirations to enter the profession: 'At school I'd appeared in *Joseph and the Amazing Technicolor Dreamcoat* (my portrayal of Pharaoh is still being talked about today!) and I'd also been in several productions by the local repertory company, The Kapiti Players: I was the Mad Hatter in *Alice in Wonderland*, the Second Voice in *Under Milk Wood* and as for my Big Bad Wolf – well, all I can say is they *loved me!*'

Ken Hammon and Pete O'Herne were among the first members of the film crew when shooting began on 27 October 1983 in Makara, not far from Wellington, with a shot of Giles consulting a road sign. The signpost (complete with AA logos) had been made by Peter and looked sufficiently authentic to cause a memorable brush with the law. With the shot in the can, the team were taking down the sign when they were spotted by a public-spirited citizen who decided to report their act of vandalism to the local police!

Fortunately the crew were easily able to show that the sign was their own as opposed to public property, if only because of the clearly made-up destinations: in one direction, 'Castle Rock' (a place-name in a story in Stephen King's comic-book, *Creepshow*, and the recently-released George Romero film of the same name); and, in the other direction, the place where, unwittingly, Giles was to meet his grisly end – 'Kaihoro', a tasteful little joke inspired by a Maori word meaning to 'eat greedily'!

That was the beginning. But *only* the beginning…

Craig Smith reflects, 'It had all seemed nice, clean, simple and easy: six weeks work tops and we were out of there. But, if there is no script, if it's not locked down then – whether it's a five-cent

A moment captured at work at the Evening Post – *it was what we did to fill in the days!*

movie or a million-dollar movie – anarchy ensues!'

Today, Peter Jackson would probably agree (although his films have tended to allow for a greater degree of script flexibility than other directors); at the time, however, the film featured few dialogue scenes and his approach was one of shooting from a storyboard of mental images: 'There has never been a script,' he would tell the New Zealand Film Commission after fifteen months of filming. 'There has simply been no need for a script. I have gone to the locations with every shot, every angle in my head. I just direct the others according to my plan.'

The process by which *Roast of the Day* grew – or, to use a better word, *mutated* – into what would eventually become the cult movie, *Bad Taste*, is a intriguing, often bewildering, saga of plot developments and restructurings the full, intricate complexity of which are probably only of interest to the most devoted *Bad Taste* fans and are already chronicled on a variety of internet web-sites.

Suffice it to say, as Craig Smith puts it, that 'once Pete got the bit

At one point I started drawing caricatures of my Evening Post *workmates, including a self-portrait (bottom left).*

between his teeth – he just kept throwing more and more ideas into it.'

'It just kept going,' recalls Pete O'Herne, 'building and building until for some of us – though probably not for Peter – it all started to blur!' Twists and turns developed, details and gags were added and, says Ken Hammon, with no script, there was an inevitable tendency 'for simple sequences to end up much more elaborate than planned.'

> I kept shooting, shooting, every weekend and then I'd go into the *Evening Post* to do my job all week long and I'd be sitting there, bored, thinking up ideas for the next weekend's filming. It was a classic 'make it up as you go along' situation – and I had all week to make it up, before the next weekend's shooting would happen. That thinking time always led to my coming up with something new that I'd get excited about and, in that way, the story kept expanding.

Progress, however, was intermittent and entirely driven by what I could afford from my weekly pay packet. I would save up several hundred dollars in order to buy four or five rolls of film, we'd shoot for a day and use them all up and then I'd realise that I couldn't afford to *process* the film, so I'd have to put them in the fridge until I'd get my next wage-check and could afford to put the film into the lab for processing. But having to pay the lab-bill meant that I then wasn't able to buy any film for the following week, so I'd lose another weekend's filming and would have to wait for another pay-cheque in order to buy some more rolls of film.

Nevertheless, new sequences continued to be shot at a variety of locations around Pukerua Bay, including the historic Gear Homestead in Porirua, which served as the cannibals' mansion. An elegant, white-painted, clapboard house with a colonnaded veranda, the Homestead had been built in 1882 by New Zealand tycoon James Gear whose

---

Gear Homestead near Porirua served as the main location for Bad Taste. *My parents knew the caretakers and they kindly gave us free access during the weekends when there weren't weddings in the garden, which was the principal use of the old dwelling.*

fortune had come from the Gear Meat Preserving and Freezing Company – an appropriate sponsor for *Roast of the Day*!

Gear Homestead was administered by the local council but Peter's father happened to know the caretakers and arranged for 'the boys' – as Peter and his friends were referred to in the Jackson household – to shoot there on 'three or four occasions', although, by the time the film was completed, the number of filming days in or around the house had risen to a figure closer to thirty or forty!

Roast of the Day briefly became *Sapien Alfresco* before acquiring a new working-title of *Giles' Big Day*. A major development in the plot occurred when the cannibals became invading aliens hoping to make earth a source of fast food for the people of their planet who were otherwise forced to live on guinea-pigs! Then the S.A.S. suddenly burst onto the scene. When making *The Lord of the Rings*, Peter would discover that a member of his cast – Christopher Lee – was a former member of the 22nd Regiment, the Special Air Service (Motto: 'Who dares Wins'), but he had long been fascinated by stories about the exploits of the S.A.S. and they soon had a key role to play in *Giles' Big Day*.

> The SAS appearance in *Bad Taste* is directly linked to the siege of the Iranian embassy in London, which occurred while we were making the movie. I saw the TV images of these guys storming the building and put them in the movie!

Peter came up with the idea of a bunch of balaclava-wearing S.A.S operatives storming the house and rescuing Giles who was gently marinating in a barrel of herbs and vegetables with an apple stuck in his mouth! However, there was a twist: although the S.A.S. *seem* to be helping Giles to escape from the alien-cannibals and are seen killing

---

RIGHT: *This is the original Mark One design for the Bad Taste aliens. In the mid-Eighties,* American Werewolf in London *had come out with Rick Baker's brilliant transforming latex 'change-o-heads'. I tried to copy that with these designs, which were based on the idea that the S.A.S. rescuers would actually transform into aliens. Everything, including plot and designs, got overhauled following Craig's exit from the project.*

his captors, it is nothing more than a cruel joke since the rescuers eventually turn into aliens who have simply been enjoying themselves by 'playing with their food'!

The involvement of the S.A.S. required additional cast and, in addition to Pete O'Herne, Peter Jackson enlisted the help of two work colleagues at Wellington Newspapers: Mike Minett and Terry Potter. 'The rest of us,' recalls Mike, 'were into sex, drugs and rock-and-roll but Peter was just this nice, adorable guy who loved his mum and dad and was really into making movies.'

'I really liked Peter,' says Terry Potter, 'I liked his sense of humour.' Legend has it that a sign appeared in the process department of Wellington Newspapers that read: 'Who needs drugs when you've got Peter Jackson?' There were the occasional practical jokes – paper bats in the darkrooms, larks with home-made tarantulas – but those who knew Peter at the time recall him not so much as an 'outright funny guy' as someone with an engagingly quirky way of looking at things: an off-the-wall take on life seen in the Monty Python TV shows and the surreal films of The Beatles, whose music he adored.

Peter's love of The Beatles was shared by another *Post* colleague, Ray Battersby (with whom he later planned to make a TV documentary on The Beatles' visit to Wellington), and Mike Minett who, as a member of a local rock band – 'almost everybody belonged to a band in those days' – had taped his own versions of some Beatles numbers on his four-track recorder: 'Pete heard them and spent several lunch breaks – while the rest of us were sitting around playing cards – attempting to add the vocal track. He was enthusiastic and knew all the lyrics but, unfortunately, couldn't sing for shit!'

Years later, when the Howard Shore soundtrack for *The Fellowship of the Ring* was being recorded at London's Abbey Road Studios, Peter and Howard along with Recording Engineer John Kurlander (who had worked on the Beatles' *Abbey Road* album) and Associate Producer, Rick Porras, paid homage to the iconic cover-image of the 1969 album by posing for a photograph while striding across the famous nearby zebra-crossing. But long before that, as we shall see, The Beatles would have a fleeting connection with *Bad Taste…*

Mike after a hard night out on the town. I had to be careful with my camera angles on that day. Something very similar happened years later on LOTR with Viggo Mortensen, except that was due to an encounter with a surf board, not a fist!

Apart from his Beatlemania, the driving passion in his life was film. 'He was always talking about movies,' remembers Mike Minett. 'It was *movies, movies, movies!*'

'In the end,' recalls Terry Potter who admits to not being much of a cinemagoer before meeting Peter, 'he talked us *all* into liking movies and, eventually into *making* movies. It started out with our lending a hand when he needed people to help with transport and carrying equipment: it really wasn't that much hassle and, after a bit, we started enjoying it.'

'There were times,' says Mike, 'when it was terminally boring. It would be: "Just ten minutes more…" "Not long now…" "Almost ready…" We'd be waiting and waiting till it was all boredom, *boredom!* Then, instead of just helping out as crew, we got the chance to be in *front* of the camera!'

Had they but known it, Terry and Mike along with Pete, Craig and Ken, were getting themselves involved in a project that, whilst bringing them none of the usual trappings associated with being film stars, would at least give them cult-movie celebrity status. Almost twenty years on, they are still occasionally recognised and asked for autographs; Pete and Mike, particularly, are in frequent e-mail correspondence with fans all over the world, and Terry Potter, when attending the premiere of *The Two Towers*, was introduced to 'the Hobbits' and was amused to be greeted with bows from the young stars who happen to be keen fans of *Bad Taste*.

Back in 1983, such goings-on would have been unimaginable. Most of the guys who helped Peter in pursuing his hobby thought of it as no more than that: a sometimes fun, sometimes boring way of spend a Sunday, hanging around with a few mates, playing at film-making and having a few beers at the end of the day.

However, what the story of the making of *Bad Taste* shows – and confirms again and again – is that Peter Jackson was already developing the talents, displaying the personal philosophy and demonstrating the stamina and tenacity that would equip him to tackle *The Lord of the Rings* and sustain him through its making.

'Perhaps the most fascinating thing about this little amateur movie,' says Craig Smith, 'is the way in which Peter was developing his skills as a film-maker, as a special effects artist – even as an actor. It is the story of someone developing his craft from scratch and necessity…'

Over the best part of the next three years (specific datings are difficult due to the fragmentary nature of the way in which they worked and the inevitable haziness of people's memories), Peter would suc-

A home-made camera crane perched on the cliffs above Pukerua Bay. I had no way of actually seeing what I was shooting, so I'd point the camera in the basic direction and hope for the best. I'd find out how successful the shot had been when I looked at the 16mm print.

ceed in enthusing and involving work colleagues and friends (and often friends and relations of friends!) either as full- or part-time crew members or as 'extras' for those scenes involving the cannibal-cum-aliens.

Peter built his own camera equipment including tracks and a dolly for moving the camera along the ground and a home-made version of a 'Steadicam' – a spring-loaded, weight-counterbalanced camera harness designed to allow the filming of action scenes in *cinema-vérité* – which, at the time, would have cost upwards of $40,000 but which Peter constructed for just 'twenty bucks'! He also made an aluminium crane, 'put together like a giant Meccano set', that allowed – more or less! – professional-looking crane-shots...

> Once I'd mounted the 16mm camera on the end of the crane there was no way of looking through the lens, so I simply pointed in the general direction of the actors and hoped for the best! Actually, I discovered that if you used a wide-angle lens, then you'd generally get away with that sort of thing!

Peter also created the film's props, including a convincing-looking arsenal of weapons made out of aluminium tubing, cardboard and wood and 'largely held together with glue!' He particularly relished the opportunity to create the alien make-ups that were, had the world but known it, forerunners of the armies of prosthetic grotesques that would, one day, march out of Weta Workshop and onto the battlefields of Middle-earth! The foam latex was whisked up in his mother's food-mixer and baked in the family oven – the size of which was the only constraint on Peter's imagination...

> I sculpted the alien heads to a precise dimension so that I could squeeze them into the oven with about half-an-inch to spare – which is the evolutionary explanation for why the aliens all had somewhat flattened head shapes!

As Joan Jackson would later recall, 'Peter would often take over the whole kitchen. I'd have a menu planned for dinner and we'd end up

This is the gang of photoengraving colleagues I rounded up for a scene in a crowded room. We shot it in one of the darkrooms after work on a Saturday. It was edited together with reverses of Craig in the barrel, which I shot in my parents' garage. I used to buy old white shirts at the Salvation Army store and dye them blue – it was the cheapest alien wardrobe I could think of!

having sausages under the grill because Peter was using the oven!'

Peter's diverse creativity and astonishing proficiency impressed those who knew him. Work colleague, Ray Battersby, who would briefly join the ranks of 'Aliens 3rd Class', recalls, 'I was amazed at his confidence and authority on set. He was in total control, handling everything with complete aplomb. I should have known better than to have ever underestimated Peter, because he could turn his hand to just about anything: he was the Swiss army knife of creative ability!'

Not content with his various creative responsibilities off-screen, Peter had also written himself into the action as the 'scruffy, bearded, tramp-like character' with the bayonet that attacks Giles on his arrival in Kaihoro. As anyone who has ever seen Peter demonstrating to actors how a scene is to be played, there can be little doubt that had he been subjected to one or two different influences or have been given some alternative opportunities to express his imagination and creativity, he might easily have been drawn to a career in acting.

Week in, week out, on as regular a basis as possible, the guys got together and filmed. Around this time, Peter wrote, 'I love writing, I love editing, I love dabbling in special effects, but organising everyone and getting out and filming is a real chore.' Nevertheless he did and he got the other guys to do it, too.

'After all these years,' says Mike Minett, 'we are all still talking about it and, of course, we always say what fun it was and how we all established this crazy, nutcase friendship… But we all had our lives and jobs and there were times when it was hard to get up on Sunday mornings – especially if it was cold or even raining – and go off filming. But Peter couldn't afford *not* to film: he'd have got his pay-cheque and bought a few more reels of film. If he didn't film, he'd get behind schedule. So, he had to do it – and we had to help him do it.'

Craig Smith reflects, 'I often ask myself what it was about Peter that made us all get involved and go along with his schemes. Peter was something of an oddball character, but then, the truth is, we were *all* oddball, nerdy fan-boys, hanging out together, going to movies and then trying to *make* a movie… But Peter had a knack for motivating people. I believe he felt completely secure in himself – he had inherent self-belief and was always totally focused – and those are qualities that attract other people like a magnet. That's what kept hauling people in Sunday after Sunday.'

Jamie Selkirk, Peter's long-time editor and co-director of Weta Workshop, sees him as employing a similar, if refined, technique today: 'Peter has a great knack for starting people off with something that is little more than the germ of an idea. He gets people excited and committed, draws them in further by soliciting their input and then develops and embellishes the idea to a stage where they're hooked! Then he can push them, because he knows that once they've made a creative and emotional investment, they are unlikely to quit until they can deliver something with which both Peter and they are totally happy.'

By the end of 1985, after a period of fifteen months, *Giles' Big Day* had got substantially bigger…

I didn't have any editing equipment, so I just shot and shot and shot and stacked the film away under my bed. Although I knew that it wasn't finished, I was still, at the time, thinking in terms of a ten- to fifteen-minute film.

Eventually I took a week's leave from work – I was only allowed three weeks off each year – went to the Film Unit and hired a little machine, called a Pic-sync editor, and a splicer for joining the cut footage and a pair of re-wind arms so that I could manually wind back and forth through the film spools. I put the re-wind arms on an old plank of wood, which I then clamped onto my parent's dining-room table – for the week while I was editing, they had to eat off their laps in the lounge!

I had shot four hours of film and – by the end of the week – ended up with 55 minutes of edited footage. I was amazed, I'd no idea we had something that was almost already an hour long... There was a moment where I debated trying to cut it back down to the original ten- to fifteen-minutes, because I knew that there was always a possibility of showing a short movie at film festivals. On the other hand, no one would want a picture that ran for an hour – there was no market for it. It was a pivotal moment, but I figured, 'I've only got another half an hour to go and I'll have a full-length feature!' So, all of a sudden, *Giles' Big Day* was going to be a feature film... I was shocked, because I'd never even considered the idea until that point.

If the little amateur movie was now to run to feature-film length then clearly an injection of cash was required to make that possible. To date, *Giles' Big Day* had cost $8,500 (of which Peter had invested $8,000 and Ken Hammon $500) and Peter decided to turn for help to the New Zealand Film Commission. The founding of the Commission, less than a decade before, had been based on a series of proposals written on behalf of the Cultural Branch of the Department of Internal Affairs by Jim Booth, later assistant director of the Queen Elizabeth II Arts Council of New Zealand and a man who was to play a significant role in the shaping of Peter Jackson's career.

Jim Booth's proposals were for a Film Commission that would be totally 'market-orientated' as opposed to the government-sponsored film-making undertaken by the National Film Unit (where, as a school-leaver Peter had gone in search of employment) or the funding of experimental films, which was to be left to the Arts Council.

The Film Commission was to be run 'strictly on an investment basis with an eye very firmly on the market', investing in the production of films – for television and theatre – that, in addition to generating income, would provide 'cinematograph expressions particular to New Zealand' as opposed to what was seen as being a 'largely unrelieved diet of films from foreign cultures.' In addition it was hoped that such films would 'do much to announce the existence of New Zealand to the world at large'.

Jim Booth, the author of these plans, had become Executive Director of the New Zealand Film Commission in 1983 and it was two years later – on 18th January 1985 – that a fifty-five-minute videotape and a nineteen-page document entitled *Giles' Big Day* arrived on his desk from a 'Peter Robert Jackson (copyright owner)' who was applying for $7,000 'to assist the completion of filming on a low-budget 16mm Feature Film'. On the following page, the applicant refined that definition to 'Ultra low budget,' and went on: 'I would be tempted to call it zero-budget if it hadn't been for the fact that I've put $8,000 of my own money into it.'

It was to be the beginning of an exchange of correspondence that would eventually bring about a break-through in Peter's long-held ambitions to be a film-maker, but which, again and again, demonstrate the extent to which the determination and tenacity that would become hallmarks of the Jackson personality were already firmly established.

Peter's letters to Jim show him to have been a young man with strongly held views that he was not afraid of expressing, with belief in his skills and abilities – articulated with self-affirming confidence but also a total absence of arrogance – and with a positive, upbeat philosophy of life that was undimmed by momentary disappointment. The occasional typos and spelling errors have been corrected – '(excuse the mistakes)' he added in pen at the bottom of the nineteenth page – the italics, where used, are my own.

By way of introduction, Peter offered the following self-portrait: 'I am 23 years old and *all I want to do is make movies.* I've always been keen on films, especially ones of the fantasy/horror genres. Special

My bedroom in my early twenties, already starting to groan under the weight of geekdom books and videos.

effects have long been a fascination, ever since being exposed to *Thunderbirds* at the age of 5. All I wanted to be when I was a little boy was a special effects man. *Fortunately I didn't just dream*, I grabbed Plasticine and started making monsters and masks when I was still at Pukerua Bay Primary School. It is this grounding that I'm finding so useful now...'

Of the film he was attempting to make, Peter wrote: 'The movie is science-fiction/horror film with large doses of extremely black humour, some of which is quite tasteless. It is science-fiction but not in the connotations that most people have with that term (i.e. *Star Wars*, *Doctor Who* etc.) The horror is mainly in the gore field. We sacrificed potential "scariness" for humour at an early stage...'

As his mother would later report: 'I didn't think it would be quite so gory as what it is, but then as Peter said: "There's a laugh with every drop of blood, Mum. There are laughs..." I know him very well, he's always had a great sense of humour, I think that's his forte, but he covered it with horror, too...'

Despite its laughs, Peter stressed that the story, had 'its moments of suspense' and was 'aimed directly at the *Monty Python/Animal House* punters, as well as the standard sci-fi/horror buff. Someone who goes to *Friday the 13th* to enjoy eight inventive murders will have plenty to drool over in our film.' Lest the concept of drooling over grisly deaths strike a wrong chord, he added a disclaimer of the kind usually displayed on films in connection with the treatment of animals: '*Having said that, I must make the point that NO women get killed or threatened in the film.*' His point, and it is the redeeming feature of the eventual messiness that is *Bad Taste*, was that not only were its horrors tempered by humour, but that the film could in no way be accused of being exploitational.

Peter provided details of those involved in the project and what, to date, had been achieved. 'Continually giving up Sundays over such a long period of time is a lot to expect of a fairly large group, and it is to everyone's credit that interest and enthusiasm has hardly waned since the start. In fact it is stronger than ever now as in the last couple of months everyone has suddenly realised that it is GETTING SERIOUS.'

However, he went on to explain, he was now facing problems: the film contained a great many special effects and he simply did not have the time during the week to get everything made and ready for the following Sunday's shoot and the other guys in the group couldn't assist either because they didn't live close enough to 'pop around', had wives and families to think about or lived in flats that didn't have sufficient space to work. 'Above all is the simple fact that the work is so complex and requires a knowledge of materials and techniques that takes a long time to develop, as well as a fairly high level of artistic skill.'

Lest the point hadn't been clearly enough expressed, he added – using words that have a prophetic ring when one remembers the level of personal control exercised over every facet of the filming of *The Lord of the Rings* – 'I also like to be in complete control of the look and quality of the stuff that goes on screen.'

One can only speculate on the picture of Peter Jackson which must have begun to form in the mind of Jim Booth, before he even reached 'The Proposal' which was for $7,000 to enable him to take four months unpaid leave and work on 'the extensive make-up and visual effects that form the last thirty-five minutes of our already partially completed feature.'

The figure proposed comprised $4,200 for sixty rolls of film and $2,800 which would give him $175 a week for sixteen weeks: a sum that would be spent on board and keep to his parents and the purchasing of essential materials: 'paint, timber, latex, fibreglass, and sundries like glue, screws, cables etc.' Although it was apparently not possible to give a detailed breakdown of these costs, Peter, happily announced, 'All I know is that $175 per week will be quite adequate to produce the goodies I've got in mind.'

About one thing, Peter was adamant: 'A loan of the type that has to be repaid within twelve months, or whatever, is something I have no interest in. I have enough on my plate getting the film finished without having to worry about big debts... I realise that the whole financial aspect of producing a feature film is something I am going to have to face up to at some stage, with legal agreements, copyrights and everything else involved sorted out, but I want to shield myself from that side of things as much as possible until we have completed filming. It is far more important for me to concentrate on next Sunday's camera angles, with as few distractions as possible.'

A detailed synopsis of the 'Plot – Part One (filmed)' ran to five pages while 'Part Two (unfilmed)' took up *six* pages, which really ought to have suggested that the action described was likely to run for somewhat longer than the promised thirty-five minutes! The action-packed conclusion of the film featured Giles making a crazy thrill-ride escape down the gully of a stream (inspired by a scene in *Romancing the Stone*), an elaborate sequence involving an alien spaceship, a flying 'chair type thing', and an encounter with a 'vaguely humanoid creature' that would have been brought to life with stop-frame animation. Called 'the feared Troppe Marcher of Om', it was described as 'standing there, all seven feet and pointy teeth'! The *dénouement* saw Giles defeating the Troppe Marcher, destroying the aliens and their spacecraft and concluded with the revelation that even though he lost his job (having failed to collect sufficient charity

The vomit drinking scene. I had somebody help me mix the green gloop, which I'd prepared with food colouring, yoghurt and diced vegetables. I remember taking a look at it and suggesting to somebody it needed thickening up. Unbeknownst to me, they went into the garden and added handfuls of dirt – unbeknownst to them, I needed it to be consumed by our hungry aliens, so they all ended up drinking something similar to thick green mud. I had no idea why people complained about the horrible taste!

donations) 'AT LEAST HE HAD THE SATISFACTION OF KNOW-ING THAT HE HAD SAVED THE WORLD.'

'Well that's it!' wrote Peter. 'Can we do it? Yes, there is nothing there that I have not got figured out.' However bizarre this application must read, its author sounded supremely confident and disarmingly candid:

'I think I've summed the whole thing up fairly well. I've been honest and not tried to pretend we're something we're not. If you decide to support us you must realise that you're dealing with ama-teur film-makers that do not fit into the standard guidelines and film production methods established in this country. I have not made any wild claims or boasts about the film's prospects. Just how successful we have been… will be over to you to decide when you view the video.'

There was a 'Last Word', anticipating and answering any potential criticisms of *Giles' Big Day*: 'One subject I would like to touch upon is the question of "Is it culture?" Yes, it is. Cinema is an art form, and art is culture. I will get rather angry if people get on their high horse when this film comes out and moan about it not being a proper New Zealand Film, or that we "shouldn't make these types of films here". I'm a New Zealander and proud of it. I have every right to make whatever film I please and it is just as much a New Zealand Film as anyone else's. If I like horror films then I'll make horror films. If anyone objects then they should get off their bum and make their own film.'

'I've just about typed myself dry…' Peter concluded, but there was no doubting his conviction and commitment: '*If you decide that you cannot support us the film will still be made.* I will stay at work and continue to film in my spare time. I've committed far too much money to it, to back down now. The production of a feature film in your spare time is, as you can imagine, a mammoth undertaking especially while working full-time in another job that is also full of its own pressures and deadlines. I have said with pride many times that we're making a movie "with no help from anyone," but now the pressure is beginning to tell, and I'm worried that the quality of the film will suffer. And that would be the greatest pity of all.'

The six weeks Peter waited for a reply from the Film Commission must have seemed interminable. When it came it was disappointing. 'We very much admire your enthusiasm, energy and dedication…' wrote Jim Booth, 'But (and it is a big "but"), we do not think that we can assist you financially with this project. In the end, neither the film as shot, or the effects, are up to the standard which would see the Commission obtain a return on its investment.'

Peter's initial response seems to have been one of disillusionment. He wanted to know what, precisely, was wrong with the way in which the film had been shot – and was, not surprisingly, wounded by the slur on the quality of his precious special effects. Unable to bring himself to speak with Jim Booth in person – 'He assumed the role of my nemesis and I was too scared to speak with him' – Peter delegated Ken Hammon to make a telephone call to the Film Commission in order to get a more detailed critique. Three weeks later, Peter was ready to reply...

> I realise now, looking back, that my stubbornness was evident even then, because I kept right on shooting my movie and bombarded Jim with another seven-page diatribe telling him how stupid the Film Commission were to have turned me down!

It was, actually, an *eight*-page diatribe! It began innocuously: 'Thanks for your letter and the consideration that you obviously gave our proposal. As you can imagine, an air of disappointment was wafting about for a while, but it soon passed.' Peter was also careful to keep open future lines of communication: 'We are going to need plenty of help from the Film Commission in the next year, in terms of advice and information...' (No mention, wisely, of money) '...so we would certainly like to keep you up to date with the project.' Peter then added a defiant declaration of his intention to see the project through to completion: '*After all, it will one day stand as a "New Zealand Feature".*'

Then the lecture began! Peter tackled Jim Booth's reservations about the quality of the film. *Giles' Big Day*, Peter said, was not intended to compete with Stanley Kubrick's *Barry Lyndon* but with movies such as *Fiend* and *Deadly Spawn*: 'Our sole aim... has been to produce an addition to the ever-growing range of zero-budget, schlock gore video tapes, proven video favourites world-wide.... I'm not claiming our film to be the greatest thing since sliced bread, but I do think it will at least "stand out from the bunch". It has pace that few of these films can match, good intelligent humour and the New Zealand locations give it a fresh look [that is] well away from American suburbia or log cabins.'

With every paragraph pounded out on the typewriter, Peter revealed his wide-ranging knowledge of cinema (his examples are of both Hollywood and New Zealand films) and his intimate understanding of a specific film genre that he clearly thought was unknown territory to Mr Booth of the Film Commission:

'A film like *Kramer vs. Kramer* or *Smash Palace* must perform on many levels to succeed. The script must be excellent, the acting of a very high standard, the photography and sound completely professional. The stern gaze of the critics and public are on the film. If the acting is poor, or the direction sloppy, the whole thing falls apart and the film becomes a bit of a joke. With our type of horror gore film none of this really matters because the film is already a joke. Nobody takes them seriously, nor are they meant to. When I make this film, I'm saying to the audience: "Look, you know this is rubbish, and I know this is rubbish, so let's just unhook our brains and enjoy ourselves." Of course, there are people who don't see it like that, and they are either the people who hate horror films, or the critics who put the most pretentious or Freudian meanings to every scene…'

There followed a further two pages of close argument, drawing parallels with such movies as Tobe Hooper's *The Texas Chain Saw Massacre*, Sam Raimi's *The Evil Dead*, George Romero's *Night of the Living Dead* and other films that had proved to be 'just as welcome in "art-house' cinemas as in any video shop, showing that "sleazy gore films" can achieve a certain critical respect as well.' To which comment he added, as a bracketed throw-way: '(Not that it really concerns me.)'

In Jim Booth's letter, the Film Commission's Executive Director had sought to explain how the Commission worked: 'We operate in a manner similar to a merchant bank and we have to be as confident as possible that our funds have a chance of being recouped from the sale of the finished product…'

It was something that, by page six, Peter was ready to tackle head-on: 'This business about the Commission being in it for the money. Frankly this came as a surprise to me, considering some of the films that you have been associated with in the past. I realise that things are pretty grim in the film industry at the moment, with government support for the Commission slipping away. I guess that you are faced with the prospect of largely supporting yourselves from investment returns etc., so I can understand your caution…' Peter was, he now readily admits, an angry young man:

Using my parent's typewriter on the kitchen table, I'd be sitting there, late into the night, writing these interminable letters, exacting my anger on the Film Commission for turning me down!

The letter continued: 'We were not asking for, nor did we expect, charity... I really hope that in the future there will come a time when there is enough money to spare to give enthusiastic young film-makers a go, without the burden of expecting an immediate financial return.'

'I certainly feel better,' Peter confessed 'having got all that off my chest!' having done so, he felt free to adopt a slightly more conciliatory tone:

'Reading back over what I have written, there are a couple of comments I think I should make. I've felt very awkward writing this, since there's a danger of becoming precious, of sounding like a pupil lecturing the teacher. However, after spending every day for two years with this film constantly on my mind, not to mention the back-breaking work spent on it, I'm sure you will understand my determination to defend it where I think such defence is justified. You may not agree with the points I have made, but I hope it has given you a much better idea of exactly what we are aiming for. I have tried to make my comments as well balanced and constructive as possible.

'The other point I want to make is that this is neither a "sour grapes" letter, nor a "Please Mr Booth, give us another chance" letter. I hope it has not given that impression. *I'm a person that believes that everything happens for the best* and the fact that we are on our own could well be advantageous for both us and the film... As things have worked out, I now have complete freedom to film what I want, with my own money, happy in the knowledge that I don't have to put up with a lot of moans about "public money being spent on such shocking trash".

'Of course,' he went on, 'there will be complaints when the film comes out, but they can only help the box-office, since the horror film regarded as "notorious" are usually the more successful ones.' Think of all that money you are passing up, he seems to be saying and then disarmingly adds, 'There may have been a fair amount of flak coming the way of the Commission too, so it lets us both off the hook.'

Peter's concluding remark betrays a dogged – almost defiant – belief in self-determining success: 'I hope this letter has cleared up any misconceptions that you may have had about what we are trying to achieve… *If you hear or read anything about us in the next year or so, then at least you will know what it's all about.*'

Jim Booth took ten days to reply and when he did it was, on the face of it, not particularly encouraging: he heard, though didn't necessarily accept, the parallels with such films as *The Evil Dead* or *The Texas Chain Saw Massacre* and stood by his belief that the quality of what he had so far seen was simply not good enough, particularly in view of what he believed were increasing demands in the video market for 'higher standards'.

Before signing off, however, Jim Booth offered the chance to reappraise the project with a non-committal suggestion that some future assistance might be forthcoming: 'I am sure you are right when you say that the go-it-alone principle will be beneficial to achieving your aims and if we can look at the film when you have completed it to its full gory glory we can see whether we could help at post production stage.'

Reading this correspondence with hindsight, it is impossible to overlook a specific argument offered by Peter and responded to by Jim. 'Something worth mentioning,' Peter had written, 'is the status that some films have as "cult films". A cult film, particularly a cheap one, often becomes a huge financial success due to the repeat viewings from a group of hard-core fans. While I would be reluctant to make any such claims about *Giles* being "cult material", I think it contains many of the elements of the cult film, and it stands up well to repeat viewings. *Only time will tell…*'

'I'm afraid we often get the argument about "cult films",' replied Jim, 'but they are in fact the very rare exception – the ones that get some kind of lucky break.'

He didn't know it yet, but he was the very person destined to give Peter Jackson and his would-be 'cult-film' just such a lucky break – but not quite yet…

Signing off his letter, Jim Booth wrote, 'No doubt we will be hearing from you at a later date.' When he did hear, four months later in July 1985, it was in another lengthy letter (six pages this time) recounting the most extraordinary tangled tale: 'As I promised last time,' Peter began, 'a further update on the progress we are making with our rather taste-less, low-budget 16mm feature...'

Peter Jackson was, without doubt, a born storyteller with a thriller-writer's understanding of the power of suspense! 'Just before I get into my stride,' he went on, ' an apology for the overpowering typing....' Indeed, unlike his previous epistles – in which the typing had a feint, almost ghostly, quality – the present letter was so inky that every 'a' and 'e' was no more than a blob! He duly explained, 'New ribbon! (I think I might have got the wrong sort.)'

Only then did he take up his story:

'Hopefully you can recall the basic plans we had and the video that you saw containing the first hour for our movie, *Giles' Big Day*. If you can't, don't worry since you may as well forget it anyway. In the last three or four months the whole thing has gone through a complete facelift, leaving the version you saw rather outdated. Before I detail the changes, I'll briefly explain why it happened...'

It transpired that Peter had arranged to take two weeks leave from work in April, the month after receiving the Film Commission's refusal of his grant application, in order to build the considerable number of models and props required for the final part of the film. 'We mapped out a shooting schedule so I'd know what to make first and if I remember right we had hoped to have completed filming... around about now. However, it was not to be.'

On the Sunday before Peter was due to begin his leave, he had planned to take a location-recce with Ken Hammon and Craig Smith in order to block out the scenes. As Peter explained to Jim Booth, they never got around to making their trip...

'Craig broke the news that he wasn't very happy with the amount of gore in the film and could we please tone it down. On further discussion it became clear that it wasn't exactly toning down he wanted, but the removal of all violence and gore! As you can imagine... this was a bit like saying, "You can film *Ben-Hur* so long as you don't have

Craig's departure from Bad Taste. *He allowed himself to be 'written out' in a gory way. At the time, I just shot some random footage, having no idea how I would end up using it and how it would shape the finished movie. It was a big problem.*

anyone wearing a toga!" Without the "good bits" we'd have a real turkey on our hands.'

The personal circumstances that had led Craig to this decision were less sudden than it must have seemed on that Sunday morning when he delivered his ultimatum. 'At the time,' says Craig, 'it seemed like the right thing to do. I had serious health problems: I was hooked on prescription drugs, was drinking heavily and was pretty much f***** in the brain. After several months of some of the worst experiences, I became involved with some devout Pentecostalists who, as they saw it, were trying to drag me over to the light. Frankly, I was at war within myself and my involvement with the film came to seem like another of those things that I needed to change...'

To Peter, the announcement was little short of devastating:

This turn of events was a real bombshell to me. As I sunk back in my chair all I could see was eight grand, in used twenties, floating down in front of my eyes. My next fairly coherent thought was "Thank God we didn't get the Film Commission grant". We would have been in a very awkward position.

Peter and Ken attempted to 'reason' with Craig – 'the discussion was full of deep and meaningful theology and the whole thing should have been broadcast on *Credo*' – but it was to no avail. Eventually, they reached an understanding:

> I explained to him that we had a bunch of really nasty aliens on our hands and they had to be disposed of somehow. What did he think would happen to religion if they were allowed to take over the world? He relented a bit and said that he would kill them on screen, so long as they were only shot. Pointy things like axes, knives and bayonets were a no-no, and chainsaws were Right Out! I tried to make him see that more gory methods of killing off the alien baddies gave us far more scope for humour, thereby making a joke of the film. Shooting them was dull and in many respects more cold-blooded. However, he was quite adamant.
>
> *In the end, it simply came down to a situation where an actor was trying to control what a writer/director does with his film.* Even to a photo-engraver like myself, that was pretty hard to take. However noble his motives may have been, I wasn't going to allow him to censor what I wanted to do.

Recalling what was a difficult time, Craig Smith (for whom religion would later prove 'a phase' which he 'got over'), says of Peter's attitude: 'I was, at the time quite sincere about my moral stand – on one occasion, I'd even dragged Ken along to a revival meeting out of serious concerns for his immortal soul! I honestly believe that Peter tried to understand where I was coming from and, remarkably in view of what had happened, remained a friend despite having left him with a serious headache.' As Peter put it at the time: 'I always have respect for other people's beliefs, no matter what they are, so I couldn't get too angry with Craig.'

In passing, Peter hinted that the blame for Craig's decision might have been laid at the door of the Film Commission! 'I think he took the rejection of our grant application a little harder than the rest of us,' Peter told Jim. 'The idea of another year or so of filming on a rejected movie must have been a little depressing for him and he may have opted for the easy way out. I don't altogether blame him. At times I wish I had an easy way out as well! Still, whatever his motives, one thing was sure: he had a rotten sense of timing.'

Peter finally agreed to write Craig out of the film and Craig agreed to shoot for a couple more days in order to make sense of the plot changes – although, at that moment the director had to confess, he 'didn't even know what the plot of my own film now was!' Worst of all was the frustration of 'blowing two weeks leave just sitting around the house thinking.' After all, as he wryly pointed out: 'That was something that I could have done just as well at work or on the train!'

After taking several long walks over the hills above Pukerua Bay, 'trying to get inspiration from somewhere', Peter finally had it 'all sorted out'. Giles would be killed during the escape from Gear Homestead and the S.A.S. men who had previously turned out to be aliens would no longer be either S.A.S. *or* aliens, but 'a special task force set up to monitor and react to any U.F.O. activities'.

When, years later, the recasting of the role of Aragorn in *The Lord of the Rings* resulted in a lot of last-minute rescheduling, there were those who expressed surprise at Peter's apparent calmness in the face of what was a major crisis. What they didn't know was that he had been there before, but could at least console himself with the thought that, unlike *Giles' Big Day*, he hadn't already sixteen months of filmed footage in the can.

By the time he was writing to the Film Commission, Peter had cut ten minutes of footage to make sense of Craig's scenes that couldn't now be completed and had worked quite a few new 'goodies' into the scenario:

'The very first scene has one of the most disgusting things I've ever seen in a film and a little later there are some appalling things done with a sledgehammer, however, I won't go into details here. *You'll just have to wait with mouth-watering anticipation until I've got it edited!* Despite the gore, I think people will accept it for the black comedy it is. I think both of the scenes that I mentioned above are very funny, but then I might be a trifle warped!'

I figured out a lot of my Bad Taste *script problems during long lonely walks over these cliffs. I loved the wild landscape. We used to carry this crane and other equipment up the hills each weekend. Eventually we got sick of that and ended up hiding all the equipment in the bushes, hoping it would still be there whenever we returned in the next few weeks.*

Despite the sorry saga he was reporting, Peter was clearly in good spirits: with Mike, Terry and Pete O'Herne, he had taken a week's leave, during which time they hired a sound camera from the National Film Unit and – having 'figured out how it worked' – had, as Peter delightfully put it, embarked on their 'first ever experience of shooting talking bits'!

The results of these experiments with sync-sound were, the director reported, 'surprisingly… not TOO bad'! 'Remember,' he wrote, 'that these guys had done all their previous acting wearing balaclavas and shooting people. In these early scenes they are unmasked, in civvies and have to act and talk at the same time!'

It also gave Peter a further opportunity to appear on screen: in addition to playing 'Robert', the bearded, bayonet-wielding cannibal-zombie-alien who first attacks Craig in Kaihoro, Peter (sans beard) was now also playing 'Derek', a nerdy, buck-toothed 'alien-buster', wearing spectacles and a school scarf and out to save the world from an invasion of 'extraterrestrial psychopaths'. Peter's comments (in the role of Derek) about himself (in the persona of the alien Robert) are an amusingly apposite piece of character description: 'There's something strange about him – like he's got a screw loose or something…'

Whilst Craig's sudden departure from Bad Taste *is widely known to fans, Terry also asked to be written out. He was emigrating to Australia and couldn't carry on, so I devised and shot an Ozzy death scene, which involved a basic impalement through the body with a metal spike. Several months later, Terry arrived back from an unhappy time in Oz and offered to rejoin the group. Fortunately things had not advanced that far in his absence, and I wrote him back in as if he'd never left!*

Doubtless there were times when people, witnessing the filming of *Bad Taste*, must have thought that they *all* had a screw or two loose!

Playing two roles eventually led to Peter engaging in a cliff-top fight with himself, perilously filmed above Pukerua Bay. As Peter would later tell the fan-site, The Bastards Have Landed (named from *Bad Taste*'s defining quote), whilst the scene was most certainly dangerous, the results were less spectacular than he had envisaged: 'I was always disappointed with the footage, because it felt way more scary being there, than it looked on film!'

The fight – in which Peter was seen both bearded and clean-shaven – was shot in two sessions with the best part of a year between, rather as Elijah Wood and Sean Astin would eventually film their scene on the Cirith Ungol stairs in *The Return of the King*, while the fact that Ken Hammon was required to stand in for back-of-the-head-shots of Robert (or Derek as the case may be) meant that the sequence was filmed in a similar way to some of the scenes in *The Lord of the Rings* involving scale doubles. Unlike many moviemakers, whatever Peter Jackson asks or expects of an actor, the chances are he has sometime done something similar himself!

Nevertheless, the overall situation with *Giles' Big Day* was scarcely any less serious than when Peter had first approached the Film Commission: several more months work, an investment of a further $3,000 and still only an hour of completed film. It was, he said, 'a bit like running on a treadmill.' That said, he was convinced that it had all worked out for the best.

'Peter has always had confidence,' says Ken Hammon, 'he's always been optimistic. He has an unwavering sense that things will always work out.' Or as Craig Smith puts it: 'Peter was always going to be a film-maker. Failure was simply not an option.'

Moreover, as Peter told Jim Booth, he considered the new version of the film as nothing short of an improvement:

'The revamping of the film was a situation that was forced on me. I would like to say that I did it of my own choosing, but I can't. It was the best thing that ever happened to the film. It made me look at the project from a different vantage point and it was only then that I saw it for what it was and was able to chop out the dead wood and inject new life into it. *A valuable lesson has been learned.*'

It had indeed and it was one not easily forgotten...

As for Craig Smith, he takes a similar line, albeit from a self-mocking perspective: 'By taking my moral stand, it turned it into a damn sight better film. So, really, if it hadn't been for me...!'

Only one issue remained – apart from the need for money – and that was the title: *Giles' Big Day* was clearly no longer appropriate. 'After much banging of our heads,' wrote Peter, 'we finally came up with the moniker *Bad Taste*. This seems to sum it all up rather well. It has a double meaning. Not only does it describe the aesthetic qualities of the film, but [also] works in with the main plot device of a bunch of aliens with a taste for human meat... The other name that we considered for a while was *Dirty Creatures*, but *Bad Taste* it will be.'

Bad Taste it was; and, when eventually completed, it would prove to be the film that launched the professional movie-making career of Peter Jackson.

3

A MATTER OF TASTE

'All of a sudden, out of the gloom, leaped this damn great gorilla!' Bob Lewis, manager of the processing department of Wellington Newspapers, was minding his own business, passing the camera darkrooms, when he found himself unexpectedly confronted by an enormous ape. Convincing though it looked – and it was scarily authentic – the simian attacker was, in fact, only a man in a costume. At the time, he was just Peter Jackson, one of the paper's photoengravers; later, however, he would become Peter Jackson, film director, whose movie projects would include a remake of that classic monster-movie, *King Kong*.

Peter had begun making the gorilla costume whilst recuperating from the operation on the pilonidal cyst that had developed following his accident amongst the rock-pools, whilst playing Sinbad. Made of rubber and covered in hair, the ape suit was a highly impressive piece of work. One day, 'for fun' he decided to wear it into work. His first 'victim' was his manager, Bob ('Mr') Lewis: 'I guess Peter thought,

---

TOP RIGHT: *My finished gorilla suit. It was never used in a movie but it started a series of life-changing events.* BOTTOM RIGHT: *Building my gorilla suit in my bedroom. It was made from carved foam and glued together with carpet glue and latex. I was sleeping in a cloud of fumes every night. I think every* Famous Monsters-*inspired kid who has experimented with building monsters has similar stories to tell. I'm sure it alarmed my parents, who must have been copping the fumes as well since our house was so small.*

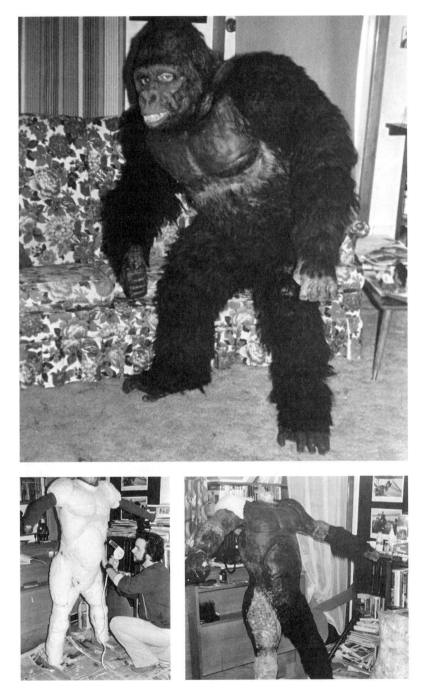

"Let's see if we can give the boss a fright," and he certainly succeeded because I must have jumped a foot in the air!'

News of Peter's escapade percolated up to the journalists on the *Evening Post*, who decided it would make a fun story. Staff photographer, Ian Mackley, snapped Peter in costume, emerging from the bushes onto the roadside near his home in Pukerua Bay. The photograph, which included a passing car (with presumably a seriously baffled driver!) eventually ended up on the front page of the *Post* under the headline 'PETER THE APE MAKES THEM GAPE'!

This startling image happened to catch the eye of Paul Dulieu, a props buyer on a television series entitled *Worzel Gummidge Down Under*. Based on the characters in Barbara Euphan Todd's popular books about 'The Scarecrow of Scatterbrook Farm', the series had originated on British television in 1979. Written by Keith Waterhouse and Willis Hall (of *Billy Liar* fame) Worzel Gummidge starred former 'Dr Who', Jon Pertwee, as the scarecrow and Una Stubbs as Aunt Sally, his temperamental inamorata.

In 1986, Worzel was given a new lease of life 'down under' with Pertwee and Stubbs reprising their roles in two twelve-episode series. A two-part story in the first series ('Two Heads Are Better Than One' and 'Worzel to the Rescue'), involved a sinister character called The Traveller, some spooky voodoo-rituals and a couple of zombie-scarecrows – an appropriate storyline to have involved Peter Jackson!

As a result of the photograph in the *Post*, this guy Paul Dulieu called me up and asked if I would be interested in making a couple of rubber voodoo dolls that were required for the scenes in which the Traveller enslaves Worzel. Later, they were required to burst into flame when Worzel's guardian, The Crowman, rescues the scarecrow and releases him from the enchantment.

I couldn't believe it! This was my first contact with real film people and it was the most exciting moment for me. I remember Paul Dulieu coming to our house and meeting my mum and dad. He asked me: 'How much do you want for these things?' I was rather nervous: I'd never talked about money with anyone like that – in fact, I'd never done anything where anyone was prepared to pay me! – so I really didn't

A key moment in my life. My first encounter with 'professional' film-making was these little latex voodoo dolls I made for Worzel Gummidge Down Under. *They came directly from my gorilla suit being featured in the newspaper, and in turn led to me meeting a whole series of people who would change my life, both professionally and personally.*

know what to ask. In the end I said something like: 'Oh, about $25…'
And he reached into his back pocket and pulled out a big wad of notes
and peeled off a hundred bucks and said: 'Now, look, here's a hundred
dollars – I've got this money so you might as well take it!'
   That was the first professional income I ever earned from films…

Paul Dulieu invited Peter to visit the set of *Worzel Gummidge Down
Under*, which was on location in the Hutt Valley, and so he drove
down to take a look at what was going on. That visit would result in
several significant encounters, the first of which was with Costa
Botes, a name that Peter immediately recognised from having read
his regular film reviews in *The Dominion*.

I was a little starstruck when I met the unit's Third AD. This lowly position is the guy who stops traffic between takes, but I knew his name
from his *Dominion* reviews. When Costa asked what I was doing and I
said: 'Oh, I've been making a movie…' I told him how I'd shot seventy-

One of the first results of my gorilla building was my parents offering to build a workshop for me under the house. Dad and I built it together – that's the workshop on the lower right – and my parents got a nice patio out of it too

five minutes of footage and had asked the Film Commission for financial help but had been turned down, that it was all rather depressing but that I was still boxing on, trying to finish the film. He seemed genuinely interested and actually asked if he could see the footage. I was a little nervous, since I'd been reading his film columns for a few years. It was one of those memorable moments – my first visit to a real movie set, and somebody wants to see my film.

I also noticed a pretty young woman sitting in the corner of a greenhouse talking about the script with Bruce Phillips, the actor who played The Crowman. I didn't know who she was or what her job was, and I didn't even get to meet her on that day, but I'll always remember the fact that she made a striking impression on me, with her long black hair.

She was Keith Waterhouse and Willis Hall's New Zealand Script Consultant on the first *Worzel Gummidge* series and her name was Frances F. Walsh.

Costa recalls: 'My first impression of Peter was of a rather bedraggled, shaggy-looking guy, wearing an awful cardigan (like Starsky used to wear in *Starsky and Hutch*) and a backpack. I hadn't heard Peter's name, but I had read something in the local film journal, *Onfilm,* about a bunch of loonies shooting a movie out at Pukerua Bay.'

The coverage in *Onfilm* had been a piece of publicity that Peter had managed to get for *Bad Taste* at a time when the group were feeling somewhat less than buoyant:

It was tough going on *Bad Taste*: we'd been shooting for years and had failed to get any official support. I thought it would provide a morale-booster for everybody if we were mentioned in what was a film industry journal. So, I wrote to *Onfilm*, told them what we were doing and sent them some photos and they printed a cool little story. It was the first ever bit of press about the making of *Bad Taste* – suddenly the fact that this movie was in production was 'official'!

It also represented the first official announcement of the 'film company' making *Bad Taste*. Once Peter had started filming on 16mm, the exposed footage had to be sent off to the laboratory to be developed, accompanied by a form that had a space for the name of the production company. Filling in the form to go with the first reel of film, Peter had to make a decision: did he leave that part of the form blank or did he pick a name for himself?

> I didn't want anything that sounded too pretentious or self-important, like 'Imperial Pictures', so I decided to come up with something that sounded really dumb! I settled on the stupid name, 'WingNut'.

The inspiration came from… *a rabbit*! Mike Minett had a pet rabbit which he had named 'Wingnut', because its big floppy ears had reminded him of the flared sides – or 'wings' – with which you loosen or tighten a wingnut. Apart from its literal meaning, 'a wingnut' has also long been a slang expression for a person with sticking-out ears

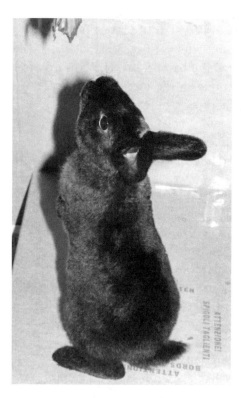

or someone whose behaviour is a bit crazy or off-the-wall. In any event, Mike took Wingnut the rabbit into work to give it to his boss to take home and keep. Sadly, a few weeks later, the rabbit had an encounter with a ferret from which it didn't survive. But, happily, its name is now memorialised as one of the most successful film production companies in the world!

This is Wingnut. For a few days he was kept as a pet in our photoengraving department at the newspaper. We made his pen from my favourite cardboard boxes. He disappeared as quickly as he arrived and I know little about him, but I stole his name for my film company.

The workshop coincided with work picking up on Bad Taste *after Craig's departure.
Probably four or five months had gone by without any filming going on. For a while it felt
like another project started but destined never to finish. The fact that I had never really
finished a movie really concerned me and certainly fuelled my determination to complete*
Bad Taste, *even though it had now changed from ten-minute short to feature film. Here
I'm making a head cast in my new workspace, having decided I didn't like the alien designs
done a couple of years earlier.*

Wingnut made his appearance at the *Post* around the time that I was
trying to think of a name to fill in on the laboratory forms and 'WingNut
Films' seemed nice and dumb! My only edict was to make WingNut one
word with a capital 'N' in the middle.

The news item in the 'Short Ends' column of the August 1985 edition
of *Onfilm* carried a photograph of a scene from *Bad Taste* being filmed
on the cliffs at Pukerua Bay, with Pete O'Herne in front of the camera,
Peter Jackson behind it and Dean Lawrie managing the sound-
recording equipment. 'WingNut Films,' ran the text, 'at work on *Bad
Taste*, a sci-fi/horror 90-minute 16mm feature for the video market,
described as "A mindless movie for the discerning armchair merce-

I met Costa Botes on the Worzel *set, which led to a* Bad Taste *cameo for him and a lot of advice, assistance and introductions for me.*

This is the photo I sent to OnFilm *magazine, our local trade paper. At the time, I wanted to give the guys a morale boost, and seeing our project in print for the first time certainly made it seem real. By now, I had figured out and written a new storyline to use as much existing footage as possible.*

nary"… begun in October 1983 and worked on every Sunday since.'

The item gave details of those involved – billing Peter as producer, writer and director – and went on: 'Although the team are all newcomers and part-timers working without pay, Jackson stresses it is not "some sort of Mickey Mouse home movie", as it has already cost $10,000 (of their own money), and he estimates final budget at $30,000.' This was the piece that had caught Costa Botes' eye: 'I remember laughing and thinking, "What is all that about?"' Anyway, I got chatting with this guy who showed up on the *Worzel Gummidge* set – because when you talk to someone who is really into movies you almost always hit it off – and when he mentioned the fact that he was making a film at the weekends, I put two and two together and figured out that he was one of those loonies I'd been reading about!'

The film had continued to go through various ups and downs: there were precious film days lost due to bad weather and, for Peter, the frustration of having to compete with rival obligations on the part of some members of the team…

> There was a social soccer club at the *Evening Post* and Terry Potter and Mike Minett, who were sporting guys, were members of the team. It was often the case that I couldn't do any filming on a Sunday until the afternoon, because they'd be playing a match in the morning. That bloody soccer club was the bane of my life! I still remember one day, spent at Gear House, waiting for any of the guys to show up. I had the film gear, props and costumes. My parents dropped me off at 9.00am, and came back at 5.00pm to collect me. I was still sitting in the same spot. None of the guys had made it, and in the days before mobile phones I had no idea. I just sat there all day, waiting for anybody to show up, and no one did. I was almost in tears in the car driving home.

Various comings and goings, over the years, continued to ensure that the scenario for *Bad Taste* remained somewhat flexible. Terry Potter spent some time in Australia, but later returned to New Zealand and rejoined the project as, sometime during mid-1986, did the film's original leading actor, Craig Smith, whose marriage had come to an end and who was now free of his dependency on alcohol, prescription drugs and religious convictions.

At the same time that Stephen Sinclair called me, we were welcoming Craig back into the Bad Taste *team. His role as Giles had stayed in the film, although in an altered form, but he was game for anything. Here Cameron Chittock is strapping him into an alien costume.*

'When I decided to leave the team,' says Craig, 'the plan had been for Giles to die during the escape from Gear House and we filmed me being impaled on a tree branch. When, a year later, "the prodigal son" returned to the fold, the death scene was ditched – Peter cut away just before my impaling and Giles survived until the end of the film. I went back to doing all the jobs I had been doing previously, plus donning alien costumes from time to time – the only real change was that Giles was no longer the central character. I fitted back into the team as though I had never left and it's a tribute to the boys that, even today, they don't tease me about it and have made a point of never talking about it to anyone outside the group: it's always been strictly between us – which shows what a very close-knit group we were and, in many ways, still are.'

In July 1986, following his chance encounter with Peter, Costa Botes arranged to view the *Bad Taste* footage on a Steenbeck film editor at the National Film Unit. Also present was the producer of *Worzel Gummidge*, Graham McLean, a former TV director whose credits included *The Ray Bradbury Theatre*, which had featured numerous moments of terror and suspense; he had also worked as an Assistant Director on a creditable New Zealand horror film, entitled *The Scarecrow*. Peter has never forgotten that day:

> It was a little nerve-wracking... It was the very first time that anyone had seen anything from *Bad Taste*: I'd never screened it for the guys who were making it – I'd never even shown my parents – it wasn't finished and it didn't have an ending...

'Peter arrived at the Film Unit,' recalls Costa, 'and produced a big roll of untidy looking film. We threw the reel onto the Steenbeck and sat and watched this extraordinary mishmash – at times quite brilliant, at times quite odd, but always kind of funny... I remember Graham's response was a sort of astonished, "What the hell...?" The thing that struck me, however, was that, even though Peter was obviously struggling from a lack of resources, this guy was a very, very good film-maker with an amazing facility for putting together action sequences.'

Costa's recollections of seeing this footage are significant, and a reminder to those who find it hard to make the link between *Bad Taste* and *The Lord of the Rings*, that film-making is, as Costa observes, as much about sensibility as it is about subject: 'You often see amateur films that

---

My newly revised plot needed the addition of one new character, so Derek was born. I cast myself, having literally run out of friends who could help, and I licking my wounds after Craig left: I figured that at least I would always show up for filming each Sunday!

look amateur, *play* amateur and don't go beyond the obvious. But *Bad Taste* is not like that and I could tell, even from the very early rough-cut, that it was clearly the work of a well-developed talent.

'Above all, Peter's sense of humour is what shines through. I only found out later that he was a great fan of silent comedy and of Buster Keaton in particular, and when you view *Bad Taste* with that in mind you can begin to join up the dots and see that you have a person who is very good with a camera creating comedy out of responsive materials. Peter will take a few bodies and a couple of props, set up a little bit of conflict, and come up with some really good jokes.'

At the end of the screening Costa and Graham McLean wanted to know what Peter was planning to do next: 'Was he looking to finish it, we asked? Peter said that he was and then stammered out that he had tried to talk to the Film Commission, but they weren't very interested. I just remember saying to him: "Then you've got to go back, you've got to actually *show* them this footage."'

Fired by their advice, Peter decided to write another letter to the Commission's Executive Director. Sue Rogers, partner of the late Jim Booth, remembers him talking about his continuing correspondence with the young Peter Jackson: 'Jim always said that much of the credit for the fact that he finally backed *Bad Taste* was down to his assistant, Cindy Treadwell, who, whenever she brought a new Jackson missive into Jim's office, would ask: "When are you going to do something to help this young man?" The fact that Cindy kept on at him encouraged him to encourage Peter.'

Ever since Peter's riveting account of losing his central character and having to restructure the film previously known as *Giles' Big Day*, Jim had tried to suggest (without making any absolute commitments) that the Film Commission door remained open to him: 'I am very pleased to hear that you are still pushing on with the project,' he wrote in one letter. 'I hope you continue to do so and I look forward to seeing the film on the bench when you have an assembly.' Another letter concluded: 'I would like to say how much I admire your enthusiasm and dedication to the project and wish you all the best with its future development.'

It was now time for Peter to knock on that door one more time:

'We have finally got all the early scenes of *Bad Taste* filmed and edited,' he now wrote to Jim. 'In a couple of months we will start shooting the climax... I'm fairly happy with the results we've got. I think the seventy-five minutes could be tightened up a bit... and there are a few changes I want to make, but I won't go into it now. I'll wait until you've seen it and we can have a chat...'

Peter casually mentioned having done 'a few little special effects things' for the *Worzel Gummidge* series and that he had screened the film for Graham McLean and Costa Botes: 'The comments and advice they gave were very helpful. I think the most pleasing thing was the fact that they found the gore to be very funny, especially Costa, who seems to have the same dark sense of humour as I do...' Peter ended by saying that he was now looking forward to screening the footage for Jim: 'You've already seen about half of it on the video, however, so much has been changed or tightened up since then that I'm sure you'll agree that it is much improved...'

That screening eventually took place on the afternoon of 7 August 1986:

> I had my first appointment with Jim Booth in the screening-room. I'd had a two-year, somewhat antagonistic, relationship with him but we'd never actually met. When we did, of course, I found he was a really nice guy! I screened the footage and he said: 'Ah, now I get it! Now, I see what you're doing! Okay... Let me have a think about it...'

Jim Booth reported his views on *Bad Taste* to several of his colleagues at the Film Commission. Deputy Chairman (later Chairman) of the Commission, David Gascoigne recalls Jim's enthusiasm for finding a way to help Peter, if only because, unlike most aspiring film-makers who applied to the Film Commission for a grant, he had already demonstrated his initiative by starting to make the movie on his own. 'Jim described what he had seen of the film,' says David, 'as being raw and rough, but also energetic, vibrant and, in an anarchic way, very funny. He knew, however, that several members of the board were conservatively inclined and unlikely to resonate with some of the images in the film.'

Another introduction via Costa was Stephen Sinclair. After meeting him and enlisting his help in painting sets for Bad Taste, *Stephen called me out of the blue and pitched the idea of* Braindead. *He had developed it as a play but was keen to collaborate with me on a film. My world was suddenly becoming more interesting and exciting: it was a time I'd been dreaming about for fifteen years.*

Indeed, Lindsay Shelton, the Commission's then marketing director, remembers a general response from those to whom Jim described the plot of *Bad Taste* as being along the lines of 'You must be *joking*! Are you seriously suggesting the Film Commission gets involved with this film?' Another six weeks or so passed and Jim requested a further screening in order to get a report on whether the film could be technically released: 'Our criterion for providing you with funds would be that we have some realistic chance of recouping that finance from sales.' Jim also decided to get a second opinion, asking television producer and director, Tony Hiles, to assess *Bad Taste*'s commercial prospects.

Meanwhile, Costa Botes asked Peter if he could screen the film for a couple of friends who were scriptwriters. The screening was at a production office in Wellington where Costa was editing a short film of his own. When Peter arrived with his reel of *Bad Taste* under his arm, he was introduced to Costa's friends: one was playwright, Stephen Sinclair, whose co-authored *Ladies Night* – about a bunch of unemployed guys who become strippers – had opened to considerable acclaim in 1987. Costa's other friend was, at that time, Stephen's partner. 'I recognised her immediately,' says Peter. 'She was the girl with the long dark hair who I'd seen on the *Worzel* set.'

Fran remembers the impression Peter made on her when they

finally met at the screening: 'At first I thought he was Greek! Or perhaps Italian! He had sallow skin and dark hair. But his name was
Jackson so he couldn't be Greek or Italian! Frankly, I didn't quite
know what to make of him although I immediately took a liking to
him: he was just a nice guy, a really nice, funny person; there wasn't
any pretence of any kind, no duplicity and no agendas.'

And what did Fran make of the film? 'My first impression of *Bad
Taste* was of its being completely uninhibited and unrestrained. True,
it didn't have any really usable sound – you could hardly hear what
people were saying – but because it was such a visual piece it didn't
really matter! What was so extraordinary was that, despite having
hardly any money, the guys hadn't allowed that fact to stop them
from doing what they wanted to do. That was really impressive and I
couldn't believe that it wasn't getting supported by the industry.'

Recalling the screening, Costa says: 'Fran and Stephen shared my
own reaction to *Bad Taste* and to this lunatic fan-boy who had made

---

*Through Costa, I met a great group of local film-makers and writers. I wasted no time in
getting them to help me build and paint sets. That's Fran Walsh in the middle, standing on
the chair and wielding a paint brush.*

Tony Hiles was wonderful at not only steering me through film-making politics but in rolling his sleeves up and getting stuck in. Here, he and Bryce Campbell ready a smoke-belching miniature of Gear Homestead for take-off.

it. I think we all looked on him as a kind of lovely fool, a brilliant idiot, a uniquely talented savant who was capable of coming up with amazing ideas and images. But I have to be honest and say that I really had no inkling, at that point, that he would go on to create cinema with real maturity and depth. Not really. That only became obvious a little later...'

Bad Taste came a step closer to getting Film Commission support when, in September 1986, Tony Hiles submitted his assessment of *Bad Taste* to Jim Booth. Tony had met with Peter at an editing suite at a company called, appropriately, 'Mr Chopper', run by Jamie Selkirk who had worked on *Worzel Gummidge* and, years later, would pick up an Oscar for editing *The Return of the King.*

Tony's first reaction to the film and the film-maker is interesting: 'Something which impressed me was that whilst the film needed a lot of work, Peter understood that I required specific details and infor-mation and, unlike most new film-makers who usually talk too much over their film, he told me exactly – and *only* – what I needed to know.'

At the end of the screening Tony had decided that he was going to recommend *Bad Taste* and that he would offer to help produce the film. 'I had to think carefully about whether to get involved in somebody else's film, but Jim and I were good pals, and I was always interested in shaking the tree! Besides, how could you not choose to get involved with this crazy little film? I thought "The Boys" were great – I'd never seen such a loose pack of hopeless heroes in my life, but I really wanted to watch them on screen! *Bad Taste* was new, it was renegade…'

Tony would subsequently write, in defence of the project: 'The rough-cut that I viewed and assessed was a fair reflection of a filmmaker growing through the production process. Despite the shortcomings of the film itself, the story was there and, most important, there was a feeling of inventiveness and cinematographic understanding in Peter Jackson's work. There were other reasons for my support for the film – it is a product of determination, humour and individualism – no formula stuff here, a thoroughly New Zealand film with strong appeal made by, potentially, a new feature director with a pleasantly nasty sense of humour.'

At the time of filing his assessment, Tony described *Bad Taste* in the following terms: 'Potentially, this film could be the Ultimate Low-Budget A+ Splatter and Squelch Movie. So far it has been shot and cut with such an OTT sense of humour and style that it could become a steady earning cult movie – but work needs to be done and it will soon be time for a little professional supervision to move the product economically to completion.'

The 'school report' assessment of Peter that followed was particularly revealing for the picture it gives of him at the time: 'I think Peter Jackson deserves encouragement for his determination and skills. He is a very good special fx maker and, in addition, displays good basic skills in camera operation and editing. Given the constraints under which he has been working, including a re-cut after the departure of his hero, he has already shown himself to be resourceful and dedicated…'

I built a steadicam camera mount using plans from a US home movie magazine, CineMagic. *Like the crane, it was a point, shoot, hope for the best device, but ended up working quite well.*

Comparing him to one of the success-stories of New Zealand film, Geoff Murphy (who would later serve as Peter's second unit director on *The Lord of the Rings*), Tony Hiles described him as 'one of those people who will make films whether he gets any help or not.'

He went on: 'I find his attitude worth encouraging – he has plans to get into special effects for film and does not appear to have super-big ideas about himself – a refreshing change from the usual starry-eyed tyro who thinks the world owes him a living, or at least enough money to make a film.'

The appraisal ended with a couple of caveats: 'There is a lot of untangling to be done and it won't be that quick – but I'm sure it's worth the effort, especially initially, as this will allow us to find out enough about him to know whether it's worth continuing.' And on the subject of money: 'I recommend that any Film Commission investment is stage by stage, drip-fed, keeping the project reasonably lean and hungry, otherwise it could go all over the place, just like the aliens' brains…'

Tony Hiles' evaluation was to prove the turning-point in Peter's career: it reinforced Jim Booth's impression and provided independent evidence that would help convince the board of the Film Commission when the time came to approve investment in the film.

At the end of his report, Tony wrote: 'I look forward to continued involvement with this Sheep-offal Saga.' He had already warned Peter that the Commission might ask him to oversee the film's progress to completion and when Jim Booth wrote to Peter, on 6 October 1986, with the news that the Film Commission was 'now definitely interested in assisting you to complete the movie', he added, along with requests for budgets, that the Commission wanted to appoint Tony as a consultant. In reply, Peter indicated that he was 'very happy with the idea of working with Tony,' although, as Tony pragmatically observes, 'If I'd been a one-legged gorilla he'd have probably still said, "Yes!"'

In his letter to Peter, Jim Booth wrote: 'Once again, I would like to congratulate you on your energy and the results obtained to date. A most commendable effort.' Peter's response was suitably expressive of his obvious gratitude:

'Many thanks for the consideration that you have been giving to my movie over recent weeks. As you can imagine, I was delighted to receive your letter… I realise that my project doesn't follow the normal pattern or accepted procedures, or whatever. The Film Commission's support in spite of that makes me all the more grateful and, I should add, determined to produce something really worthwhile…

'The next six months are going to be a great learning experience for me, far better than going to film school, and at the end of it we'll have a finished film. I'm looking forward to all the learning, and I'm also looking forward to working within a set budget and schedule, a discipline I've never needed before.

'So thanks again for the faith you have shown in me. I won't let you down.'

After signing off – 'Kind regards, Pete Jackson' – he added an engaging, and suitably tantalising, postscript: 'If you liked the movie so far, then don't go away. The best is still to come!'

For a while, Bad Taste *had a very different climax, featuring a chase scene on alien hover vehicles (this was 1985, so I was no doubt inspired by* Return of the Jedi*). I built this model of Craig and hover car at about half scale. Eventually the idea was scrapped and a new ending devised when the NZ Film Commission came onboard.*

Following Tony Hiles' recommendation, Jim Booth began drip-feeding the continuing production of *Bad Taste* with a payment of $5,000 made from the director's discretionary fund and therefore not requiring the approval of the full board of the Film Commission. Jim acquainted David Gascoigne with what he had done and, a little while later, mentioned that he was intending to advance another $5,000. This, as Jim was well aware, was bending the rules, which allowed the director to spend only a maximum of $5,000 per picture, as opposed to making repeated payments on the same project, which would normally have required approval by the board.

'I was knowingly complicit,' admits David, 'because it was a case of Jim having a good idea – he was a great believer in (with capital letters) Having Good Ideas! – and I not only didn't intervene, I gave him tacit encouragement. Today it would be different, but then we were inventing a system of film support as we went along.'

As for Peter, he now reached an important decision about his future career:

> I decided that if Jim was going to be able to give me these payments, then the moment had finally come to start working on the film full-time. So, I went into the Film Commission and picked up the cheque – made out to WingNut Films – for $5,000. It was the most money I had seen in my life; the following day I handed in my notice at the *Evening Post*.
>
> I kept filming for the next six or seven months: I could only shoot at weekends because all my actors still had full-time jobs, but at least I was now able to build props, masks and two different scale-models of the Gear Homestead, which we had now decided was in fact the aliens' spaceship and would have to take off at the end of the movie. Being able to devote all my time to the project meant that I was not only able to accelerate the schedule but also to step up the production values.

Peter had been introduced to Cameron Chittock, a Christchurch model-maker and puppet-builder who was attempting to break into the film industry. Cameron flew up to Wellington, visited Peter at his home in Pukerua Bay and showed him examples of his work.

Cameron was given a tour of the Peter Jackson workshop – a basement room that Peter and his father had dug out under the house and built by hand, and which Richard Taylor would later describe as 'a Batman's lair'! Cameron was staggered at the professionalism, and the sheer quantity, of the creations packed into the room, from Peter's stop-motion puppets for *The Valley* through to the weapons, props and masks, which he had been building for *Bad Taste*. He also got his first glimpse of the film itself:

'I loved it! It made me laugh: I'm not especially interested in horror movies or films with a lot of blood-and-guts, but I found Peter's angle on the genre irresistible. The thing that really attracted me to him was his sense of humour and what you might call his outrageous behaviour on film – he had a rebellious streak in him and he attracted other rebels and provided the focus for a bunch of people in the film industry who were wanting to stir things up a bit!'

Recognising Cameron as someone who was not only skilled but who shared his own passion for special effects, Peter offered him the job of being his special make-up effects assistant. 'I moved to Wellington,' remembers Cameron, 'and, within a few days, was working twenty-four hours a day, seven days a week trying to keep up with Peter!'

Cameron's early recollections of Peter accord with those of many who knew him at this early stage of his career: 'If you didn't know him, you might have thought him quite shy with people, even withdrawn, but as soon as you put a camera in his hands or gave him a paintbrush or bottle of latex to work with, he became incredibly confident and self-assured.'

Until he found accommodation of his own, Cameron lived with the Jackson family and has strong memories of Peter's parents at this time when their son was embarking on his career as a professional film-maker: 'The Jacksons were really delightful people. The moment you met them you realised that Peter had grown up with a very loving and hugely supportive home life. Mr Jackson was calm, warm and generous, a good-natured, jovial man whose company I really enjoyed. Mrs Jackson was very motherly, doing everything possible to make me feel at home and part of the family and clearly dedicated to supporting Peter, even though she couldn't really relate to the weird movie he was busily making! Both parents were obviously happy that Peter had found what he wanted to do in life and were going to do everything they possibly could to help him achieve it.'

As the story began to circulate about the little amateur film that had been three years in the making and was still being filmed, various people began lending their help: Costa Botes met an unpleasant death as an alien; Tony Hiles appeared as the shadowy controller of the anti-alien unit 'Coldfinger' (a reuse of the punning name from Peter's early, uncompleted James Bond spoof); while Stephen Sinclair and Fran Walsh wielded hammers and paintbrushes on the construction of a scale replica of Gear Homestead.

Two more friends of Stephen and Fran's joined the increasingly expanding group that was now pushing *Bad Taste* towards completion. Bryce and Grant Campbell were brothers who worked with special effects gear. They were dragged off to watch the footage already shot which, says Bryce, 'felt about two and half hours long' but which had

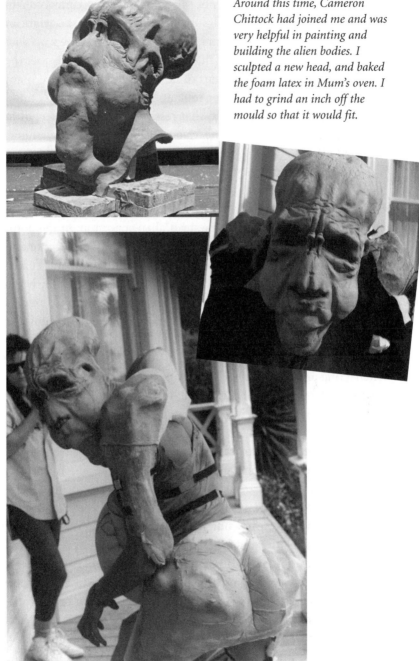

Around this time, Cameron Chittock had joined me and was very helpful in painting and building the alien bodies. I sculpted a new head, and baked the foam latex in Mum's oven. I had to grind an inch off the mould so that it would fit.

the most extraordinary moments: 'There was an interminable gun battle that must have run for almost forty-five minutes, but then an amazing shot of somebody having the top of his head blown off that was so unbelievably convincing that it made you wonder whether the guy who'd filmed it was some sort of homicidal maniac!'

In fact, Bryce and his brother took an immediate liking to Peter: 'He was totally driven and somewhat reserved but, when you got to know him, you realised that he was this big, enthusiastic, super-obsessed kid!'

The Campbell brothers were soon involved giving practical assistance to the project: Grant blew up a car (and a sheep) while Bryce helped with rain and wind effects and had a near-death experience with the model of the Gear Homestead/alien spaceship. At the point when the house 'blasted off', the model was lifted up on a crane and smoke had to pour out from beneath like a rocket taking off: 'I had a smoke machine and Peter built a contraption using a rubbish bin that was intended to collect the smoke and feed it to various outlets within the model. Unfortunately, the pressure built up and the container exploded and a big piece of wood came swishing down on Peter and me like a helicopter blade. Fortunately it missed!'

Reflecting on the support which people in the industry had shown towards *Bad Taste*, Tony Hiles wrote, 'The response was extraordinarily gratifying and at either minimal or (usually) no charge we mustered labour, equipment and building sites… I think my colleagues supported the project because they saw it as… adventurous, risky, crazy, oddball, inventive, humorous and above all – fresh.

'Certainly part of its freshness comes from its raw quality – the often amateurish camera-work is just the start – but I have always felt it is a film with great heart and great integrity. Whether you actually get off on spoof splatter and non sequitur ironic humour is irrelevant because there are a hell of a lot of people who do. It's a risky film but that is one of its great strengths – it will, when complete, be appalling to some and brilliant to others but it will never be average or ordinary…'

While new footage was being filmed to strengthen the story and deliver a *dénouement*, Peter was working with Jamie Selkirk on editing *Bad Taste* into shape. 'It was a fun project to be involved with,'

Cameron and I built a couple of smaller models of Gear Homestead for different shots. Here I am with the smaller models in front of the half-scale house. The filming of Bad Taste *was entering its final days.*

My last day filming Bad Taste – *it was actually a night shoot and we finished about 3am. We shot in some old farm buildings and there were no showers. I actually drove myself home – about two hours away – looking exactly like this. The whole way home I was praying that I wouldn't get stopped by the police!*

says Jamie, 'but who knew what would happen afterwards? Peter Jackson might go on to other things or he might just drop away. At the time, the impetus was simply to get the movie finished! Peter had a great deal of self-belief, but *Bad Taste*, as it then existed, was pretty rough round the edges so I took over the editing: tidying it up and tightening it up; showing Peter where it didn't work, where things jarred or flagged and where continuity didn't match.'

After his first viewing of the film, Jamie had identified one or two places where the pacing would be improved if a shot could be extended for a few seconds. 'I really needed to see what Peter had edited from the film, so I asked him if I could see his other material: the trims and out-takes, anything he had shot that wasn't in the cut. He kept saying, 'Yeah, yeah, they're at home somewhere... I'll bring them in.' The following day, Peter arrived with a huge paper rubbish-bag which he dumped on the floor. It was filled with a great mass of bits and pieces of twisted, tangled film, all stuck together with tape.'

Jamie had the off-cuts and out-takes spliced together and assembled into a rough order, and rescued a number of useful bits and pieces from the jumble: 'I felt that, being a splatter movie, we needed to push it along and that anything at all extraneous had to go. Peter often clung to shots that he wanted to use but which were holding up the film and, in a good-spirited way, I'd have to try and coax him into letting go of stuff that he really didn't need.'

Jamie Selkirk, who still edits Peter's films, admits that not a lot has changed over the years: 'Every movie I've ever cut for Peter has been too long – it's just got trickier as the budgets have got bigger! Very often, Peter will write a scene in one line, such as "Minas Tirith – the battle begins…" One line on paper; fifteen minutes on film! And, no matter how much he shoots, he always cuts together all the scenes he's shot before making any decisions about what finally stays and what goes. We've spent a lot of time cutting a lot of footage that I *knew* wouldn't end up in the picture, but Peter's feeling is that it must be put in first; it's how he works, how he crafts a film.'

Back in 1987, by the time it had been edited, *Bad Taste* had cost $17–18,000 of Peter's money

My cat Timmy poses with four years' worth of Bad Taste *film. This was the original negative, which I had stored under my bed. By the time we made our final prints of the movie, some reels were damaged by mould, which proved very difficult to remove. A couple of shots in the finished movie even have mould stains on them. Sometime soon I'll do a digital clean-up of the movie and finally repair the damage from my sloppy storage!*

and $15,000 of Film Commission money, which Jim Booth contributed to the project in instalments. To complete post-production with a vocal soundtrack, effects and music and a blow-up of the 16mm film to a 35mm print was expected to cost in the region of a further $200,000. This was far too large a sum to be slipped to the film-maker out of some discretionary fund. 'For that money,' Jim told Peter, 'you will have to screen the movie for the board of the Film Commission.' It was another nerve-wracking experience, worse even than screening his raw footage for Jim Booth, because, if the board refused to approve the funding, then *Bad Taste* was unlikely to ever be completed.

> All the members of the Film Commission board were sitting there, seeing *Bad Taste* for the first time. This, of course, was Jim's plan: show them the film in its most polished state; don't let them see it in the state that *he* saw it in, but let them view it as a finished cut so that it feels more like a proper movie...

David Gascoigne's memory of meeting Peter the first time is of someone who was 'pleasant, fun and imaginative but who also had a level of magical persuasiveness! I liked him but "liking" isn't enough, I thought there was evidence of real ability.'

Lindsay Shelton agrees: 'Over the years, the question has often been asked, "How could the Film Commission have ever invested in a splatter movie?" Actually, it's easily answered: they were backing talent; they took a look at what was on offer and decided that this was a talent that they wanted to assist. And they were right.'

'They were a bit shocked by the footage,' says Peter, 'but I think they saw that there was a film there...' As David Gascoigne recalls: 'Seeing the footage was a cathartic experience! Of course some members were concerned or had reservations – being dependent on public money, the board had to consider how the film would be viewed on the political landscape, because if you offend too many politicians then you won't get any more money and that hurts the industry. Happily, despite some nervousness, the board approved the post-production funding without significant dissension.'

A major issue in post-production was the vocal performances of the cast. It was the view of some that 'The Boys' needed to be dubbed by professional actors and it was an issue that Peter had tackled in his original nineteen-page approach to the Film Commission:

'If needs be, me and the others will go out and tape all the sound effects, use our voices and compose and record our own music (a couple of the guys are in bands) BUT I don't really want to do that. The sound plays such an important part in this film (many times I've said to the others, "Don't worry if it doesn't look too great, the sound will carry it through,") so I want to make sure that it is as best a job as can be done under the circumstances. I would like to hire two or three professional sound recordists and editors and I'd like to get professional actors to provide the voice characterisations...'

In the event, Tony Hiles convinced everyone that The Boys should dub their own voices and, though initially a little apprehensive, they quickly mastered the technique and provided strong vocal perform-ances that now seem an essential ingredient of the film's 'home made' appeal. Only Lord Crumb, the head alien, who had been played by Doug Wren, one of Peter's older colleagues at the *Post* and an amateur actor, was dubbed by a *real* actor, Peter Vere-Jones, a man with the fully rounded tones of an old-school thespian. Vere-Jones also served as voice-coach to The Boys, who treated the whole experience with characteristic level-headedness, especially any attempt to get them to open the vowels and enunciate correctly! Mercifully, The Boys (who refused to join the actors' union) stayed completely themselves and the contrast that they provided to Vere-Jones' plummy old alien is one of the joys of *Bad Taste*.

Everyone was in agreement about the importance of finding the right film score for *Bad Taste*. At first, Peter had thought he might be able to incorporate numbers by his favourite group, The Beatles, and former work colleague and fellow fan, Ray Battersby, remembers Peter talking about using the group's 1964 number, 'I'll Get You' ('So I'm telling you, my friend,/That I'll get you, I'll get you in the end,/Yes I will, I'll get you in the end') over the closing credits. Rights and permissions made this proposal impossible, although The Beatles did manage a 'guest' appearance in the film. When the 'brain-dead' Derek

LEFT: *As Jamie laboured away on the final edit, the cast had to rerecord all our dialogue. Here, Pete O'Herne and I try to match our lip movements from a few years earlier. Brent Burge did our final sound mix for* Bad Taste. *Recently, Brent did a brilliant job designing the gorilla vocal sounds for our* King Kong *movie.*

pursues the aliens in a bizarre-looking saloon car with an 'upper deck' (having been adapted for a disabled driver), the passengers in the front seats are life-size cardboard cutouts, painted by Peter, of The Beatles in their 'Sgt Pepper' outfits.

In Peter's first letter to the Film Commission, he had written of his musical ambitions for the film: 'Above all I want a good musical soundtrack. That is the most important thing of all. A soundtrack that carries the film along, smoothing over the rough bits, providing a mirror to what the people are seeing, amplifying the different moods the film contains. Mike and Terry (our two band members) may well be able to come up with something good: they play rock music, and one of my pet hates is a rock soundtrack. Mike had a go at some mood music with his electric guitar and various gizmos a couple of months ago, and it wasn't bad, but I'd love a more orchestral-sounding score if I could get it. A good example of what I like are Brian May's two *Mad Max* soundtracks – overly loud, overly dramatic.'

The first that Wellington composer, Michelle Scullion, heard of the project was an intriguing telephone call: 'Tony Hiles said that he was working on a project with a young guy who was making his first feature. All he said about it was that it was "unusual", that it might be my kind of thing and suggested that I have a look. So, I had a look…'

Tony and Peter screened half an hour of edited footage for Michelle on a Steenbeck machine in Jamie Selkirk's editing suite. 'That first ever meeting,' says Michelle, 'I remember lock, stock and barrel, clean as a whistle, clear as a bell! Peter had messy hair, quite a stammer and a certain coyness about him. The film was incredibly wacky and even though the acting wasn't brilliant, it was honest and had an innocent "boys own adventure" charm.'

There was no sound, but Peter and Tony provided an aural sound score to the movie, creating the effects with mouth noises! 'I was in hysterics; hooting; tears running down my face! It grabbed me and reminded me of going to the local "bug-house", as a kid, to watch giant versions of John Wayne and Donald Duck when, if anyone messed around or made too much noise, the film would be stopped and we'd be told if we didn't quieten down we'd all be sent home!'

At the end of the screening Tony asked if Michelle wanted to work on the film. 'Of course I wanted to work on it! Not because I wanted to work on a feature film – it was to be my first – but because I wanted to work on *this* film!'

Michelle did her research: 'When I work with a film-maker, I want to get into their mind, know what they're thinking of in relation to the score. Peter told me he was a great fan of The Beatles and would have loved to use Beatles songs on the soundtrack; I also discovered that he was a fan of James Bond, so I went off and watched about nine Bond films and some zombie splatter movies that Peter lent me

---

I was worried about copyright issues involved in using an existing image of The Beatles, so I painted these myself. I'm not a great artist but the silliness of it all gets the laugh I was after. For a long time I harboured a dream of including one or two Beatles songs on the Bad Taste *soundtrack, but that could never have happened.*

Three key collaborators in Bad Taste – *from the left, editor Jamie Selkirk, producer Tony Hiles and composer Michelle Scullion. Concentrating on the newspaper crossword at that moment, they were the perfect team to help me when I needed it.*

from his collection! I felt that what it needed to be was a big score, plenty of full-on, wall-to-wall music and – thinking "blokes", "cars", "guns" – went off on a misguided "heavy metal" tangent, before changing course to a more "classical" approach.'

As the score developed and began to be recorded, Michelle was intrigued by Peter's intuitive grasp of the process: 'Peter sat on my shoulder the whole time. He may have lacked musical vocabulary, but he had all the words necessary to explain the shape and the emotion of what he wanted. I was surprised that someone so new to the film business could do that, but he was not only smart, he was an incredibly quick learner: each step was just another thing to be taken in by his huge sponge-brain that soaks up experience and uses it; in turn, I learned to go with him and let him guide me…'

Reflecting on Peter's subsequent career, Michelle Scullion says: 'I won't jump on the bandwagon and say I knew then that he was a film-making genius, but I will say that it was clear that he was totally dedicated and had ambition. *Bad Taste* may have started out as a weekend "guerrilla film-making" project, but I don't believe that it was ever truly a hobby in Peter's mind.'

The score for *Bad Taste* was richly varied to match the moments of insidious menace and relentless pursuit; for the scene where the aliens feast from a bowl of regurgitated pea-green 'gruel', Michelle wrote a subdued jazz score with a muted trumpet: dinner music for chuck-eating; while the climactic battle scene had all the energy of a full-on, rock-and-roll number.

In July 1987, as Michelle was completing her score and the sound effects were being added, a rough-cut of the near-completed film was screened for the New Zealand Film Commission. Internal reports reveal a mixed reaction that veers between arch condescension and blatant dislike. Seeing *Bad Taste*, it seems, had left its audience with something of a bad taste...

The film was disparagingly described as 'a backyard 16mm feature film made by Peter Jackson, a former employee of the *Evening Post* Circulation Department'. Whilst 'its very explicitness should ensure that it can earn some money from the grosser end of the international video market' it was thought to lack 'style and verse' and suffer from various weaknesses including 'minimal acting talent and characters who are unsympathetic and crude.' The report went on: 'The film includes a lot of misjudged humour, which could be enjoyed by the crassest of audiences, but very probably not, because much of the dialogue is incomprehensible, especially so for anyone outside New Zealand.'

Jim Booth defended the project, saying that 'viewing a film with only an unedited dialogue track (and no atmosphere or effects sound) is an unusual experience and perhaps gives a false impression of the finished film', but it was left to Tony Hiles to ride to the defence of the project on which he had been serving as Consultant Producer.

In a document sent to the Film Commission entitled '*Bad Taste*: Report on an Experience', Tony presented not only a vindication of the support which had been shown towards *Bad Taste*, but a moving, often prophetic testimony of belief in Peter and his incipient talent:

I worked with Sue Rogers on the Bad Taste *poster design. I always liked the image of the alien jabbing his finger up, and had attempted to shoot it myself several times. This is a shot I did at the end of my parents' garden. Eventually a professional photographer, Rob Pearson, came onboard and shot the final memorable image on the coast at Moa Point near Wellington Airport. Cameron Chittock was wearing the alien costume.*

'I see him as an amiable mixture of Steven Spielberg and Woody Allen – he is creative, inventive, a good actor and he loves film. However, I do not see him as some sort of messiah. He has a hell of a lot to learn – his comprehension of story and scene structure is limited, as is his ability to utilise his time and that of his co-workers in a fully economic fashion. But these things will change, as he learns fast…'

Countering murmurings that the Commission ought to insist on more changes being made to the film, Tony continued, '*Bad Taste* is an individual film with both the strengths of a film-maker with talent and the weakness of a film-maker with limited experience – and that is exactly why *Bad Taste* essentially works and should be left alone to work in that way.

'*Bad Taste* is more than a New Zealand film, more than a regional film, it is a Pukerua Bay film. For what it will ultimately cost, *Bad Taste* is an extremely low-budget film, which should return its investment if correctly marketed. I believe the actions and support of the New Zealand Film Commission to be an excellent example of how to assist and encourage a new film-maker.

'The whole project is really based on taking a risk; Peter started taking the risk nearly four years ago and the Film Commission took its risk on Peter almost a year ago. Completing the exercise will prove that risks are worth taking.'

Bad Taste was completed and without any further demands for changes.

The song accompanying the end credits – as the survivors drive away into the sunset in Derek's eccentric car – was composed and sung, not by The Beatles, but by Mike Minett with a backing group that included Fran Walsh and Michelle Scullion. It caught the renegade spirit not only of the *Bad Taste* Boys but also of the film and its director…

> *We're gonna be winners, this time we will;*
> *We've got a good team, unbeatable.*
> *This time unite, we'll be as one,*
> *Our private army will never run.*

The last Bad Taste *photo, taken to promote Tony's* Good Taste *documentary. In its own way, it sums up the spirit of the preceding four years quite well.*

We've got the reason to believe,
We've got the power to succeed;
But the minute you let me down,
You'll leave a bad taste in my mouth.

Let's get the permission,
Let's do it right,
License to kill,
License to fight.
We're only Human,
We're only Boys,
We're only… Dispensable toys.

After four years, it was finally over. The little weekend hobbyist film had been given the necessary professional finish. The exhausting, occasionally tedious, week-in-week-out regimen had ended with a flourish of high-energy activity, an injection of much-needed cash and the involvement of people who worked in the real film industry.

It was a moment that marked not just the completion of a movie-making project, it was also the close of an era and that closure had different consequences for different people.

Of The Boys, one or two entertained the hope that they might have a role to play in future Jackson projects, but it was an unrealistic and unrealisable hope. The very qualities in Peter Jackson that had drawn others to him, had made them pitch in on the *Bad Taste* project and, more or less, stick with it for so long, had finally carried him out of their orbit. As participants in what would rapidly be considered a cult movie, they would acquire their own unique cult status: they were, and always will be, 'The *Bad Taste* Boys'. Otherwise – despite having helped save the world from being consumed by aliens! – it was, for them, the end of the road. Most of them embraced their fate philosophically; one or two, perhaps, thought they were, in the words of the film's closing song lyric, 'only dispensable toys'.

Peter was, and still is, deeply conscious of his indebtedness to the group: '*Bad Taste*,' he says, 'was an endurance test. I have great admiration for the guys because they showed up week after week in order to help me get that film made.' There would even be talk, over several years, of a sequel to *Bad Taste* being made and, five years on, WingNut Films would indeed present the New Zealand Film Commission with a proposal for a project to make *two* such sequels, back-to-back. It is a project, however, that has yet to get off the ground...

Reflecting on that 'endurance test' today, Peter sees several similarities between *Bad Taste* and *The Lord of the Rings*:

Both took four years to shoot and both employed the same film-making techniques. The way we made *Bad Taste* was not a bad way to make a film and that is why I adopted a similar approach to *The Lord of the Rings*. Neither was made using the principle: 'Lock a script down, rush off and shoot it without any changes, cut it and release it.' I don't think a rule that says you get one crack at a script and that it never changes is a particularly smart way of making films. I prefer an approach that enables you to pause every now and again and say, 'Yes, this is working okay, but I could really do with a scene that does this, I'd like to put in a sequence that does that, or I need to explain this a bit more...' and you then go and shoot those things as we did with the pick-ups we filmed for *The Lord of the Rings*. Handcrafting a film has always appealed to me: refining, finessing, streamlining as we go along – it's a process that started with *Bad Taste*.

For Peter, in 1987, completing *Bad Taste* was not so much an ending as a beginning. It was, as one observer puts it, now the moment for Peter to move on; he was now a professional film-maker; the talent would soon be recognised, the promise and the ambition fulfilled; it was time for him to step up to bigger challenges.

Although completed and delivered, the Film Commission decided not to show *Bad Taste* prior to screening it at the 1988 Cannes Film Festival. Doubtful of the film's ability to succeed, the policy was to hold back release in order to get the maximum publicity from any response at Cannes – however unlikely that might be! For Peter, the opportunity for *Bad Taste* to become a possible topic of conversation along the length of the Promenade de la Croisette, represented the hope that offers of other work might follow. There was, however, one snag...

> The Cannes Film Festival takes place in May which, at the time I finished work on *Bad Taste*, was still several months away. I'd left my job, was unemployed and had no income. There was nothing to do, except wait...

Wait... *and* come up with new ideas!

Peter had become close friends with Stephen Sinclair and Fran Walsh following their introduction from Costa Botes. Two more of those film industry rebels who were attracted to Peter, they had given him encouragement on *Bad Taste* (as well as lending a hand when the scale replica of Gear Homestead needed painting) but, more importantly, the three of them were already working on a film script together. Throughout 1987, the final year of making *Bad Taste*, they were writing what would eventually become *Braindead*.

> One day Stephen had pitched me an idea about a young man who lives at home with a domineering mother who turns into a zombie – that was the story. It had started life as an idea for a play (and would eventually be staged as *Brain Dead: The Musical* in 1995) but Stephen was also interested in developing the idea for a film with me as director. I thought it

was a great idea; I've always thought that zombies are fantastic and I was, and still am, a huge zombie film-fan.

Zombie pictures are as old as popular cinema and Bela ('Dracula') Lugosi had starred in what was probably the first of the genre: *White Zombie*, made in 1933. Several cult zombie films had appeared in the Sixties and Seventies, including *Night of the Living Dead* and *Dawn of the Dead*, but by the 1980s it had reached plague proportions with *The Evil Dead*, *Re-Animator* and many others. Indeed, during the two years from 1985 to 1987, over twenty zombie-themed films were released, many of them low- or no-budget pictures with such improbable titles as *Night of the Living Babes* and *Bloodsuckers from Outer Space*.

Braindead went through several drafts during 1987 and was budgeted as requiring in the region of $2.5 million, making it a relatively expensive project at that time. Peter, Stephen and Fran submitted an application for development finance to the New Zealand Film Commission:

'*Braindead* is a zombie movie. It is also a parable about breaking away from family ties and emerging into adulthood. As a satirical tale of life in the suburbs, the film is a study of emotional repression and social propriety. There is an inversion of the usual sex role stereotyping: Lionel, our hero, is trapped in a fraught domestic situation until he is rescued by Cathy, who offers him the chance of another life.

'The splatter aspect of the film is highly stylised and tends more towards farce than naturalism. It is more in the style of Monty Python than Sam Peckinpah. Similarly, the characters should not be read as naturalistic. Lionel and Cathy are naïve innocents in a world populated by the bizarre and the grotesque.'

We were very aware that, whilst we had a script, nothing was going to happen with *Braindead* before *Bad Taste* was screened in Cannes, but it was a strategic decision to have a prospective next project to capitalise on any attention that *Bad Taste* might pick up at the festival. Nevertheless, I was still faced by this five-month period of unemployment...

More plans were hatched at regular meetings at Fran and Stephen's flat over a Chinese restaurant in Courtney Place, past which, years later, Peter would ride in the triumphant motorcade *en route* to the premiere of *The Return of the King*.

Cameron Chittock, who joined in many of these sessions, recalls: 'Basically, we would get together and conspire to make evil projects!' One of these dubious enterprises would eventually carry the unlikely tag line: 'Sex, Drugs and Soft Toys'. While working on *Bad Taste*, Peter had coined the term 'splatstick' to describe something that combined the gory messiness of the splatter movie with knockabout laughs of a slapstick comedy. Now he was thinking of another combination-genre by grafting the ever-appealing splatter movie with – *a puppet film*. The new idea was for a 'spluppet movie'!

In the Seventies and Eighties puppets had achieved a new world-wide popularity through the work of Jim Henson, whose contribution to the American educational television series, *Sesame Street*, had led to the international hit TV series, *The Muppet Show*. The premise of a group of puppets producing and starring in a vaudeville show – with intriguing glimpses of backstage tantrums and traumas – not only made household names of Kermit the Frog, Miss Piggy, Fozzie Bear, Gonzo, Rowlf and the rest of the gang, it catapulted them into a series of big-screen adventures beginning, in 1979, with *The Muppet Movie*, which was followed by *The Great Muppet Caper* and *The Muppets Take Manhattan*.

With each of the Muppet feature films, the characters became increasingly liberated not simply from the confines of their puppet-theatre home but also from their puppeteers, to the extent of finding it possible to take a cycle ride through London's Hyde Park. It was a conceit that Peter and his 'co-conspirators' wickedly seized upon…

My initial idea was a very simple image: an all-singing, all-dancing Muppet-style TV show, except that back-stage there are no puppeteers taking puppets off their arms; the puppets are not puppets at all, they are real: they walk into the dressing-room, rip the tab off a can of beer, light up a cigarette and say, 'God, that was a terrible show tonight!' As for the show itself, that was just a piece of cheesy entertainment put on

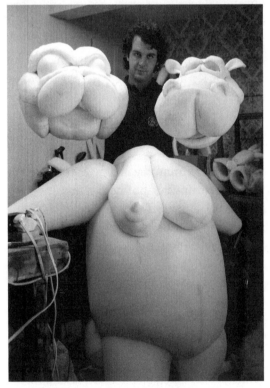

Following the completion of Bad Taste *in November 1987, there was an agonizing wait until the film was to be screened at Cannes in May 1988. I was unemployed, broke and still living at home, so I filled in the time writing* Braindead *with Stephen and Fran, and devising the idea for* Meet the Feebles *with Cameron. Eventually Cameron and I started building puppets to bring our ideas to life.*

by these characters that have the same flaws and weaknesses as any human being.

Unlike the mild-mannered Muppets – whose frailties and idiosyncrasies are charmingly portrayed and utterly inoffensive – the Feebles, as the puppets in this version were to be called, were to be blatantly into anything and everything that was either illegal or immoral, or both! Although the name suggested that this devious, dubious bunch of crooks and perverts were somehow related to the clean-living characters created by Jim Henson, Peter never saw the idea as being a parody of *The Muppet Show*.

> Essentially, the Feebles were satirising human greed and weakness; we were sending up human beings and human nature, not puppets themselves.

The original concept for using the Feebles had sprung out of a suggestion by Grant and Bryce Campbell for a possible late-night television show hosted by an elderly, cantankerous character called Uncle Herman who would tell a series of unlikely (even unsuitable) bedtime tales.

> *Uncle Herman's Bedtime Whoppers*, as we called it, was to be a series of outrageous one-off, half-hour films devoted to different subjects, featuring different actors and probably made by different film-makers. In fact, they'd have nothing in common other than being introduced by Uncle Herman. Talking with Cameron, Stephen and Fran, we decided that this puppet thing featuring the Feebles might be a good candidate for one of Uncle Herman's Whoppers!

Stephen and Fran roped in another of their friends, writer, actor and cabaret comic, Danny Mulheron, who had directed Stephen's satiric musical, *Big Bickies* and was collaborating with the playwright on an outrageous farce, *The Sex Fiend*. Described as possessing an 'unstoppable curiosity and twisted perception of the world that is truly frightening and thoroughly entertaining,' Danny was a suitably anarchic talent to be invited to join in the creation of the Feebles' madhouse of mutated Muppets. Danny joined Peter, Stephen and Fran in writ-

ing the script as well as contributing lyrics for songs while Cameron
Chittock began designing the stars of the show that was now being
called *Meet the Feebles*.

Peter was feeling decidedly happy with life.

> I thought, 'This is fantastic! This is a five-month project that will keep me
> busy until May when I go off to Cannes and get the money for
> *Braindead*.' We applied to the Film Commission for some funding – not
> much, $30–40,000 – convinced that it was a pretty much guaranteed cer-
> tainty. After all, I had finished *Bad Taste*... True it hadn't yet been released
> or sold anywhere, but they'd *seen* it and knew what I could do. They were
> hardly going to turn us down for an inexpensive half-hour TV show.

But they did. The Film Commission declined the application on the
grounds that Peter had assumed would make them assist: *Meet the
Feebles* was not a feature film project, but a one-off TV programme
which was never going to have any sales in the film marketplace. The
money requested might have been relatively small, but it was an
unsound investment. The group explained that *Feebles* would be part
of a TV series, but it was a series that had yet to be commissioned and
funded.

> We had a council of war and were very angry with this – as you always
> were in those days, whenever we got turned down or knocked back!
> Stephen, Fran, Cameron and me decided that we would fund it our-
> selves. It felt a bit like *Bad Taste* all over again, except that we were going
> to be doing it on a reasonably professional level: we were going to have
> a small crew, shoot it in a block and get it done. So we drew up a
> minimal budget of $25,000 and all chipped in equal shares. We put
> together a crew and Cameron and I started building puppets, getting
> together each day in the basement under his flat, chopping up foam and
> carving and sculpting these characters.

Characters like Bletch the Walrus, a lascivious impresario and, literally, a 'cat-lover'; Arthur the Stage-manager, a cockney worm in a flat
cap and jumper (knitted by Peter's mum); Wynyard the Drug-and-
war-crazed Frog with a perilous knife-throwing act; and the star of

Stephen and Fran came on board Meet the Feebles, *not just as writers but also co-financing a self-funded* Bad Taste-*style short film shoot. It was another case of everyone pitching in – here one of our puppeteers, Eleanor Aitkin, and Fran build sets for the forthcoming mini-production.*

'The Fabulous Feebles Variety Hour': Heidi, a 'gorgeous hunk of hippohood', played by Danny Mulheron inside a huge, pink foam-rubber hippopotamus suit.

As is done with animated films, the Feebles' dialogue was recorded prior to the beginning of filming so that the puppeteers would be able to perform to a pre-recorded voice-track. The vocal cast included Peter Vere-Jones, who had provided the voice for Lord Crumb in *Bad Taste,* as Bletch and Brian Sergent, who would later play Ted Sandy-man in *The Lord of the Rings,* as Wynyard the amphibious heroin addict, haunted by the horrors of Vietnam.

Unable to afford a studio in which to film, the group took over the upstairs rooms of a somewhat decrepit Victorian house in the Wellington suburb of Thorndon where Grant and Bryce Campbell were living. Not long before, the Campbells' landlord had evicted a group of drunkards and derelicts and offered the vacated rooms to the brothers on the understanding that they clean up what was several years' unsavoury mess. Peter took on the responsibility in return for permission to use the space as a studio for shooting *Feebles.*

> Everyone was supposed to help, but I remember it was mainly me doing it! I cleared out piles of old newspapers and absolute filth too disgusting to talk about. I had buckets of bleach and I scrubbed and washed and mopped for days on end. Finally, I cleaned up three bedrooms, and a lounge, and a loo – and that became our *Feebles* studio.

Shooting the short version of Meet the Feebles *was a sharp shock. A very small team worked incredibly hard to complete the filming just before I jumped on a plane for Cannes in 1988.*

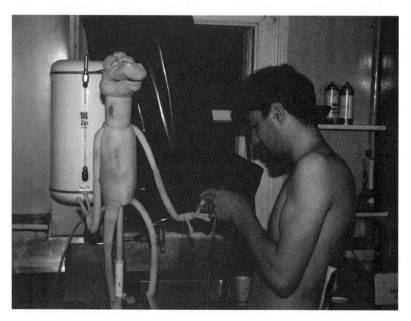

The cleaning process and some major structural renovations took time and shooting on *Meet the Feebles* didn't finally begin until a little over a week before Peter needed to depart for Cannes. Filming with puppets proved more complicated, and therefore slower, than had been anticipated and the shoot ran behind schedule, resulting in only two-thirds of the thirty-minute show making it onto film by the deadline. *Feebles* had to be put on hold until Peter's return and he headed off for the south of France.

Peter travelled to Cannes with Tony Hiles, a curious journey via Los Angeles, Amsterdam and a series of milk-trains to the city on the Riviera whose motto is 'La Vie est un Festival' ('Life is a Festival').

Looking back a few years later, Peter's father, Bill Jackson, would recall: 'I told Pete, don't be too disappointed if it isn't a success at Cannes. It's a heck of a lot to achieve – if it *is*, all to the good, if not don't be upset by it... I was thinking: having put four years into something, no one could be told that it was a failure...'

'It was,' says Peter, 'a real "Dad" thing to say!' But *Bad Taste* was anything but a failure. Peter and Tony promoted the film in every possible way: a rash of garish stickers (hot red with a black splat in the middle and the words *Bad Taste*) broke out all over Cannes and, having been produced using a particularly strong glue, stubbornly resisted removal!

'We wondered whether the foreign audiences would get the jokes,' recalls Tony. 'But we showed the film to the French girl who was working on the New Zealand stand at the Palais des Festivals and, having watched the scene in which Derek puts his own brains back in his shattered cranium, she commented, in not great but *interesting* English: 'Oh, the head! And poor Derek, he was not very well *before* that!'

Bad Taste was greeted with a standing ovation and generated much enthusiastic interest. Despite the New Zealand Film Commission's fears that the picture was 'unsaleable', it sold to ten countries in six days and went on to sell to twenty more.

The French distributor invited Peter to attend the seventeenth International Festival of Fantasy and Science Fiction that was due to be held in Paris a couple of weeks later and offered to pay his expenses to stay in France.

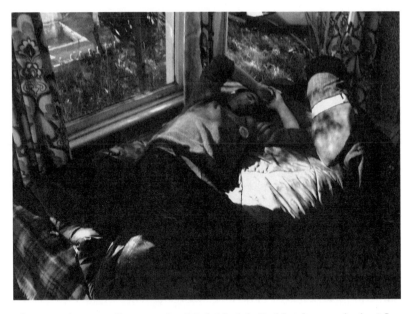

These two pictures really go together. We finished the Feebles *shoot on the day I flew out to Cannes. Here, a shattered Cameron Chittock is crashed out on the couch at our Hawkestone Street shooting location, whilst a few days later I'm having my first taste of international cinema in Cannes, May 1988.*

Tony Hiles headed back to New Zealand alone: 'My job was done, but Peter was clearly going somewhere – I didn't have a clue where – but I just tried to give him a helping hand to go there... I always thought of working with Peter as like driving along a desert road in an old Citroën DS, when up behind me comes this really fast little red sports car and I wave it on...'

The opportunity that Peter had been hoping for came when the Spanish producer, Andrés Vicente Gómez, buying *Bad Taste* for distribution in Spain, expressed interest in seeing any other projects that Peter might have in development. Gómez read the script for *Braindead* and began discussions with the representatives of the New Zealand Film Commission about the possibility of a Spanish/New Zealand co-production. It was suggested that if the film's hapless hero were to have a Spanish girlfriend, it would help any deal, so Peter telephoned Stephen and Fran, who agreed that if casting a Spanish actress was a route to getting *Braindead* in front of the cameras, it was one that should be pursued!

Peter travelled to Paris and introduced the screening of *Bad Taste* at the Festival of Fantasy and Science Fiction, which was held in the 3,000-seat Le Grande Rex Cinema where, fourteen years later, *The Two Towers* would receive its European premiere. *The Auckland Star* reported Peter as saying of the event: 'It's full of crazy Frenchmen, and there are guards at the door. Everybody that comes in gets searched. When the film's screened, there is a continual barrage of chanting and screaming, clapping and cheering. I had to go on stage before *Bad Taste* was screened, which was an experience...'

As the *Star* journalist wrote, the whole event was 'an eye-opener during an eventful year for the 26-year-old Wellingtonian'; topped off by the fact that *Bad Taste* went on to win the coveted Prix de Gore.

Following this triumph, Peter flew to Madrid to meet potential Spanish actresses for the romantic female lead in *Braindead*. One of those who auditioned for him on video was Diana Peñalver, who had appeared in a number of successful films including *El Año de las Luces*, (*The Year of Enlightenment*), which had been produced by Andrés Vicente Gómez and written and directed by Fernando Trueba,

The Olympia Cinema in Cannes. Home of our Bad Taste *screening, and thirteen years later the very same cinema screened the first footage from* The Lord of the Rings *to the world's media. If I had a lucky cinema, I guess this would be it!*

who would go on to make the celebrated romantic comedy, *Belle Epoque*.

Peter decided that, despite her lack of English, Diana Peñalver was ideal for the role of the girl whose destiny was to save Lionel from his tyrannical mother. Then, after so many excitements, it was time for Peter to return home.

> Everything had happened very quickly: I was supposed to go to Cannes for eight or ten days and ended up being abroad for two months. I arrived back on the day *Bad Taste* was having its New Zealand premiere as part of the Wellington Film Festival. I was exhausted but I went straight to the midnight screening at the Embassy Theatre where, fifteen years later, we would hold the world premiere of *The Return of the King*.

The Festival programme note on *Bad Taste* read, 'If Laurel and Hardy had decided to make a film about flesh-eating zombies from outer space, this is how it might have turned out.'

It was a description that might have seemed guaranteed to attract only the most dedicated of fringe audiences, but reports of the film's success in Cannes and Paris ensured that the film-makers were local, if somewhat maverick, heroes!

Mike Minett remembers that night: 'The theatre was packed; everyone was cheering and applauding! It was crazy! None of us had ever expected that kind of reaction. We had no idea that *Bad Taste* would end up being shown around the world, which is why we were willing to do all those mad things and make fools of ourselves – willing to fall out of a tree twenty-five times if that was what was needed! We didn't care! We just did it! We could only be ourselves and maybe that's why *Bad Taste* worked. That night, I had tears in my eyes and thought, "Pete's finally done it! He's broken through! He's going to be famous...

Four of the NZ film industry players at Cannes 1988 – from the left, John Maynard, Jim Booth, Lindsay Shelton and Barrie Everard. Jim was the Executive Director of the NZ Film Commission, and I had gone the full nine rounds with him getting funding for Bad Taste. *In the end it resulted in a great respect, love and partnership with this very funny, brave person.*

We're going to be famous!" Well, anyway, Pete got to be famous…
And I love him and am proud of him.'

The following day, Peter's old employer, the *Evening Post*, raved:
'*Gore… Blimey!* There's heaps of it in Peter Jackson's simply spiffing
splatter movie, *Bad Taste…* An eager audience delightedly lapped up
the offal action as a team of dedicated Kiwi E.T.-busters machine-
gunned, macheted and chain-sawed their way through a swag of
galactic nasties.'

In Tony Hiles' report to the New Zealand Film Commission, submitted as *Bad Taste* was approaching completion, he had written:
'The film will soon be finished, but for Peter it is just the start – his
next few films are going to be most interesting.'

How true that was…

4

SPLATTER AND SPLUPPETS

'Let's not waste any money on this!'

That was one person's verdict when an application for $10,000 development funding had landed on people's desks at the New Zealand Film Commission at the beginning of 1988.

The proposal, for a film variously titled *House Bound* – or, more ominously, *Braindead* – had been submitted by Peter Jackson, Stephen Sinclair and Fran Walsh and was described as 'a tongue-in-cheek zombie genre movie' intended to exploit 'the characteristics of that genre in an over-the-top way.' The proposal went on: 'It will achieve that combination of gore and humour which was foreshadowed in *Bad Taste*, but this time with a script and the backup of a small professional crew.'

Some of the recipients of this proposal were singularly unimpressed: 'Peter Jackson has some talent as a film-maker,' one grudgingly admitted, 'but he has fallen into the trap of selling himself short on "sensation" rather than "soul" and "intelligences".'

The film certainly featured its share of 'sensation': severed limbs and exploding body-parts; an ear in a bowl of custard; quantities of pus, gore and other bodily emissions; a rabid rat-monkey whose poisonous bite is the primal cause of the zombie infestation; and Baby Selwyn, a murderous zombie-tot in a striped romper suit, whose terrifying behaviour is as lethal as it is ludicrous.

Nevertheless, the script assessments that had been carried out were, given the ingredients, surprisingly positive: 'A highly entertaining, funny, gory, horror-love film,' read one report, 'it could emerge as a strong blend of both black comedy and horror...' While another read: 'The visual potential, excellent. The script is good... While the story indulges in lots of bloodthirsty violence, the writers haven't indulged themselves in any off-the-point navel-gazing. I believe this script could well make a successful film.'

Shortly afterwards, *Bad Taste* had become the toast of the town in Cannes, Paris and Wellington, and the odd doubting Thomas was, if not silenced, then at least only permitted muffled protests!

Hedging its bets, the Commission finally settled on a compromise and advanced $6,000 instead of $10,000. But, by July 1988, Peter was back with a new request for financial assistance with his 'touching story of a young couple's relationship placed in jeopardy by a swarm of zombie relatives.'

On this occasion, Peter was asking for $31,300. The money was required in order to rewrite the script with a Spanish female lead, following the decision to cast Diana Peñalver. As a result, the character originally called Cathy would eventually be rechristened Paquita – conveniently the same name as the role Diana had portrayed in the celebrated *El Año de las Luces*.

Since the film was to feature 'a swarm' of zombies, money was also required for 'necessary development of zombie manufacture', which was, Peter explained, as important and as time-consuming as the scripting process.

The balance of the funding application was to pay for the advice of the American script consultant, Dr Linda Seger, who, a few years earlier, had established a reputation by defining 'script consultancy' as a useful – even essential – adjunct to the process of screenwriting and who would go on to write a number of best-selling handbooks, including *Making a Good Script Great*.

The emergence of Linda Seger and other screenwriting consultants and experts was part of a new awareness of the importance of script-to-movie that sprang, in large part, from the work of a man who would become Hollywood's guru of gurus: Robert McKee.

Now known to the cinema-going public through being portrayed as a character in the 2002 Nicholas Cage film, *Adaptation*, Robert

McKee's career was founded on both academic study and practical experience – as an actor and director – of theatre arts. He attended film school, wrote and directed short films and, moving to Los Angeles, wrote scripts (and analysed other peoples' scripts) for United Artists and NBC. In addition to feature films, McKee contributed scripts to such TV favourites as *Kojak*, *Columbo* and *Quincy, MD*.

In 1983, McKee joined the faculty of the School of Cinema and Television at the University of Southern California, where he first presented his groundbreaking seminars on Story. Within a year, McKee was opening the three-day seminar – thirty-hours of intensive concept-broadening tuition over three days – to the wider public. It was the start of a twenty-year career, during which McKee would teach his principles to over 40,000 aspiring screenwriters – like Nicholas Cage's character, Charlie Kauffman, in *Adaptation*.

In 1988, the New Zealand Film Commission invited Robert McKee to Wellington and Peter Jackson, Fran Walsh and Stephen Sinclair signed up for the seminar.

I hadn't heard much about McKee, but the opportunity came at an important time because we were working on the script for *Braindead* and we thought it might be a useful exercise.

There were a lot of rumblings at the time of McKee's visit, with people saying, 'Why should this American come here and tell us how to write our films? What does *he* know about telling Kiwi stories? He doesn't understand anything about our culture…' Which is true: but what he understands, and what he teaches, are the fundamental theories of narrative momentum, within a screenplay. These theories are universal, and transcend borders and national pride.

And McKee goes to great pains to say that, once you know the theories, you can apply them to any subject matter in any cultural context. You can make them your own. But he also makes it clear that if, as a film-maker, you choose to ignore the principles and theories he teaches, then you will have a flawed film. And he's right; analyse all the great movies and, in terms of screenwriting, they all, more or less, adhere to a basic structure.

What was fascinating for me was that the Film Commission had given him a videotape of *Bad Taste* and he really loved it! I didn't think he would, since it's without structure, but he was incredibly enthusiastic about it.

For their part, Peter, Fran and Stephen were equally enthusiastic about what McKee had to offer. Drawing on cinematic examples from over 100 films, he illustrated his thesis on story structure, which briefly put (in McKee's words) rests on the following twin hypotheses:

'*Story is Supreme* – Characters are what they do. Story events impact the characters and the characters impact events. Actions and reactions create revelation and insight, opening the door to a meaningful emotional experience for the audience.

'*Structure is Character* – Story is what elevates a movie, transforming a good film into a great one. Movie-making is a collaborative endeavour... but the screenwriter is the only original artist on a film. Everyone else – the actors, directors, cameramen, production designers, editors, special effects wizards, and so on – are interpretive artists, trying to bring alive the world, the events and the characters that the screenwriter has invented and created.'

> McKee taught us that a film story is made up of different 'acts', like the acts in a stage play, each of which has certain things to achieve. He talked about establishing the turning-points in a screenplay; how the set-up should be handled and what he calls 'the inciting incident', which is the moment, about ten or fifteen minutes into the film, when you suddenly realise what the film is *about* and the viewer says, 'Right! So *this* is the story...'
>
> In *The Fellowship of the Ring* it is the moment where the Ring passes to Frodo. At that moment our story defines itself – it's the tale of Frodo Baggins and the powerful ring he possesses.
>
> *The Lord of the Rings* was not just written, but also edited, with McKee's principles of story structure in mind. When, as we did, you begin editing the film during the course of shooting and then spend time shooting pick-ups, the structure can easily get a bit loose. So, what we did on *Rings* was to take a look at our first cut, where you actually have everything you've shot in the movie; you then reappraise it again, using McKee's theories.

This was where most of my time was spent, writing Braindead *and then* Meet the Feebles *with Stephen Sinclair and Fran Walsh. We worked in a little flat above a restaurant in Courtney Place.*

In 1988, Peter and his collaborators began to apply McKee's lessons to the writing of *Braindead* and the story development showed a new understanding of character and motivation: the domineering mother who has kept her son both under her thumb and out of the clutches of womankind, has a dark secret: not only was her late husband of hallowed memory a shameless womaniser, she had murdered him together with one of his mistresses.

'In a final confrontation with his snarling zombie mum, [Lionel] presents her with the lie she has forced him to believe. She reacts by literally exploding in an angry storm of bile. The house burns its mess of mutilated zombies as Lionel and Cathy make their escape. *The Underlying Human Truth*: Guilt Sucks.'

The content and layout of the application itself demonstrated how swiftly Peter was picking up the ways of the professional film-maker. He was, as so many people noted, a quick learner. The Commission approved the finance and work began on the script and on building the unstoppable horde of zombies needed to create what Peter referred to as the film's 'grisly chaos'.

Meanwhile, *Bad Taste* was continuing to garner reviews ranging from the critic of *The Hollywood Reporter* who declared: 'I've never seen a movie that's so disgusting – it's great!' to the description included in the programme for the forty-third Edinburgh International Film Festival:

'The title is an understatement. Blood cascades, heads fly, torn-out guts are slurped underfoot, brains leak, green vomit is joyously imbibed. *Bad Taste* reduces schlock *ad absurdum*, but Peter Jackson is a film-maker with more than a hint of inspiration and fearsome dedication. No situation, no effect is too outrageous for New Zealand's own Sultan of Splatter... The wonder of it all is that *Bad Taste* doesn't look anything like a home movie, far from it... Most feature length films consist of about 800 to 1,200 separate shots. *Bad Taste* has closer to 2,500. You might need a sedative by the time it's over.'

It was around this time that what would prove a significant development in Peter's career took place. Jim Booth, the Film Commission's Executive Director – or 'Ex-Di' as he called himself – decided to quit his job and set up as an independent film producer, taking on the responsibility for producing the films of Peter Jackson.

Recalling his late friend and colleague, David Gascoigne says: 'Jim Booth was a good chum, a long-time person and one of the people I miss most in life. It's dangerous to make friends too closely with people with whom you work, but with Jim you simply couldn't help it!'

Jim's partner, Sue Rogers, catalogues some of his attributes: 'He was kind and had intelligence, integrity and an impish sense of humour. He had no pretensions, but was an enthusiast who was willing to take risks. He possessed a good sense of self-esteem and was a generous, positive force in that he also topped up other people's self-esteem.'

'Everyone loved Jim,' says Lindsay Shelton, the Commission's former Marketing Director. 'He was very bouncy and eager. After spending much of his life as a back-room bureaucrat he became the Film Commission's second Chief Executive and had a wonderful time, using the considerable flexibility that the staff had in those days to help people and make things happen. In his decision to leave the Commission and become Peter's producer, there was also a certain ambition.'

Jim Booth's decision was doubtless taken for a variety of reasons: those close to him recall Jim espousing the philosophy that a job need not be held for life, or at least for any longer than it gives satisfaction. At the age of 43, he may also have decided that it was time to be more intimately committed to the day-to-day creativity of filmmaking as opposed to the arm's length involvement at the Film Commission. Having recognised Peter Jackson's potential (and had his somewhat cavalier backing of *Bad Taste* finally vindicated), Jim doubtless saw Peter's future career as being in need of help, guidance and support that it would be difficult for him to give if he remained within the bureaucratic restraints of the Film Commission.

> Jim asked if it would be of interest to me if he were to come on board *Braindead*. I liked him and he'd been a great help to me with *Bad Taste* and in talking with Andrés Vicente Gómez about the co-production deal for *Braindead*. At the time, I didn't have a producer but I knew that I needed one because the budget for *Braindead* was going to be significantly larger than the cost of making *Bad Taste* and Jim's help was going to be invaluable.

'I think Jim gave Peter a huge amount of encouragement and confidence,' reflects Lindsay Shelton. 'Financing a movie in New Zealand, other than with money from the Film Commission, is a mammoth task that takes knowledge, experience and a lot of effort. Jim was equipped to be able to do that and was a producer in the best sense of the word, in that he enabled Peter to focus on what he wanted to achieve without having to worry about the mechanics involved.'

Following Jim Booth's resignation, he and Peter started work together on advancing the film. Script consultant, Linda Seger, had submitted a positive report, which concluded: 'A good rewrite... Have fun filming the blood and gore and gristle and dead furry animals!' Aiming to do just that, they had found premises in a former railway shed to serve as a studio, and were already scouting for locations, casting roles and assembling a crew.

Two more key people entered Peter's life at this point: Richard Taylor and his partner, Tania Rodger, who would later become the creative backbone of Weta Workshop and oversee the staggering miniatures, prosthetics and weaponry used on *The Lord of the Rings*.

Richard and Tania had first met Peter during the latter days of the *Bad Taste* project when their friend, Cameron Chittock, had invited him to visit a studio set where the three of them were working on a TV commercial. Richard recalls: 'We were building massive trees, vast jungles, futuristic cities and all sorts of stuff. We only talked with Peter for a few minutes but we took to him immediately as being a really pleasant guy. He was clearly genuinely interested in what Tania and I had been doing in setting up our company and trying to earn a living from building models, props and puppets and I was very interested in hearing how he was trying to make his own movie at weekends.'

Richard and Tania made puppets caricaturing politicians and celebrity figures for *Public Eye*, a satirical television show in a similar mould to British TV's equally anarchic and generally offensive *Spitting Image*. 'Several months passed following our meeting and we never thought anything about Peter. However, he had seen our puppets for *Public Eye* and had obviously logged away in his mind that there were two young people in Wellington who were very interested in working on this kind of thing and so, when *Braindead* went ahead, we got the call...'

Braindead opened with a scene set on a mysterious island that was the habitat of the rat-monkey carrying the zombie-creating virus that would plague the life of Lionel Cosgrove. There was to be an ancient fort on the island and Richard and Tania's first contribution to *Braindead* was building a massive cannon for the battlements.

The island scenes as they would eventually be represented in the film (sadly, *sans* fort and cannons) were filmed at the Putangirua Pinnacles in the Wairarapa, a few hours out of Wellington, where a decade later Peter would film the scenes in which Aragorn, Legolas and Gimli travel the Dimholt Road to the Paths of the Dead.

It's a very evocative location and I figured that, because so few people in the world have seen *Braindead*, we could get away with using it a second time in *The Lord of the Rings*. I had decided that the rat-monkey was to be captured on an exotic island near the coast of Sumatra and, of course, there was only one island that fitted that description – Skull Island!

Not shown on any map or chart, it was a name that had captured Peter's young imagination from the first time he saw *King Kong* and the island, with its sinister skull-shaped mountain peak, loomed up out of the mist. One day he would go there again in search of a creature rather larger than a rat-monkey...

By 1989, Peter had left his parents' home in Pukerua Bay and was living in a small, two-roomed bungalow in Seatoun, just a short drive from the centre of Wellington. Richard and Tania began socialising with Peter – or, as Richard puts it, 'just hanging out together' – as often as two or three nights a week.

'Richard and I didn't own a television,' remembers Tania, 'but Peter had the biggest TV we'd ever seen! He also had huge, beautiful couches, and because the room was really quite small it meant that you were virtually sitting on top of the television set! On Friday nights, Peter would invite us around to watch the latest video that he'd got from the States and we'd grab a big bag of fish 'n' chips and a big bottle of Coca-cola and sit inches from the screen eating supper and watching some really gory, over-the-top movie! I remember seeing the American Civil war film *Glory*, starring Matthew Broderick, Denzel Washington and Morgan Freeman, and Peter fast-forwarding to all the gruesome battle scenes!'

'Because the bungalow was right beside a footpath,' adds Richard, 'we'd often look round and find a group of passers-by standing outside, looking through the window getting a free view of the movies. It was bloody funny!'

In October, Jim and Peter flew to Milan, venue for the annual International Film and Multimedia Market (Mifed) where they joined the Film Commission's Marketing Director with the aim of generating pre-sales for *Braindead*. Jim was becoming anxious about financing the project since, with a budget of $2.5 million, it was not possible for

In 1988 I finally bought a little cottage of my own. My parents loaned me most of the money. I thought their house was small – this was half the size and I had trouble finding room for all my stuff.

the Film Commission to single-handedly underwrite the picture and the hoped-for co-production deal with Spain had failed to materialise. Jim had an investor interested, but promoting the film to international buyers at Mifed was crucial if *Braindead* was to remain alive.

The producer and director had a supply of flyers with an image, designed as a poster concept by Cameron Chittock, showing Lionel's Uncle Les – a deeply unpleasant superannuated swinger who blackmails his nephew over having zombies in the cellar – pursuing Baby Selwyn with a motor-mower. The resourceful Peter also packed a videocassette in his suitcase.

> The tape contained fifteen to twenty minutes of *Meet the Feebles*. After returning from Cannes, while we were starting to prepare for *Braindead*, I took a look at the *Feebles* footage and decided I better get it edited into shape. It was incomplete and it didn't have a climax but it gave an idea of what it would be like.
>
> I had already met and got to know quite a few of the international distributors because of *Bad Taste*'s success at Cannes, so while at Mifed I showed *Feebles* to anyone who'd take a look. One of them, Mack Kawamura, the Japanese distributor of *Bad Taste*, was to my great surprise particularly interested – I really hadn't imagined there would be a market in Japan for a film about puppets into sex and violence! He was, however, only interested if *Feebles* was a feature film, which was not something we had considered or – with *Braindead* about to go into production – could even *begin* to consider.

Peter and Jim returned from Milan but, as 1988 drew towards its close, unexpected political and economic factors conspired to deal *Braindead* a serious blow. The finance minister for New Zealand's Labour government, Roger Douglas, had been the author of a series of economic policies aimed at controlling inflation, cutting subsidies and trade tariffs and privatising public assets that were regarded, by many, as a betrayal of left-wing ideologies. There were serious differences between Roger Douglas and New Zealand's Prime Minister, David Lange, and after months of growing dissent within the cabinet – heightened by the effects of the previous year's 'Black Monday' Stock Exchange crash – the Prime Minister dismissed one of Roger Douglas'

Cameron designed and illustrated this Braindead *flyer, intended to raise market interest in the film before it was made. Ultimately, this version of* Braindead *was never produced.*

prime supporters, causing the finance minister to resign from office.

It was an unexpected lesson for a young film-maker: the realisation that political ups and downs can have an adverse – and totally unexpected – impact on the arts. Jim Booth was forced to advise the Film Commission that the resignation of the country's Minister of Finance had 'given our proposed investor the collywobbles' and that, as a result, the proposed commitment to *Braindead* was 'postponed'.

The timing could not have been worse since the Commission had just agreed to a major investment in the film of $1.5million, but that sum needed to be matched with a further $1million from elsewhere. Various banks and finance houses were approached for investment; meanwhile the film was already heavily into pre-production, with model-making and set-building, and Jim was faced with the need for an adequate cashflow to keep the zombies alive until a funding deal could be struck.

An appeal to the Commission, a few days before Christmas 1988, to either underwrite the entire venture or to keep it going until the end of January was met with a refusal. The language was regretful – there were references to a 'fine project' and 'talented people' – but the Commission had already advanced $300,000 towards the film and was not going to pay out more money without any guarantee of a film being made as a result.

At the beginning of January 1989 Jim sent a long, passionately argued letter to the Commission analysing the state of New Zealand film-making, reminding them of their responsibilities and repeating his appeal for sufficient funding to keep *Braindead* active until the end of the month. 'Rather than giving a shove to a New Zealand film,' he told his former colleagues, 'I feel that I have my bare foot wedged in a door, which is being vigorously slammed. It hurts a lot.'

The Film Commission reconsidered and relented, agreeing to advance the project two weeks' sustaining funding. Those two weeks passed in a flurry of desperate activity but, two days before the Commission's money was due to dry up, no investor had been found and it was clear that *Braindead* was just that – *dead*.

On 20 January 1989, the cast and crew were handed a letter telling them that it had been necessary to postpone the start of filming on the film. All those involved remember their feelings when the blow fell: 'We were devastated,' remembers Richard Taylor. 'We had been working for a number of years to try and become film-makers and suddenly we were on our first feature film with a guy that we really liked, and just as suddenly it was all over and we were out of work. We went home, opened a bottle of wine and drowned our sorrows.'

Whatever the disappointment experienced by the crew, it was worse for Peter Jackson: 'He was,' says Richard, 'clearly heartbroken.' After riding high on expectation, he had seen his first professional film indefinitely postponed before filming had even begun.

> It was one of the most disastrous days of my professional life. Jim and I met with the crew at lunch. Jim did all the talking, telling them that, hopefully, it was just a delay; that we were going to try and get the money together and do what we could; but we were having to send everyone home because we couldn't pay them any more.

Somehow, I knew that, for me, this was a historic day. I thought, 'One day this will be a memory and it won't be as disastrous as it is at the moment...' I had a camera, so I took a photo of Jim addressing the crew: I wanted to make sure I had recorded the memory of that day for posterity.

That memory would return, several years later, when Peter experienced another such catastrophic day in his career, but Peter's determination to remember the bitter taste of defeat in a way that most people only wish to relish the sweet flavour of success, shows maturity, self-awareness and a sense of fortitude that would see him through many vicissitudes in his later film-making career.

> *Braindead* had crashed and burned. That afternoon, straight after the meeting, I went back to Stephen and Fran's flat; we were totally destroyed and sat there thinking, 'Oh my God, what do we do now?' Then, fuelled by the feelings of rejection and failure, we looked at one another and said, 'Let's make *The Feebles* as a feature film!'

After all, a Japanese distributor at Mifed had expressed an interest in a feature-length version of the spluppet project and twenty minutes of footage was already on film...

The events of the next day have taken on mythic status and are told by many of the participants with varying detail but a consistent desire to associate themselves with what was clearly a significant development in Peter's unfolding career.

Early in the day, unbidden and without pre-arrangement, people began to turn up at Peter's little home in Seatoun: first one, then another (the order varies slightly depending on who is doing the telling), until a crowd of twenty or thirty people were packed into the two-room bungalow: Cameron Chittock, Jamie Selkirk, Richard Taylor and Tania Rodger, Fran and Stephen, Jim Booth... 'We all had the same thing in mind,' recalls Cameron. 'How can we turn the disaster around and turn it into something positive?'

The Feebles with its tale of 'the lives and loves of the puppet world' seemed the perfect solution.

There were, of course, questions... The New Zealand Film Commission had already declined any involvement with *Meet the Feebles* – which had resulted in its being personally financed by Peter, Cameron, Stephen and Fran – but, ironically, the man who had refused that investment was Jim Booth, and not only was he no longer at the Commission, he was now Peter's producer! What's more, he had good contacts with his former colleagues at the Commission, who would need to be brought on board to help fund the project.

A more pressing issue was the script: the Commission would need to see a script – to know that the twenty-minute squib about puppets behaving badly could realistically play out at the length of a feature film. Peter began the process by brainstorming with Cameron, who recalls: 'We took a walk along the beach in Seatoun to shoot the breeze, thinking of more and more characters that could be introduced through the film to keep the story developing and interest alive... I came up with every outrageous character I could think of without expecting Peter to take them seriously but, a few days later, they were part of the film script!'

> Cameron went away and started furiously building more puppets and would come in with sketches and ideas – such as a duck who was a 'quack doctor' – and we'd decide if we were going to work them into the script, give them a name and settle on their personality. We'd say, 'The elephant looks a bit sad and depressed and looks like someone who might be called Sid...'
>
> Rather than come up with characters and then get Cameron to draw them, his drawings led the whole process: we'd work back from Cameron's drawings, figuring out who the characters were and what their role was in *The Feebles* show. Then Danny, Stephen, Fran and myself would work day and night on writing them into what needed to be a ninety-minute script.
>
> We figured out that in order to have the film completed for delivery to the Japanese at Mifed, we had three weeks to write the script, and needed to be shooting three weeks after that!

In this organic manner, *Feebles* grew in length while its texture of gross and grotesque detail became more complex, ranging from the

Here, and on the next few pages, are a few key members of our Feebles *team: Cameron Chittock – Cameron carried on designing and building new puppet characters for the feature length version.*

satiric addition of a (literally) fly-on-the-wall paparazzi, constantly feeding off the Feebles celebrities' dirt, to the calamitous storyline following Heidi Hippo's addiction to Black Forest gateaux, her declining career and her waning relationship with the obnoxious Bletch. This full-blown tragedy dramatically concluded with a failed suicide attempt and an apocalyptic revenge on the world, which – in a torrent of blood and bullets – shows that 'hell hath no fury like a hippo scorned!'

The script also contained occasional flashbacks that are among the most stylishly realised sequences in the final film: a smoky, black-and-white memory of Heidi's early career as a nightclub singer, with the once-svelte hippo crooning a Billie Holiday-style number by avant-garde composer Peter Dasent (formerly of The Spats and The Crocodiles), who scored *Feebles* and Peter's next two pictures, and which wittily captures the period mood while foreshadowing Heidi's later pie-and-cake obsession:

> *You want a slice of the action,*
>   *but you're not actin' very nice.*
> *You want a slice of the action,*
>   *but you don't wanna pay the price.*
> *You're gonna end up in traction, if you don't take my advice.*

You want a piece of the pie,
  but you don't want to share with me.
You want a piece of the pie,
  but you never get nothin' for free.
You better watch what you say, 'cos that ain't my recipe…

There are also a series of flashback scenes telling the tale of Wynyard the Frog's days in Vietnam, complete with heroics under fire and torture in the jungle at the paws of Vietcong mongooses given to subtitled outbursts of communist ideology which spoof *Platoon* and any number of other Vietnam war movies and, with its game of Russian roulette, Michael Cimino's *The Deer Hunter*.

'Everyone made their own unique contribution to the process,' says Cameron, 'but Fran's vital input was in insisting that the film needed straight characters who could provide a sympathetic contrast to all the insane, horrible, dirty, ugly characters!' Thus were born Robert the Hedgehog, 'a naïve young chappy from the back blocks with a dream of making it big in showbiz' and Lucille, 'a pretty young fur seal'. Their romance would provide the antidote to the rather more sleazy goings-on between the Feebles veterans…

Before any Commission funding was in place, Cameron was busily building puppets with the unpaid help of Richard and Tania. It was soon clear that the original footage that had been shot between the completion of *Bad Taste* and Peter's trip to Cannes was unusable.

> We had created new characters, changed the design of others, and it was all filmed in an entirely different space (the upstairs rooms of the Campbell brothers' house) and with different sets and lighting. Not a single frame of that footage ever appeared in *Meet the Feebles* – and it remains, to this day, its weird, bastard, alternative twin!

Jim Booth contacted Mack Kawamura's company, Compass International, in Japan who confirmed their interest in *Meet the Feebles* and a further distribution deal covering the remaining world markets was made with Perfect Features in London. By 17 February 1989, less than one month after the collapse of *Braindead*, the Film Commission were considering a weighty document containing a budget, a script breakdown, pages of Cameron's engaging character sketches (which seriously belied the character's despicable habits!) and preceded by an emotive aide-mémoire from Jim Booth:

'The Commission has to invest in the future of the New Zealand film industry – particularly at this time of crisis.

'Peter Jackson is a good investment – if not our best investment.

'This project involves some of the best young, yet proven writing talent in New Zealand – Fran Walsh and Stephen Sinclair.

'The film-makers have jumped through all the hoops. With their own money they have developed the script, made the puppets, gone to the world and found at least a third of the money.

'The project can be delivered to Mifed in October.

'What more can be asked for, at this time, for $457,000?'

If nothing else, *Meet the Feebles* promised to be a lot cheaper than *Braindead*.

Desperate times call for desperate measures and when it came to meeting with the Film Commission, everyone pitched in to sell the idea:

> There was a strong cultural awareness at the Commission, so Stephen, who speaks Maori, opened for us with an impassioned twenty-minute speech in fluent Maori! Throughout the monologue, everyone in the room looked very sombre, but I think there was probably only one person who actually understood what he was saying. Still, quite a way to start!

The Film Commission finally agreed to finance *Meet the Feebles*. After all, *Bad Taste* had sold well and generated a lot of international interest and the money involved was much less than would have been gambled on *Braindead*. There was doubtless also a feeling of wanting to support and encourage Peter following the collapse of that project.

However, whether articulated or not, there were certain anxieties that would quickly find expression over the weeks that followed. There were those at the Commission who had been decidedly unsympathetic to the horrors of the *Braindead* proposal and there

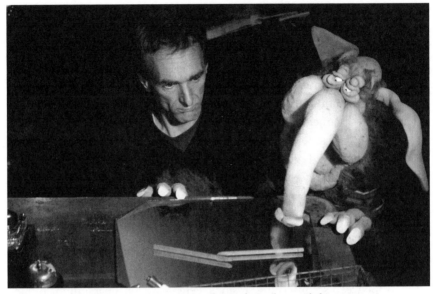

Jonathon Acorn – an excellent puppeteer who performed several characters.

was, no doubt, a degree of nervousness about Jim Booth as the producer of a film that had not only failed but had done so with $300,000 of public money.

Then there was the subject of this new project: even before they had read the full script they knew that the 'Feebles Variety Hour' was peopled by debauched, degenerate, dissolute characters who were into sex, drugs and violence. Only later would such ingredients become the cause for alarm when the explicitness became manifest and, as was inevitable with a Peter Jackson project, more extreme even than had been hinted at in the original scene breakdown.

No one seems to have wondered whether a film demanding the complex interaction of marionettes, glove puppets and costumed characters, as well as the deployment of a great many special effects, could be pulled off in what was to be a seven-week shoot.

For Peter and the team, however, getting the go-ahead to start work on *Feebles* seemed, at least at the time, an opportunity to get busy and get working...

The project was an extraordinarily democratic venture with everyone – from the runner to the producer and director – being paid the same weekly wage of $600. Richard Taylor recalls, 'Tania and I were young, enthusiastic and keen as mustard. There was a wonderful camaraderie, a real feeling of equality, a sense of everyone mucking-in together. It was an incredible experience for any new film-maker.'

During the lead-up to *Braindead*, Richard had noticed that some of the seasoned professionals working on the pre-production of the film didn't seem to give Peter the credit or support that Richard believed were due to the director, despite his youthfulness and limited experience. When filming began on *Feebles*, however, he noticed a marked difference: 'Peter immediately took command and everyone grew to respect that we were working with someone who was really clever and really visionary. As sad as it was that *Braindead* fell over, the fact that it led to *Feebles* was so fortuitous for Peter's development and for all our careers.'

Between scriptwriting sessions, Peter – with his passion for model-making – joined Cameron and Richard in producing puppets. 'He was an excellent puppet-maker,' recalls Richard, 'although not experienced with the equipment we were using. We sculpted the puppets using a commercial sanding belt: it was very wide, very course and ran at about 10,000 revolutions per minute. By holding a block of foam rubber against the sander you could create any shape you wanted. However, it took care and practice to use the sander effectively and safely. Peter started work on a puppet of Arbee Bargwan – an Indian contortionist who disappears up his own bum – snipping out his first piece of foam and putting it on the machine with all the confidence with which he confidently does everything! The foam rolled under and his fingertips went straight onto the moving belt, sanding off the skin from all ten fingertips. He had to build the rest of the puppet with band-aids on all his fingers. It was very funny – sad, but funny!'

Despite moments of levity (however painful), filming *Feebles* proved gruelling and exhausting. 'Making it,' says Cameron Chittock, 'was a nightmare!'

The film was to be shot in the railway shed that had been hired for the filming of *Braindead* and on which Jim still had a lease. It proved to be the 'studio' from hell.

Richard Taylor and Tania Rodger – I first met Richard and Tania in their tiny fume-ridden bedroom/workshop and immediately found some kindred spirits.

The disused railway shed was a former hangout of a notorious motorbike gang, known as the Mongrel Mob, and, if the area was insalubrious, then the interior was worse! 'It was,' says Peter, 'an appallingly horrible place.' For one thing, it was so cold that the team habitually wore three pairs of socks, two pairs of pants and two coats plus hats, gloves and scarves.

There were also health hazards: pigeons had got into the building and, in addition to quantities of pigeon excrement, the number of dead birds lying around – combined with a rat population and visitations by wild cats – had resulted in an infestation of fleas. 'We suffered terribly from flea bites,' remembers Richard Taylor. 'I actually felt poisoned by them. We wore plastic rubbish sacks on our legs, wrapping them up around our knees and taping them on and then spraying ourselves with dog-spray in an attempt to keep the fleas at bay. It was shocking.'

'Even some of the puppets became infested with fleas,' says Cameron, 'and others started to get eaten by the rats. It was insane!' It also

The old rat-infested, pigeon-infested, cat-infested, flea-infested railway workshop buildings where Braindead *had a false start and the* Meet the Feebles *feature was eventually made. Several years later, the new Wellington Sports Stadium was built right on this site. I can never watch an All Blacks test match there without thinking of the nutty time we spent on that 'hallowed ground'.*

puts the lie to the disclaimer at the end of the picture, which reads: 'The producers wish to advise that no puppets were killed or maimed during the production of this film'! Indeed, as Peter would admit in a later interview: 'I would not mind working with puppets again, but the way that we abused and treated them, I doubt whether they would want to work with us!'

Once the shoot began, Peter quickly realised that filming with the *Feebles* cast-members was going to be a laborious task:

> The puppets were a technical nightmare. By the end of the first day's shoot, on 23 April 1989, I was already half-a-day behind schedule. I had begun by shooting the scene where Heidi the Hippo tries to commit suicide by hanging herself but is so heavy that the noose breaks and she falls through the floor. It was incredibly arduous. Within a few days we were falling significantly behind schedule...

This was bad news. A schedule that was slipping by the day left the production in a vulnerable position, especially in view of the fact that a month before filming had begun Jim Booth had gone back to the Film Commission requesting an additional $37,000 to 'enhance' the production with some location shooting and the addition of mechanised puppets that would be able to 'blink, twitch or otherwise convey emotions'.

The Commission were not sympathetic to this request – especially since it included a fee for someone to undertake accounting and management tasks while Jim was in Cannes and mention of the fact that the two-week break planned for the middle of the shoot was being reduced to one week.

Alarm bells rang. Jim's successor as Executive Director, Judith McCann, appears to have suspected *Feebles* of heading for an overrun before filming had even started. Her response prompted Jim to reply, countering such fears and asking the members of the Commission to visit the studio in order to 'obtain some idea of the extraordinary production being created down here on the smell of an oily rag'. He closed in conciliatory terms ('I remain your humble and obedient producer'), but it was to be the beginning of an exchange of correspondence between Jim and Judith McCann which rapidly degenerated from good-humoured skirmishes into full-blown hostilities.

The anxieties at the Commission were rooted in their experiences with *Braindead* where additional sums of money had been provided without the film ever going into production. Jim's application was seen as a potential 'early warning signal' that financial management of the *Feebles* project was not what it should be. This situation, combined with the fact that the explicit nature of the film suggested limited sales potential, was a discouragement to investing any further sums of money.

However, the Management Committee finally agreed to the additional advance, but with reservations expressed by the Executive Director in the most serious of terms: 'In making this decision, the Commission expressed its disappointment with the development of this project, and warned that further requests for additional investments would not be approved.'

George Port – George performed the role of Bletch and became a founding member of Weta.

There was also considerable concern over the content of the final script that had now been submitted and which, as Judith McCann wrote, had 'diverged significantly' from the original outline: 'The story as now portrayed is sexually exploitative, verging on the pornographic'. It was, perhaps, an extreme reaction to such sequences as that involving the filming of a porno bondage movie, starring Daisy the Cow (a.k.a. 'Madame Bovine') and a cockroach, which was too absurd to be truly offensive. *Meet the Feebles* was a puppet film equivalent of Ralph Bakshi's *Fritz the Cat* and other 'adult' animated movies. It was an irreverent idea conceived in the style of underground comics created by Robert Crumb and others. To criticise it by any other standard was to miss the point.

As Peter would put it, during an interview on the film's release: 'It's not undergraduate humour, so much as... well, the term I'd use would be "naughty schoolboy humour", I guess. That obsession with bodily functions, all that kind of excessive crudity. And that kind of physicality suits *The Feebles* really well, since you wouldn't normally associate those kinds of bodily things with puppets, so you can do with them the most disgusting, gross things possible, and get away with it. Had we been working with human actors, I don't think we would have taken it nearly as far as we have, because it probably would have been quite sick. But *The Feebles* are only puppets, they are just bits of material, really, so I have no qualms about treating them in the most dreadful ways!'

These two pictures have a special significance to me. My mother is walking me through the bush near Mt Egmont. She was great at creating off-the-cuff stories about the trolls in the woods or goblins who lived high in the branches. Here, I'm clearly captivated by a wild story she's concocting – and thirty-five years later, here we are on the set of The Return of the King, with her son having turned those wild stories into something of a career. With a different mother, it would almost certainly never have happened. Her health was going downhill fast by this stage and, despite trying to hang on, she died just three days before The Fellowship of the Ring was finished. The first ever screening of the finished movie took place for my relations on the afternoon of Mum's funeral. Dad had died in 1998, so neither of my parents, who had been so supportive, got to experience The Lord of the Rings craziness.

LEFT: *Me shooting a close-up of a creepy hand rising from a fog-shrouded grave. I did this type of shot alone at night – aim the camera on the tripod, set it going, then quickly do the 'hand acting' in our family's bath tub.*

BELOW: *This is one photo that makes me pinch myself a little. I know the 21-year-old Peter was looking out across the Universal backlot, dreaming of becoming a 'real film-maker'. In 1982, working in Hollywood was the only real option, but I had no idea how I was ever going to make it.*

I've always been the product of films I've seen and that have excited me. From Thunderbirds to King Kong, James Bond, WWII and Hammer Horror films, I spent my youth stockpiling the influences that I carry around as a film-maker today. Growing up with Harryhausen's movies, seeing the animated The Lord of the Rings in 1978 and then reading the book, and the arrival of movies like Conan the Barbarian all resulted in me building this troll head in the early Eighties. I had just bought a 16mm camera and for a while the brutal barbarian vs. troll fight-scene was going to be my first 16mm movie. I built a complete troll suit but eventually I moved on to what became Bad Taste.

I rented a sound camera from the National Film Unit for the first few days of filming Bad Taste. Holding that camera made me feel like a real film-maker – here I'm trying really hard to look like one too! Years later, when I bought the Film Unit and we sold off most of the old equipment, I made sure this camera was kept in the company for sentimental reasons.

Fran in full zombie mode for Braindead. *The fun thing about making zombie films is how everyone, no matter how unlikely, gets into the spirit and wants to play a zombie. During* Braindead, *most of the crew and a lot of our friends and relatives came along to do the undead shuffle.*

Richard and Tania clowning around with Tim Balme at Cannes in 1992. We would head out each day at the crack of dawn, papering the entire town with Braindead *flyers. Anything to get your movie noticed!*

One the puppets I made for Meet the Feebles. *As crazy and tough as that film was, I loved being able to build some of the characters, although Cameron Chittock and Richard Taylor did most of the puppet work. Apart from making a few model trams for* Braindead, *it was the last time I've been able to be hands-on involved in the special effects – which is the reason I wanted to make films in the first place.*

Bad Taste *was fuelled by the great Kiwi tradition of fish 'n' chips. Back in those days, it was all we ever ate!*

LEFT: *During the period between* Meet the Feebles *and* Braindead, *I met a whole lot of people: some were idols who had influenced my life, like Ray Harryhausen, here at a German film festival; others were people who would become friends and profoundly affect my future.*

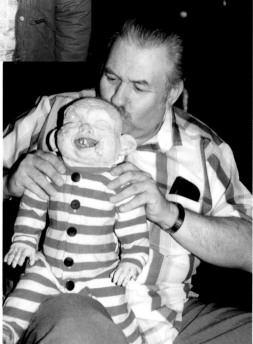

RIGHT: *Film collector and passionate historian Bob Burns, who had just been presented with Baby Selwyn to look after in his museum in LA. Selwyn's still there, and Bob came down to New Zealand recently to visit us and do a cameo during* King Kong.

LEFT: *In 1990 I travelled to Turkey to visit the Gallipoli battlefields during the seventy-fifth anniversary. Here I am with an old tin can lid, found after scrambling up through the gorse of Shrapnel Gully. Being able to stand on 'S Beach', seventy-five years to the day after my grandfather stormed ashore there, was an emotional experience.*

LEFT: *My thirty-fourth birthday on the set of* The Frighteners.

RIGHT: *During our 1992 trip to Sitges, we visited the nearby Barcelona Zoo with Rick Baker, who introduced us to Snowflake, the world's only albino gorilla. Snowflake had such a wonderful face and made a huge impression on us – to the point that we used him as our unofficial model when designing King Kong thirteen years later.*

LEFT: *Our first draft of King Kong required a 1917 Sopwith Camel aircraft and I managed to track an airworthy example down. Trouble was, it arrived in New Zealand one day after Universal had shelved the movie! Putting the aircraft together provided a welcome diversion from the stress and, without a movie to star in, it has since become a regular performer at local air shows.*

Mum and Dad visiting the set of Heavenly Creatures *in Lyttelton.*

The first award I ever received for The Lord of the Rings *was a Bafta in 2002. In some respects it remains my fondest memory, since it was the David Lean Directing Award and it was presented by Kate Winslet – both had great personal significance for me.* (Image courtesy of Dave Hogan/Getty Images)

This book wouldn't be complete without poo-eating, so here it is, courtesy of my favourite character, The Fly.

The Commission, necessarily conscious of their responsibility as custodians of taxpayers' money (and possible accusations of its misuse), put the script out for review. The report did not make encouraging reading: 'This story left me totally confused and somewhat sad at the fact that someone with Peter Jackson's potential could create such a worthless project... There are no protagonists, no one to cheer for, no real story, no depth to any character... It's not just the script – it's the content, style and execution, no pun intended... I have serious doubts as to whether this film will pass the censor... Peter Jackson is a very talented film-maker with the ability to do well in any country, but I don't think this project is necessarily going to advance his career...'

With the possibility of money being withheld, script changes were made but there were angry allegations of 'censorship', which were strongly countered. The frequently acrimonious correspondence – comprising official as well as off-the-record 'Personal and Confidential' letters – was hampered by several misunderstandings and crossed purposes that indicated a lack of mutual trust.

There were the occasional positive glimmerings as when Grace Carley of the distributor, Perfect Features, faxed the Commission with a letter of support for *Feebles*: 'The screenplay of *Meet the Feebles* far exceeded my expectations in terms of originality and structure. The writers have done an admirable job in creating and sustaining a pacy, cohesive story which avoids being episodic or repetitive...'

And, on the issue of possible bad taste: 'Excess is a common thread running through satire or spoof in all media, and is acceptable as part of that genre... The marketing approach on *Meet the Feebles* is that it is a cutesie puppet show with sex and drugs, rock 'n' roll and violence. Its very nature dictates that it be somewhat racy although in a comical way – and it must be accepted that it won't be everyone's cup of tea. If it loses it's hard edge by having to compromise to a potentially sensitive audience, it runs the risk of becoming neither one thing nor another and consequently of no interest to anyone...'

Meanwhile, the film-makers were battling on with filming while marksmen were called in to pick off the pigeons and bug-exterminators tackled the fleas.

Marty Walsh was unit manager on the film: 'It was all pretty nutty.

Chris Short – our first AD on Feebles. *If ever any role needed a sense of humour it was this one. Fortunately Shorty has humour in spades.*

People got sick, simple injuries turned septic and quite a few folk seriously lost the plot! Art director Mike Kane, staged a short-lived protest against the cold by lighting an open fire – on a wooden floor! It was total madness: there was no money for smoke-machines for the Vietnam battle scenes, so – crazy though it sounds – we burned old car tyres! The place stunk of acrid smoke and if you happened to be downwind of it, you ended the day with a face like a panda!'

The memories of those involved are varied: 'We worked twelve to fourteen hours a day, six days a week' recalls Cameron. 'We had no life apart from making the film…'

'Despite everything,' says Tania, 'it was very exciting to be involved with the project, even though there were some hard moments… I remember the food not being particularly grand, probably because the catering budget was some ridiculous amount like $7 a day, which meant that we pretty much lived on mince! Most of the crew were constantly griping about the food because they had worked on other

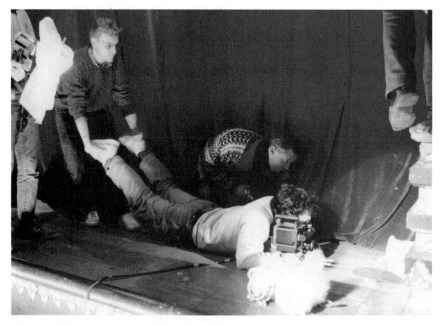

Marty Walsh – our second AD. That's me shooting and Marty dragging me backwards to create a very low budget dolly move. Marty has gone on to become the AD running all the miniature shooting on Lord of the Rings *and* Kong.

movies and noticed the difference, whereas Richard and I were actually grateful that food arrived each day and the fact that it was free was an absolute bonus!'

However, as Tania also remembers, the chef's supplies were hardly sacrosanct – at least not when the artistic requirements of the model-makers were involved: 'We didn't have sufficient budget to buy everything we needed so, after hours, Richard and I would carry out a purge of the catering store – pinching various ingredients, like rice, frozen vegetables, milk and yoghurt – to turn it into vomit and other unmentionable things!'

To help keep up the team's morale – and supplement the not over-generous catering – Peter's mum would often pop in around teatime with piles of scones or apple slices for fifty hungry people. The support that Joan and Bill Jackson gave to their son automatically extended to those with whom he was working, without apparently, a moment's pause over the antics of the fornicating, urinating, expectorating Feebles!

'Looking back,' reflects Richard, 'I still think of the time spent in that railway shed as the best time of my working career, although Peter really can't believe it, when I say it! Of course, we were too young to understand all the politics that was going on. We just thought it was the way all film-making was done!'

Peter, of course, *was* aware of the politics – even though Jim tried to shield him from the worst of it; and he knew that, as far as the Film Commission were concerned, *Meet the Feebles* was *not* being made according to the way film-making was usually done!

> We kept on filming, but we were over-running and over-budget. After seven weeks we were still nowhere near completing the shoot. I felt panicked. There was a real sense at the Film Commission that I'd gone out of control, there were threats that I would be removed as director.

'The threat to remove Peter,' recalls David Gascoigne, 'was probably intended as shock tactics to get some level of compliance; Peter could not have been replaced without the agreement of the entire board and I doubt that would have ever happened – apart from which, I can't imagine who on earth we would have got to finish it!'

Jim Booth attempted to salvage the situation by asking the Commission for a bridging loan of $148,000 on the guarantee that he and Peter would personally underwrite the overrunning budget on the strength of their personal assets, including their houses, Jim's car and life insurance policies and Peter's income from *Bad Taste*.

The loan was granted on various conditions, one of which was the appointment of a 'completion supervisor' to see the shoot through to its end at, ironically, a cost to the Commission that was greater than financing the shoot through to its conclusion.

The person handed this poisoned chalice was feature film director John Reid, who had recently made *Leave All Fair*, a film about Katherine Mansfield starring Jane Birkin and John Gielgud. Jim ought, perhaps, to have known John Reid's presence on set was hardly likely to be acceptable to a director who was already under serious pressure.

> Everything began looking very grim. I was determined to make the best
> film I could, to finish it properly, but it was so very hard. The Commis-
> sion developed a really bad attitude towards me, not that I was rude...
> No... I *was* rude actually!
>
> John Reid showed up on a Sunday night as we were about to begin a
> night shoot. He had been sent in to tell me what to do to get this film
> finished, but I was so angry at his presence that I screamed and yelled
> at him and he turned and walked off, and never reappeared. John is a
> really nice guy and I feel very embarrassed when I remember how I
> behaved towards him, but I was stressed to the max and I just didn't
> want this guy around, so I'm afraid I sent him packing...

John Reid clearly found the situation untenable but felt no malice
towards a fellow director so heavily under the cosh. Nevertheless, his
arrival and instant departure had an immediate knock-on effect.
Judith McCann wrote a letter of admonition to Jim Booth, bristling
with, as the Commission would have seen it, justifiable anger:

'The Commission is of the view that it cannot rely upon you to
work in an open and willing manner with the Commission in order
to complete the film... Accordingly, we advise you that you are in
breach of the Production and Loan Agreement...'

Although the circumstances were such that the Commission had
the right to take over production and completion of the film, it
decided against such action, advising Jim, 'You can continue, if you
wish, to complete the film. However, you are in default until such
time as you fully repay the loan and interest.'

In what was a stinging rebuke to her predecessor, the Executive
Director wrote: 'As you will be aware, this is the first time the Commission has had to take such a drastic and regrettable step. While the
Commission has an obligation to encourage film-making, it also has
an obligation to safeguard its limited funds by ensuring its contracts
and agreements are complied with... Producers who are successful in
obtaining the Commission's approval have a moral obligation to
their fellow producers and to the industry as a whole to comply with
the responsibility they assume in accepting the Commission's production financing.'

WingNut Film's response of a few days later, signed by both Jim and Peter, was passionate: 'We were stunned to receive your letter… We consider the decision extraordinarily harsh, precipitate, and we dispute the grounds upon which it was made…' Seizing upon the one conciliatory note in Judith McCann's letter ('The Commission's door is not closed…'), they went on to outline a solution to the problem which was that all parties accept Jamie Selkirk as Post-production Producer and for Jamie to take on the responsibility of ensuring 'the completion of the film on time and on budget.'

The Film Commission agreed to this proposal and that, as far as finishing off *Meet the Feebles* was concerned, *should* have been that. However…

> There were still some key scenes to be shot, but the Film Commission were insisting that we stop filming and start editing the movie. At this point, Stephen, Fran and I got together and thought, 'F*** them! We'll finish the film the way we want!' So, we chipped in $20,000 of our own money to fund the remainder of the shoot.

This response is indicative of Peter Jackson's determination to do what he does 'his way'; to make the film he has envisioned as fully as possible – however *impossible* – brooking no obstacle and holding on to the commitment and sense of shared endeavour of those with whom he works. As Marty Walsh observes: 'Peter is a film-maker, not a poseur-director. He is the real deal. There are no duplicitous agendas; there is no tyrannical, egocentric power-play. He is only there to make the film. That is his mission and it is the opportunity to *share* in that mission that earns him the loyalty and commitment of others.' That approach was first demonstrated during the marathon that was *Bad Taste* and again during the nightmare that was *Meet the Feebles*.

> We couldn't allow the Film Commission to find out that we were still shooting, so we got the crew together and told them we would pay them to carry on but in *total secrecy* and, of course, they were all on board – loving the fact that it was all being done undercover!
>
> During the day I had to be seen going into the cutting room to work on the edit with Jamie. But at six o'clock every night, I would go down

Another ace puppeteer, Ramon Rivero, operating the dead fish off-camera. Every conceivable method was used to bring these little bastards to life. This scene was being shot during our 'secret week' when the Film Commission thought I was in the cutting room.

to the railway shed... We'd park our vehicles out of sight and have sentries posted outside to keep a lookout for any Film Commission people, while we, literally, locked ourselves in and shot in secret.

One of the last days was incredibly stressful as we had to shoot a scene on a golf course in broad daylight with the entire crew – plus actors in full-size puppet costumes as Bletch the Walrus, Barry the Bulldog and Cedric the Warthog – hoping to hell that nobody saw what we were up to!

'The infamous secret shoot on *Meet the Feebles*,' says Costa Botes, 'was an indication of Peter's strength of purpose, his dogged, determined, never-say-die, my-way-or-the-highway attitude! It also demonstrated his ability to inspire the troops; why else would those people do what they did, working through the night to finish the film? Then as now, Peter generates a fierce loyalty within those who work with him.'

When the time came to send the negative that we'd shot during the secret shoot off to the laboratory to be developed, we obviously couldn't label it *Meet the Feebles*, so we gave it a code name and called it *The Frogs of War*!

Apart from the amphibious links to the military career of Wynyard the Frog, the punning reference to the 1981 film version of Frederick Forsyth's novel *The Dogs of War* was appropriate since it told the story of a revolutionary coup staged by a mercenary!

Marty Walsh remembers the last day of shooting when the production reached an all-time level of absurdity: 'We were filming in the overgrown gardens of the local hospital, which doubled for the Vietnamese jungles. By this stage there were only three or four of us left and we were filming Wynyard running away from the Vietcong.

This was a reasonably simple Feebles *shot compared to most. Heidi's cables operated her eyes and eyelids. Danny did a brilliant job with the rest.* Meet The Feebles *was the last film I operated the camera on, a job I love doing. I'm in awe of directors like Ridley Scott and Robert Bodegas, who make complex films and still manage to operate their own camera – something I'll have another go at doing one day.*

Peter was manipulating the puppet with one hand, holding the camera with the other while running backwards through the undergrowth. Depending on your point of view, it was either amazing to think of Peter being, simultaneously, actor, cameraman and director, or just bizarre to see what was, effectively, a film-maker shooting his own hand!'

The nuts-and-bolts of filming holds little mystique for Peter. Think of more or less any job on a movie and he will, at some point in his career, have done that job himself: model- and prop-maker, set-builder, special-effects technician, actor, animator, cameraman and director. As a consequence he knows what he is asking of every member of the crew.

Meet the Feebles was finally completed and a fine cut was screened for the Film Commission towards the end of July 1989. Quite a lot of what they saw took them by surprise – especially scenes about which they had already expressed concern and one or two that they didn't expect! There was full-frontal hippo nudity, acts of fellatio and the introduction of a quite unexpected musical number. Where, in the original script, the Feebles' director – a camp fox named Sebastian – sang a song entitled 'How Low Can a Hobo Lobo Go?', he now appeared on a set decorated with phallic columns singing an altogether different song. Written by Danny Mulheron, it began, 'Sodomy, I think it's very odd of me, that I enjoy the act of sodomy…'

The Film Commission's response was, perhaps not too surprisingly, somewhat cool: they were disappointed, they said, but in view of the time constraints prior to delivery of the film, had decided not to intervene over what was or was not included in the final cut, knowing that 'the validity of your judgement on this and other aspects of the production will lie with the censor (and, subsequently, with the market place)…'

As final closure on what had been a stressful few months, the Commission declined to receive a credit on the film.

'In the Commission's defence,' says former Chairman, David Gascoigne, 'it would have been a really bad idea to have invested public money in a film that was banned and couldn't be shown. The Commission would very probably have been accused of irresponsibility.

Danny Mulheron – Danny had the pivotal role of Heidi the Hippo, and was always a key member of the writing team on Feebles. *Heidi's voice was supplied by Mark Hadlow, so with a guy performing inside and a guy doing her voice, we all got a kick when she was nominated for Best Female Performance at the local film awards!*

It might have also damaged the industry if there had been so much fuss that the Film Commission had failed to survive.'

A difficult child that had several times been almost cut off with out a penny, *Meet the Feebles* was now to be tossed out into the world as a bastard...

It hardly mattered. From its premiere screening at Mifed in October 1988, it found plenty of people ready and willing to adopt it!

Over the next few years, *Meet the Feebles* (or, as it is known in the USA, *Just the Feebles*) picked up various international awards: Le Prix Très Special in Paris; the Audience Prize for Most Popular Film in Madrid; and, at the Fantafestival in Rome, Best Director, Best Special Effects and (for Heidi the Hippo) Best Female Performance!

Similarly, the *Feebles* have found plenty of reviewers – in many parts of the world – ready and eager to sing its praises:

'Wildly original, deliriously sick stuff. Disgusting, vile, and outrageous – and we mean that lovingly...'

'*Monty Python* meets *Sesame Street*...'

'Perfect for mutant children of all ages...'

'Take your sense of humour (and perhaps your sick-bag), and leave your delicacy (and your children) at the door...'

'An adult puppet movie with something to offend everybody...'

'Terribly funny, and terribly sick...'

'So tasteless that it scrapes genius...'

Years later, the man whom an Australian magazine had dubbed 'the Scorsese of scum' walked on stage at the seventy-sixth Academy Award Ceremony in Hollywood to receive one of his Oscars for *The Lord of the Rings: The Return of the King*. In his acceptance speech he mentioned two of his earlier movies, *Bad Taste* and *Meet the Feebles*, which, he quipped, 'were wisely overlooked by the Academy at that time.'

For some it may be difficult to see *Meet the Feebles* as being a step towards *The Lord of the Rings* – beyond, perhaps, the obvious sharp and painful learning curve of dealing with the politics of film-making – but it was during the making of his early films that Peter first articulated the philosophy that focused his vision as a film-maker and which would, indeed, one day turn its gaze on Middle-earth. In a contemporary interview, Peter expressed what could be called the Jackson mantra:

'I like doing things that are pure to film, that have no actual exis-tence outside of cinema. That's what I find the challenging thing – making these little daydreams look convincing and real.'

'*Meet the Feebles* is what it is,' says Costa Botes, by way of reassess-ment. 'It is episodic with moments of brilliant invention and inspired satire, as well as moments of gross tastelessness and utter nonsense! But it was a film that was necessary for Peter, because it allowed him to see that episodic brilliance is not enough, that he actually had to have the dramatic through-line in order to make a connection to an audience. Watching *Feebles*, you're sometimes up in the air and then you're dropped and have to pick yourself up again; the storyline soars and it sags, and – despite the genius of individual sequences – it is, ultimately, an unsatisfying experience. But Peter was still developing as a talent: not exactly an immature talent, but not yet fully devel-oped either. Peter's progress crosses a couple of the movies following *Bad Taste*: they form a kind of crucible into which all these droplets go, and what comes out at the end of the process is measurably dif-ferent to what went in.'

Sitting on the plane en route to Milan in October 1989, Peter was reading a copy of *Fangoria* magazine that he had bought at the airport bookstall in Auckland. Founded in the United States in 1976, *Fangoria* was internationally regarded as the horror-gore-fantasy-sci-fi world's official organ (pun intended) and was, and still is, one of Peter's favourite magazines. This particular issue contained an 'on-set diary' with writer David J. Schow during the shooting of *Leatherface: Texas Chainsaw Massacre III*, the second follow-up to the 1974 shocker that had fired Peter Jackson's taste for terror and which he had later spoofed in Derek's final crazy chainsaw assault on the aliens in *Bad Taste*.

Jeff Burr was directing *TCM3*, but to Peter's utter astonishment the article mentioned that among the names that had been originally pitched as a possible director for the picture was … 'Peter Jackson'!

> I still felt like a kid: I had made *Bad Taste* and just finished *Meet the Feebles*, but that was all. Yet here I was reading in *Fangoria* that somebody had been pitching my name for *Texas Chainsaw Massacre III*, which, of course, I had never heard anything about! *Wow!* I felt quite proud, but I could hardly believe it! That was the first time that I had ever read my name in a magazine in connection with any film project.

Had Peter but known, there was already a growing Jackson-awareness in Hollywood, and especially at New Line Cinema, the studio which was producing *TCM3*, where Peter had a champion in the person of Mark Ordesky. Years later, Mark would be intrinsically involved in the process of making of *The Lord of the Rings*.

'Before I was with New Line,' remembers Mark, 'I was at Republic Pictures and I had a weekly ritual: I would bring home a supermarket bag full of videos I had been sent in by various companies and I would sit and watch them, looking for the odd one that might be worth buying. One of these videos was *Bad Taste*. I fell in love with it: I thought it was just unbelievably innovative, clever and propulsive. In fact, I tried desperately to get my bosses at Republic Pictures to let me buy it, but they – probably wisely – said, "Are you out of your mind?! You want us to buy a film about flesh-eating aliens from outer space attacking New Zealand? No way! Forget it!" So I failed at that, but the name "Peter Jackson" was logged in the memory bank.'

One of the friends I made in LA was Mark Ordesky, who had a lowly position at New Line Cinema. I took this photo as a joke, since Mark's job seemed to consist of being on the phone all day. Eventually he moved up the New Line hierarchy and championed The Lord of the Rings *through the company. Back in 1990 we had no idea that our paths would cross again in such a dramatic way.*

Mark Ordesky moved on to New Line and, based on his response to *Bad Taste*, pitched Peter's name as director of *Leatherface: The Texas Chainsaw Massacre III* while David Schow was working on the script. That suggestion didn't get approval, but Mark continued to follow Peter's career and, when he received a videotape of *Meet the Feebles*, arranged a screening in New Line's preview theatre, which David Schow still recalls: 'After seeing a lot of dismal movies, I saw two in the same week that literally changed my whole screenscape: John Woo's *Die xue shuang xiong* (*The Killer*), and Pete's *Meet The Feebles*. They were a turning-point.'

'On seeing *Meet the Feebles*,' says Mark, 'I was further thrilled and excited and, once again, tried to buy a Peter Jackson film. But I was told, "Are you out of your mind?! You want us to buy a pornographic puppet film? No way! Forget it!" At that point I thought this man is someone I've got to know...'

Someone else who recalls his response to *Meet the Feebles* is Peter Nelson: 'I was shocked and surprised by that movie as anybody would be, in varying shades of blue, purple and pink!'

It was not, however, Peter Nelson's first awareness of Peter Jackson. He was a Los Angeles-based entertainment lawyer with a growing practice – but, he says, 'hardly on the map in Hollywood terms' – and one of Peter N's clients, during a visit to New Zealand, had passed his details to Peter J who had contacted the lawyer and asked if he would take a look at 'a backyard movie' he had been shooting. Whilst nothing immediately resulted from that contact, Peter N recalls being impressed by what he saw: 'I thought it was excellent, very funny and the use of a driving story was promising. In fact, I thought, "This guy's a film-maker." That movie, of course, was *Bad Taste*.'

Meet the Feebles confirmed that judgement: 'It ratified my belief in Peter: if he could make a film peopled with crazy puppets and make it so compelling and involving, I was convinced he could direct anything he wanted.'

The first and only time I've been yachting – this is with Peter Nelson, an LA entertainment lawyer who offered to help me after Bad Taste *and represented me for free for years.*

Peter Nelson negotiated the tricky manoeuvres to secure a distribution deal for *Feebles*. As an X-rated film, it wasn't widely released, but where it was seen it made its impact: '*Feebles* branded Peter – albeit in very limited circuits – as a genius and I was personally never reticent to use that term, as I honestly felt that is what he was.'

Describing himself at the time as Peter Jackson's 'beachhead in Hollywood', Peter N would make a point whenever he was in town on his way to or from New Zealand, to introduce him to people he ought to know. One such introduction led to a proposal to create a television series in the style of *Meet the Feebles* for the still-new Fox network, where *The Simpsons* had found fame in 1990. Innovative though Fox were, they could not conceivably launch a series that was as extreme as *Feebles*; however, Peter's co-writer on *Feebles*, Danny Mulheron, was teamed with Mark Saltzman, who had written for *Sesame Street* and *The Jim Henson Hour*, and the two men came up with a script that was funny but too groundbreaking for any television network.

'The script went through various drafts,' recalls Peter Nelson, 'and each time it became increasingly dumbed down and homogenised. There was one hysterical scene featuring an enormous diva who wanted to reduce her weight and decided to do this by liposuction. The problem was, when she lost weight, she also lost her ability to sing, because the talent was all in the fat! The liposuction took the fat down into the gutter where it had a second life as a singer while the unfortunate diva went around without her voice! It couldn't have ever made its way to network television, but the script retained much of the irreverent sense of humour that is a feature of the original film.'

The contact made with Peter Nelson eventually led to his becoming Peter Jackson's legal adviser and representative: one of several major steps in moving Peter from a niche film-maker from New Zealand to a major player in the international movie game.

Meanwhile, Mark Ordesky was pursuing the idea of working with Peter: 'I decided to seek out a relationship with him by writing the classic fan letter; eventually this led to our meeting up and getting to know one another. In those days, I was insistently insane and I kept

During my visits to LA I became friends with writer David J Schow. It was a lot of fun to meet people who loved the same films I did, who were obsessed with the same monsters I was. The world was suddenly getting a whole lot smaller for me.

talking and talking about this guy Peter Jackson in New Zealand in the hope that New Line's Chairman and CEO, Bob Shaye, would eventually give me a chance to hire him!' And, eventually, that chance came along…

On one of Peter's periodic stop-offs in Los Angeles, on this occasion in company with *Feebles* co-writer (and Heidi the Hippo's alter ego) Danny Mulheron, Peter met David Schow, the man whose script for *TCM3* he might, in different circumstances, have directed: 'Peter and I had a lot in common,' he says, 'we were both equally interested in film-making as a process, quite apart from the yield of the finished product. Getting to that finish is a process of having two thousand headaches that you actually court and enjoy! What kind of people would *do* that?'

David was also interested in the fact that Peter's origins were not those of most young film-makers: 'He did not spring from the then-usual well of music-video and commercial-directors who stepped up to features. Pete was a "from-the-ground-up" film-maker who would, for *Bad Taste*, shoot a hundred feet at a time with a hand-wound Bolex (so no take could run more than that limit), build AK47s out of wood and cure latex monster heads in his mum's oven. Lacking actors, he'd shoot a fight scene with himself and make it work in the cutting. That kind of dedication-level is something you'll only find in a person who embraces the headaches of zero-budget production because he or she simply *loves* movies. Seeing that quality in Pete was incredibly refreshing.'

Another contact made was Frank Darabont, a young film-maker who had yet to direct his first feature film but who had made a short student film based on a story by Stephen King. The source material, *The Woman in the Room*, was not one of King's ubiquitous tales of horror and the supernatural, but an emotional story about euthanasia. Made with King's blessing (the author allows students and independent film-makers to adapt his short stories for a $1 fee and the promise of script approval), *The Woman in the Room* would, years later, result in the author approving Darabont as writer and director of two highly successful features based on his work: *The Shawshank Redemption* and *The Green Mile*.

One day when Frank had to visit the offices of New Line, Peter tagged along and had his first encounter with Mark Ordesky, who expressed his great enthusiasm for *Bad Taste* and *Feebles* and his desire to work with Peter. Over frequent dinners at 'Pane Caldo' on Beverly Boulevard, a simple bistro with a stunning view of the Holly-wood Hills, Peter, Danny, David, Frank and Mark spent time talking movies and Peter showed his American friends a fantasy script he had been working on with Danny.

Entitled *Blubberhead*, it has been variously and tantalisingly described by those who have read it either as a cross between *Monty Python* and *Indiana Jones* or as a fantasy set in a *The Lord of the Rings*-type realm of dwarves and giants…

This *was* a very *Monty Python* style fantasy tale, which looked at the absurdities of a very particular taxation system at work in a medieval-style fantasy township. Very Terry Gilliamesque, it would have made an interesting film. The intention was to use stop-motion animation to bring creatures to life, and I actually met up with Randy Cook in LA and spoke to him about the project in 1990. Years later, I finally worked with Randy when he became Animation Director for the *Rings* movies.

Mark Ordesky recalls reading the script: 'I loved *Blubberhead* but although I couldn't get any New Line traction on it, I did convince Bob Shaye that we should hire the "crazy New Zealander" to write something else for us.'

Released in 1984, Wes Craven's *A Nightmare on Elm Street* introduced the world to Freddy Krueger, memorably portrayed by Robert Englund with his striped jersey, trilby hat jauntily set on a hideous burned face and a glove with knife-blade fingers; it also spawned a franchise that was to run to seven movies.

1989 saw the release of the fifth *Nightmare* movie, *The Dream Child*, and whilst Freddy's box-office takings remained good, the series had, as Mark Ordesky puts it, 'begun to wane in terms of its creative innovation'. Maybe the crazy film-maker from New Zealand with his flesh-eating zombies and porno-puppets might be just the person to breathe new life into the ongoing supernatural-slasher-horror-fest.

'In those days,' says Mark, 'we hired multiple writers, because you never knew who would come up with a great "Freddy" story that might be, if not the next film, then a future episode. So I convinced New Line to let me hire Peter for Writers Guild of America scale-pay – which, at that time, was around $20,000 US.'

I suggested to Danny that he get involved in it and we write it together. Mark was pretty honest and up front, telling me that they were developing two scripts at the same time and that New Line would make whichever one of the two they thought best.

If they liked my script I'd get to do the movie, but I'd have to make it in the States, which was fine by me because I felt pretty confident that I could do that. So there were no guarantees – maybe we'd make the film or maybe we wouldn't – but, at any rate, it would be fun…

There was no brief other than 'Come up with a cool idea for us…' And the idea we came up with was, I think, pretty cool!

The *Nightmare on Elm Street* mythology established by Wes Craven in his original film centred not on a flesh-and-blood villain but a spectral serial killer who haunts the dreams – or *nightmares* – of his young victims and slays them in their sleep.

Peter's cool idea was set a few years on from Freddy's last rampage, at a point when his powers appear to be losing their potency. A bunch of obnoxious local thugs meet up in Freddy's derelict house, take drugs to put themselves into dope-induced sleep and – in a clever reversal of the usual *Elm Street* premise – enter Freddy's dream world, track him down and beat him up in what Peter describes as '*A Clockwork Orange*-type mugging'.

A policeman is sent in to break-up the drug-ring, but in the meantime Freddy has managed to kill one of his assailants and, in doing so, become fully rejuvenated. The policeman goes to Freddy's house, gets trapped when a fire breaks out and ends up in hospital in a coma.

> Unlike the other movies, it's not a case of him falling asleep and having experiences, he is actually permanently trapped in Freddy's dream world. He can't escape; it's him against Freddy and Freddy is out to get him…

The script was written in New Zealand, but it was necessary for Peter to travel to Los Angeles for meetings and script discussions. 'New Line was so cheap in those days,' recalls Mark Ordesky, 'that Peter's *per diem* ran out almost immediately and he ended up crashing on the couch of my ratty apartment around the corner from New Line.' Peter also remembers 'blobbing out' at Mark's apartment and, in particular, learning to play the board game, *Risk*.

Devised in France as *La Conqueste du Monde*, the game was introduced into America in 1959 under a succession of titles, including *Risk: The World Strategy Game* and *Risk: The Game of Global Domination*. Like *Monopoly*, *Risk* has been thematically repackaged and, in 2001, a new movie-inspired version appeared entitled *Risk: Lord of the Rings*!

Under Mark's tutelage, Peter became a proficient player at *Risk* –

certainly Richard Taylor and Tania Roger remember being soundly defeated whenever they played him at the game. Describing Peter today, Richard calls him 'an incredible strategist', but back in 1990, Peter's Hollywood power-play wasn't quite as impressive.

'We had several creative meetings at New Line,' notes Mark, 'where, basically, no one took us particularly seriously! I'm sure Bob Shaye really thought Peter was very talented, but I don't believe he really thought anything would come out of the *Nightmare on Elm Street* idea. But I was persistent and he let me do it and Peter turned in what was a really amazingly innovative script.'

Meanwhile, an alternative script was also being developed by New Line staff member Michael De Luca, who had a proven track record on and around Elm Street, as Production Executive on the fifth *Nightmare* and Executive Consultant on the TV series *Freddy's Nightmares*, as well as having scripted *The Lawnmower Man*, based on the story by Stephen King.

Michael De Luca would eventually rise to the position of President and Chief Operating Officer of New Line Productions and, on the day in August 1998 when New Line announced their intention to produce *The Lord of the Rings* trilogy, would be quoted as saying: 'Peter's creative foresight, technological prowess, and passion for the project uniquely qualify him to translate one of the world's most imaginative novels to the screen.' Back in 1990, however, in the battle for the scripting of *Elm Street 6*, Mike De Luca was the clear favourite to win.

When we learned that the other script was being written by Mike de Luca, we thought the writing was pretty much on the wall, but we knocked out our script very quickly and really just saw it as a quick gig as well as an opportunity to get paid some much-needed money.

We were in this lull between finishing *Feebles* and hoping *Braindead* would get made. I wasn't earning any money at all. In fact, *Feebles* had *cost* us money: we had put our own money into making the half-hour TV version of it and ended up putting our own money into finishing the feature-length version!

So *Freddy* turned up at a very good time and helped me survive during a difficult year.

Apart from the money, the *Freddy* experience had brought Peter into contact with other young American film-makers and given him an invaluable insight into the differences between power-brokering in Hollywood and the rather more parochial politics of the New Zealand film world.

Ultimately, New Line went with Michael De Luca's script and 1991 saw the release of *Freddy's Dead: The Final Nightmare* – though it was not *quite* final, since Freddy's creator, Wes Craven, eventually returned to Elm Street to direct the true coda to the series, *A New Nightmare.*

'Even though we didn't make Peter's version of *Nightmare*,' reflects Mark, 'it was enough to show Bob Shaye that this guy was as clever as I said he was! So, Peter went on to make *Braindead* – another one we didn't buy… And *Heavenly Creatures* – but we didn't buy that either! Eventually, however, our time would come!'

> I don't recall feeling particularly devastated when we didn't get our *Freddy* film made, because – pretty neatly as it turned out – by the time Mark was breaking the news that they were going with Mike De Luca's script, *Braindead* was back on its feet and I was very happy about that. It was unfinished business and let me stay in New Zealand. It was not the last time a project came together at the eleventh hour and let me stay home instead of working in the US.

The task of returning *Braindead* to the land of the living had not been easy. After various prospective investors had backed off, Jim Booth finally succeeded in securing finance from distribution pre-sales in Japan and an investment from Avalon Studios, once the state-run home of TV New Zealand.

When they had opened in 1975, Avalon was the largest studio in the southern hemisphere – and known by a variety of nicknames including Buck House, The Factory and The Taj Mahal. The home of telethons and such popular game shows as *Wheel of Fortune*, Avalon had, at the time of its investment in *Braindead*, been recently privatised and as part of the deal the film was to be shot on their studio complex, which was a significant improvement on a flea-ridden, rat-infested railway shed!

Christian Rivers and Richard Taylor get under way on a 'Mum-monster' hand for Braindead. *Christian was a very young school kid who had written me a fan letter with some of his art. As a result, he did storyboards for all my movies from* Braindead *onwards, working at building up his skills with Richard and Weta's digital department. This resulted in Christian winning an Oscar as an animation director on* King Kong, *fifteen years after this photo was taken. He supervised all aspects of Kong's performance. Fran and I are currently working with Christian on a movie for him to direct.*

Despite the 'bad boys' reputation that *Feebles* had earned Jim and Peter at the New Zealand Film Commission, the request for production investment financing was given unbiased consideration. The script-assessment, which was to help the Commission reach a decision to support *Braindead* for the second time, was written by Costa Botes. After several pages of detailed analysis, he concluded:

'The imagery in *Braindead* will be gross and violent, and will certainly be beyond the pale for many people. This film isn't meant for them. For those who enjoy fantasy and horror genre pictures, there is still a fine line between tasteless crudity or cheap shock, and genuinely inspired black humour.

'Peter Jackson has already demonstrated twice that he knows

where to draw that line. *Bad Taste* and *Meet the Feebles* have both been notable for the positive reviews they have drawn from critics and audiences not normally responsive to splatter films. Part of the reason is that Jackson is a movie fan himself, an enthusiasm which equals his love of actually making films. He respects his audience, odd as that may sound, and is not at all interested in brutalising them. Humour, not brutality, is the abiding impression his films leave in the mind.

'Jackson has no equal amongst New Zealand film-makers in terms of sheer bravura cinematic style. *Braindead* is full of opportunities for Jackson to unleash his manic brand of slapstick... but now, for the first time, he also has a cohesive script to work from.'

The script Costa was assessing was Peter, Fran Walsh and Stephen Sinclair's final revision of the material. As Costa Botes notes today, 'There was clearly a massive shift in the quality of the writing pre- and post-*Feebles*. In the finished script of *Braindead* you see a definite move towards the classic paradigm of screenwriting. It was as if they had come away from that seminar by Robert McKee with a whole new bunch of tools and they were learning how to use them.'

A crucial decision was that of moving the story from the present day back to the more innocent era of the 1950s.

> It meant that we could get away with a lot of hi-jinks that people would believe in to some degree – if 'belief' is the right word in connection with something like *Braindead* – because the Fifties is regarded as an age of innocence where boys could still live at home with their mother and not be scorned and when you could believe that unspeakable things could be going on behind the closed doors of suburbia, without the knowledge of the neighbours, let alone the rest of world...
>
> Stephen is an essentially satirical writer and part of his interest in *Braindead* was satirising the stiff, formal conventions of 1950s New Zealand society and then turning a load of zombies loose into that environ- ment!

Despite the fact that the film was being largely funded with New Zealand money, Peter, Fran and Stephen decided against reverting to the original scenario, which had featured a New Zealand girlfriend for Lionel. 'Cathy' had become 'Paquita' and even though there was now no requirement to maintain a 'Spanish connection', the writers considered that it gave the script an interesting and individual flavour and – since the story also featured Paquita's mystical, tarot-reading grandmother – a quirky touch of exoticism.

Once the choice had been made to keep Paquita, it was then a simple decision to keep Diana Peñalver, the actress who, more than a year earlier, had been cast in the role. An inspired piece of casting, Diana added a charming sense of bemusement, as her character becomes embroiled in the unbelievable gruesome events unfolding at her boyfriend's family home.

Tim Balme, a stage and television actor, would make his impressive feature film debut in *Braindead*, playing Lionel Cosgrove.

The role of Lionel's domineering mother, Vera, went to Elizabeth Moody, an actress who was also known as a regular panellist on *Beauty and the Beast*, a popular TV show in which a team of four women and a token male gave agony-aunt advice to viewers' problems.

My mother was a big fan of Liz Moody because she was outrageous, opinionated and not the sort of person to suffer fools gladly. Liz was rather formidable but she was also funny, with a pretty dark sense of humour.

She was the perfect choice to play the mother from hell! Later she would appear in *Heavenly Creatures* and play a cameo in *The Fellowship of the Ring* as Bilbo Baggins' hated cousin, Lobelia Sackville-Bagg

The cast also included *Feebles'* voice artists Peter Vere-Jones and Brian Sergent (later Ted Sandyman in *The Lord of the Rings*) and another local actor who would go on to appear in *Rings* as the Orcs, Sharku and Snaga: Jed Brophy.

The cameras rolled on *Braindead* for the first time on 3 September 1991. The Film Commission, with whom good relationships had been restored, sent two fax messages to the director on the first day of shooting. Commission Chairman, David Gascoigne wrote:

'Dear Peter… This is to wish you and Jim and all your cast and crew the very best of luck with your despicable, rotten, appalling, dis-

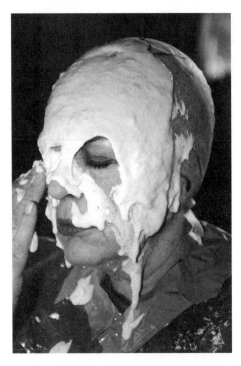

Liz Moody disappears under alginate during her head-cast. Liz was a lot of fun to have around and gave us the perfect 'Mum' performance in Braindead. *You certainly need a good sense of humour to go through this.*

agreeable, we-wish-we'd-never-heard-of-it project, *Braindead*. Actually, we are all looking forward to being soothed by its discreet charm and grace…'

Another fax, signed by all the staff at the Commission, simply read: 'Break a leg… and an arm … and a skull!!'

Braindead was Peter's first experience of directing professional actors (other than those who had provided the voices for the stars of *Meet the Feebles*), and he seems to have intuitively understood the process both in terms of what he required as director and what actors need to be given to do their job well.

Former work-colleague, Ray Battersby, received a telephone call: 'Want to be a zombie?' and found himself on the set of *Braindead*. 'Having previously watched him directing on *Bad Taste*, I was aware that he was now a "proper director" – professional, authoritative, obviously in control, but still the friendly guy who had directed his mates in *Bad Taste*. Perhaps that was part of his secret: having learned to deal with people – cast and crew – as friends.'

Jed Brophy describes Peter's directorial style: 'There is no second-guessing how Peter will direct a scene, but he wants you, as an actor, to bring something to the set – some idea or approach with which he can work. The more you give him, the more he will let you give and, as a result, characterisations become fuller, more rounded. I remember him saying on *Braindead* that the actors had made more of the characters than he could have imagined and he thrives on that approach. By the same token, Peter will shoot until he's happy with what he has on film, which can be exhausting but which is also satisfying because, in the end, what is on film is the best that everyone can do. Peter is the only director I know who gets on screen what he has in his head. And I have never worked with a director who has had so much fun directing!'

> It *was* fun! It was a good time. I look back on both *Feebles* and *Braindead* as a time of great freedom, because the Film Commission funded these movies and, essentially, we had no masters.
>
> In the case of *Braindead* we were living in an era that had seen some classic zombie movies, such as Stuart Gordon's film of H. P. Lovecraft's *Re-Animator* and Sam Raimi's brilliant comedy-horror movie, *Evil Dead II*. There was this great feeling of trying to top the previous zombie film – to go as far as possible beyond what they had done – and without any concern about what censorship or ratings were going to do to you: it just didn't matter because these were always going to be un-rated films.

Braindead was a proving ground not just for the director but also for Richard Taylor, who was responsible for the 'creature and gore effects'. 'The ambition of it was huge,' says Richard. 'When *Braindead* had originally gone into pre-production before its collapse, Peter had hired in an effects company from Australia who had designed and built various props and effects that never got used. When we came to work on the picture, following on from *Meet the Feebles*, Peter gave us complete control of the effects. It was a challenge: we didn't use a single thing that had been made the first time around, but instead started anew and created everything completely from scratch.'

There were pustulating wounds and errant body parts to be created and Selwyn the psychopathic baby in a candy-striped romper suit as well as miniature sets of period streets with model cars and trams. 'We made phenomenal amounts of stuff,' recalls Richard, 'while at the same time learning a lot, which was great.'

One challenge, as Richard explains, was the stop-frame animation required to bring the vicious rat-monkey to life: 'Peter had experimented with animation in the films he made as a child but I'd never

Another dream realised – to have a stop-motion creature appear in one of my films. Richard and I took turns animating a couple of shots each. The year after Braindead *came out, the first computer-generated dinosaurs stomped into film history in* Jurassic Park, *and everything changed.*

stop-frame animated anything. Pete's solution was to create live-action reference footage on which we could base the animation. So, using his Bolex camera, I filmed Pete acting out the role of the rat-monkey in the back garden of the house where he used to edit the films. We then got it transferred to video and had a video player next to the animation table so we could play it while we were animating: study the performance, analyse the movements frame-by-frame, and attempt to replicate them with the puppet. It was a few years before motion-capturing Gollum, but it worked really well.'

For Peter and Richard, *Braindead* was the beginning of a professional partnership that would, eventually, help make *The Lord of the Rings* a consummate achievement in special effects and cinematic design. Jed Brophy has witnessed the relationship between Peter and Richard from *Braindead* onwards: 'If Peter wants something, Richard will deliver the goods – even if he and his colleagues have to stay up twenty-four hours, day and night. What Richard has is the satisfaction of knowing that Peter will use what he has produced in a way that is the most exciting and dramatic.'

'It is true,' says Richard. 'I've gone along with Peter's every wish and Tania and I have had our company taken to the brink but we've always tried not to panic about the risks, because we trust Peter and the fact that he knows where he's heading for and what he's going to do. Somehow or other, he will always pull it off and it will be beautiful and successful. It is a testament to Peter's ability to capture people's imaginations and grab them up into his dreams. It's something he's incredibly good at. It is Pete's train-set, but you've been asked along to help build some bushes or a station building or a level crossing; you have been invited to join in and play and, of course, you *will* because actually there's nothing in the world you'd rather do…'

The filming of *Braindead* was, as Peter describes it, 'smooth sailing' and 'fairly uneventful', although he acknowledges that the hardest aspect of the picture was the mounting carnage in the final reel and the bloodbath that attended it. When, in a desperate attempt to purge his home of an ever-increasing number of zombies, Lionel resorts to attacking them with a motor lawn mower, the flesh (offal and pork fat) and blood (maple syrup dyed with food colouring) really flew.

The set for the hall and staircase where the zombie slaughter takes place was constructed with a floor raised three or four feet in order to allow for the operation of the puppet Baby Selwyn, as well as various zombiefied heads, limbs and organs. This feature proved useful in controlling the excessive flow of blood from the pumps that were used to create the eruptions of gore at five gallons a second. A hole was cut in the middle of the floor and, after each 'take', the blood was mopped down the hole into waiting buckets ready to be recycled.

It got to the point where at the end of each day's filming the blood and the stuff had flown around the set to such a degree that it was pointless even trying to clean it off, and anyway, we'd have to put it back there on the following day for continuity. So we just left it there and, day after day, we'd add more to the already existing layers of blood which got thicker and thicker. Eventually, the entire set was covered in congealed maple syrup to the extent that if you stood still for more than two or three seconds the soles of your shoes glued themselves to the floor!

One of those who had to keep moving or get stuck was stills photographer Pierre Vinet, who recalls having to wash the blood-spattered filters of his camera after every single take.

Pierre's involvement had begun with a telephone call, as he remembers in his strong French-Canadian accent: 'They asked me: "Have you heard that there is a man in New Zealand doing this blood thing who needs a photographer?" So I came and met Peter. And my first impression? *Visual!* This is a totally visual guy!'

For Pierre – like his future wife, make-up supervisor Marjory Hamlin – *Braindead* was to be the beginning of a long association with Peter Jackson. On his first day on set, Peter's instructions were very simple: 'Shoot everything!' Pierre did just that. 'By the end of the first day, I went to Peter and said, "Guess how many rolls of film I shot? *Ten rolls!*" Someone with Peter said, "*Ten rolls!* You shouldn't shoot more than two rolls a day. Ten is far too much!" But Peter said, "No, no, no! Ten rolls is good… It's just about enough…"'

By the end of *Braindead*, Pierre had shot more than 20,000 photographs, a figure that pales into insignificance when compared with the 150,000 he shot during the making of *The Lord of the Rings* – many of which have become iconic images of the trilogy, recognised throughout the world: 'Every day I am working with Peter as a photographer brings some reward; all day long I am spoiled for visuals, but always, before the day is over, Peter gives me a surprise: The Grand Visual… *The Shot*…'

One of Pierre's fondest memories is of Peter's mother arriving, as she had done on *Meet the Feebles*, with a batch of fresh-baked scones and then sitting down to watch the filming and knitting woollen hats for the crew with the word 'Braindead' incorporated into the pattern. Many of those who worked on *Braindead* still have those hats. 'It was,' says Pierre, 'the best gift I have ever been given: it was given me by the director, but it was made by family.'

Pierre's other abiding memory of being on the bloodstained set of *Braindead* is the smell – something that Peter has also never forgotten.

This is how we used to do things back then: if we needed a bunch of model cars I'd take the parts home at night and build them myself on my kitchen table. We had such tiny budgets, any savings would help. I also made the trams from scratch.

Worse was the fact that, under the heat of the lights, the syrup gave off a sugary-sweet odour that would get in your hair and your clothes so that you'd go home stinking of it. In fact my overriding memory of *Braindead* is that maple syrup smell.

The smell – not just of the fake blood, but also that of the fibre-glassing process used to make zombie-parts – was one of the things that other users of Avalon Studios objected to about having Peter Jackson and his crew around the place. But there were also other disruptive and displeasing activities: Jed Brophy recalls the disquiet expressed by some of those using the canteen over having to share their meal breaks with a bunch of decomposing zombies; while Richard and Tania remember testing exploding heads by dropping them down one of the stairwells in the building. 'The old timers,' says Richard, 'just couldn't believe what we were doing to their building!'

What they did to the building, albeit accidentally, was – as befits the nature of zombies – not pleasant...

The people at Avalon Studios had no experience of anyone making a horror film there! Unfortunately, we rather disgraced ourselves... During the lawn-mower massacre scene, the blood was being pumped furiously around and it sent great sprays of blood splattering up, beyond our set, onto the walls of the sound stage – and way too high for anyone to clean! People tell me that, to this day, the bloodstains are still there on the studio walls!

The other mishap, which was also a bit unfortunate, concerned the carpets in the corridors at the studio. The make-up and wardrobe rooms and the green room for the zombie extras were located at the opposite end of the building from the sound stage. Between takes the zombies would be walking back and forth down nicely carpeted corridors dripping blood and gore as they went. By the time we were finished the carpet was completely trashed.

Avalon demanded the carpeting be replaced; Jim Booth maintained that it was an insurance issue for the studio. As a result, there was for a while a residue of, literally, bad blood...

Tim Balme and Jed Brophy between takes – I hope that Tim didn't need to use the loo! Jed went on to portray a series of orcs in The Lord of the Rings *movies.*

In the manner of the alien scenes in *Bad Taste*, the zombie extras included as many friends and relations as could be persuaded to get bloodied-up, among them was *Bad Taste* crew-member, Ken Hammon, and former *Post* colleague, Ray Battersby, who took Peter a magazine about The Beatles (at the time, the two men were talking about the possibility of making a TV documentary about The Beatles' 1964 visit to New Zealand): 'I remember watching him sit on set, in the middle of all the mayhem of preparing for a shot, reading the magazine with complete concentration as if he were in a personal cone of silence, locked off from the distractions of the activity around him.'

It is an interesting observation and an indication of something that would later impress many who worked with Peter on *The Lord of the Rings*: his ability, amidst preparation for a complex scene, to focus his entire attention on some totally unrelated issue such as a line of script under review, a design detail requiring authorisation or a video of second-unit photography needing approval.

Though no longer a key actor in his films, Peter managed a Hitchcockian appearance as the deranged assistant to Peter Vere-Jones' undertaker. Others who gave cameo performances included Jim Booth in photographs, as Lionel's late, lamented father; Fran Walsh as a horrified 'Mother at Park' witnessing Lionel trying to dispose of the fiendish baby Selwyn; Jamie Selkirk (with his son in a push-chair) as visitors to the zoo; Joan Jackson giving a squeal of disgust as Vera Cosgrove despatches the rat-monkey; and Tony Hiles in a scene-stealing moment as a creepy zoo-keeper with a sensational tale of how rat-monkeys were used in witchcraft ceremonies in Sumatra and how they were descended from tree-monkeys that had been raped by rats from the slave ships!

Peter had unsuccessfully tried to persuade David Schow to visit New Zealand and make a guest appearance, although he did achieve a notable coup in securing a cameo from one of his adolescent idols: the legendary Forrest J. Ackerman.

'Forry' (as Forrest was known to friends and fans alike) is a sci-fi and horror writer, editor, publisher and collector. One of Forry's most renowned publications, *Famous Monsters of Filmland* had, for Peter, long been a source of information – and inspiration.

Over the years, Forry had made numerous cameo appearances in the movies of film-makers who admired his contributions to chronicling and celebrating a popular, but critically neglected, art form.

> Forry's cameo appearances became quite renowned particularly since he would always go on at length about them in his magazine!

Apart from looking in on dozens of dubious B-pictures – *Evil Spawn, Curse of the Queerwolf, Nudist Colony of the Dead* – Forry popped up in a number of films directed by Joe Dante, among them *The Howling*, and several by John Landis, including an appearance as a zombie in the final frame of Michael Jackson's music-video, *Thriller*.

In June 1991, three months before shooting was due to begin on *Braindead*, the thirteenth New Zealand Science Fiction Convention was held in Wellington and was designated 'Forrycon' as a mark of respect to its guest of honour.

One of my favourite people visited me in my tiny cottage during 1990: Forrest Ackerman, editor of Famous Monsters of Filmland *magazine, which I'd avidly read since I was about 12 years old. One of Forry's passions was collecting film props and he brought with him the original Pteranodon model from the 1933* King Kong. *Here I'm holding the Pteranodon, with Forry holding my copy of the* Famous Monsters *cover that featured the exact same scene. I get goose bumps doing things like that. Years later, when Forry decided it was time to part with some of his collection, he kindly offered me his original* Kong *models. I'm now the custodian of them and hope to get them into a museum.*

I finally got a chance to meet and be photographed with Forry and with Willis O'Brien's original model of the Pteranodon from *King Kong*, which he'd brought with him in his suitcase.

He was only in Wellington for three or four days, but I invited him to my house and got to know him a little. I was thinking, 'God, what a shame the timing didn't work out so he could have had a cameo in *Braindead*...' Then I thought that perhaps there was something we could shoot in advance and drop it into the film later, and what about the scene at the zoo...?

When Lionel takes Paquita on a date to the zoo, his overbearing mother pursues and spies on the lovers until she is bitten by the rat-

Forry's trip was sponsored by a local sci-fi convention, but I took the chance to fill another childhood ambition and have Forry do a cameo in one of my films. He had appeared in nearly 100 sci-fi or horror films over the years and would always feature his cameos in Famous Monsters. *We were still a few months away from shooting* Braindead, *but I grabbed my* Bad Taste *Bolex camera and a roll of film and took Forry to the zoo to shoot some reaction shots I knew I could edit into the sequence we'd shoot there months later. This is him holding a copy of* Famous Monsters of Filmland *No. 1, which would have been out in 1957, the year* Braindead *was set. It was Forry's own copy – I couldn't afford to buy the expensive collector's item.*

monkey and begins her descent into zombiedom. Grabbing his Bolex camera and a reel of film, Peter kitted Forry out in an overcoat and trilby borrowed from his father, and drove to the zoo, where he bought two tickets so they could go in as ordinary members of the public. Once inside the gates, however, out came the camera…

Forry had a copy of *Famous Monsters of Filmland*, No.1 – the very first issue and very collectable! – so Peter posed him against a rail outside the lions' cage, reading his magazine, and began filming: directing him to react as if hearing the mother scream when the rat-monkey bites her and snapping off a photo as the mother clubs the rat-monkey to death.

In the middle of all this, a zoo official came striding up and demanded to know what I was doing filming in the zoo without permission. I told him it was for a home-movie, but he got really irate and was convinced that it was for some sort of professional movie – which actually, of course, it was!

I remember being really embarrassed because there was Forry – this really famous guy – and there I was, involved in this big argument with an angry zoo manager. I can't remember whether we got thrown out or we just upped and left, but it didn't matter, because I'd already got the shots in the can and, eventually, used them in the movie.

Peter has remained an admirer of Forrest Ackerman and on several of his later visits to Los Angeles he and David Schow would visit Forry at his house, with its famous street sign outside reading: 'Horrorwood, Karloffornia'. Forry (of whom it was once said, 'if he had not existed it would have been necessary to invent him') has continued making cameo appearances despite, at the time of writing, approaching his ninetieth year. It is entirely fitting that one of them should have been in a Peter Jackson movie.

Between the collapse and resurrection of *Braindead*, the American B-movie horror-meister, Roger Corman (who apparently never does title-searches because they cost too much!), had turned out a low-low-budget film of the same name. There was, for a while, talk of renaming the Jackson film and someone came up with the engaging, alternative title *Unstoppable Rot*. Eventually, since Corman's film had only received a limited theatrical release, *Braindead* opened in 1992 under its original title. Ironically, however, when it was released in the United States it would be blandly rechristened – without Peter's knowledge or approval – *Dead Alive*.

Over the next few years, the film amassed awards at film festivals in Rome, Montreal, Avoriaz and Sitges. In the New Zealand Film and Television Awards it scooped Best Film, Best Director, Best Male Performance (for Tim Balme), Best Screenplay and Best Contribution to Design for the special effects.

Trailing some extraordinary reviews (a 'necrophiliac's wet dream') and accompanied by a fluttering of flyers ('a Love Story with Guts' and 'Laughter, Slaughter and Gore Galore') *Braindead* went to Cannes and wowed the glitterati along the Croisette, while advertising ribbons

Jim with two of our Braindead *team, Michelle Turner and Nicola Olsen (above), at Cannes in 1992. These seemed like happy days at the time, but none of us knew what fate was about to dish up. Diana and I (below) celebrating* Braindead's *first public screenings at Cannes.*

for the film, with which the New Zealand contingent decorated the palm trees, were quickly purloined by French youngsters to tie onto their scooters!

Braindead was screened at The Olympia, where – nine years later – the Cannes crowd would get their first sneak peak at footage from *The Fellowship of the Ring*.

David Gascoigne recalls: '*Braindead* was a resounding success in the market at Cannes. Usually at screenings you start out with a cinema that is maybe 40 to 50 per cent full and, by the time the lights go up at the end, there are about ten people left in the audience! There were three screenings of *Braindead* and not only were people fighting to get into them but, when the film ended, everyone was still there in the theatre – something I'd never before seen happen to any New Zealand film.'

It had taken a long time for *Braindead* to get made and be successful. Like *Bad Taste* and *Meet the Feebles*, it had been a testing – often exhausting – uphill struggle.

> Looking back, I feel as though it is almost as though the films, in themselves, are not as important as the fact that they actually got made!
>
> Over a period of ten years we fought enough battles and worked through enough politics in order to make those small films, which ultimately equipped us to take on the biggest challenge of all: getting *The Lord of the Rings* made.

Following the screening of *Braindead* at the Olympia, director and producer took David Gascoigne for a celebratory ice-cream sundae. 'Over the *coupe de glace*,' remembers David, 'Peter and Jim – who did an incredible double-act between them – told me about another project they were interested in: a true story of two schoolgirls in New Zealand who commit a brutal crime. It was a story I had heard about when I was a kid and I remember my parents trying to hide the newspapers from me. It seemed to be a terribly unlikely subject for a film – particularly a Peter Jackson film. But as Peter talked he worked his "magical persuasiveness" and I began to think that maybe, after all, it was a film that he *could* make…'

That film, *Heavenly Creatures*, begun as another stepping-stone in Peter Jackson's career, eventually turned out to be a milestone.

Concluding his appraisal of *Braindead* in 1990, Costa Botes had written: 'It is beyond my brief to comment on Jackson's future prospects, but I do believe he has the potential to follow in the foot-steps of directors like David Cronenberg and Roman Polanski; his talents and interests are by no means restricted to horror films.'

Heavenly Creatures was to prove that assessment true.

5

ISSUES OF LIFE AND DEATH

'Having just come off seven months' intensive work on *Braindead*, I feel as if I'm only just starting to figure out what film-making is all about. I want nothing more than to launch myself into another movie right now!'

Peter Jackson was writing to the New Zealand Film Commission in May 1992 with a proposal for a very particular movie, which he wanted to make 'as soon as possible' – although he was already enough of a pragmatist to add, 'I'm sure every film-maker says that…'

When you're a young film-maker and you're trying to get a momentum going and movies made, the best time to float a new project is when people are being enthusiastic and saying nice things about your previous one! If you're selling people a film at Cannes or Mifed, that's the perfect opportunity to tell them your latest idea and show them the next script. To strike while the iron is hot!

I had developed a pattern of starting writing my next movie while I was in post-production of the one before: Fran, Stephen and I had written *Braindead* – and come up with the idea for *Meet the Feebles* – while *Bad Taste* was being completed; and, while *Braindead* was in post-production, Fran and I settled on an idea for another film.

By that point, certain personal dynamics had changed: Stephen and Fran had amicably ended their relationship the previous year, and Stephen had moved back to his native Auckland. Subsequently, Peter and Fran became partners and would be, for a while, sole collaborators.

As with so many aspects of Peter Jackson's life, coincidence and chance seemed to jog the hand of Fate. 'It is very curious,' says Fran, 'but my grandmother's sister lived three doors down from Peter's family in Pukerua Bay, and when I was 4 or 5 years old, my grandmother used to take me on visits. Peter's mother knew my aunt well and we must have passed each other on that street in our pushchairs.'

At the time of writing to the Film Commission about the movie he wanted to make 'right now', Peter had, in fact, several potential film projects in various stages of development. There was *Blubberhead*, 'a very big expensive project', the script for which Peter was revisiting with Danny Mulheron ('Leaving scripts alone for a few months always works wonders…'), and there was *Warrior Season*, being written with Costa Botes.

> *The Warrior Season* was a Kung Fu western, set in the NZ Gold Rush of the 1870s. It was born out of an idea of Costa's, blended with my new-found love of Jackie Chan movies. My LA friends, Dave Schow and Mark Ordesky, had introduced me to some of these amazing Hong Kong movies like *Police Story 2* and *Project A*. I'd never liked this type of film before, but Jackie Chan had so much in common with Buster Keaton – brilliant physical comedy – that I became an instant fan.
>
> At one stage, *The Warrior Season* was a film I was hoping to make. I remember Costa and I talked about me directing it, and I wanted Timothy Dalton to play the villain. It was not to be, but the script still exists, so who knows? We used the title as a private in-joke much later in *Forgotten Silver*.

There were also early stirrings on an idea that Peter had been playing with, on and off, for a number of years and still not quite relinquished – *Bad Taste 2*.

At various times – on *Bad Taste*'s release and, later, when it was issued on video – reviewers seemed to be of the opinion that the story of The Boys and their alien adversaries was not yet over. As one critic put it: 'If ever an ending cries out for a sequel, this one does.'

'When *Bad Taste* was first released,' wrote Peter in 1992, 'I felt some pressure to do a sequel... It seemed people expected me to jump straight into it... That made me all the more determined not to! I wasn't going to allow myself to be pigeonholed so early in my career. I was keen to learn about scriptwriting, work with experienced people and professional actors. I made a promise to myself at the time that I would only do it when I wanted to – when I was excited by the idea...'

Now, it seemed, he was finally getting excited: 'I've been thinking about it more and more lately, and the urge to have a go at *Bad Taste 2* is getting strong, so I guess now is the time. After all... none of us boys are getting any younger!'

Life had recently been busy – completing *Braindead* ('Finished, hallelujah!') and researching future projects – but Peter had somehow managed to find a little time for contemplating what mayhem might be unleashed in a possible *Bad Taste 2*: 'Things have been pretty hectic, and at the end of the day I'd collapse into a hot bath. Most of the best ideas for *Bad Taste* came to me when I was laying in the bath, so I decided to try thinking up stuff for *Bad Taste 2*...'

The results of 'those nocturnal soaks' were suitably anarchic and with the prospect of becoming even more so: 'The original *Bad Taste* was shot over four years, with the story and gags developing constantly over that time. I obviously can't repeat that, but I do want to have the ideas bubbling away for a long time before things start to get nailed down... I have concentrated on trying to come up with a reasonable narrative that can be used as a backbone for a lot of action and humour... When I first set out, I had three elements I wanted to work into the story... An alien attack on Wellington, Santa Claus and a giant Weta. The mix may not be quite right yet, but at least they're all in there!'

As indeed they were, along with Derek's experiences among their fast food outlets on the alien planet, Nailic Nod; Giles being consumed by the giant Weta and reborn as an insect with a human head; The Boys defending Wellington against extra-terrestrial invasion; a Santa's workshop (relocated to the *South* Pole) complete with elves; a phoney alien, Santa; an assassinated Rudolph and a reindeer brain-transplant (with antlers) for the brain-dead Derek!

It had every indication that it was a story still in development but with all the makings of one that would be filled with wild and wacky nonsense. About one thing Peter was adamant; *Bad Taste 2* was to be a low-budget exercise: 'The second film must be shot with the same flavour as the first… *BT2* must not look glossier and flashier than the original. Certainly a lot of the technical and directorial flaws that are apparent in *Bad Taste* can be eliminated, but the tone and style (which has rough edges) must not.'

Peter also intended 'to toy around' with slightly offbeat production methods… possibly a very long shoot with a small crew: 'I have gained valuable experience working with normal-sized crews on *Meet the Feebles* and *Braindead*, but ironically some of the best scenes in both movies were shot with tiny crews.' Peter had been most recently inspired by an experience towards the end of the *Braindead* shoot: having uncharacteristically run under budget, he had had enough spare money to finance an extra, un-scripted sequence that was filmed on the fly and with a lot of improvisation.

The sequence, dubbed 'Selwyn Loose in the Park', featured the zombie baby, with Lionel in pursuit, going on the rampage through the innocent world of kiddie-swings and nursing mothers. This episode – like that of Wynyard the Frog on the run in Vietnam in *Feebles* – was shot with a tiny crew, which for Peter had definite advantages: 'The atmosphere is relaxed and you generally get twice as much shot as on a normal day.'

BT2 was, as well as being a possible answer to the 'numerous enquiries and requests' received 'from magazines and fans around the world,' an opportunity for Peter to get back to his roots: being fully hands-on and in total control of his film-making. It was the way he had started – his one-man-film-school approach – and some elements of it had doubtless been hard to relinquish.

Several of those involved in *Meet the Feebles* recall Peter's insistence on being behind the camera as being seen by some as a breach of the accepted, or expected, procedures of professional film-making (even in the relaxed atmosphere of New Zealand), where a director does not also do the job of the director of photography. With *Braindead*, Peter had surrendered the job of camera operator, but

BT2 offered a possible return to the amateur-auteur ways he had enjoyed on his first film.

Despite his obvious desire to get back together with The Boys and, once again, save the world – or at least Wellington – from the aliens, he was also beginning to feel the need to make a very different film from what, by now, was seen as a genre he had made his own.

> After finishing *Braindead*, I thought, 'Where is there to go now with splatter films?' I had just made what I thought was the *ultimate* splatter film! What else could I do: make another one and set it in a different place, a different time? It would just be more splatter.

As he wrote to the Film Commission in 1992, 'After *Bad Taste*, *Meet the Feebles* and *Braindead*, I have to admit to being slightly worn down by all the mayhem and splatter! I'd like to have a crack at something different. Working with the actors on *Braindead* was fun and the idea of doing a movie that is less gimmicky, with real characters, greatly appeals to me at this time...

'My interest in film-making goes deeper than gag-driven "splatstick" films. I feel I have more to offer than the limited skills needed to keep turning them out. I love the horror/fantasy/action genres and intend to continue working in that field, but I would also like to diversify once in a while and make something with a little more substance. I feel that this is a good time in my career to do that.'

And he already had the ideal project with which to diversify...

In July 1954, the newspapers in New Zealand were full of reports of a brutal murder committed in Christchurch, a city not usually known as a place of sensational events. The crime, which rocked Christchurch society and shocked the entire nation, was according to the florid rhetoric of the Crown Prosecutor: 'A callously planned and premeditated murder committed by two highly intelligent but precocious and dirty-minded girls.'

On 22 June, during a walk in Victoria Park, 16-year-old Pauline Parker and 15-year-old Juliet Hulme had battered Pauline's mother to death using, as a weapon, a brick in a stocking. Details of what rapidly became known as the 'Parker–Hulme Murder Case' were captured in colourful headlines that were soon splattered across not just the front pages of New Zealand's newspapers but also across those of the British Press.

Despite class differences, the girls both possessed highly developed intellects, fertile imaginations and a considerable creative talent for writing, drawing and model-making. Together, they became caught up in a world of shared fantasies and grandiose delusions, born out of mutual emotional dependency and carrying them to a heightened state of ecstatic euphoria.

Concerns about the possibly 'unhealthy' nature of their relationship led to attempts to part the girls; as a result, the murder of Pauline's mother – seen as the chief obstacle to their being together – was cold-bloodedly planned and executed.

Found guilty and being too young to be hanged, the girls were imprisoned but were released five years later, taking on new identities and disappearing from the public gaze. Hardly surprisingly, the case was, and has remained, a cause célèbre.

> There was a lot of curiosity about their outrageous and inexplicable crime, but even more so about where the girls were now and what had become of them, which had kept interest in the story alive for almost forty years.
>
> Fran had been fascinated by the Parker–Hulme case since she was young. At the time, I hadn't heard of the case but Fran kept mentioning it, telling me about books and newspaper stories she had read on the subject and insisting that the story of Pauline and Juliet would make a great film. Initially, I didn't believe her: I just thought, 'Two girls kill one of their mothers, it's a pretty grim story, why would anyone ever want to go and see a movie about that?' But Fran didn't give up and eventually we began to research the case together. As we did so, I became more and more interested, not so much in the murder as in the character of the girls and, finally, I started trying to find the movie...

Various films had been made over several decades based on celebrated twentieth-century murder cases, including the Christie killings that took place in *10 Rillington Place*; the story of Ruth Ellis (the last woman to be hanged in Britain) in *Dance with a Stranger*; and an account of the miscarriage of justice that led to the hanging of Derek Bentley for a crime he did not commit in the film *Let Him Have It*.

> They were all rather gloomy, depressing films without any joy or humour in them. I said to Fran that I wouldn't want this story to be told like that – it was the obvious, easy way to go. I would want it to have more life, more heart and that meant trying to find out *why* the girls did what they did.

Their research began with contemporary press accounts of the trial that were prosaic – even simplistic – and which reduced a complex case to a series of journalistic tag-lines: 'No Remorse', '"Intense" Friendship', 'Legally Insane?' And most of what had been written subsequently had simply rehashed those accounts.

Evidence was presented at the trial that sought to question the girls' sanity and extracts from diaries kept by Pauline were quoted to stress what was seen as abnormal behaviour. Adolescent rituals, such as making little temples in the garden for the candlelit worship of famous matinee-idols, were interpreted as being cult-like and sinister; while the girls' obsessive devotion for one another was interpreted – in veiled hints, typical of the times – as being indicative of a lesbian love-affair, a social evil not far short of murder. There was a general feeling that the girls were, therefore, inherently evil.

Apart from the trial reports, writings about the case were few and far between and ranged from a lurid 1950s pulp-fiction novel based on the thinly disguised real-life events and subscribing to the prevailing 'demon-daughter' theories, to a 1990s socio-political study, *Parker & Hulme: A Lesbian View*, exploring the homosexual hysteria attending the trial.

> Fran and I talked about what we had read so far and I remember saying, 'We can't base a movie on this stuff. We have to research the real events for ourselves…' So, we started to do exactly that: ignoring all the newspaper accounts and going back to the original sources, such as court papers and trial transcripts.

Whilst Peter and Fran began to uncover details that had been forgotten, suppressed or distorted in the various accounts of the murder, they made another discovery:

> It came as quite a shock to us to find that there were two other prospective film projects based on the same story: one to have been produced by Dustin Hoffman's company and the other to have been directed by Niki Caro, who would later make the award-winning *Whale Rider*.
>
> Such a situation was very unusual for a country this size, but that wasn't all: in addition to the possible films, there was also a stage play, *Daughters of Heaven* by Michelanne Forster, which had been performed in Christchurch in 1991 and was being talked about as the basis of a possible TV film. We were now aware that there were other people who were thinking about this as a film subject, which motivated Fran and me to think, 'God, if we want to do this ourselves, we'd better be pretty quick, or someone else is going to get there first!'

It was only a matter of months before Peter was to take *Braindead* to the Cannes Film Festival, which was the obvious forum in which to announce his interest in the Parker–Hulme story. Peter was in the cutting-room during the day, finishing editing on *Braindead,* but in the evenings he and Fran would work on their new screenplay and within just five or six weeks had produced a draft script for what was to be called *Heavenly Creatures.*

> We wrote right up until the eve of going to Cannes and I took the script with me to the Festival, hot off the press, as it were.
>
> No one knew anything about what we'd been doing and I remember sitting in a hotel room in Cannes one afternoon with Richard and Tania and reading them the entire screenplay of *Heavenly Creatures.* I was quite proud of what we had written and was keen to have their opinions and get some feedback.

'What was wonderful about *Heavenly Creatures,*' says Richard, recalling that afternoon, 'was the realisation that the world had now accepted Peter as a George Romero–Sam Raimi gore-meister and had assumed that that was to be his future; and yet here he was, planning to turn round and slap them in the face with a beautiful, poignant, incredibly intimate, revealing story of female teenage angst which – just from Pete's reading of the script – was obviously going to be an incredible work of art.'

That determination to play against people's preconceptions signalled a talent who was determined to define himself, rather than be defined by others; this should have been remembered when, a few years later, people expressed surprise – even alarm – that Peter Jackson was about to attempt the conquest of Middle-earth.

In 1992, Peter's producer, Jim Booth, wrote of the *Heavenly Creatures* proposal: 'Some may be surprised at Peter taking on this subject. I am not. Peter's storytelling skills are based on a genuine ability to recognise the universal, the myths, and the fantasies which lie behind all stories. It is the childlike quality of the fairytale; it is the talent of the Spielbergs of this world...'

At Cannes, Peter met with German film producer Hanno Huth of Senator Films, who had produced the Dennis Hopper thriller *Eye of the Storm* and the film about The Beatles' early, pre-fame days in Hamburg, *Backbeat*. Huth bought *Braindead* for distribution in Germany and was interested in knowing whether Peter had another film he wanted to make. In fact, he offered him one: *Invasion of Privacy* – a social thriller written by Larry Cohen about a man who kidnaps a woman carrying his child and holds her to ransom in a remote house in order to prevent her from having an abortion. Peter turned down the project and, instead, showed Huth the script for *Heavenly Creatures*, which the German read, liked and agreed to help finance as co-producer.

When the New Zealand Film Commission's Chairman, David Gascoigne, heard the pitch for *Heavenly Creatures* (over that ice-cream sundae in a Cannes café) he was surprised not just by the proposed subject matter but also by the fact that, unlike earlier projects, Peter had developed a script before approaching the Commission for funding. As Peter later explained: 'I didn't think I would be taken seriously if I started blabbing about it before I had written a script. "The Sultan of Splatter" doing the Parker-Hulme story is a difficult concept for people to accept, and I felt I had to produce a script as proof of my integrity when dealing with this subject matter.'

Having established that integrity, Peter wanted urgent funding for Fran and himself to continue their researches in Christchurch. He realised that to secure the Film Commission's support he needed to address the issue of exactly what the 'Sultan of Splatter' thought he was up to. His application to the Film Commission tackled this question head on:

'WHY ON EARTH AM I ATTRACTED TO THE PARKER–HULME STORY? I can hear the journalist's question now, and will hear it a hundred times if this film gets made – at least it will give me a break from the usual "Did you have an unhappy childhood?" (Come to think of it, it probably won't!)

'First and foremost, it is a great story, with great characters. Beyond that, it has one compelling attraction that is guaranteed to intoxicate film-makers: it is a very well-known but totally misunderstood chapter in New Zealand criminal history.

'Pauline and Juliet were two very imaginative but normal girls. They did nothing that most of us haven't done – kept diaries, played fantasy games, sneaked out at night, had imaginary friends, planned impossible trips, experimented with sex... even fantasising about killing your parents. What has set them apart from the rest of us is that they went one step further...

'I have taken no sides, no political stance; the story is not about sexual politics, it is not about "lesbian killers" or "lesbian martyrs". Once you learn who Pauline and Juliet were and why they acted the way they did, it all becomes very clear. I have tried to tell a complex psychological story in a way that I think represents the truth in a very accurate manner...'

At the end of his proposal, Peter concluded with a typical, 'straight-up' Jackson comment: 'Re-reading the last couple of pages, I realise that this is coming across like some sort of personal crusade... and it's not really. In the end, I'm a movie-maker and I know this story could make a great film, and I would love to have the chance to do it. The fact that it is a true story with real people has excited me in a way that has never happened before with scripts I've worked on.'

Supporting the *Heavenly Creatures* proposal, Jim Booth wrote:

Jim Booth at an industry function in 1992. Jim and I assumed we would be partners in film-making for many years to come.

'Peter is a serious film-maker. This is not a departure for him, but a logical progression. His work with the actors in *Braindead* turned an essentially "comic-book" film into something much more, and the potential of Peter with this script is very exciting.

'It will not be an earnest, "worthy" film. But it will be a worthwhile film because it is true to the people involved; to the humour and pathos, foolishness and mistakes that surround this tragedy.

'Peter will always strive to make films which appeal to audiences. This does not trivialise or demean the subject. In fact the reverse; the core of his work is based on universal precepts which will entertain, surprise and involve the viewer.'

In just a few years the 49-year-old Booth had gone from being perceived as the archenemy at the Film Commission who was preventing the completion of *Bad Taste* to being Peter's producer and advocate. Peter had come to rely on Jim as a sounding board for his ideas, as a litmus test for his scripts and as someone who would help him achieve what he wanted to do by releasing him from many of the less appealing, time-consuming tasks that go along with making a movie. Above all, they had become not just colleagues, but friends.

It was therefore all the more devastating when – a couple of weeks after the triumphant response to *Braindead* in Cannes and the anticipation that had been stirred up for *Heavenly Creatures* – Jim broke some unexpected bad news to Peter.

He told me that he'd just been diagnosed as having bowel cancer and that he had suspected that something was wrong while we had been making *Braindead*, but hadn't wanted to go to the doctor because he didn't want to do anything to jeopardise the film. I was shocked at the news and appalled that he had put off seeing a doctor. I remember saying, 'Oh, Jim, you should never have done that... Why did you do it? We would have coped, okay.' I was totally, utterly stunned...

A colostomy operation followed, which Jim faced with characteristic fortitude and matter-of-factness, inviting friends round for a pre-op get-together, which he jestingly referred to as a 'Disembowelling Party'.

While Jim was recovering from surgery the Film Commission approved the advancing of finance for Peter and Fran to continue their researches into the Parker–Hulme case in Christchurch. Visiting many of the real-life locations – the girls' school, the Hulme family house and gardens, the tea-rooms in Victoria Park close to the murder site, even the consulting-rooms of the doctor who alarmed Pauline's mother with his talk of 'homosexuality' – brought history vividly alive and convinced Peter and Fran that, as far as possible, the film should be shot at the actual places where the events occurred.

Whilst some Christchurch people still viewed the case as an embarrassment, others readily shared their memories: neighbours of the two families and retired teachers and fellow students at the school attended by Pauline and Juliet, as well as the two people who were the first to be confronted with the results of the girls' crime:

We met Ken Ritchie, the caretaker at Victoria Park in Christchurch, who found the body, and Ken's wife, Agnes, who was in the tea-room at the top of the Park and who served the mother her last cup of tea before the girls took her down a wooded track and killed her. It was Agnes who had confronted the hysterical girls when they came running up, covered in blood, after committing the murder. That scene, which we showed at the beginning of the film, was based entirely on Agnes Ritchie's own personal account.

We also found a very close friend of the Hulme family, Nancy Sutherland, who was then an elderly lady in her nineties and who gave us a huge amount of practical advice and very intelligent insights into what went on and why. She told us about Juliet's mother having an extra-marital affair, which had caused the break-up of the family and provided the catalyst for the murder of Pauline's mother.

Nancy had never spoken to journalists but we won her trust and she decided to tell us everything, perhaps because she knew she was approaching the end of her life, but also, I think, because she felt that the truth had never really come out. From our contacts with all these people, we were able to base the movie not just on contemporary records, such as the court papers and Pauline's diaries, but also on personal reminiscences.

In June 1992, Peter was in Los Angeles where he met with a man who was to prove another major player in his future career. Peter's American lawyer, Peter Nelson, had decided to use the completion of *Braindead* as an opportunity to 'supplement the team with a Hollywood agent.' In fact, Peter had already had a relationship with a Los Angeles agency. 'They were,' says Peter Nelson, 'a good agency. They had signed him post-*Meet the Feebles* for all the right reasons but they fell asleep: at that time he wasn't making them money, so they didn't pay enough attention and that agency missed out on a rather significant opportunity! Peter brought *Braindead* to Hollywood and we invited agents and distributors to a screening, as a result of which we had offers from five agencies.'

One of those who attended the screening was Ken Kamins of InterTalent, who had joined the agency just three months previously after working for eight years as Vice-President at RCA/Columbia Pictures Home Video: 'What I saw in *Braindead* was tremendous confidence: the special-effects work is obvious, but it was more than that; it was Peter's willingness to almost look the audience dead in the eye and wink at them! *Braindead* is a big wink; Peter is giggling along with the audience all the way through, as if he's sitting in the seat next to you and saying, "Can you believe this?" I thought that showed enormous confidence, which would translate in whatever direction he decided to go with his movie-making.'

Following the screening of *Braindead*, Peter met with the interested agencies and the last of those meetings was with Ken Kamins: 'We had lunch on the last day before he got the plane to go back to New

Zealand. He was very inquisitive, and rather than sitting back, looking to me to make a presentation, he was asking a great many questions. I think he saw genuine enthusiasm on my part and maybe a candour and honesty about where he was in the marketplace and what might have to be done to get him to different places, and I think the truth is, in 1992, he didn't really know who he wanted to be in the business. Of course, Peter knew he wanted to make movies, wanted to do as much as he could himself and wanted to remain in New Zealand; he was, I think, initially somewhat uncomfortable about the idea of having to come to Los Angeles to get his work.

'I talked about possibly setting up a round of meetings with important studio executives and producers: I told him that *Braindead* would appeal to the likes of Spielberg and Zemeckis and that I would like to set up meetings with their companies. I've never forgotten his response, "Yeah, that would be great, but you know who I'd *really* love to meet? Sam Raimi!" That's absolutely the truth! He wanted to meet the director of *The Evil Dead*. For Peter, *The Evil Dead* was the Holy Grail!'

In fact, Hollywood was already beginning to show interest in Peter and even made occasional approaches with possible projects. The Disney Company, where – unlikely though it may seem – *Meet the Feebles* had been given a viewing, offered Peter a script in the wake of *Braindead*. A teen-zombie romance with the working title 'Johnny Zombie', it made an uncomfortable stab at social satire by presenting the various attitudes displayed towards the back-from-the-grave, undead hero in terms of racial prejudice. Peter wisely turned down the project, which was eventually released by Touchstone Pictures under the anodyne title *My Boyfriend's Back*.

Peter returned to New Zealand and, a few days later, called Ken Kamins to say that he would like to work with him. Peter Nelson reflects: 'Ken was a brilliant choice: he's an intelligent guy, but he has a humility that goes well with Peter's worldview. It would have been hard for any agency not to have done an acceptable job for Peter, but Ken has done an extraordinary job.'

Choosing an agent was a very personal decision. I was lucky enough to have meetings with all the big agencies, and ended up choosing the person I liked best, who happened to work for the smallest agency, InterTalent. Within a few months, they were absorbed into ICM so I ended up there with Ken. I think Ken assumed I would jump into an American movie, but he quickly learned how serious I was to make films at home. I'm grateful that he has always supported that, and never tried to turn me into something I'm not.

'Whatever Peter's answer might be as to why he signed with me,' says Ken, 'I believe that, unlike most of the other agencies who looked at *Braindead*, the one thing I *didn't* tell him was that what he needed to do was direct *A Nightmare on Elm Street* or a *Friday the Thirteenth* movie or some low-budget horror genre picture.'

> The Hollywood machine has pigeonholed a lot of very fine film-makers – which is frightening! It can take a Tobe Hooper, a John Carpenter or a Wes Craven and force them to stay in that genre because Hollywood is a very unimaginative town and pigeonholing is one of its specialities! It's all too easy to be stifled by the genre you're in and never really be offered anything else. Working in New Zealand made it easier to avoid being pigeonholed because we were generating and driving our own projects.

It was one of those projects that Peter had spoken of to Ken Kamins: 'He told me about a movie, a true story of matricide in New Zealand that he really wanted to make. And, if I'm not mistaken, I believe I was the only agent who told him he should make it!'

By early September 1992, the script for that story had gone through several more drafts and a submission was made to the Film Commission for production investment. The *Heavenly Creatures* proposal was a sophisticated and compelling document – to then-chairman David Gascoigne, it was simply one of the most impressive submissions he had read. Illustrated with period photographs and containing detailed notes on character and story structure, it was a far cry from documents that Peter had been sending the Commission about *Bad Taste* less than ten years earlier.

Peter once again addressed his reasons for wanting to film what he was now describing as 'a murder story with no villains': 'A lot of people will attribute this choice of project as an attempt by me to break out of typecasting – "to gain respectability" – or the old favourite, "to be taken seriously as a film-maker." Not so. They are making an assumption that my career choices are governed more by what I want to be seen to be, rather than what I actually want to do. I naturally find that rather annoying. I've had a long interest in the Parker–Hulme story… I'm a film-maker, so the notion of making a Parker–Hulme film is perfectly natural to me, if not to anybody else…'

> What I find curious is that if people like two or three splatter movies that you've made then they somehow can't get their head around the fact that you can possibly make other types of films and, if you do, then it comes as a total shock to them. They say, 'How did you make this? It's just so *different!*'
>
> I can understand why people say it, but it really doesn't have a great deal of bearing on reality, because if you are a film-maker nothing is really that different. The subject matter, sure, and the genre; but for the rest: you've still got to show up on set at seven o'clock in the morning and decide what lens to use and where you're going to put your camera, and you have a script that has to achieve something – whether it's a zombie film or *Heavenly Creatures* or *The Lord of the Rings* – and your task is to read the pages you're shooting that day, and figure out how best to cover them and bring them to life.
>
> Obviously, those scenes are dictated by what's on the page, which in turn is dictated by what the movie is, but the job itself is exactly the same. If you can make a good splatter movie, then you can probably make a good cowboy film or musical. If you can't it's because other people have ghettoised you, and not given you the chance! Staying in New Zealand, and making low-budget, independently financed movies allowed me to control my career path and make my own decisions in a way that would have been impossible in Hollywood.

Aware of how he was perceived as a film-maker in 1992, Peter was at pains to give as clear a picture as possible of the approach he intended to adopt in filming *Heavenly Creatures*: 'I don't intend to make a dark, brooding, little murder film. That would be the obvious, clichéd way to go. It holds little interest for me. More importantly, it belittles the characters involved in the story.

'So much of Pauline and Juliet's friendship was positive, and that is the tone I intend to take with the movie: a celebration of a remarkable relationship. It has a tragic ending, but to portray it as "doomed from the beginning" would be a mistake. For the most part it was a joyous, exhilarating relationship, filled with humour, intelligence and two wonderfully hyper imaginations…'

Those hyper imaginations had led the girls to create their imaginary kingdom of Borovnia and to develop a perception of themselves as belonging to a mystical dimension or altered state which they described as the Fourth World: a schizophrenic state of mind that prompted Pauline to write of Juliet and herself:

I worship the power of these lovely two
With that adoring love known to so few.
'Tis indeed a miracle, one must feel,
That two such heavenly creatures are real.

The fantasy realm with its invented characters and the girls' equally fantastical obsession with movie heartthrobs, and in particular Mario Lanza, star of such movies as *The Great Caruso* and *Because You're Mine* and the owner of a magnificent voice, which Arturo Toscanini described as the 'voice of the century', all offered promise of a rich visual and musical approach to the telling of the story.

'With character dramas such as *A Room with a View* or *Angel at My Table*,' wrote Peter, 'we are used to quite laid back, static camera angles. *Heavenly Creatures* will burst into life with a fluid, lively style. Camera movement and editing will build up to near manic levels during some of the more exalted sequences. The Mario Lanza music will help create this mood. Who knows, we may even get "The Donkey Serenade" back into the charts!'

Such claims (with the exception of that relating to 'The Donkey Serenade') are a not-uncommon feature of 'proposal-speak'. In the case of *Heavenly Creatures*, however, Peter Jackson's claims would be vividly realised with wildly dynamic, highly energised scenes that force the viewer to share in the girls' heightened emotional states, whether joyous or murderous. What Peter hadn't specifically promised but, nevertheless, spectacularly delivered were sequences of breathtaking beauty – especially those in which he gives the sense of the relationship between people and landscape that foreshadow many such moments in *The Lord of the Rings*.

Sensible of his growing status, Peter ended his submission with a courteous but firm request for an early decision from the Commission. He pointed out that he had been 'turning down several directing offers', the latest of which had been from director Sam Raimi and producer Rob Tapert: 'I'm going to decline without even reading the script simply because it clashes with our plans for *Heavenly Creatures*. It is my risk and I'm happy about that... I mention it only to illustrate my point that I need to know in October if I should stick with *Heavenly Creatures* or look elsewhere for work. I need to have a "yes" or "no" from the Commission. I will have to take a deferred decision as a lack of confidence in me and my script and move on to other things...'

In conclusion, Peter spoke of attitude towards future work: 'I have a strong commitment to the New Zealand film industry and hope to continue to be based here. If I ever get involved in a Hollywood project, I will be vigorously promoting the idea of shooting it in New Zealand, or shooting SPFX here, or doing post-production here. To make those sorts of demands in Hollywood I need a reasonable amount of clout, and I believe that *Heavenly Creatures* could be successful enough to give me a lot of clout over there.'

There may have been some who read that passage and thought that it was nothing more than an attempt to push them towards a positive response on *Heavenly Creatures*. Time alone would show that Peter meant – and would stick by – every word.

Nevertheless, apart from the offer to work with Peter's hero, Sam Raimi, there had been word of another project from 'over there' that was equally right in Peter's backyard: a new *Planet of the Apes* movie for Twentieth Century Fox. As a youngster, Peter had been inspired by the first of the five *Planet of the Apes* pictures to make his own ape masks and to pay homage to the movie's famous climax in his juvenile film, *The Valley*. Now, over twenty years later, he was in the frame to write a new title for the franchise.

Ken Kamins had floated the proposition to Peter, who had immediately started putting together a script idea with Fran, which became a three- or four-page treatment. It was October 1992 and Peter and Fran, who were still awaiting a decision on *Heavenly Creatures* from the Film Commission, were on their way to the Sitges Film Festival in Spain. Ken set up a meeting with producer Harry J. Ufland (whose films included *The Last Temptation of Christ, Night and the City* and Michael Jackson's *Bad*) so that Peter could pitch the *Apes* proposal, which was for an original story rather than a remake of the first film, as would eventually – and pointlessly – be undertaken by Tim Burton. Peter had been particularly keen to write a part into the script for Roddy McDowall, who had had a key involvement in the five *Apes* movies and the subsequent television series.

> Fran and I had devised a storyline that continued the *Apes* saga from where it left off in the fifth movie. We imagined their world being in the midst of an artistic Renaissance, which made the ape government very nervous. It was a time of amazing art and we wanted Roddy McDowall to play an elderly chimpanzee that we based a little on Leonardo da Vinci. The plot involved the humans rising in revolt and had a half-human, half-ape central character that was sheltered by the liberal apes, but hunted down by the Gorillas.

Harry Ufland was excited enough to arrange a meeting between Peter and Fran and Roddy McDowall on their homeward journey from the festival.

In Sitges, Peter met Ralph Bakshi who – almost a decade-and-a-half on from directing the animated version of *The Lord of the Rings* – had just made *Cool World*, a live-action/animation answer to *Who Framed Roger Rabbit*. Peter and Fran also met and became friends with Quentin Tarantino, fresh from directing *Reservoir Dogs*, and Rick Baker who had been responsible for the make-up effects on such films as *The Howling, An American Werewolf in London* and the appalling 1976 re-make of *King Kong* in which, uncredited, he had donned a monkey-suit in order to play the giant ape!

Peter and Rick Baker talked about the *Kong* movies and Rick's

I was visiting the Sitges Fantasy Film Festival in 1992 when we heard that the NZ Film Commission had approved funding for Heavenly Creatures. *Amongst the many guests at the festival was Ralph Bakshi, who had made the animated version of* The Lord of the Rings *fifteen years earlier. The thought that I'd one day be adapting that same story hadn't even entered my head when I asked Ralph for this 'fan photo'.*

work on other ape and gorilla projects such as *Greystoke: The Legend of Tarzan, Lord of the Apes* and *Gorillas in the Mist*. Peter also talked about the *Planet of the Apes* script idea that he was pitching to Fox and which Rick responded to with much enthusiasm.

While at Sitges, news came from Jim Booth in New Zealand that the Film Commission had finally green-lit *Heavenly Creatures*. The film that Peter had long set his heart on directing was to go ahead and filming was to begin early in 1993.

On the way home via Los Angeles, Peter and Fran met up with Harry Ufland once again and had lunch with Roddy McDowall, prior to going on to meet with executives at Twentieth Century Fox, the owners of the franchise.

McDowall, then in his early sixties, had read their *Planet of the Apes* proposal and warmed to the fact that they had created a new chimpanzee character with him in mind and which felt like a comfortable grey-haired version of Cornelius, his first Apes role.

We lunched at the Ivy with Roddy, who was very sweet. He had seen and really liked *Heavenly Creatures* and was kind of excited about the idea of working with us. He said, 'I had never wanted to be in a *Planet of the Apes* film again, but I love your idea and I'd love you guys to make it. We should do it!'

The group then went on to the Fox studios.

Walking from the parking lot to the office where the meeting was to be held, Roddy gave us a running commentary on the history of the studio where he had worked for over fifty years since his early films as a child star. He'd point to a sound stage and say, 'That's where we shot *How Green Was My Valley*...' and he'd say, 'This was the street that we used for this film... And so-and-so was shot over there...' He was full of amazing memories and in just taking that short walk with him we experienced this fantastic first-hand insight into Hollywood.

The meeting with the Fox executive Tom Jacobson did not go well. When Harry Ufland had previously discussed the possibility of bringing an *Apes* project to Fox, it had been with Joe Roth, who

Fran and I at lunch with Roddy McDowall and the Ufflands. Over the course of several years, we tried very hard to make a new Planet of the Apes *film, but it was not to be.*

had now left the studio to work for Disney. Jacobson was certainly interested in a *Planet of the Apes* movie, but less so in Roddy McDowall – Peter's memory is that he really didn't seem to know anything about the veteran actor or understand his emotional involvement with the film series.

> It went incredibly badly, but in the process we learned a useful lesson in Hollywood politics. Harry Ufland and Joe Roth were good friends and obviously Joe had been happy to help Harry with his *Planet of the Apes* project. However, Tom Jacobson was not committed to any previous discussions that may have taken place. So, when Harry made remarks about Joe having said this or that, he just looked up and said, 'Joe is not here anymore...' And at that point we realised, okay, there are no allies! No matter what Fox think about a *Planet of the Apes* movie, they are not interested in Harry Ufland being Joe Roth's old buddy and they don't care about Roddy McDowall.
>
> And as for us... *Heavenly Creatures* hadn't been released at that stage, which left us with *Bad Taste*, *Meet the Feebles* and *Braindead* as our films, and they were films that none of these people had seen. So we walked out and somehow, at that meeting, the project died...

Though it was not *quite* the last to be heard of *Planet of the Apes*...

Back in Wellington, Peter went straight into pre-production on *Heavenly Creatures*, on which much had to be accomplished in a short period of time – not least in the area of special effects.

In contrast to the gore and gunk of the previous films, Richard Taylor and Tania Rodger's talents were now going to be needed to help create the girls' imaginary kingdom of Borovnia, which was peopled with life-size versions of the figures of mediaeval knights and ladies that the girls modelled from Plasticine. It was an effect that had made members of the Commission nervous when they had read the Borovnian sequences in the script, but Richard produced models and costumes that not only convincingly created the illusion that Pauline and Juliet had entered a realm of the imagination, but also paved the way for the advanced prosthetic work involved in fashioning the creatures that would inhabit Middle-earth.

The film was also going to include some limited computer effects

*Richard Taylor and his crew made a crowd of Plasticine figures (above) using rubber suits.
I still get asked questions about this scene, with most people assuming they were computer
generated. Shooting* Heavenly Creatures *(below) at Port Levy, near Christchurch.*

– specifically to produce the hallucinatory effect of the Christchurch beauty spot, Port Levy, morphing into an ornamental garden with gargantuan butterflies when the girls have an ecstatic vision of what they called the Fourth World. These moments in *Heavenly Creatures* were to be the birthplace of Weta Digital.

> The truth was, we didn't *really* need computer effects on *Heavenly Creatures*... I was honest enough to admit that to myself, but I thought, 'God, what the hell! Why don't we just get a computer and do some stuff, because this is a great excuse to learn about how these computer effects work!'

The equipment was a single computer and was very expensive. In fact, it was so expensive that it had to be financed with a loan that was still being paid off seven years later – long after the machine itself had been overtaken by *new* technology! The machine was operated by George Port who had first got to know Peter during the making of the TV pilot version of *Meet the Feebles*. 'It was all Cameron Chittock's fault!' recalls George. 'We knew one another from working for an animation studio and Cameron told me about this anarchic puppet film that he was involved with and invited me to pop in and watch them filming. When I arrived, they said: "Here, put on this elephant suit!" and I was one of the Feebles.'

Despite the fact that, by his own admission, he was not a very good puppeteer, George was enlisted to work on the feature-length version of *Feebles*. Half-way through the shoot he also bought a video camera, with which he shot hours of behind-the-scenes footage for what is, to date, an unfinished video-diary and a precursor of the 'appendices' that would later become a feature of *The Lord of the Rings* DVD releases.

Like many others, George was impressed and intrigued by Peter's grit and determination. After filming the secret *Feebles* shoot with its ever-dwindling personnel and resources, George came to the conclusion that 'it wouldn't actually have mattered, in the end, whether or not anyone else had been with him: he would have still finished the film – if necessary, on his own!'

During *Braindead*, George had stepped in for another actor who was unwilling to have a head cast made and, as a result, it is George's head – sliced horizontally in two – that is seen being kicked around the floor during the zombie carnage. Between spates of bloodletting the film-fans on the team talked about James Cameron's recently released *Terminator 2: Judgement Day* and bemoaned the fact that the computer effects in that film could never be produced by film-makers in New Zealand.

When *Heavenly Creatures* began to be discussed, with its need for convincing fantasy sequences, the topic of computer effects came up once more. 'It was obvious,' says George, 'that we weren't going to be asking George Lucas' Industrial Light and Magic to create the effects – one shot would have eaten up our entire visual effects budget! So, Peter and Jim allowed me to do some research and with the aid of Kodak and some dodgy computer salesmen we leased a film scanner and recorder and a Silicon Graphics SGI computer.' The process was very much one of trial and error: 'The film scanner didn't have a manual,' recalls George, 'just two pages of photocopied instructions – which were wrong!'

Whatever other production issues were on Peter's mind, the first – and most urgent – task to be tackled on his return from Sitges was to cast the film.

Peter and Fran flew to London, since part of the original proposal allowed for the casting of English actors in the roles of Juliet and her parents – they had moved from Britain to New Zealand when the father, a mathematical physicist, became Rector of Canterbury University College in Christchurch. The casting agents, John and Ros Hubbard (who would later be involved in casting *The Lord of the Rings*) assembled 175 teenagers for the part of Juliet Hulme, one of whom was a 17 year old with considerable experience in theatre and television but who had yet to make a film and who was currently working in a deli in her home town of Reading.

> I remember John Hubbard saying, 'I really want you to meet this young actress because – mark my words – she is going to be a star one day!' Her name was Kate Winslet.

> Kate was amazing: she gave a vibrant audition and, by the time we
> had left London, we had offered her the role of Juliet.

Clive Merrison, a veteran of stage, film and television was cast as
Juliet's father, Henry Hulme – to whom he bore an uncanny resem-
blance – and the experienced theatre actress Diana Hart was cast as
his wife, Hilda.

Anna Quayle, one of the actresses who auditioned for the role of
Hilda Hulme, was to point Peter and Fran in the direction of further
research. To their astonishment, Anna had announced that her
parents had met Pauline and Juliet in New Zealand, shortly before
the murder.

Actors Sir Anthony and Lady Quayle were with a touring Shakespeare company and, while visiting Christchurch, had been guests at
a garden party that Mr and Mrs Hulme had held in their honour –
an event later incorporated into the film. Sir Anthony had died a few
years earlier but his widow, Dorothy Hyson, was still alive and shared
her memories with Fran and Peter:

> Lady Quayle had clear memories of the house and the parents and, par-
> ticularly, of the father showing them the gardens and of the two girls
> following them around, sniggering and laughing at them from the bushes,
> making rude noises and having fun.
>
> So, even when we were at the stage of casting the film, we were still
> researching and researching…

Although Honora Parker, the murder victim, was a New Zealander,
there had, for a while, been talk of casting a British star-name in the
role and mention had been made of Pauline Collins who was still hot
from her Oscar-nominated role in *Shirley Valentine*. Eventually, the
part would go to Sarah Peirse, who had impressed Peter and Fran
with her work in the period TV drama series, *A Woman of Good
Character*, and who had won a New Zealand Film and TV Award for
her role in Vincent Ward's 1988 feature film, *The Navigator: A
Mediaeval Odyssey*, which had for several years been New Zealand's
most acclaimed movie.

'I regard Sarah's performance,' Peter later commented, 'as a real triumph – the strength of her performance turns the story into a true tragedy. It was very important to Sarah that she honour the memory of Pauline's mother, and I think that this is evident in her compassionate and intelligent reading of the character.'

Other roles were cast from among established New Zealand actors and Jed Brophy returned to work with Peter again as the gauche young lodger with whom Pauline loses her virginity. The weeks passed and the cast was virtually assembled, with one major exception – a young actress to play opposite Kate Winslet. With just a month until the start of filming, the picture had, as yet, only one of its heavenly creatures.

The part of Pauline was obviously pivotal to the film, but the intensity of her character made the casting a challenge, especially since Peter was determined that the actress should be as near as possible to the age of Pauline Parker at the time the events took place. New Zealand casting agent Liz Mullane had already auditioned some 500 teenagers for the role – a number eventually whittled down to two or three potential contenders.

> We kept refusing to make a decision – kept putting it off – because we really felt in our hearts that none of the shortlisted actresses were really going to be right for the film. I remember Fran getting so frustrated and saying, 'This film really relies on the perfect bit of casting and we haven't got it, Peter, we haven't got it!' And I said, 'No, I don't think we have…'
>
> We realised that we were probably going to have to work with someone who had never acted before, which was scary for two reasons: not just the fact that she hadn't acted, but also we still had to find her.
>
> It was just absolute, utter despair.

While Liz Mullane resumed her search in Auckland, Fran decided to get personally involved in the search, telling Peter, 'Well, I'm just going to go out there and find her!'

Accompanied by Bryce Campbell, who was one of the Campbell brothers in whose house the first version of *Meet the Feebles* had been filmed, Fran set off with a map, a mobile phone, a pile of telephone directories and a video camera. As they approached a town, Fran

Fran and I outside the old Christchurch Girls High building during the 1993 production of Heavenly Creatures, *with our movie class '3A'.*

would call ahead to the local schools, explain what they were doing and ask whether they had any 15-year-old, dark-haired pupils who might have done some amateur dramatics and, if so, whether she could meet them.

The response from the schools was positive, with Fran meeting a number of girls who, if they seemed at all likely, would be given an instant audition on video with Bryce operating the camera. After about three days on the road, they arrived in New Plymouth and were invited to meet the pupils of the Girls' High School. Fran walked into a room full of 15-year-olds, saw a particular girl sitting in the class and asked if she might talk with her?

The girl's name was Melanie Lynskey. She had taken part in some school dramatics and was interested in acting. On went the video camera...

I was in Christchurch in the middle of pre-production, gearing up to make the movie, and Fran phoned me up and said, 'I think I might have found her, I think I've found our Pauline! But, we've got to figure out if she can act.'

Fran got parental permission for Melanie to fly to Christchurch in order to meet Peter. Deciding that it would be unfair to expect Melanie to audition again without some tuition, Peter and Fran asked their friend, actress and director Miranda Harcourt, to provide some coaching. Miranda (who had played the role of Pauline's mother in the Wellington production of the stage play, *Daughters of Heaven*) took Melanie to the original girls' high school building, which was no longer being used for teaching, and talked to her about Pauline's character and the mood of the story.

Peter was pleased with the results: Melanie was a novice, but also clearly had a quality that was suited to Pauline's intense – 'outsider' – temperament. However, Melanie flew home to New Plymouth without knowing whether she had won the role as Peter and Fran had not wanted to build up her hopes in case her parents, not unreasonably, baulked at having their 15-year-old daughter plucked out of school in order to fly several hundred miles away for twelve weeks of filming. It was an anxious moment when – in the midst of a research trip to the local tram museum – Peter put in a telephone call to Melanie's mother.

I told Mrs Lynskey we wanted Mel to be in the movie but that before we spoke to her we wanted to know how her parents felt about it. She had just the right sort of attitude and said how proud and pleased they would be. And then she handed the phone to Mel and I said, 'You've got the part, Mel, you're going to be in the film.' It was a great moment and someone snapped a photograph of me making that vital phone call!

A few days later, Fran and I took Kate Winslet to Christchurch airport to meet Mel's plane and, as she walked off the aircraft, Kate rushed up and gave her a huge hug!

The two girls quickly bonded and the more experienced Kate took Melanie under her wing and was generous and supportive to her co-performer. Kate's maturity and Melanie's willingness to learn was combined with a great deal of care shown towards both girls – in *loco*

Kate Winslet and Mel Lynskey came to Heavenly Creatures *with differing levels of experience, but both were fearless when they tackled the tough scenes. As much as I try to help cast members capture the right moment on film, I'm learning such a lot about acting and directing with every movie. Movie-making is one continual film school.*

parentis – by Peter and Fran as well as by Jim Booth and his partner, Sue Rogers. Several things inevitably followed: *Heavenly Creatures* featured two outstanding juvenile performances, Kate Winslet moved a little closer to that stardom which John Hubbard had foreseen for her and Melanie Lynskey took her own tentative steps towards a notable screen career.

The film reunited Peter with several members of the crew of *Braindead*, including (in addition to Jamie Selkirk and Richard Taylor) make-up supervisor Marjory Hamlin; stills photographer Pierre Vinet; storyboard artist Christian Rivers; sound mixer Mike Hedges; sound editor Mike Hopkins; sound recordist Hammond Peek; and production assistant Linda Klein-Nixon. All of these individuals would still be working with Peter when he came to direct *The Lord of the Rings*, as would several of the 'newcomers' to the team, among them production designer, Grant Major; costume designer Ngila Dickson, and first assistant director Carolynne ('Caro') Cunningham.

On set with my first assistant director Carolynne Cunningham. Caro has been a terrific support to me, steering us through the complex filming of The Lord of the Rings. *She recently produced* King Kong *with Jan Blenkin.*

There's a tradition in New Zealand that requires a film crew to cross dress on one day of the shoot – 'Frock Day'. We generally have a hard time keeping a straight face – although here we're shooting one of the film's most intense scenes.

The film's exquisite cinematography was by Alun Bollinger, who would work on Peter's next two movies, while the Steadicam-operator, John Mahaffie, would later serve as second unit director on *Rings*. This extraordinary role-call – and the fact that many of these people have since continued the association by working on *King Kong* – is a testament to the two-way loyalty that Peter both exhibits and generates.

In the week before shooting began, Peter and Fran took Kate and Melanie to meet some of Pauline and Juliet's school contemporaries whom they had interviewed while researching the film. It was a unique form of preparation for the young actresses, helping them inhabit their roles.

> Kate asked one of the friends how Juliet walked and she described her as having a slightly haughty way of walking. I remember Kate saying, 'Show me, show me!' and the woman giving a demonstration and Kate learning how to walk like Juliet there and then in the lounge of one of her former school friends.

Anxious to help the girls over the daunting practicalities of being on a film shoot, Peter preceded the first day's filming with a *dummy* first day's filming.

> There is a certain amount of learning and familiarisation that you need to get over before you actually start shooting a movie – needing to understand that you are really going to be *in* the camera, *on* film – and I didn't want the first time that the girls had ever experienced a film crew to be our first day of shooting.
>
> So, we set up a whole day's filming, not using the real script or the real locations, but simulating all the conditions of being involved in a film, which was especially important for Mel who had never been on a film set before in her life.

In proposing *Heavenly Creatures* to the Film Commission, Peter had written: '*Heavenly Creatures* will be a very hard film to make. Every day will provide many challenges: difficult scenes to be shot, difficult decisions to be made. The characters are wonderfully complex. They have great emotional depth. Directing the film will keep me on my toes all the time, while also providing the chance to develop my film-making skills way beyond anything I've yet attempted.'

Acknowledging the existence of those challenges shows considerable maturity and self-awareness. Meeting them with confidence was already the 'Jackson way'. Which is not to say that filming certain sequences of this particular story didn't present tensions and anxieties and none more so than when it came to recreating Pauline and Juliet's murder of Honora Parker.

Arriving on location at Christchurch's Victoria Park, Peter and Fran followed in the steps of victim and murderesses on that fatal day in 1954.

> The track down the hill from the tea-rooms was, and is, still there. It hasn't changed from the day of the killing. We walked down the path and knew exactly where the murder had taken place. We had read the police files and we were able to identify the precise location. As Fran and I stood on the murder site we knew that there was no way that we could recreate the murder on the spot where it happened. The place had a weird vibe and energy, and I just couldn't face the idea of staging the scene there.
>
> So we found another, identical-looking path on another hillside in the park. It was enough that we were recreating the murder on film; to do that in the place where it had really happened would have been going too far…

As it was, the murder scene was the one episode that everybody was beginning to get stressed about filming. Kate, Melanie and Sarah Peirse were already gearing themselves up for the sequence and Peter had felt 'the tension starting to build up' before they arrived at the Victoria Park location. There were several scenes to be shot in the park: Honora and the girls having tea in the tea-rooms, the trio walking down the path, the moment when the girls rush back, covered in blood and, finally, the murder itself. On the weekend before shooting was to begin, Peter telephoned Jim Booth.

> I told Jim that I wanted to film the murder first thing on Monday. I asked him to alert Make-up and Wardrobe, but that nobody was to tell

In the world of low-budget films, you can't afford more than one costume – so I wanted to make sure the bloodstains on Kate's coat were what I imagined them to be.

Sarah or the girls. I didn't want to give them those extra few days to get themselves wound up about it. So, we surprised them: they thought they were going to be shooting the scene in the tea-rooms, and I went into their trailers and told them we were going to shoot the murder right now, and get it over and done with. It was very, very emotional... It took all day, and by the time the scene was finished that evening, everyone was a wreck.

I had filmed lots of deaths in *Bad Taste, Braindead* – even *Meet the Feebles* – but they were different, they were make-believe: this was a scene recreated from real life. Not only that, but we had become immersed in the lives of these people and we felt what I guess I can only describe as guilt. There's no way round it: you are making a movie, which is ultimately designed as a piece of entertainment and yet, at the same time, it is based on somebody's murder; you can't help but feel that you are exploiting those people who were affected by that murder and especially those who are still alive.

I guess we justified it by saying to ourselves that if we are going to do this film we had to make it as real and truthful as possible; that, after forty years of this killing being described as inexplicable and the girls as being evil, if we could somehow show what happened and what was in their minds – and *why* it was in their minds – and what state they had wound themselves up into in order to do this, then maybe we could actually bring a level of understanding to the case that had perplexed people for so long.

The search for truthfulness became of paramount importance to the film-makers with even the script's fantastical episodes being inspired by the events and characters depicted in the romantic fairy-tale entries from Pauline's diaries and eyewitness descriptions of the girls' Plasticine figures.

> We got to a point where we didn't want to make anything up or put any-thing in the movie just because it suited us. I was reminded, much later, of the experience of making *Heavenly Creatures* when we made *The Lord of the Rings*.
>
> With *Rings*, we were constrained by the book – and maybe we broke the shackles of the book more often than we should have done – but with *Heavenly Creatures*, whilst it wasn't adapted from a book, we were basing it on our researches into the real life events to an extent that we ended up with our own version of a Tolkienesque bible that we then had to stick to when making the film.

Despite their desire to be true to the historic events, Peter and Fran had decided not to seek out any of the surviving members of the families nor indeed to attempt to communicate with the girls them-selves.

They had become aware of the names under which Pauline and Juliet were living following their release from prison when, during their researches, they were inadvertently shown files that should not have been made available to them. In his first approach to the Film Commission in May 1992, Peter stated, 'In the course of my research, I uncovered Pauline and Juliet's new identities and their whereabouts. I have no intention of contacting them and will keep the information totally confidential. They are entitled to their privacy.'

The revelation, made in the wake of the film, that Juliet Hulme was now living in Scotland as Anne Perry, a highly successful writer of period crime fiction, and the subsequent discovery, a few years later, that Pauline Parker was now Hilary Nathan, a retired schoolteacher living in a Kentish village in Britain, reawakened interest in the events of the Parker–Hulme case and also, inevitably, focused on the Peter Jackson film-version of those events.

At the outset of the project, Peter had written, 'The moral issue of making a film about the murder of Honora Parker is one I have thought long and hard about. The story is part of New Zealand's history and is certainly valid material for film-makers… I think it is very important that the film has integrity and treats the key people involved with a degree of understanding that has thus far been denied them.'

During filming, Peter discovered that Juliet Hulme's new identity was already known outside of the prison service, since one of the actors on the film who had also been a cast member of the stage play, *Daughters of Heaven*, revealed that the Hulme-Perry connection was a well-known fact to those involved in the Christchurch run of the play.

Appropriately, Peter – who 'felt indirectly responsible' – refused to capitalise on the exposures and wrote to the Film Commission asking them not to make film stills available to journalists covering the 'outing' of the two women: 'WingNut Films will not be involved in any intrusion into the adult lives of Pauline and Juliet.' Later, however, when the film received its American release, Miramax – to Peter and Fran's disgust – promoted the film under the poster tag, 'Murder she wrote! The true story of the mystery writer who committed murder herself.'

Despite Peter and Fran's best intentions, Anne Perry clearly laid a degree of blame at the film-makers' door and, whilst not having seen the film, strenuously denied its premise that it was the threat of being parted from Pauline that had led her to take part in the murder on Honora Parker, preferring the explanation that she had feared Pauline would commit suicide if she failed to kill the mother.

Subsequent events would make it difficult for some people to view *Heavenly Creatures* dispassionately and the arguments as to whether it should have been made or made differently (perhaps rewritten as a work of fiction) or, indeed, how another film-maker might have approached the material, if Peter hadn't made it, will doubtless be re-played from time to time. What *was* clear as the film came together in editing was that it was a mature and powerfully-structured drama.

Several scenes in *Heavenly Creatures* were set in a sanatorium (Juliet Hulme contracted tuberculosis) and among the background extras were Jim Booth as a patient and his partner, Sue Rogers, as the nurse looking after him. The poignancy of this detail, unnoticed by the average audience member, is that Jim's state of health was consistently and seriously worsening. The colostomy operation had failed to stem the advance of the cancer...

> Jim produced the movie and was with us in Christchurch every day throughout the making of the film, but all the time he was becoming weaker and sicker as the cancer took hold. He fought bravely, but was being slowly overpowered by the disease.

Jim Booth watching us shooting Heavenly Creatures. *Although Jim's health was failing him during this time, he still produced the film with his trademark good humour and irreverent spirit.*

Heavenly Creatures went into post-production, which involved the new experience of grappling with the time-consuming frustrations of the Silicon Graphics SGI computer! 'There was so little storage space on the computer hard-drive,' remembers George Port, 'that effects could only be created one frame at a time!' The forty-odd digital shots occupied George, seven days a week for seven months.

It may have been the case that computer effects weren't strictly necessary for *Heavenly Creatures*, but with a director whose boyhood ambition had been to become a special effects technician, it was likely that his future films *would* require special effects and as the blockbuster movies coming out of Hollywood increasingly demonstrated, special effects now meant *computer effects*. Seeing the digital dinosaurs in Spielberg's *Jurassic Park* in 1993 made as dramatic an impression on Peter Jackson as his first encounter with the stop-motion monsters created by Willis O'Brien, sixty years earlier, for *King Kong*.

On a practical level, WingNut needed somewhere to house its computer work while Richard Taylor's company, RT Effects, was seriously in need of a permanent workshop in which to create models and prosthetics. Although now known throughout the world as a multi-Oscar winner, Richard and his company had very modest beginnings.

> When I first knew Richard and Tania they were making puppets in a one-bedroom basement flat full of toxic fumes! Then, when he started working on my films, Richard became an itinerant: constantly having to work out of different premises and, every time we would go on to a new film, having to shift all his stuff to some other workshop or rented space.
>
> Eventually, a group of us who'd been working together – Richard Taylor, Tania Rodger, Jamie Selkirk, George Port, Jim Booth and myself – decided it was time to join forces, consolidate our talents and form a special effects company that could work on my movies as well as other people's. After *Heavenly Creatures*, it felt like a good time to do it.

Jim Booth bought a shelf-company called Firefly, although it was soon to be re-named after a rather different bug – the weta. Known

We were lucky to get one of the rare native New Zealand unicorns for a brief, dream-like sequence in Heavenly Creatures.

by the Maori as 'wetapunga', or 'God of ugly things' (or as Richard Taylor prefers, 'New Zealand's coolest little monster!'), the weta is a highly resilient insect.

Wetas are capable of considerable growth (the giant weta has been known to grow to be three times heavier than a mouse) and possess a matchless survival record, having been around, virtually unchanged, for some 100 million years. Worthy attributes for any aspiring company!

Various accounts of the naming process exist ranging from the likely 'because we couldn't think of anything else' to the probable post-rationalisation that it was an acronym of 'WingNut Effects and Technical Allusions'.

A company, a mission and (however it was arrived at) a name – what Weta didn't have were premises out of which to operate. 'We spent several months,' recalls Richard, 'looking at different, potential sites. It was fun looking but it is actually frightening to think of some of the places we looked at. There was an old police barracks, a disused food warehouse and a former bacon factory! Most of them were completely inadequate.'

Exactly who finally found the premises on Weka Street, Miramar, is open to debate. Richard and Tania remember noticing that the building was up for sale while cycling past it on their way to the near-by garden centre, while Peter's recollection is that he was driving past in his car and spotted the 'For Sale' board outside. Whoever saw it first, it was to become the home of the now world-famous Weta Workshop...

No. 1 Weka Street had, as Richard explains, a fascinating, if chequered history: 'Originally, it was an aquatic fun-park with a huge swimming pool and water-slides; then, at the turn of the century, it was filled in and turned into a mental institution: an ugly, spartan place with tarmac floors and open beams. During World War II, it became a hospital for the families of American GIs; after which it became, first of all, an industrial unit turning out Exide batteries, then a pharmaceutical factory making Vaseline and talcum powder. And then, finally, we bought it and turned it back into an asylum!'

After these myriad uses and years of abandonment, the building was in an appalling condition, but it had plenty of space and great potential. 'We expected it to be completely out of our price range,' remembers Tania, 'but, because it had been neglected for such a long time, it turned out to be a feasible option and that was when the real sense of excitement started! Richard adds, 'We loved it, and from the moment we walked in we knew that we could do great things there!'

The one sadness was that Jim Booth was, by now, too ill to visit the building. Instead, Peter videotaped a tour and took it to Jim and Sue's home and showed it to the man whose help and encouragement had done so much to bring Peter, and his associates, to that point in time.

While *Heavenly Creatures* was in post-production, Peter and Fran, as was by now their habit, had started work on another project; although, on this occasion, the initiative had come from elsewhere. Sometime in 1992, Peter's agent, Ken Kamins, heard on the Hollywood grapevine that Robert Zemeckis was looking for a movie script. Zemeckis, who had directed *Romancing the Stone*, *Who Framed Roger Rabbit* and the three *Back to the Future* movies, was also an executive producer, and occasional director, of the TV series, *Tales from the Crypt*, based on the famous – *infamous* – Fifties comic book.

Bill Gaines had launched EC Comics' legendary *Tales from the Crypt* in 1950 to the joy and delight of all right-minded horror and fantasy fans and to the disgust and loathing of all wrong-minded guardians of public morality! The puritans' hatred of the magazine's resident storyteller, the Crypt Keeper, and his chilling (and often ludicrously gory) tales of morgues and mausoleums, zombies, vampires, ghosts and ghouls contributed to the establishing of the Comics Code Authority, which banned titles using words such as 'horror', 'terror' and 'weird'. Bill Gaines, defeated by city hall, folded *Tales from the Crypt* and concentrated his efforts on the less shocking (but still irreverent) *Mad* magazine.

After languishing for years only in the memories of devoted fanatics, the original *Tales from the Crypt* comics were rediscovered and reprinted as collector's editions, winning a new generation of fans, including Peter Jackson, who was even known to occasionally sport a *Tales from the Crypt* t-shirt. In 1989, the Crypt Keeper's tales were brought to television by an extraordinary raft of talent including directors Zemeckis, Richard Donner, John Frankenheimer and Tobe Hooper and a cast-list that included Christopher Reeve, Brooke Shields, Tom Hanks, Dan Ackroyd, Tim Roth, John Astin, Arnold Schwarzenegger, Michael J. Fox, Yvonne de Carlo, Bob Hoskins, John Rhys-Davis and Brad Dourif.

Following the *Tales from the Crypt* TV series, there was talk of a possible motion-picture spin-off with Zemeckis and others each directing a low-budget, genre movie with *Crypt*-style stories. Ken Kamins told Peter that Zemeckis needed a script and asked whether he happened to have any likely story ideas. Of course he did!

It was an idea that I'd had some time before and which Fran and I had been kicking about and it concerned a guy who advertises himself as being a psychic investigator, a ghost-buster who, for a fee, rids haunted houses of their spooks. It is obvious that he's a charlatan. But then the twist is that while he *is* a charlatan, he is also a genuine psychic who is sending ghosts into people's homes to scare the hell out of them and then earning his money by getting rid of them again!

Ken Kamins passed a three-page outline to Zemeckis, who asked to meet with Peter. As *Braindead* was to have a midnight screening at the Sundance Festival in January 1993, it was agreed that Peter and Fran would fly on afterwards to Los Angeles. Over lunch in Santa Monica, they pitched the idea to Zemeckis, who liked both them and their story and asked them to write a script. Peter explained that they couldn't start writing immediately since he was then only weeks away from beginning the shoot on *Heavenly Creatures*.

Until that point, according to Ken Kamins, Zemeckis was unaware that Peter was also a director, but was anyway happy to wait for the script since he was also about to direct a movie: a picture with Tom Hanks called *Forrest Gump*. 'When you're done,' he told Peter, 'give me the script and we'll hook up.'

So, while *Heavenly Creatures* was being cut, Peter and Fran began work on the script, which was to be called *The Frighteners*.

Fired by Peter's inexhaustible energy and enthusiasm, encouraged by Fran and steered by Jim Booth, WingNut Films were also planning for the future. Towards the end of 1993, earnings on *Braindead* were heading for NZ$3,000,000 and Peter was able to say with complete confidence, 'I have reached the point that my films can attain good prices based on my name.' Those films may not have been 'mainstream movies' but they had undeniably made a name for themselves – *and* for their director.

It was now becoming increasingly obvious to the world what Jim had seen in the raw footage of *Bad Taste*: that Peter had an exceptional future ahead of him. Having a Hollywood lawyer and agent helped and, even before *Heavenly Creatures* was finally edited, word was out and a Hollywood studio was interested in getting involved in its distribution.

Miramax Films, the company founded in 1979 by brothers Robert (Bob) and Harvey Weinstein – and named for their parents Miriam ('Mira') and Max – became rapidly successful at distributing independent, foreign and art-house films that were not rated as commercially viable by the major studios, such as Merchant Ivory's *Mr and Mrs Bridge*, Tim Robbins' *Bob Roberts* and the Whoopi Goldberg picture *Sarafina!*, as well as re-releases of a diverse backlist of titles, among them *Belle de Jour, Apocalypse Now* and *A Hard Day's Night.*

In 1993, the Walt Disney Company bought Miramax, on a price tag of around US$75 million, in a deal which left the Weinstein brothers running the show but with Disney having the power of veto over their releases. Despite issues between the companies over controversial titles such as *Priest,* Miramax notched up an impressive hit list that included such diverse pictures as *My Left Foot, Sex, Lies and Videotape, Muriel's Wedding, Bullets Over Broadway, The Crying Game* and *Pulp Fiction.*

The quest to find new talent to be corralled in the Miramax stable was unceasing and global. As former executive Tony Safford told the *New York Times*: 'We went to work with passports in our bags. We didn't know where we'd be going that day. That's not hyperbole, that's how it was.'

For David Linde, then Miramax's senior Vice President of Acquisitions, the trip one day was to Wellington, New Zealand to view an early cut of *Heavenly Creatures.* Liking what he saw, Linde bought the distribution rights for the United States and later negotiated a deal with Hanno Huth of Senator Films, who had co-financed the movie with the Film Commission, to acquire various European rights in the film for Miramax; subsequently he also bought the New Zealand and Australian rights from the Commission.

Jim Booth must have relished the rich irony of seeing a director whose movies the New Zealand Film Commission had frequently been embarrassed about having to distribute, suddenly being courted by a major Hollywood player. Indeed, Linde's colleague, Tony Safford assured WingNut that they had 'a home at Miramax'.

Apart from the interest being shown by Miramax, Hanno Huth was so encouraged by the success of *Braindead* in Germany and by the way in which the edit of *Heavenly Creatures* was coming together an offer that he made to co-finance a package of WingNut films.

'It was time to use the 'Peter Jackson' name and his growing reputation to do two things: advance and consolidate Peter's personal career and, by association, assist the careers of other New Zealand film-makers. As Jim Booth explained in writing to the New Zealand Film Commission, it was time for vision.

'WingNut Films has now established itself as a regular producer of quality New Zealand films. We have achieved that very hard thing: making proudly Kiwi films that work well in both the national and international marketplace.

'We have always felt a strong commercial responsibility and have done as much as we could to ensure our film return the NZFC's investment. In the very near future, every cent of the approx $5.5 million the NZFC has invested in four WingNut feature films will have been returned with what we hope will be a decent profit. It is a record we are proud of.

'*The question is: Where to from here?* WingNut Films has achieved all this based on the movies directed by Peter and produced by Jim. However, to continue using WingNut Films just to make Peter's films seems to be limiting our potential and is not taking full advantage of all our international contacts.

'We have amassed a lot of experience in film production and, more importantly, in script writing. Fran Walsh and Peter Jackson are now establishing themselves as a writing team with good credentials. It is WingNut's intention to start to use this production and script writing experience to help other New Zealand directors. We do not intend to invite an open cattle call of projects or scripts.

'WingNut's plan is that the scripts will be co-written by Fran and Peter. Sometimes they will work with the director, sometimes the director will not become involved until after the first draft. The director will be handpicked by WingNut to suit the script – or the script will be handwritten to suit the director!'

Although the scheme, as outlined by Jim, would never materialise, WingNut had already taken one or two of tentative steps towards the vision of a Jackson-led consortium of talent.

In 1992, Jim and Peter had produced a fifteen-minute short, *Valley of the Stereos,* directed by George Port and co-written with Costa Botes. Made with minimal use of dialogue (which, one critic felt was, its 'universal power') the story concerns River, played by *Feebles* collaborator Danny Mulheron, who runs Tranquillity Records, a one-man outfit creating music from animal sounds recorded near his home – until, that is, the only other house in the vicinity is bought by a very noisy neighbour.

The following year, 1993, WingNut backed *Jack Brown Genius*, a first feature by Tony Hiles, the former TV director who had played an important role in helping *Bad Taste* realise its full tasteless potential! With Jim on board, and the Jackson–*Bad Taste* associations, it was almost a formality for the project to get the support of the Film Commission and Senator Films in Germany.

Jack Brown Genius was conceived as a whimsical romantic comedy with a wacky premise: Brother Elmer, a tenth-century monk who died whilst trying to prove the feasibility of man-powered flight, finds himself condemned to an eternity in hell as a suicide. Elmer has one hope of salvation: if, before 1,000 years have elapsed, he can persuade another mortal to convincingly prove his theory before God, his soul will be liberated and sent to heaven. Enter the story's hero – nerdy inventor with a ruthless corporation – Jack Brown, genius.

Jim Booth had been a friend of Tony's for many years, liked the story and offered to produce the film, suggesting using WingNut. He also suggested involving Peter and Fran to help with reviewing the script, a process that led to what Jim described as, 'a total page-one rewrite'. So began what, for everyone involved, would ultimately become a chapter of life that they would rather forget…

But, 1993, that was in the future. Other possible films under discussion included a thriller to be directed by Costa Botes as well as projects to be directed by Grant Campbell (of the Campbell brothers) and Harry Sinclair, later to become a successful director as well as appearing as Isildur in *The Lord of the Rings*.

Jim Booth's proposition to the Film Commission concerning the future of WingNut accompanied a major application for financial investment in a Jackson project going under the enigmatic code-name *Jamboree*. It was the first use by Peter as a moniker borrowed from Merian C. Cooper who, in 1933, had used it to camouflage the fact that he was filming his *King Kong* sequel, *Son of Kong*.

Jamboree would later become famous as the shooting title for *The Lord of the Rings*, but in 1993 it was intended to conceal a sophisticated variation on the project formerly known as *Bad Taste 2*. It was, however, a considerably more ambitious and elaborate proposition than the one that had been floated the year before. In fact, Peter was asking for NZ$3.5million to match a similar investment by Hanno Huth.

The reason for the inflated budget and the imposition of secrecy was because the project was now not simply for a *Bad Taste 2*, but for a *Bad Taste 2* and *3* – the two films to be shot back-to-back, but with the second sequel only to be announced when the first one was released.

'Why two sequels?' asked Peter, before answering his own rhetorical question: 'Because it's harder… It gives me great freedom to develop an epic saga… It would be a lot of fun to have a second sequel following hard on the heels of the first… It makes economic sense to make *Bad Taste 3* at the same time as *Bad Taste 2*…' It was, after all, the way in which Robert Zemeckis had filmed *Back to the Future II* and *III*.

Peter next asked 'Why do I want to make it at all?' and his answers provide a fascinating pen-portrait of how he then viewed his talents and his future:

'I want to make a couple of absolutely entertaining, fast-paced, funny action films that will delight and surprise audiences, break special effects boundaries and send fans of the first film into spasms of joy.

'That's the simple, most obvious answer; however, it does go deeper than that. Why could I not make an entertaining, fast-paced, funny action film with completely new characters and story? Why return to something I left behind me over six years ago? There are several reasons…

'I think of myself as a writer as well as director. I feel very comfortable with storytelling and story structure. I know that in the six years since *Bad Taste* was finished, my script-writing skills have vastly improved.

'However, in that time I don't feel I have made the same significant strides as director. Sure, my subsequent films have looked a lot flashier, had much more production value and tighter scripts and better performances, but I really feel that some of my favourite directing is still in *Bad Taste*. I see *Jamboree* as an opportunity to build on and improve my directing skills.

'I am trying to create a rare opportunity for myself – one which in practice does not usually happen. Feature directors usually get locked into a pattern of bigger films, bigger budgets – a pattern which I myself have followed: *Bad Taste, Meet the Feebles, Braindead* and *Heavenly Creatures* – all bigger than the last.

'At this point in time, I want to break out of that pattern, return to a much simpler form of film-making. *Bad Taste* was my film school. In a very short space of time I taught myself everything I needed to know to enable me to make my subsequent films, but I still think I have a long way to go. I'm always learning, but with the pressures of a tight schedule and forty crewmembers standing around, there is little opportunity to try new things. I always punt for the same and sure.

'Now, six years after *Bad Taste*, I want to return to my film school. I want to give myself the freedom I need to push myself and make significant advances as a director that will pay off in the years ahead.'

Peter then added one of those characteristically frank statements that, despite the gore and splatter in his movies, always endeared him to the Film Commission: 'Don't think for a minute that *Jamboree* will be arty, obscure or self-indulgent... All my instincts are commercial and I will make two very commercial films. When I say I want to make strides as a director, it's in the direction of James Cameron or Steven Spielberg, not Peter Greenaway!'

The story for *Bad Taste 2* and *3* was very similar to that which he had outlined in his submission of the previous year – with some inevitable embellishment! The plan was now for The Boys to go to the planet Nailic Nod, find Derek, have 'a climactic encounter with the aliens on their home turf' and escape home. The third film was now to feature the aliens' 'massed revenge attack on Wellington' with a finale described as featuring 'a spectacular aerial battle over the city with dozens of flying houses, Buzzy Bees [New Zealand's beloved pull-along toys] and Santa Claus.'

After such a synopsis, it may have been superfluous to point out that *Jamboree* was to be 'a visual comedy, rather than a character based comedy.' Once again, Peter stressed the time-consuming and improvisational nature of creating good visual as opposed to verbal comedy, and took as an exemplar his favourite film director: 'In all the reviews of my movies, my favourite comment is from one critic who described me as "the Buster Keaton of gore"; I am very proud of that, since Buster Keaton is my all time movie hero.'

Keaton had been his icon since his first youthful viewing of *The General* and he knew, and envied, the comic's film-making methods: 'He was supplied with a permanent film-crew – assigned to him all year round. When Buster wanted to shoot a scene, they went out and filmed it. When Buster wanted to take a couple of weeks off to dream some new gags, they sat around (on full pay) waiting for him. His films were therefore worked and re-worked; scenes shot and re-shot. This was an amazing (and expensive) luxury, but it did lead to the creation of some of the greatest visual comedies ever made…'

With a paradigm such as Keaton it should never really surprise us when we read of Peter Jackson adding, altering and developing scenes on the studio floor or reassembling casts and crews for pick-up shoots. It is all part of a Keatonesque pursuit of perfection.

'There *will* be a script,' Peter reassuringly advised the Commission, lest alarm bells start ringing. 'It will detail the plot of *Jamboree* very clearly. That storyline will be adhered to during the shoot. What will be largely missing from the script will be all the detailed stunts and gags

'For instance, the script may read: "DEREK escapes from the alien's fast food factory, runs through the restaurant and finally makes it aboard the spaceship. He immediately takes off with two alien space-ships hot on his heels."

'Only four lines of script, but it may be a four–six minute sequence. It will contain several elaborate sight gags, a complex series of special effects shots, maybe even a surprise monster attack!

'The point is: I want to have the entire shoot available to me to come up with all the gags and ideas – "the gravy" as I call it. That is the point of doing it this way. To say that all that stuff must be in the script from day one is robbing me of the greatest advantage I have in making these couple of really imaginative, unique, crowd-pleasing movies.

'I guess you have to decide whether I can be trusted to come up with a lot of funny visual gags. I hope that my track record speaks for itself. Some people would say it is what I do best.'

There was a sop to those for whom the wholesale bloodletting in *Braindead* had been a gallon or two of gore too far: '*Jamboree* will be made with greater audience accessibility in mind. It will not compromise in the stuff the cult fans love, but audiences will not be overwhelmed with gore. It will be good natured and silly but with none of the amateurish problems of *Bad Taste* and without the huge quantities of red maple syrup, the very thought of which frightened some people off *Braindead.*'

Peter was still talking about using the original cast of mates (all of whom were now getting on with the rest of their un-showbizzy lives) and of shooting the movies with a small – 'second unit'-sized – film crew. However, post-*Heavenly Creatures*, he was envisaging a far greater sophistication in the area of special effects.

The bravado of his statement belied the serious challenges that George Port had been wrestling with over the past several months. What they had achieved to date, said Peter, was 'a gentle introduction into the computer effects world and a chance to figure out how it all works', and what they needed was an opportunity 'to further develop the techniques…'

The hype was running high, but this was, after all, Peter's first love – special effects: 'The *Heavenly Creatures* effects are low key, as they should be for that movie – but in *Jamboree*, we will really let rip! It would give us the chance to produce effects of a quantity and quality that would rival advances that Industrial Light and Magic have only recently made. The only limit to computer effects is the imagination of the film-maker – and I have a fairly vivid imagination!'

In the event *Jamboree* – or, at any rate, this project with that name – never got any further than a twenty-two-page proposal and a detailed scenario. Even so, the idea lingers on.

In answering the question 'Why two sequels?' Peter had given as an additional reason to those of its being more fun and more economic, that if they didn't make the movies soon the '*Bad Taste* Boys' (himself included) would 'all be too old and fat to make any more.'

Nevertheless, ten years later, while in the middle of editing *The Return of the King*, Peter had not yet finally ruled out the possibility, saying: 'I still have a real desire to do a *Bad Taste 2* and I actually think, as the years go on, it could get more interesting. It would be quite fun to do a sequel where everyone is older and fatter but all still having to do the same things. I keep toying with ideas for the plot line and have quite a good little idea ticking away in my head...'

In 1993, in a covering letter to the Film Commission, Jim Booth had written, '*Jamboree* is a follow-on from *Bad Taste*, but of a sophistication undreamed of in *Bad Taste* and with an emphasis on fantasy and special effects which will take New Zealand into an international arena which we have not previously been able to contemplate.'

Jim's passionate enthusiasm both for *Jamboree* and for his vision of WingNut providing a launch pad for other New Zealand talents was what might have been expected of a man in the prime of life with a reasonable expectation of seeing some of those things come to pass. This, however, was far from the truth.

The submission was made to the Commission in late November 1993, by which time Jim's health had taken another serious downturn: his office was now his bedroom and despite his courageous battle against the cancer, it was clear that his life was moving towards its end.

Meanwhile, Peter and Fran were working on that script for Robert Zemeckis.

> Writing *The Frighteners*, which was all about death, funerals, ghosts and the afterlife, when we knew that Jim was dying felt really weird and wrong. We were committed to the script, so we had to carry on with it but I remember our thinking, 'God, this is the very last subject matter we want to be writing about at a time like this...'

Over the Christmas holiday, there was a further, dramatic deterioration in Jim's condition. Although he and his partner, Sue Rogers, had been determined that, with nursing care, he would see out whatever time was left him in his own home, that was now no longer possible. A lifelong asthmatic, Jim's lungs had finally succumbed to the cancer, and the need for assistance with breathing and effective pain-management precipitated his move to the Mary Potter Hospice.

It was a deeply distressing period, not just for Sue and for Jim's children, but for his many close friends. Rotas were drawn up to make certain that Sue had round-the-clock support. It was a time both of great sadness and much selflessness. Sue, who had been given a low fold-away bed alongside Jim's regulation-height hospital bed, recalls the day when Peter and Tony Hiles rearranged the beds in the ward in order to create an almost double-bed for a couple who were anxious not to be parted from one another.

At the time, Jim was the only patient in a four-bed ward, so the support team virtually camped out in the hospice, ensuring that there was always one of them awake, while the person on the next shift slept on one of the spare beds. 'Those last days,' remembers Tony Hiles, 'exposed a great many raw nerves. We *lived* at the hospice, doing what little we could, watching Jim vomiting black blood and fighting for his life.'

> Jim was courageous and, although desperately sad for Sue and his sons, had absolutely no self-pity. He was someone who was clearly dying and yet, at the same time, was refusing to feel sorry for himself – almost as if he were refusing to accept death.
>
> Even towards the end, he was still talking about the future, giving me advice and discussing all the things we were going to do, and I was sitting there thinking, 'God, you're not going to be around, Jim; you're not going to be around…'
>
> There was this poignancy about seeing somebody who was so keyed up about the future when his own future was slowly slipping away, getting shorter and shorter by the day.
>
> You had to admire his bravery and the absolute positivism of his attitude, but it was also heartbreaking.

Shortly before the end, which came on 4 January 1994, Peter was sitting with Jim so that Sue had the opportunity to snatch an hour or two of much-needed rest. Jim was, by then, in a distressed and feverish state, tossing and turning and throwing off his bedding, and Sue remembers Peter's concern to take care of Jim and help him maintain his human dignity.

> It was the night before he died, and I sat with him from about eleven o'clock at night until six in the morning. He was quite delirious, thrashing around and drifting in and out of consciousness.
>
> I had never seen anyone dying before, never been with somebody as they slipped away…

And Jim was the first dead person I ever saw. It may sound strange, but I was happy about one thing: if I was going to see a dead body for the first time, then I was glad that it was someone that I knew. I really didn't have any qualms about it because it was my friend, Jim.

'The loss of Jim,' says Tony Hiles, 'was devastating. At his funeral, a lot of effort went into celebrating a death that could not be celebrated.' It was a day that would reveal the depth of people's feelings.

Instead of the mourners symbolically scattering a handful of earth onto the coffin, it had been suggested that they should be invited to fill in the grave. Many of those attending the funeral were taken aback by this unconventional conclusion to the ceremony and none more so than Peter.

I just remember finding myself with a spade in my hand and I remember chucking in the first shovel-load of dirt, and the sound of it hitting the coffin with a wooden reverberation. It was a terrible sound, like something out of a horror movie, and it made me feel really sick. And then I just got to it and shovelled away and kept shovelling until the bloody hole was full...

Others by the graveside, uncertain about what to do, were stunned by Peter's zeal and devotion in almost single-handedly tackling and completing the task. It was a bizarre event that, for several of them, remains an unforgettable memory of a sad day.

It was an odd experience and something I really didn't expect to do. But it was also moving and I actually felt all right about it at the end because I thought, 'Well, if I were lying there in the coffin, I would rather my friends fill me in and pat the dirt down than for it to be done by complete strangers.' But it took quite long time... Twenty or thirty minutes... It was hard yakker.

'Hard yakker', the ANZAC slang for hard work, derived from the aboriginal word 'yaga', aptly summed up Peter Jackson's approach to life: get stuck in and do the job.

It was precisely this determination and dedication that had caught the imagination of Jim Booth and prompted him to throw in his lot with the amateur film-maker from Pukerua Bay. In just a few years, Jim had seen Peter mature from an enthusiastic photoengraver, making a weekend movie with his mates, into a world-class director with a potentially brilliant future ahead of him.

In the many thousands of interviews Peter has given during and after the making of *The Lord of the Rings*, the name of Jim Booth has seldom if ever been mentioned. Nor would it be... Jim had nothing to do with that project. And yet, as Peter is well aware, without the kick-start that Jim gave to the Jackson career, it might never have happened. There can be little doubt that Peter would have still succeeded as a director, but whether the game would have played out in quite the way it did, remains one of the great unknowns.

> I don't want Jim to be 'the forgotten person' in my career and, just because he's not around anymore, it shouldn't deprive him of the right to stake his place in my story. He was there for me at just the right time... and had he lived, I'm certain we'd still be partners today. Since Jim's death, I've never really settled down with another producing partner. It has a left gap in my life that I still feel today.
>
> My lasting regret is that Jim died when things were just starting to go well for us and, if you can ever talk about somebody's death in *business terms*, then I think the biggest bummer of all was the fact that Jim checked out just when things were starting to take off.

Eight months after Jim's death, *Heavenly Creatures* received its premiere at the Venice Film Festival. Before the film's prologue and title sequence there appeared on screen the two words, 'For Jim'. As the closing credits rolled, the audience rose to give the film a ten-minute standing ovation. When, at the end of the festival, Peter accepted the Silver Lion, the Jury Grand Prize, he referred to the award as being 'truly a tribute to the producer, the late Jim Booth.'

Perhaps an even greater tribute was that, for Peter, it was just the start of more hard yakker and more movies.

6

CHEATS, SPOOKS, HOBBITS AND APES

'Fear, like your imagination, has no limits.'

Peter Jackson was talking about *The Frighteners*, the ghost story that he and Fran had been writing for a film to be directed by Robert Zemeckis. They had completed the script in early January 1994, not long after the death of Jim Booth.

The original story idea of the double-dealing, psychic con man had developed into a far more sophisticated, cross-genre story: it now incorporated elements of the thriller when fraudulent ghost-hunter, Frank Bannister, sets out to investigate a series of mysterious deaths, and a touch of romance when Frank falls for an attractive doctor who is the widow of one of the dearly departed. Other ingredients now included sinister unfinished business resulting from a gruesome serial killing in the past, the meddling machinations of a loony FBI agent and several scary, heart-stopping interventions by a being that appears to be none other than the Grim Reaper.

Peter sent the script off to agent Ken Kamins on what seemed like a decidedly inauspicious date: 17 January 1994 – the day on which Los Angeles was devastated by the Northridge Earthquake – and waited for Zemeckis' response.

Meanwhile, Miramax had rushed an early print of *Heavenly Creatures* to the selection committee at the Cannes Film Festival, hoping for the film to be included in competition. When, instead, they were offered a midnight screening out of competition, Miramax decided to withdraw the film, wait several more months and premiere it instead at the Venice Film Festival in September.

> We were all in this holding pattern: Melanie Lynskey had gone back to school; Kate Winslet had returned to making sandwiches in her local deli, because she didn't have another acting role and no one had yet seen her performance in *Heavenly Creatures*; and Fran and I were waiting for people to see and react to what we had made.

As always, Peter had various possible projects 'ticking away', as he likes to put it, but early in 1994 he had other responsibilities, one of which was to honour Jim Booth's commitment to Tony Hiles' film, *Jack Brown Genius*. T. S. Eliot once observed that 'between the conception and the creation… falls the shadow' and that can be as true of movies as of any work of art.

Maybe what was essentially a fairytale about two characters, separated by a thousand years, who need to prove that a man can fly didn't really require as many special effects as it was given. Perhaps the combination of the WingNut name, Peter's contributions as co-writer, producer and second-unit director combined with the casting of *Braindead*'s Tim Balme as the film's eponymous hero suggested far too strong a link to the Jackson opus. There is little doubt that everybody did what they did with the best of intentions, but most of the parties involved were either novices in their various roles or else were reluctantly discharging their duties as a debt to Jim Booth.

For whatever the reasons, *Jack Brown Genius* was misapprehended and, eventually, misjudged as a failure. As a result there were some regrets and a few recriminations and long-standing friendships were tested, strained and, in some cases, irreparably damaged. 'It was very sad,' reflects one of those involved. 'After all it was only a damned movie…'

Oddly, seen today, devoid of the expectations and disappointments that cursed it a decade ago, *Jack Brown Genius* is wistful and zany. The locations create an off-the-wall sketch of daily life in Wellington and there are strong, energetic performances from the cast, notably Tim Balme as the engaging and sympathetic Jack and

Marton Csokas (later Celeborn in *The Lord of the Rings*), in his feature debut, as Jack's best mate.

When it was first screened at Cannes, the film had its advocates: *Variety* described it as 'wonderfully loopy… exciting and funny' and praised Tony Hiles' direction for keeping 'the action and the comedy bubbling along'. Subsequently, it would acquire the status of being a poor – even bad – movie. Now, however, occasional internet critics are chipping away at that reputation (a 'charming, if thoroughly bizarre little film… I don't know what they put in the water in New Zealand, but it's time they started exporting it!') and it is tempting to suggest that, one day, *Jack Brown Genius* will be reassessed, if not as a work of genius, then at least as anything but an ignoble failure.

What is astonishing about Peter's career at this period is the way in which certain projects came and went and, sometimes, came back again; the way his expectations sky-rocketed only to plummet and be dashed before, against all hope, getting resuscitated! With every new Jackson movie to be released, the publicity sound bites offered by cast

A group of the friends we make films with: construction foreman Norm Willerton, Director of Photography Alun Bollinger and Art Director Dan Hennah.

and crewmembers repeatedly focus on Peter's equanimity and his ability to remain single-mindedly focused. It was a lesson he learned early on.

When Peter and Fran had left the offices of Twentieth Century Fox after pitching their idea for a *Planet of the Apes* movie, it had seemed that that particular door had closed, but with the passing of time [(and executives)] it opened for a second time. Accompanied by Ken Kamins, Peter met with two of Fox's senior personnel, Peter Chernin and Tom Rothman, over lunch at the Hotel Bel-Air to discuss his script idea for *Apes*.

> We re-pitched exactly the same idea to these two high-powered Fox executives who'd never heard it before. Once again it was met with a lot of enthusiasm but then they launched into this long explanation about how they'd spent a lot of money developing a potential *Planet of the Apes* film – though not with us because we'd worked on spec and never earned a cent! – and how they already had one or two failed screenplays.
>
> We heard of various versions including one by Terry Hayes, who wrote *Mad Max 2* and *3* and went on to write *Vertical Limit*. Anyway, at the end of this preamble, they said that they'd like to use our story, have Fran and I write the script and me direct but they also wanted James Cameron to produce it and for Arnold Schwarzenegger to star in it.
>
> 'We have had a real commitment,' they said, 'for this to be a vehicle for Schwarzenegger. Why not meet with James Cameron before you leave town and pitch him your ideas? We think as a group you'll make a great team…'

Back at their hotel, Peter and Fran discussed the proposition and were of one mind.

> It felt bad. Not because I don't like Cameron or Schwarzenegger, I'm actually a big fan of their films, but Fran and I are incredibly independent spirits, you know, and we are very protective of our work. We thought that if we had James Cameron as the producer and Arnold Schwarzenegger as the star, I would have absolutely no power, and if, for example, there were a conflict with Schwarzenegger then Cameron

would be likely to back him rather than me. I didn't know for certain, it was just assumptions, but it didn't feel like a work situation that we should put ourselves into.

So we declined to take the meeting and, this time around, it was us who passed on the project.

I finally met Jim Cameron for the first time in 2005, and found him to be charming. I couldn't help wondering what might have happened if we'd said 'Yes' to the deal...

In July 1994, Miramax's David Linde proposed that Peter and Fran should sign an exclusive three-year 'first-look' deal with the studio, which required them to give Miramax first refusal on any film projects they initiated during the period of the contract. 'A first-look deal,' says Ken Kamins, 'means that a studio pays your overheads, so you can function and come up with ideas but with the caveat that the studio gets first crack at making those ideas into movies.'

The agreement also called for Peter and Fran to act as Miramax's 'eyes and ears' in New Zealand. Harvey Weinstein was quoted as saying: 'Some of the most compelling and unique film-making is emerging from New Zealand and this relationship provides us with an extra opportunity to access the wonderful talent there.'

However, other factors were in play. Allegedly, Harvey Weinstein was under some pressure from Jeffrey Katzenberg, then Chairman of the Walt Disney Company, to sign some of the artists with whom Miramax were working to 'first-look' agreements in order to keep budding talent on the Miramax-Disney team. Similar proposals would be made to fellow New Zealander, Jane Campion, following the success of *The Piano*, and to Quentin Tarantino after *Pulp Fiction*.

'The Miramax deal,' notes Ken Kamins, 'was useful in giving Peter an initial grounding in America: people would say, "Oh, Peter Jackson's made a movie that's strong enough for Miramax to give him a first-look deal".'

Before Peter got around to offering any projects to Miramax, Robert Zemeckis responded to the script for *The Frighteners*. Initially, Peter was bitterly disappointed by the director's reaction.

He said that it wasn't really the type of thing that he was looking for and that it didn't really feel like a *Tales from the Crypt* movie. I thought, 'Oh, s***! Well, that was a waste of time...' But then he said that he really liked the script and how would I feel if he was to produce it and I was to direct it?

As it transpired, Zemeckis never did direct a *Tales from the Crypt* movie and only two titles ever appeared: *Demon Knight* and *Bordello of Blood*. As for directing *The Frighteners*, Peter agreed – on one condition:

By the time Fran and I had finished the script, I really liked what we had written and I thought it would be fun to make... So I said, 'Well, I'll do it, if I can make it in New Zealand.' I really didn't have to think about whether or not I *wanted* to do it, but I *did* say that I didn't want to go to America to make it. I remember Bob saying, 'Well, does New Zealand look anything like America?' And I said, well, for the small town depicted in *The Frighteners*, I'm sure it could...

There was one other factor involved in committing to Zemeckis and Universal – the first-look deal with Miramax. As Ken Kamins explains: 'Obviously, a studio doesn't want to have a first-look deal with somebody who is unproductive or where no movies result from the relationship. Although, at the point when Peter was offered *The Frighteners* by Zemeckis, Harvey hadn't had any movies from Peter, he simply said, "Fine, since we don't have anything right now, we'll suspend and extend..." This meant that the deal was suspended for an agreed period while Peter made *The Frighteners*; afterwards, the terms of the deal would come back into play, but be extended by the same length of time as the suspension so that Miramax wouldn't lose out.'

September 1994, the Lido, Venice, Italy: Chairman of the Film Festival's jury, David Lynch (*Eraserhead, Blue Velvet, Twin Peaks*) presented Peter Jackson with the Festival's Silver Lion.

Mel, Kate and Sarah Peirse were with us and there were hugs and sobs afterwards; it was a very emotional experience because Jim wasn't there and we were all feeling that really heavily...

This was borne out by reviews, first at the film festivals at Venice and Toronto (where 600 members of the international journalists gave it the Metro Media Award) and, subsequently, in Britain:

Venezia La Nuova called Peter Jackson 'New Zealand's Spielberg' while the *Toronto Globe and Mail* declared that 'Never has the reinvention of adolescence seemed more haunting, more frightening, more wickedly credible…' Hugo Davenport in London's *Daily Telegraph* wrote: 'Jackson has confounded expectation. Though familiar ingredients are present – murder, fantasy, a satirical view of New Zealand society – they yield a film of memorable atmosphere and originality'; while Christopher Tookey in the *Daily Mail* wrote: 'Astonishingly… Jackson has turned out a film unrecognisable from the rest of his oeuvre – mature, sensitive and profound.'

The American press were uniformly ecstatic with a preponderance of such words as 'startling', 'original', 'exhilarating', 'stunning,' 'compelling', 'powerful' and, not surprisingly, 'troubling'. *Variety* praised Peter's 'drop-dead command of the medium' and the film's marriage of 'a dazzling, kinetic techno-show and a complex, credible portrait of the out-of-control relationship between the crime's two schoolgirl perpetrators.' Kenneth Turan in *The Los Angeles Times* described it as 'adventurous and accomplished, burning with cinematic energy' with 'the ability to get inside hysteria and obsession, the skill to make us feel sensations as intensely as its protagonists…' There was hardly a review that didn't try to emulate the ecstatic mood of the film: 'a mesmerising black diamond', 'a fever nightmare', and 'a pathologically autobiographical fairy tale…' *Heavenly Creatures*, wrote the reviewer in the *Oregonian*, was a film that elevated Peter Jackson 'from the ranks of genre film-makers to the ranks of major directors.'

At the Wellington Film Festival, *Heavenly Creatures'* premiere screening received a tumultuous reception from the art-house cineastes who, a few years earlier, had probably avoided the renegade attraction offered by a midnight serving of *Bad Taste*.

It was a reception that left at least one of Peter's associates feeling decidedly queasy: 'They got up en masse at the premiere screening at the Wellington Film Festival and gave Peter a standing ovation, and I just remember feeling sick to my stomach that some of those same people had been not terribly supportive of him a year or two earlier. But now that he was suddenly making "the right kind of film" it was acceptable to jump up and call him a hero. Well, no, I think if you love cinema then you love all kinds of films and you see that there is no "right kind of film", there are just good films and bad films...'

In proposing his *Bad Taste–Jamboree* project to the Film Commission, Peter had articulated what he knew would be the question on everyone's lips: 'Why take a giant leap backwards – especially since *Heavenly Creatures* could establish me as a SERIOUS FILM-MAKER???' The answer? 'I want to spend my career making the films I want to make at any given time – not the films other people think I should make... One of the greatest advantages of working in New Zealand is the freedom I feel I have to make my own films... It's a freedom I relish and appreciate.'

What Peter did next was to exercise that freedom...

Forgotten Silver runs for fifty-two minutes – the shortest of all Peter's professional films – yet it had a lengthy gestation period and was nurtured and coaxed into life through the combined passions and imaginations of Peter Jackson and Costa Botes.

Costa knew about film; he was a respected writer *on* film but he also wanted to *make* films of his own. He had made some short subjects and wanted to stretch himself to a feature length film. It was 1988, Peter Jackson was writing *Braindead* with Fran Walsh and Stephen Sinclair when American script guru, Robert McKee, had made a flying visit to New Zealand and shaken up their ideas about film-making. Costa had missed the seminar, but had listened to tapes and talked with Peter and pored over the copious notes which Fran had made during the three-day course.

'What McKee offered in a nutshell,' says Costa, 'was the whole mystery of how you write a feature film: why some films work and others don't; why you can find yourself halfway through a script and it's turned into a ghastly, inescapable maze... There are no simple answers, but experiencing McKee's seminar helps you go back to basics and ask yourself the right questions, at the very least gives you a vocabulary with which you can talk to other writers.'

Costa began talking to Peter about a script he had started writing and for which Jim Booth, then still the Executive Director of the New Zealand Film Commission, had advanced a small amount of development funding. This was the script for *The Warrior Season*, a gold-rush-era Kiwi 'Western'. Costa and Peter collaborated on a couple of drafts of the scripts and came up with 'great action stuff – really good gravy – with really unexpected and interesting little twists and turns', although Costa was already aware that Peter's career was set on another trajectory. 'That's one of the most useful experiences of my professional life: sitting in a room, writing a script with Peter. His whole process was so fertile; he'd constantly be coming up with all kinds of ideas, and I was just aware of this little figure miles in front of me and of me going, "Jesus, how do I keep up with this guy?" Working with Peter brought me up to a whole different level, but I'd constantly feel left behind by him: he's out of the box; he's way, way ahead…'

Working on Costa's script for *The Warrior Season* led to another collaboration and one that would result in a classic piece of film-making about *film-making*…

The inspiration sprang out of a British television documentary which Costa had seen in 1977. Entitled *Alternative 3*, it set out to investigate the so called 'brain-drain' of scientific talent which, it had previously been assumed, was caused by scientists leaving Britain for more lucrative jobs overseas. *Alternative 3* presented the alarming discovery that many of the scientists seemed to have actually vanished off the face of the planet as part of a plan by the world's governments to protect the best brains against an inevitable coming destruction of humankind. 'Alternative 3' was an intellectual 'Noah's Ark' possibly located on Mars!

The documentary was, in fact, what is now commonly called a 'mockumentary', a genre popularly epitomised by Woody Allen's *Zelig* and the 1984 classic, *This is Spinal Tap*. However, in 1977, the term 'mockumentary' had not yet been coined and *Alternative 3* made a powerful impression on Costa, demonstrating how dangerously easy it can be to blur the line between film's ability to present fact and fiction and what happens when the documentarian decides to tell lies…

Costa remembers: 'The *Alternative 3* programme and the impact it had sat in my brain like a dormant seed until years and years later, about 1990. I was fishing round for ideas and I thought it would be great to create something of my own along the lines of *Alternative 3*. I came up with two ideas, one involving UFOs, and the other one recreating the life of a fictional forgotten film-maker which would also involve creating his movies.'

At the suggestion of George Port, Costa discussed the idea with Peter, whose immediate reaction was that a film investigating the lost legacy of a non-existent New Zealand film pioneer was 'a fantastic idea'. They quickly came up with a name for their forgotten movie-maker – Colin McKenzie: 'Colin' borrowed from Costa's father-in-law and 'McKenzie' added by Peter as sounding like a good Scottish-bedrock New Zealand name!

> I thought we wanted the most innocuous, normal name we could come up with, something very plain and ordinary. I was thinking about the sort of names that All Blacks are called and 'Colin McKenzie' sounded like a Kiwi-bloke kind of name!

Costa already had several ideas for elements of the story, such as linking McKenzie's career to a real life Kiwi hero by having his lost films include footage of pioneer aviator Richard Pearse making a flight in a heavier-than-air craft in March 1902, nine months before the Wright Brothers' history-making flight at Kitty Hawk. Peter told Costa that he needed 'something else' and instantly added an ingenious embellishment of his own:

> I had recently read a story in the paper that really intrigued me about a group of cinema archaeologists who had gone out into the Californian desert and uncovered ancient artefacts recovered from buildings that looked like they dated from antiquity, but which were actually Cecil B. DeMille's movie sets for the 1923 silent version of *The Ten Commandments*.

The City of the Pharaohs, 720 feet wide and 120 feet high, had been dismantled at the end of the shoot and, on DeMille's orders, had been buried in the sands of the Guadalupe-Nipomo dunes. Peter immediately began to speculate on the idea of there being remains of an epic movie set hidden deep in the New Zealand bush. 'I thought it was a fantastic image,' says Costa. 'I couldn't get over the idea of us setting out with machetes and hacking our way through the jungle and finding another lost city, this time the set of a biblical epic to rival those of DeMille and D. W. Griffiths – but built in New Zealand!'

Costa suggested the title *Forgotten Silver* (a reference to silver nitrate used in the manufacture of film stock) and Peter recalls trying to hitch Colin Mackenzie's story to another project that had been lying undeveloped for a few years:

> Remember the mythic, never-gotten-off-the-ground television show, *Uncle Herman's Bedtime Whoppers*, the ridiculous idea with the funny name that had part of the inspiration for *Meet the Feebles*? At some stage during the long window following the completion of *Heavenly Creatures*, I got another phone call from Bryce and Grant Campbell suggesting that we really ought to try to get *Uncle Herman's Bedtime Whoppers* up and running and asking if I had any ideas.
>
> I mentioned the idea of a spoof documentary about a New Zealand film pioneer who does amazing work and invents all this pioneering cinema stuff but can't make it happen because he just doesn't have the ability to follow through or somehow manages to get it not quite right. I pitched it over the phone, but I could hear that Bryce and Grant really weren't buying it…

Undaunted, Peter and Costa began elaborating Colin McKenzie's story. 'I sat down and wrote an initial document,' remembers Costa, 'a short summary of everything we knew about Colin McKenzie and all the ideas we'd come up with, not concerning myself with narrative, just putting down ideas for gags. Then we'd play about with it, tossing it around, throwing it backwards and forwards. We talked with Jim Booth, who was really sick at the time but who thought it was a fantastic idea – I remember him lying in bed and saying something really nice: that this was one of the few things that had really cheered him up lately. Jim encouraged us to carry on with it, but the real problem was that what we were talking about was so ambitious and expensive – big special effects, big crowd scenes – there seemed to be no reasonable chance of our ever getting sufficient funding to make a short film on that scale.'

Not only that, but funding a hoax was obviously a suspect proposition both for television networks and the Film Commission. Then, after several negative responses, New Zealand on Air, the state television service, invited submissions for a series of one-off TV dramas, to be sponsored by the Montana winery.

Forgotten Silver was one of 150 proposals submitted for consideration and, no doubt helped by the fact that *Heavenly Creatures* had confirmed Peter Jackson as a film-maker of the 'right kind of films', was accepted as one of the dramas for the Montana Sunday Theatre season.

The timing, however, was really not good since *The Frighteners* was finally about to go into pre-production with a Hollywood star name, Michael J. Fox, in the lead role.

> And it was like, 'Oh my God! Holy s***! I can't do this. I can't make it… I've got no time!' We were about eight or nine weeks away from actually starting shooting *The Frighteners*. But there was also the realisation that my involvement had helped get the idea accepted and that if I now pulled out, they'd drop *Forgotten Silver* and take someone else's idea. So, we worked out a way, divvying up the responsibilities between us, with Costa directing all the interview material while I shot the original footage for Colin McKenzie's 'lost' movies.

First, however, a completed script was required. Costa prepared a draft and then each evening for a month he would meet with Peter and Fran after they had been doing advance preparation for *The Frighteners*: 'We'd go through the script page by page and exhaustively rewrite and rewrite. A heck of a lot of work went into the screenplay: three drafts, all superimposed on each other. A lot of the ideas in the finished films had their beginnings with me but were all inspiringly tousled up by Pete and Fran. If you looked at the draft script you wouldn't see a single page that wasn't heavily worked over. Pete's big contribution to the whole thing was the sense of drama: he kept saying over and over that it had to be dramatic, it had to have a flow and a shape, it had to be engaging dramatically; that it didn't matter how clever we were with individual gags, if we didn't give it an overall shape it was going to be a one-joke idea.'

The films-within-the-film involved a number of genres: ranging from the *cinema-vérité* of the war documentary (filmed on the beaches of Gallipoli, of course) to the knockabout, custard-pie nonsense of slapstick comedies and the biblical epic so beloved by the early film-makers and which, in Colin McKenzie's case, took as its theme the story of *Salome*.

Working together, Costa, Peter and Fran came up with ever more ludicrous twist and turns, such as having Colin McKenzie make the first ever film with synchronised sound but have him choose as a subject a story about China so that, although the characters were all talking, no one watching the film understood a word of what they were saying! Then there were entanglements with a gang of Mafiosi (the Palermo Brothers, named after the Sicilian capital and location of a historic Mafia summit) and the authorities in Stalinist Russia, who agreed to finance McKenzie's ailing production of *Salome* on the understanding that it was reworked to exclude religion and promote communist ideology!

But there were moments of deep emotion and tragedy that leavened the gags and added to the story's credibility: Colin McKenzie's despair at his repeated failures, the death of his wife (and leading lady) Maybelle in childbirth and Colin's own death trying to save a wounded soldier in the Spanish Civil War, filmed by his own fallen camera…

> Fran was really hot on this: all the time she would be saying to Costa and me, 'It's got to be emotional; you can't just show documentary stuff and think you've done a good job, you actually have to turn it into something that makes the audience *care* about Colin McKenzie, moves people – perhaps even to tears.'

Initial fears about the cost of making *Forgotten Silver* were quickly confirmed: the available budget was NZ$400,000 but a first pass at the budget showed it needing a figure of $1million. As Costa remembers, they decided to go over the figures again: 'We thought, "What could we do it for if we forget the true cost of paying people, if we do deals, ask people to do it for a little bit less? But it was still over NZ$700,000. So then we did another pass on the basis of hardly any of us getting paid and just doing it for love and it was still sitting around $620,000…'

Peter and Costa met with Caterina de Nave, Executive Producer of the 'Montana Sunday Theatre' series, and put the figures on the table but, seemingly, there was nothing to be done. The Film Commission couldn't contribute more money and the relevant committee at New Zealand on Air weren't due to meet for some time; whereas for Peter it was crunch-time: he had to confirm his involvement with *Forgotten Silver* and start work or it would be time to begin filming *The Frighteners* and the moment would have passed. But Caterina de Nave couldn't give them an answer and, at that point, the realisation dawned that 'the project was dead in the water.'

'I went into a kind of mourning for the project,' remembers Costa. 'I had nothing to go on to and that was very hard. But the thing that hurt the most was that I wasn't going to see this character, Colin McKenzie. For the first time in my career I'd worked on something where I knew the character inside out, I'd imagined everything about him and suddenly it wasn't going to happen, he wasn't going to come alive.'

Then, after a day and a night of misery, Costa received an early morning telephone call from Caterina de Nave to say that she had talked her committee into an early meeting at which they approved the NZ$620,000 budget. 'They would never have done that if it wasn't for Peter,' reflects Costa; 'they wanted the 800lb gorilla so badly they were prepared to bust through all manner of bureaucratic protocol, step outside their meeting times and then give us 50 per cent more budget than the other films in the series.'

It was clearly the time for any remaining doubters in the arts and media of New Zealand to forget the spilt blood and scattered brains, the bloody deeds with chainsaws and power mowers: the *enfant terrible* was now an award-winning film-maker.

'*Forgotten Silver* exists,' says Costa, 'because of Peter. I came up hook, line and sinker with a lot of the original material but, creatively, the project would not be what it is without Pete and certainly in practical terms it wouldn't even be a project without him; he's absolutely, totally embedded in that film.'

Regarding Peter's gift for extending the budget (and not just on *Forgotten Silver*), Richard Taylor comments: 'Pete knows the movie he wants to make. People aren't necessarily willing to put up the money for that movie, so he begins with the knowledge that he has to settle initially for the movie that they have the money to pay for. But, as the process goes on, he cleverly generates such passion and enthusiasm for what he has envisaged, that he is able to draw them further along on the journey until they are so caught up in what he wants to do that they agree to fund the project at a higher level than they had ever expected.'

Over-arching all the many historical and movie-making gags in *Forgotten Silver* was the sustaining story of Peter and Costa's quest to discover the truth about Colin McKenzie. It would begin with Peter explaining how he had first uncovered a cache of old films in a shed at the bottom of the garden of an elderly neighbour of his parents in Pukerua Bay and conclude with finding the lost city of Colin McKenzie: the giant sets originally built for *Salome* and which – like DeMille's *Ten Commandments* sets in the California sand dunes – had lain undiscovered for decades.

Two further elements would contribute to the veracity of the story-telling: firstly Nick Booth, son of the late Jim Booth, undertook historical research into the period and events referred to in the script, following which further rewrites used this material to add authentic embellishments, often supported by genuine archive film.

Secondly, there needed to be a cast of interviewees to add veracity to the proceedings – all of whom needed to be able to lie with total conviction! The first contribution came from Kiwi star, Sam Neill. Early in 1995, the actor invited Peter to take part in a documentary that he was making on the history New Zealand film, called *Cinema of Unease*.

I told Sam, who I had never met before, that he could interview me as long as I could interview him for *our* film! He said, 'Sure,' so I then said, 'And by the way, Sam, ours is a very low budget picture, so can I use your crew and your camera gear when you come round?' And, fortunately, he still said, 'Sure…'!

Before he became an actor, Sam Neill had worked at the New Zealand Film Unit, so he invented a story about an old guy whom he had met there: a technician who was a bit damaged by all the chemicals he'd had to handle, but who actually remembered working with Colin McKenzie.

According to Sam, the technician was Stan Wilson, a former vaudeville comic who, as 'Stan the Man', travelled the country delivering a series of well-aimed custard pies – including one into the face of the New Zealand premier – all of which were covertly filmed by McKenzie using a candid camera concealed inside a suitcase and exhibited as actuality-slapstick comedies.

So I did the interview with Sam Neill, then swung his own camera back on him, and that 'swapsie' was the first thing that we ever shot for *Forgotten Silver*.

Costa Botes and Sue Rogers who, following Jim's death, was producing the film felt that Sam's interview gave legitimacy to the McKenzie story; shortly afterwards another opportunity to solicit contributions presented itself when the nominations for the 1994 Academy Awards were announced and included one for Peter and Fran for Best Original Screenplay for *Heavenly Creatures*.

Fran was in the final stages of her pregnancy with our first child, Billy, and wasn't going to be allowed to make the trip, so I was going to have to fly to the ceremony alone. But I thought, 'This is the perfect opportunity to grab a couple of interviews about Colin McKenzie.'

So, I thought I'd start with Harvey Weinstein: we'd just done our first-look deal with Miramax, so we were all part of the family. I called Harvey up and even though this wasn't anything to do with Miramax, he agreed to do an interview.

Peter's next call was to Rick Baker, who he had met at Sitges and who was a near-neighbour of the Hollywood critic, film historian and tele-

With Fran, just before I left to attend the 1995 Oscars. This is our office at home, where we'd write scripts sitting side by side at the computer.

vision personality, Leonard Maltin. Rick agreed to approach Leonard, and Peter soon had the internationally known movie commentator lined up for an interview. With a film crew booked in Los Angeles, Peter flew off for his first Oscar ceremony.

> Being nominated for the Oscar was a huge thrill – one that exceeded even the thrill of the nominations for *The Lord of the Rings*. It was the first time and felt absolutely unbelievable.
>
> It was very exciting: it was the year that Bob Zemeckis' *Forrest Gump* won Best Picture and we were going to be making *The Frighteners* for Zemeckis. *The Shawshank Redemption* was also up for Best Picture, which was the feature debut of Frank Darabont, who I'd got to know on my first trips through Hollywood. It was the year of *Pulp Fiction* – which eventually beat *Heavenly Creatures* in the Best Screenplay category – and Quentin Tarantino had been another friend we had made at Sitges when he was just this kid with a film called *Reservoir Dogs*…

Peter had been hoping to get Tarantino to join the Colin McKenzie 'talking heads' but, having just won an Oscar, he was caught up on an

endless party schedule and Peter never managed to get him in front
of the camera. As for the interview with Harvey Weinstein, that was
set up for an incredibly early time on post-Oscar morning.

> I'd rung Harvey the day before and asked what time I should show up,
> and he looked in his appointment book and he said he'd do it at some
> ungodly hour – like half past six in the morning – and I said, 'Harvey,
> it's the Oscars the night before, *are you really going to be up by half past
> six*?' Next morning I arrived with the crew and he was not only up but
> proved a wonderful bullshit artist!

After interviewing Harvey, Peter dashed off to the TV studio where
Leonard Maltin broadcast and had an hour with someone who proved
a supreme storyteller: the lies fell from Leonard's lips like pearls of
truth! Peter describes him as 'a wonderful showman', as anyone who
sees him delivering his shameless deceptions in *Forgotten Silver* will
agree. His interviews, says Costa, are 'perfect gold'. It was appropriate
that when *The Return of the King* had its Hollywood premiere in
2003, the person conducting the interviews for the telecast was
Leonard Maltin.

Back in Wellington, cast and crew were assembled in order to
shoot the 'discovered' film footage, with *Heavenly Creatures'* cinematographer, Alun Bollinger, behind the camera, and the authentic
looking 'archive' photographs and film stills that were taken by Chris
Coad and then mixed in with genuine period photographs including
pictures of Costa's wife's great-grandfather and family.

The young man chosen to play Colin McKenzie was given the
part in compensation for an earlier missed opportunity: Thomas
Robbins was a Christchurch actor who had been cast for a role in
Heavenly Creatures that was eventually cut from the finished film.
The sequence featured a teenage social and dance attended by Juliet
Hulme, at which – through a series of parental connivances – a
young lad, Colin, had been delegated to dance with Juliet in the
hope of awakening her to masculine charms as an antidote to her
intensifying relationship with Pauline Parker. Colin's overtures –
being a somewhat nervous lad – were unsuccessful and, as Peter

puts it, Juliet 'chewed him up and spat him out.' Unfortunately for Thomas Robbins, the scene was cut from the final edit for pacing reasons.

> It's something you hate doing – especially to a very enthusiastic young teenager who's told all his family he is going to be in this movie and then, right on the eve of it coming out, learns that his scene has hit the cutting-room floor. So when we came to look for a Colin McKenzie, Fran and I decided we should give the role to Tom: partly out of guilt, but also because we knew he was a good actor and, very importantly, because we knew that if we were to sustain the spoof, his face had to be unknown to TV audiences.

So convincing was his performance that, as Thomas recounts, he watched the finished broadcast with a group of mates who were oblivious to the fact that the Colin McKenzie on screen was their friend! Eight years later, Thomas Robbins would be seen in the opening moments of *The Return of the King* as Déagol grappling with Sméagol over possession of the One Ring.

Two other member of the *Forgotten Silver* company to appear in *Rings* were Peter Corrigan (playing silent comic, Stan the Man) who would be seen in the extended version of *Fellowship* as Otho Sackville-Baggins and Sarah McLeod who was cast as actress Maybelle – Colin's Salome and wife – and who would subsequently play the love of Sam Gamgee's life, Rosie Cotton.

Other industry interviewees were lined up – in addition to those Peter had already got on film – including veteran New Zealand film-maker John O'Shea. Beatrice Ashton, a neighbour and close friend of Fran's aunt, assumed the role of Colin's second wife, Hannah McKenzie, who while serving as a Red Cross nurse in Algiers had married the pioneer despite his being twice her age and their having only one night together before he went off to fight in the war! A retired headmistress, Beatrice's phoney recollections of what her late husband had told her of his life and work were to provide the chronological and emotional cement to hold the story together.

Now, however, it was clearly a race against time:

We were terrified that Universal would find out about *Forgotten Silver* in case I was in breach of my contract by working on anything else. I guess I could have argued, since it was started long before we knew I would be directing *The Frighteners*, that technically it was already a work in progress. But we certainly hadn't told them about it!

Much had to be filmed and even though some of Colin Mackenzie's films were only represented in extracts (or surviving snippets), they were complex to shoot: Richard Pearse's flight (with a full-size replica plane and a model built by Richard Taylor); the Chinese 'talkie' (which also happened to be the first 'kung fu' movie!); the various 'Stan the Man' comedies and the war footage in Gallipoli and Spain. There were also a great many scenes from *Salome* including John the Baptist preaching and getting arrested, the crowds in revolt and fighting with Roman soldiers, the Baptist in the dungeon and his eventual execution, as well as Herod and his entourage in the throne room, where Salome performs her beguiling 'dance of the seven veils' and, in the film's final moments, is crushed to death.

There was just one week in which to get all Peter's 'lost McKenzie film sequences' shot before he was under contract to Universal and locked into pre-production on *The Frighteners*.

By the second week of filming, things were beginning to get perilous. Universal sent a development producer named John Garbett down to New Zealand to represent the studio through the filming of *The Frighteners*. Looking back, Peter recalls thinking, 'Holy Hell! How are we ever going to get through this?'

Interior scenes for *Salome* were being shot at the studio and Costa Botes' memory is that they managed to hold off John Garbett's arrival with a story that there had been a serious – and highly dangerous – gas leak on the studio lot that was going to take three days to fix!

There were also several major crowd scenes to be filmed – some of which were being shot at the Massey Memorial, a marble forum-like structure in memory of former Prime Minister William Ferguson Massey. Costa remembers: 'I'd written four or five closely typed pages that was halfway between a script and a prose treatment – and had given them to Pete to have a look through and see whether any of the ideas – such as the people's revolt which I'd added to the original story – might be a way of coming up with the sequence. The next thing I know, he's on set directing with these seriously scrunched-up pieces of paper and saying, "I'd better not lose these, they are all I've got!" It was actually a very faithful adaptation of what I'd written. I hadn't done a lot of writing for other people, so it was interesting for me to see a director taking these notions – which really weren't all tied together and had some pretty big gaps in between – and making it work on film.'

The Massey Memorial was located at Point Halswell, not far from the city but safely away from prying eyes. However, the remaining *Salome* exteriors used the towering Carillon at the National War Memorial on Buckle Street in the heart of town. There were a hundred milling extras in biblical robes, phalanxes of marching Roman soldiers and a camera crew on one of the main routes into the city from the airport.

> The production runner went to the airport to collect John Garbett and drive him into the city. We had warned the runner that I was going to be out filming and, whatever he did, *not* to take John anywhere near Buckle Street... Unfortunately he completely forgot – until he drove round the corner and saw, straight ahead, this film crew and me directing a whole load of guys in Roman uniforms! The runner immediately threw the car around, skidding into a U-turn – with a squeal of tyres and John clinging on for dear life – and zoomed away in the opposite direction! I don't think John suspected anything, though God knows why!

After that Peter showed up at the studio for a couple of days to work on *The Frighteners*. There was, however, still one of Colin McKenzie's movies to shoot. In the increasingly implausible scenario of Colin's life, it was established that he had produced the first ever colour film (using berry extracts for dyes!), the subject of which had been life in Tahiti. Typically for McKenzie, things did not go to plan in that his film, showing bare-breasted Tahitian maidens bathing in a pool, was adjudged lewd and banned while Colin himself was sentenced to imprisonment with hard labour.

The Tahitian maids were to be filmed in front of the palm-fringed ponds in Wellington's Botanical Gardens. Technically, Peter had weekends off, so the shoot was scheduled for a Saturday morning. On the day before, Peter learned something that made him very anxious…

> John Garbett happens to be a nice fellow and he was very good to us all the way through *The Frighteners*, but on the Friday before the Tahitian shoot in the Botanical Gardens, I was chatting to John and he said, 'I really like it here, Peter. You know, every morning I get out of my hotel and go for a walk through the Botanical Gardens.'
>
> I was still terrified that Universal would find out that I was filming *Forgotten Silver* on the side, so the following morning we posted scouts on every bloody pathway anywhere near where we were shooting, in order to warn us if John Garbett was out on his morning walk. We were planning to run into the bushes and hide, until he had gone by, but as it turned out there was no John Garbett sighting that day! Still, I remember thinking, 'God, I'm on *another* secret shoot; why do I always end up on secret shoots?'

Whatever the anxieties, it would probably be true to say that Peter was at least a little excited by the secret shoot. 'It tickled his funny bone,' says Costa; and, like the secret shoot on *Meet the Feebles*, it was daring, risky and slightly naughty fun; it was the Kiwi 'buck-the-system-and-do-the-impossible' philosophy; it was the Jackson way.

It was one thing to conceive the idea of creating film footage that looked as if it had been shot seventy years earlier, another thing to then do so with such authenticity that it might be taken for the real thing. It was a challenge that required an understanding of many factors: the nature of early film acting and the style of art direction, the technical limitations of pioneering cinematography and how they affected the look of early movies and the effects of the ravages of time on old film stock.

> We studied old film very closely, trying to pick out all the intricacies of how it looks and why. One of the things, which people faking film don't usually manage to duplicate, is the way it goes bright and dark and fluctuates, which was caused by the cameras having a variable shutter speed.

So when we were shooting I'd keep my finger on the iris of the camera, where you set the f-stop and, as it was rolling, I'd keep turning it up and down all the time. I wanted to avoid camera moves that looked too even and mechanical and on one occasion, when Alun Bollinger was filming a shot moving along on a dolly, I remember going up behind him, shaking his shoulders and saying, 'Too smooth, too smooth!'

The scenes of war reportage were all filmed, hand-held, using the 16mm Bolex camera on which Peter had shot *Bad Taste*. Then, when it came to processing the footage, the Film Unit made a unique contribution to the antique look of the film.

'What, for me, came as a revelation,' says Costa, 'was viewing genuine old movies in the Film Archive and realising that some of the stuff looks absolutely gorgeous – it isn't all scratched and horrible. The reason we have a stereotypical idea of what old film looked like is because it was often treated so badly. We looked at footage of New Zealand troops departing for the Boer War and it could have been shot yesterday: you could see their faces clearly, their hair waving, it looked fantastic. We decided to have some film that looked quite crappy but other examples that had been better preserved and that, as we moved through the years, we'd create different looks for the different periods. Pete was great at inspiring the Film Unit to keep aiming for perfection: sending stuff back, he'd say: "It's not good enough… try again!" And they got into the spirit of it and it became a badge of honour for them that they could deliver the best possible results.'

They did a brilliant job of ageing the film and experimenting with ways of making modern film stock look like old nitrate film. They used chemicals that would bubble up or eat the emulsion and, where we wanted it to look scratchy, they'd actually chuck the film on the floor and walk about all over it for a day till it was scratched to hell!

Once the McKenzie film footage was shot and developed, Costa began editing: 'Peter was most valuable to the project at that point: he was able to look at the rough-cut and make a few really telling suggestions about how we could trim and cut and organise the material. He also pulled the strings necessary to get the broadcaster off our backs long enough to go and re-shoot some stuff. Re-shooting in New Zealand was regarded as a bit of a "no-no" – probably a legacy of our Colonial days – in that you plan the film and go out and shoot it and if you need to go back and re-shoot anything then that's an acknowledgement of failure. But early on, Pete looked at Hollywood and said, "Hang on a minute, re-shooting is fairly common over there and you do it to make it better because not everybody is right first time. So why cut off the opportunity to have another tinker, another play?" So with *Forgotten Silver* we tinkered and we played…'

Throughout the process, however, Costa – like the *Bad Taste* Boys before him – became increasingly aware of Fate determining a new path for Peter Jackson: 'I felt Pete slipping away from me, shifting into another orbit. It was a little hard, but not as hard as it might have been in that I've always felt that Peter was quite special. His success is purely based on talent and nothing else: there is no bullshit, no pretence, it's all about doing the straightest job you can and staying as true to yourself as possible. It would have felt a lot harder if I'd believed that I were of equal talent or that my abilities were just as developed. So, whilst others might find Peter's incredible progress depressing, I find it inspiring: I see it as a reassurance that, some-times, nice guys don't finish last; that sometimes talent actually does bring its own reward. We all make our own way in life, according to our own strengths and weaknesses, and I've learnt from Pete to play to my strengths and not get too hung up about the other stuff.'

As *Forgotten Silver* approached completion the two writers/directors had their first and only real disagreement. The television slot where the film was to be screened was called 'Sunday Theatre' and every other programme in the series was a drama as opposed to something, which – even if it *wasn't* – *looked* like a documentary. Peter wanted to maintain the hoax to the very last, finishing up with fake end-credits: 'For their generous assistance with research, thanks to Beatrice Aston, Thomas Robbins etc…' not to mention references to 'Field Workers', 'Archaeological and Military Advisers' and a credit reading 'Antique Film Equipment & Memorabilia – Richard Taylor, Tania Rodger…' Costa, on the other hand, believed that the credits should

Checking in on Costa Botes' Forgotten Silver *post-production work during* The Frighteners *shoot.*

be accurate and should have a cast list – 'Hannah McKenzie – Beatrice Ashton, Colin McKenzie – Thomas Robbins': the 'real' people finally being shown to have been actors. 'It would have allowed the audience,' argues Costa, 'to correctly interpret everything they'd just seen and come to the conclusion that they'd been "had", but that, now that they knew it was a spoof, it was okay and had been fun. In the end, however, Peter's way of doing things won out. It's far too long ago to worry about who was right and who was wrong, but it did contribute to what happened when the film was televised…'

What happened was every prankster's paradox: for the joke to succeed it must be done seriously; if it is taken seriously, some people will not see the joke. Worst of all, there will be those who will not see the funny side of having been fooled…

On the day before *Forgotten Silver* was broadcast, the hoax was given a boost by the weekly New Zealand magazine, *The Listener*. Denis Welch, a journalist friend of Fran Walsh, happily helped thicken the plot with a story entitled 'Heavenly Features' which began,

'Film-maker Peter Jackson still can't quite believe it. It's nearly two years now since he finally yielded to his mother's urgings and promised to look at some old films a neighbour had stashed in a garden shed. "I was expecting possibly some old home movies, that I would politely say, 'These are fascinating', and go and drop them off at the Film Archive and that would be the end of it," Jackson recalls. Instead, he found a treasure trove that has changed his life, and – he believes – the history of cinema, not just in New Zealand but worldwide…'

Despite fuelling the deception with interview quotes from McKenzie's widow, Welch's article was simultaneously 'tipping the wink' to any of *The Listener*'s readers willing to read between the lines: 'What now, then, for the McKenzie heritage? Jackson confirms that Harvey Weinstein of Miramax films – the American company that backed *The Piano* and Jackson's own *Heavenly Creatures* – has secured the international distribution rights to McKenzie's films and plans to launch them at next year's Cannes festival. After that… Jackson wants nothing less than full recognition for McKenzie: "After this documentary, this guy should be appearing on our banknotes. They should create a $3 banknote just to put his face on it. He is postage-stamp material."'

The article concluded by giving what now seems like a fairly blatant clue to the true nature of *Forgotten Silver*: '…To viewers wondering what a documentary – however sensational – is doing in the "Sunday Theatre" slot, Jackson explains: "It was actually the Film Commission which suggested it. They had already got involved in funding it and they felt that the Montana Theatre would be just right for it. There was some pressure on us at first to possibly dramatise some aspects of Colin's life, but frankly, even though it's a documentary, the events of his life were so dramatic that the word drama is not inappropriate." Adds Botes, "It's as gripping as any fictional story."'

Fictional story… It couldn't have been more plainly put. *Could it?*

> *The Listener* article sealed it for a lot of people: they read it, saw the film was screening on the Sunday night, and thought, 'God, I must watch this!' And so they went into it totally believing it…

They did. When the audience for New Zealand on Air's 'Sunday Theatre' tuned in to watch *Forgotten Silver* on 29 October 1995, almost to a man, woman and child they took the bait. With so many people in on the joke – including all those Roman extras at the War Memorial in Wellington – the film-makers partly expected word to have got out before *Forgotten Silver* ever went to air. They also supposed that the hints and clues had been broadly enough plotted from Peter's first exploration of Hanna McKenzie's garden shed through to the finding of the lost *Salome* footage inside a huge sarcophagus, the lid of which was carved with the image of a charging bull. *Forgotten Silver* had, literally, led people 'up the garden path' to discover 'a load of bull'.

Not so. 'Minutes after the screening ended,' recalls Costa, 'someone I knew, a very venerable educator, rang up to congratulate me on a very fine documentary. As I hung up, I realised that this guy whom I really respected had thought it was real and I felt horrible!'

It was just the beginning... Descendents of aviator Richard Pearse rang WingNut Films grateful to have finally seen the vindication of their ancestor's claim to be the first man to fly. A Christchurch media lecturer (who deserves less sympathy than Pearse's relatives), confronted by students who wondered why their teacher had never told them about New Zealand's pioneer film-maker, foolishly assured them that he knew all about McKenzie and would be teaching about him later in the film-studies syllabus. It is even rumoured that one of the curators of the still-being-planned national museum Te Papa Tongarewa announced that he wanted to devote exhibition space to Colin McKenzie. Clearly some people were going to be hurt and others made to look foolish.

On the Monday morning, the nation was just abuzz with this thing. It was snowballing. Within twenty-four hours it was obviously getting out of hand. Costa and I were getting very concerned about the fact that the story was growing and building and that no one was actually dispelling it. TV New Zealand said that they needed to run a story, revealing the hoax. I had already started filming *The Frighteners*, so they came and interviewed us on one of the sets and we came clean, told everyone that Colin McKenzie was made up and that his story was nothing but lies.

As a result there was a very angry backlash. Some people were embarrassed that they had fallen for it and turned their embarrassment into anger towards the people who'd pulled the prank. Others were upset because they had become emotionally involved in Colin McKenzie's story – even shed a few tears – which was, of course, one of the things that we really set out to do. I think those people felt really betrayed at having been manipulated in the most private way.

For others it was simply the case that we'd created and given them a new national hero and, within twenty-four hours, had destroyed him…

The journalists were largely on the film-makers side: reporting the furore, but pointing up the film's brilliance. The headline in the *Evening Standard* a few days later read: 'FORGOTTEN SILVER A DELICIOUS HOAX' with writer Dave Mahoney remarking: 'As McKenzie's amazing story unravelled. I kept thinking that I was watching the most exciting piece of New Zealand television ever made and upon reflection, maybe I am near right…'

Several commentators took the opportunity to suggest that *Forgotten Silver* was a timely reminder that the camera can lie and that all people should be wary of believing all that they read or see. Joanne McNeill, in an article in the *Northern Advocate*, wittily entitled 'FORGOTTEN SILVER FOUND TO BE FOOLS GOLD', wrote of the gullible believers: '"But Leonard Maltin was in it," they said, dismissing any argument that movie critic Maltin and all other television personalities are creations, powdered, primped and prompted images, as opposed to whoever they may be at home picking their noses. Surely, aware of this duality in his own personae, Maltin would be delighted to lend his complicity to any cheeky creation of illusion? It should have gone without saying that everything on television is illusion – a shiftless parade of provenance-free images made of artifice, sound waves and insubstantial light which viewers, with the aid of perception and experience, realise as whatever they seem to be.'

'Mind you,' McNeill's article concluded, 'there's a fine line between illusion and deception and… those who cross it deliberately had better watch their backs.'

The proof of that came in a torrent of letters received not just by the film-makers (bizarrely including death-threats!) but also by most of New Zealand's newspapers and magazines. The programme was denounced as 'tomfoolery' and Messrs Jackson and Botes as 'cheap confidence tricksters'. 'The role of the documentary,' wrote one furious correspondent, 'is to reveal and educate, and the programme does not qualify. It *does* reveal that intellectual arrogance is to be found among those whose vocation it is to entertain or inform…'

'An outrageous waste of money', screamed one letter; 'heads should roll in Television New Zealand,' declared another. Someone calling themselves 'Celluloid Sucker' wrote, 'Following Peter Jackson's litany of lies, it now only requires New Zealand on Air to inform him that their offer of funding from the broadcasting fee was just a hoax, and could they please have their money back? (Correction, OUR money.) The look on his face would go some way to compensating our family for now not knowing what to believe, and henceforth caring even less, about early New Zealand film-making…'

It's an old but true adage that bad reviews stick in the mind and good ones are instantly forgotten, so it is tempting to think of the entire New Zealand nation as fulminating in harmony. On the contrary, many people wrote of their enjoyment of the film.

There was the viewer who seemed to have accepted the documentary as true and then added a reference to Orson Welles and a 'certain radio play', revealing not just that an understanding of the true nature of the programme but also making an appreciative link to Welles' historic radio broadcast which presented *The War of the Worlds* as a bulletin of breaking news. One writer even offered an elaborate addition to the story by claiming to have known the illegitimate daughter of McKenzie's brother and actress Maybelle – a child named on her birth-certificate, what else, Salome!

'Congratulations to the perpetrators,' enthused one supporter, 'it was the best New Zealand entertainment in ten years!' Another wrote, 'We could only marvel at the work and ingenuity that went into this huge, hilarious practical joke…'

Forgiveness, where it was given, was granted with enthusiasm and smiles: 'I was indeed shattered to hear the next day that the documentary was all a hoax – but what a hoax! If Colin McKenzie and his brilliance never existed, then Peter Jackson created magic for me. I believed it implicitly, and loved every minute of this film. Bravo Peter and cohorts! What a journey into fantasy, which absolutely fascinated...'

Had they but known, Peter Jackson's journeying 'into fantasy' had only just begun. 'What a hoot!' wrote one delighted viewer. 'If anyone will go down in Kiwi, nay in world cinematic history, it will be this innovative film-maker...'

But who did they mean, exactly? Colin McKenzie or Peter Jackson?

In the closing moments of *Forgotten Silver*, the TV audience attended an event that had allegedly been held on 3 September 1995. A cinema marquee announced 'Colin McKenzie's "SALOME" GALA PREMIERE'. Inside, an excited audience (who had actually been filmed during the Wellington Film Festival) listened as Lindsay Shelton of the New Zealand Film Commission (and the man who, since *Bad Taste*, had been involved with selling Jackson movies overseas) told them: 'There has never been a movie which has taken so long between conception and completion. And I predict that there has never been a movie, which has given a first night audience such a voyage of discovery, as you are about to embark on now... I am greatly honoured to introduce the World Premiere of Colin McKenzie's *Salome*...' At the ending of the film as the image of the dying Salome irised away into blackness, the audience rose to its feel to acclaim the masterpiece – the first movie epic to be filmed in New Zealand.

A little over eight years later, on 1 December 2003, in the very same cinema – the Embassy, Wellington – another audience would stand to acknowledge the genuine World Premiere of a genuine epic filmed in New Zealand: *The Lord of the Rings: The Return of the King*.

When, in 1994, Universal Pictures had announced that Peter Jackson was going to be making a film for Robert Zemeckis in New Zealand, Peter had told the *Sunday Star Times*: 'It's a little bit of Hollywood coming to New Zealand. It's not me going to Hollywood, that's something I've always resisted. I just love making movies here

A fun moment of different movies crossing paths. Kate and Mel were with us in New York doing press for Heavenly Creatures *while we were meeting Michael J. Fox to discuss* The Frighteners *script.*

and there's no logical reason to change that.'

The Frighteners was variously described, as 'a supernatural black-comic thriller', and 'a ghost story that takes so many twists and turns you begin to believe anything is possible. And everything is scary…'

Zemeckis had agreed to the film being shot in New Zealand, but he had put forward a mega-star for the lead role of Frank Bannister, the dubious psychic investigator – Michael J. Fox, who had starred as Marty McFly in Zemeckis' *Back to the Future* trilogy.

> Michael J. Fox was a far bigger name than I ever imagined would be in the film. Frankly, I had expected *The Frighteners* to be a low-budget horror film and that we would be casting unknown actors, but that really wasn't what Bob had in mind at all.

Zemeckis sounded out Michael and it was agreed that Peter would meet up with the star at the Toronto Film Festival in Canada, where *Heavenly Creatures* was being screened following its triumphant premiere in Venice.

> I met and chatted with Michael in a hotel in Toronto and then he had to jump in his car to go off to the screening of *Heavenly Creatures*. As he left, I remember he said, in a funny, jokey kind of way, 'Well, I'll meet

you afterwards – and I hope I like it!' I thought, 'I hope he *does!*' Anyway, we met up again afterwards and he'd really loved the film, thought it was fantastic and asked a lot of questions about it and about the real life events. From that meeting in Toronto, he was on board for *The Frighteners*.

Trini Alverado, who had recently played one of the 'little women' in the Susan Sarandon/Winona Ryder version of Louisa May Alcott's novel, was cast as the recently widowed Dr Lucy Lynskey – a character giving a name-check for *Creatures'* actress Melanie Lynskey, who would make a cameo appearance in the film. The cast was also to include Dee Wallace Stone who, apart from being Elliott's 'mom' in *E.T. The Extra-Terrestrial*, had made the first two of several horror movie appearances in Wes Craven's *The Hills Have Eyes* and Joe Dante's *The Howling*.

The leads were joined by two legends: John Astin and Jeff Combs. Astin (the father of the future Sam Gamgee) had starred as Gomez, head of *The Addams Family* in the cult TV comedy series based on Charles Addams' ghoulish cartoons for *The New Yorker*. Astin was cast as The Judge, one of Bannister's spirit cohorts, a world-weary, Wild West gunslinger. As for Combs, he was already one of Peter's screen heroes because of his performance as Herbert West, the scientist fascinated by regenerative experiments who is the eponymous 'hero' of the seminal zombie movie *Re-Animator*. Now he was to play unhinged FBI Agent Dammers, an eye-rolling, tic-twitching, haemorrhoid-suffering performance that is both hilarious and sinister.

The cast adapted well to filming in New Zealand and Peter slipped effortlessly into directing performers used to the ways of big American studios. However, despite feeling a kinship between the lifestyle of New Zealand and that of his native Canada, Michael J. Fox suffered from bouts of homesickness:

Michael was in New Zealand for the best part of six months and he missed his family – especially since he and his wife had had twins not long before he started on *The Frighteners*. They came to visit him once during the course of the shoot and he took trips back

An ardent Re-Animator *fan getting gifts from Herbert West himself in the guise of Jeff Combs (above). John Astin shooting his six-guns in* The Frighteners *(below). A great gentleman and, after working with Sean and his daughter Ally in* The Lord of the Rings, *I can now say I've directed three generations of the Astin family.*

home whenever we could schedule him a week off.

He was very funny and generous and because he was missing his twins, he came to adopt our son Billy, who was only a few months old, almost as a surrogate child! He'd often come round to play with him – and even change his nappies!

A 130-day shoot was scheduled for *The Frighteners*, reflecting the fact that it was going to be a project that would prove demanding in every aspect of its production.

Richard Taylor and colleagues at Weta embarked on eighteen months of intensive work, building several miniature settings to help convincingly relocate Wellington to North America, devising an animatronic ghost-dog that, at one point steals The Judge's perpetually loose lower jaw ('The dog's running away with my face!'), and an elaborate costume for The Gatekeeper, a supernatural winged being who guards the cemetery but who was eventually cut from the final edit of the film.

There were also the complex make-up requirements for Frank Bannister's ghostly associates. Rick Baker, whose work was much admired by Richard and Peter, advised on the design of the particularly demanding make-up for The Judge, whose ghostly shape is in an advanced state of decomposition. 'The ghosts,' Peter observed at the time, 'are not just special effects, they're key characters in the film who happen to be dead.'

The Frighteners ceaselessly juggled the conflicting emotions of amusement and fear and, in its most terrifying moments, featured a startling representation of that harbinger of death, the Grim Reaper: a cloaked, faceless figure (a forerunner of the Black Riders of Mordor) whose appearances are a prelude to literally heart-stopping moments for his unfortunate victims.

Experiments in the creation of the Reaper included both a costumed performer and a rod puppet, operated underwater in order to create an ethereal, floating effect. Eventually, however, Weta opted for digital graphics that would enable the spook to slip and slide over the rooftops with fluid ease and to streak along roads in pursuit of speeding vehicles.

Two funny guys, Jim Fyfe and Chi McBride, who played Stuart, Bannister's ghostly assistant, and Cyrus in The Frighteners.

By using computer graphics, I think we gave the Reaper an interesting feel with the inky-black quality we were able to give to his robes. It was one of my regrets on *The Lord of the Rings* that we weren't able to create the Ringwraiths in a similar way. We considered it, but realised in the end that with nine Ringwraiths and so many shots in which they had to appear it would have put too great a burden on a team that already had to create a great many effects for the film. It's very hard to make people wearing black clothes look really scary and ultimately it only works because of the sound effects and camera angles. If we had been able to do them in the same way that we did the Reaper in *The Frighteners* I think we would have achieved a look that would have been more creepy, sinister and menacing.

'Watching what was happening throughout the making of *Heavenly Creatures* and *The Frighteners*,' notes Costa Botes, 'it was clear that Peter had taken another of his giant strides forward. He'd nudged Weta into buying their first computer, George Port had taught himself how to scan film and manipulate it using the software available and, suddenly, they had a special effects facility.'

Nevertheless, the effects for *The Frighteners* were to place heavy demands on George Port and his growing, but still small, group of technician-artists who were now installed in the recently acquired studio premises in Weka Street and were getting to grips with some of the newest Silicon Graphics hard- and software. Completing effects work on *Jack Brown Genius* had delayed some of the essential gearing-up process for the new feature and a few vital effects shots for *Forgotten Silver* had been farmed out to a small Wellington effects company called Pixel Perfect, many of whose artists would later join Weta Digital.

'*The Frighteners* became an immense laboratory,' says Ken Kamins, 'and the film really defined the expansion of Weta: the way they went about it was that you could create an ad hoc effects company by leasing equipment from Silicon Graphics and then going to unemployed animators throughout the world and enticing them to come to New Zealand. Yet they would still have an economically viable studio because Weta, at that point, didn't have the overhead charges of an Industrial Light and Magic, Digital Domain or any of the other big effects houses in the USA.'

The staggering escalation rate of Weta's contribution to Peter Jackson movies is fascinating. *The Return of the King* in 2003 would contain a staggering 1,691 special effects shots (which was double the number in *The Two Towers*) and yet Weta's beginnings, just eleven years earlier, had been by comparison incredibly modest. There were a mere forty effects shots in *Heavenly Creatures* while *Jack Brown Genius*, a year later, contained 150 shots. *The Frighteners* dramatically accelerated that figure to some 500 effects, including glowing 'auras' to surround the ghosts and the ability for malevolent spirits to reach out of walls and ceilings to grab and clutch at the living.

> It was hard: there were a lot of shots and very few people doing them. None of those 500 effects shots were particularly difficult, but we'd never done anything like it before and we were still finding our way. Fortunately Bob Zemeckis was incredibly patient and understanding.

This is what the set of The Frighteners *looked like when we filmed the ghost scenes. Spending all day surrounded by blue or green screens turns you slightly bonkers.*

And we got through it and the quality of the shots was generally pretty good. And looking at the film now it is difficult to think how we would have done some of the effects – let alone made them as dynamic as we did – without the use of computer graphics.

For Peter, *The Frighteners* was a significant, yet curious, venture: it was his first Hollywood movie and it had come about almost, it seemed, by accident.

I'd never had much to do with American studios or producers before. Jim's death had an emotional impact and it also left me freewheeling because I hadn't just lost a friend, I had lost a producer – for a while, I didn't quite know what to do.

Remembering this period, Richard Taylor says, 'Pete was reeling from the tragedy of losing Jim and his emotions were in something of a turmoil. This was the first major project he was doing without him and I think *Forgotten Silver* had distracted him a little from his normal incredible clarity of vision. Without Jim at the helm, it took Pete quite a time to regain not so much his confidence as his normal drive. There was a real necessity to get through this film, to see it made and finished so that we could move on to other things. I felt we didn't do our best work for Peter, but we were very fortunate because having Bob Zemeckis as a producer was very good for all of us.'

It was an unexpectedly 'organic' process: beginning with us thinking we would be working for Bob Zemeckis as writers with him as director but then, eventually, ending up directing the film and working with him as a producer.

I really loved working with Bob and I'm glad that my first introduction to Hollywood film-making was with him because he allowed me to stay in New Zealand and he protected me and let me make the film my way.

Bob was extremely 'hands-off': he came down here once to visit during the shoot for about a week and then he came again to have a look at a first cut and that was really the only contact that we had with him during the making of the film. I found him very respectful of us as film-makers: he suggested one or two things, but he always said, 'This is your film…' He did exactly what a good *producer* should do: he really supported us and helped make it all happen.

The film featured an evocative score by a fantasy composer with an impeccable pedigree: Danny Elfman (*Ghostbusters*, *Edward Scissor-hands* and *Batman*) and the film's design was by Grant Major with art direction by (Jackson-team newcomer) Dan Hennah: two men who would, later, make a highly significant contribution to *The Lord of the Rings* and *King Kong*.

As *The Frighteners* went into post-production, and despite the pressures they were facing, the perennial question arose: what to do next? The idea that eventually surfaced came as a direct result of the developments with Weta digital.

I was lying in bed one Sunday morning, talking to Fran, reading the newspaper and having a cup of tea, and we were kind of excited about the computer effects that we were currently doing for *The Frighteners*.

It was obvious after *Jurassic Park* that you could do the most amazing things with computers but *The Frighteners* was the first time of seeing, first hand, exactly what computers were capable of. We were very much aware that our future projects were, ideally, going to include computer effects – at least in the short term in order to get Weta on its feet.

We've always had this hope that, one day, Weta will be able to survive by doing other people's films so that Fran and I can have some time off, but, back then, we were very conscious of having thirty-five computers and that, after *The Frighteners*, the machine had to be kept fed.

On this particular morning we were asking ourselves what kind of

I just noticed that I'm wearing exactly the same shirt in all these Frighteners *photos – oops! Here I am wearing the shirt on set with our son Billy.*

films we could do with computers? What *hasn't* been done? And I said to Fran, 'You know, the genre, that's never really been done well – not for a long time – is the fantasy genre...'

For as long as he had been making movies professionally, Peter had always had in the back of his mind a desire to make a fantasy film. After all, it had been *King Kong, Planet of the Apes, Jason and the Argonauts, The Seventh Voyage of Sinbad* and other movies that had made him want to become a film-maker. Not only that, but some of his earliest film experiments as a youngster had been fantasies: an attempt to make his own version of *King Kong,* the *Spot On* competition entry, *The Valley,* and his version of *Sinbad* that he'd been trying to make when he fell and hurt his back. Science fiction and horror films were already using computer technology – there was no shortage of spaceships, aliens, robots and dinosaurs, but fantasy films of the kind made by Ray Harryhausen that had so excited Peter as a boy had really fallen out of favour with the movie-going public.

> I argued that if fantasy wasn't that popular then that was because it wasn't being done properly. A certain *type* of fantasy movie in particular – the sub-genre usually known as 'Sword & Sorcery' – is one that I don't think has ever been done very well. Why? Mainly because they don't respect the audience enough or they aim at too young an age group, or because they're just plain silly, gaudy and over-designed!
>
> I think fantasy is really one of the last movie genres to be conquered. I mean everybody's seen several great westerns, great musicals, great thrillers, great horror movies, but there have not been that many been great fantasy films.
>
> That's why it is the last genre of cinema that is open to improvement. Every time anyone sets out to make a genre movie, somebody has already made one that's better: if you film a war movie, you'll always be compared with *All Quiet on the Western Front*, which was made seventy years earlier. You are always in the shadow of greater films that have gone before – with the exception of fantasy movies.
>
> Fran asked, 'What would we write? What type of story would it be?' And I said, 'Well, it would be a *Lord of the Rings*-type of story, that's the kind of world that I'd want to create.'
>
> Of course, a lot of so-called 'Sword & Sorcery' films have been pretty blatantly 'Middle-earthish', which is not surprising, because the moment you think of fantasy, you think of Tolkien.

Suddenly, several memories flooded back… Memories of seeing that animated film which Ralph Bakshi had begun but never finished… Memories of that book with a movie tie-in cover that, while an apprentice photoengraver, Peter had bought at a bookstall on Wellington station and started reading on the long train ride to Auckland…

> So, my first idea was to make a picture in the style of *The Lord of the Rings*, but to keep it very *real:* amazing buildings and creatures but real environments, characters and emotions. It should be a story that was relatively serious, have depth and complexity, but nothing should look artificial or fake.

It should feel as if the world in which it is set has a past and a sense of history. Why should a character named Théoden, King of Rohan be any less real than Henry VIII, King of England? Why shouldn't such characters be grounded in cultures and worlds that feel genuine and authentic – even *historical*? That, after all, is precisely what Tolkien did so well in his book.

Then Fran said, 'Why would you want to create your own story when *The Lord of the Rings* or *The Hobbit* are the really *great* fantasy stories; and, anyway, we could never write anything as good as that?'

And almost immediately I found myself wondering why no one had ever made *The Lord of the Rings* as a live-action movie? Then I wondered whether some studio had the rights – Disney, perhaps, or Spielberg – and was already planning to film the book and why, if they were, we'd not heard about it. From there I moved on to wondering who actually owned the film rights to *The Lord of the Rings* and whether it might be possible to get hold of them...

'That's how it all started,' says Fran Walsh. 'It was what I call one of Peter's "epiphanies": an idea right out of the blue that, by a series of strange coincidences, would eventually come to pass.'

Of course I was thinking, 'Oh, come on! There's no way we can do that! We're not famous film-makers – we're not even particularly *successful* film-makers! How on earth would we ever get the opportunity to make *The Lord of the Rings*?

But that conversation over a cup of tea on a Sunday morning, was enough to get me to pick up the phone and call my agent, Ken Kamins, in Los Angeles, and ask him to find out what the situation was with the rights to *The Lord of the Rings*...

Within a few days, Ken Kamins had tracked down *The Lord of the Rings* film rights to a legendary Hollywood name: Saul Zaentz. Producer of the ill-fated animated version of the book, Zaentz's other – far more successful – credits included *One Flew Over the Cuckoo's Nest*, *Amadeus* and *The Mosquito Coast*.

In the early 1970s, Saul Zaentz had bought the rights to *The Lord of the Rings* from MGM who had, in turn, acquired them from J. R. R.

Tolkien for the reputed sum of £10,000. Although various directors, including John Boorman (of *Deliverance* and *Excalibur* fame), had expressed an interest in making a live-action film of the book, nothing had ever come of the idea.

> The word was that Saul Zaentz didn't seem very keen on either making a picture or selling the rights. Frankly, our chances didn't look good.

Not only that, but the situation concerning the rights was extremely complex, involving not just those concerned with making the film but also connected with any merchandising stemming from the movie, as well as issues relating to the original literary works. It was an intriguing situation: Peter had hit on a hot idea that was currently not being pursued by anyone else, but which involved having to fight through a jungle of contractual complications. Ken Kamins discussed the situation with Peter and Fran's lawyer, Peter Nelson, who remembers, 'We realised that it would make sense to have a studio involved from the beginning of any negotiations in order to deal with the other studios and individuals who held rights in the Tolkien books.'

An obvious studio was Miramax, where Harvey Weinstein was still waiting for a project under that first-look deal with Peter and Fran. However, both agent and lawyer were not convinced that this was a project that Peter was obliged to offer to Miramax. 'There is a fair amount of text and detail that goes into a writer's and director's agreement,' explains Peter Nelson, 'and we felt that the terms Miramax had were outdated. We are now talking about going into a movie that would be ten times the budget of *Heavenly Creatures* and, as a consequence, everybody's expectations about the terms under which it would be made would obviously increase. For Peter that involved issues about whether he'd have more creative prerequisites to make the movie: how much he would get paid to make the movie; how we would do, financially, if it was successful; and whether Peter would have the right to design the movie himself or whether the studio would have a ton of influence. That's how Hollywood works.'

Whilst the issue of whether or not the terms of the first-look deal still held, there was, as Peter Nelson saw it, a moral obligation to take *The Lord of the Rings* proposition to Miramax: 'We chose to look at it that we *should* take it to Miramax because, if we did, then Miramax would be honoured in its relationship with Peter and served for what the studio had done for him, particularly in promoting *Heavenly Creatures* so well.

'But if it was only a "should" rather than a "required", then we weren't obliged to introduce the project under the terms of the over-all deal, which would have been economically restrictive and unfair to Peter, Fran and the company. This is an argument we had to sell to Miramax. They preferred to view it that we *had* to bring the project to them; we said, "We don't really *have* to bring it to you, we're not bound by the terms of any existing deal, but we *want* to bring it to you and so here it is: a chance to work with Peter Jackson across this huge tableau of *The Lord of the Rings*."'

There was also a sound tactical reason for taking the project to Miramax, because Miramax happened to have an interesting con-nection with Saul Zaentz. Earlier that year, a film crew had been about to start shooting a picture in Italy and Tunisia entitled *The English Patient,* based on the best-selling novel by Michael Ondaatje. Eleventh-hour disputes arose between director Anthony Minghella and Twentieth Century Fox who were financing the movie: Fox wanted a star name in the role of Katherine Clifton opposite Ralph Fiennes – and Demi Moore had lobbied hard for the part – but Minghella had decided instead to cast the not-so-well-known Kristin Scott Thomas.

Fox finally pulled out of the film leaving the future of the produc-tion in jeopardy and the cast and crew abandoned in Italy. The hero of the hour was Harvey Weinstein who stepped in and rescued Saul Zaentz's picture by providing the finance for filming to go ahead. Eventually, of course, *The English Patient* would go on to win nine Oscars and to make a hatful of money.

Now, with Saul Zaentz owning the rights to *The Lord of the Rings* and Harvey Weinstein in a relationship with a film-maker who wan-ted to direct it, this might, just possibly, be seen as being payback time!

'October of 1995,' remembers Ken Kamins, 'we get on the phone to Harvey and pitch *The Lord of the Rings*. The idea is that Peter would make *The Hobbit* as one movie and, if successful, *The Lord of the Rings* as two movies, shot back to back afterwards.' Two films, back-to-back: Peter had already thought through the advantages of such a proposition when devising the concept for *Jamboree–Bad Taste 2–Bad Taste 3*. As Ken recalls, Weinstein's response was wildly enthusiastic: 'Harvey said, "This is great! This is a huge, fantastic idea! I'm going to call Saul and get into it now!" And immediately started in on the process of negotiation.'

And while Harvey was talking to Saul, Ken Kamins and Peter Nelson were talking with Harvey, as the lawyer remembers: 'It took a few weeks for us to iron out the question of whether or not we were required to bring the project to Miramax under the outdated terms of the existing deal and eventually we convinced them that they would need to negotiate with us for a new deal.'

It is a fascinating but characteristic tale from the labyrinthine ways of moviedom that a casting decision of a British director making a film in Tunisia should bring about a response from one Hollywood studio that would – several dominoes down the line – result in another studio having an interest in pursuing rights in a property for a director in New Zealand.

Meanwhile, however, another potential project suddenly appeared on the horizon: a suggestion which came unlooked for but with an eerie appropriateness that seems to have constantly attended Peter Jackson's career. 'What about a remake of *King Kong*?'

The question was asked by Universal vice-president Lenny Kornburg, who was working with Peter on *The Frighteners*.

> Lenny called and said, 'Would you have any interest in doing *King Kong*?' And I said '*What?!* You do realise, don't you, that this is my favourite film?'

The prospect of taming *King Kong*, the Eighth Wonder of the World, was altogether irresistible. Peter had kept faith with the great ape ever since he had first fallen on him as a boy watching the 1933 version on

TV, its primitive black-and-white footage exerting its own unique appeal, almost as if it were an old but authentic newsreel from the archives. He had read articles on the original film in magazines such as *Famous Monsters of Filmland* and, later, *Starlog*. He'd read all there was to read about Merian C. Cooper and Willis O'Brien and Marcel Delgado and Fay Wray, about the giant Kong face and hand created for the film, and the stop-motion animation that allowed Kong to battle with the dinosaurs on Skull Island and scale the Empire State Building. And as a teenager, he had read with excitement of the coming of a new *Kong*…

In the mid-Seventies, two studios announced their intention to re-make *King Kong*: Paramount and Universal both believed they had the rights to the original material and while lawyers were arguing over the paperwork, the two giants decided to start slugging it out to be the first to get their ape onto the screen. Universal planned a version that, like the original, would be set in the Thirties but would be made in 'Sensesurround' (used in movies like *Earthquake* and *Rollercoaster*) and would feature stop-motion animation by Jim Danforth, a veteran special effects creator whose film legacy included *When Dinosaurs Ruled the Earth*, *7 Faces of Dr Lao*, *The Thing* and *Day of the Dead*.

Paramount, on the other paw, were planning an updated version of the story with new characters, a new exotic and mysterious location (one of the Micronesia group of islands) and a new icon for Kong to surmount in New York – the twin towers of the World Trade Centre. Most significantly, Italian-born producer Dino De Laurentiis announced that his Kong was no stop-frame puppet, but a giant robot ape! Universal eventually retired from the fray.

> The Universal one had gone quite a long way down the track, but had finally reached a point when they realised that, because Dino was employing quicker methods of making a film and not bothering with any stop-motion sequences, Paramount's *Kong* would reach the cinemas first and that they were going to be behind the eight ball by coming out second. It was at that point that Universal pulled the plug on *Kong*.

Universal's withdrawal left the stage to De Laurentiis and a cast headed by Jeff Bridges and Charles Grodin and introducing Jessica Lange in her feature debut as 'Dwan' – the Ann Darrow equivalent, who had allegedly changed her name from 'Dawn' to make it more distinctive! There were, with hindsight, many disappointments about the new *Kong* – the lack of dinosaurs and, as it transpired, the very limited use of the much-touted robot since, for the most part, Kong was portrayed by a man in a gorilla suit. In mitigation, De Laurentiis did succeed in getting Rick Baker to be the person to put on the suit – even if he was doubly disguised by the euphemistic screen credit, 'special contributions'.

Today, De Laurentiis' *Kong* is recognised for the misguided and disappointing project that it was; when it was released, in 1976, it was greeted with anticipation and excitement – especially by eager young monster fans. On the day on which the film was due to open in Wellington, the 15-year-old Peter Jackson was at the theatre three hours before tickets went on sale!

> When the call from Lenny came asking if we were interested in *King Kong*, I was, first and foremost, excited about the concept of being involved, but secondly I was just intrigued as a fan.
>
> I thought, 'Oh, so Universal still think they've got the rights to do *Kong!*' and I started interrogating Lenny. I soon realised that I knew a heck of lot more about it than he did. In fact, he didn't even seem to know that Universal had attempted to make a version in the Seventies...

Peter's questions prompted some research at Universal into the tangled question of rights, as a result of which Lenny Kornburg was able to report back that whilst the studio didn't own the re-make rights to the 1933 film itself, they *did* own the movie adaptation rights in the original 'novelisation' of the movie! The 'book of the film' written by Delos W. Lovelace, originally published in the year the film was released and happily close to the screenplay, would be their source material on which to base the screenplay. It was a text that captured the power of the story, the power of *Kong*:

'A sense of impending fate lifted Ann's eyelids... She was aware of

... a Shadow. She turned her head. Then, while her eyes widened, the Shadow split the dark cloak of the precipice and became solidly real... Its vast mouth roared defiance, its black, furred hands drummed a black, furred chest in challenge... Ann's scream sped piercingly into the dead silence.'

To be offered the chance to create a new *Kong* seemed like yet another gift from the gods.

> I was immediately very fired but Fran had never seen the original movie, so we watched it on video together and once she saw that it could be an enjoyable project to work on, we started getting into serious talks with Universal about *Kong*.

No one could have guessed that it would be ten years before those talks would eventually result in the names of Peter Jackson and *King Kong* sharing movie poster billing.

Peter was now in the position, as Peter Nelson puts it, of having various 'ardent suitors': 'There was a tremendous amount of heat on Peter, in part because *Heavenly Creatures* had performed so well and gotten him into a broader context where he was the young writer/director with whom everybody wanted to be in business.'

It was time to start thinking about what was going to be demanded of whichever studio decided to put their money on a Jackson film.

'We decided to set the terms ourselves,' says Peter Nelson, 'because we didn't think anybody would step into the range that we thought they should. Ken and I sat down and designed a prototypical deal; we said, "The first company who will step up to make this deal with us will in fact be entitled to make Peter's next movie." We put a premium on the fact that it would be his *next* movie, because Hollywood is full of deals where people develop material that don't become movies; but if you are willing to have your client be contractually committed to turn his attention (and that of his writing partners) to a particular project next and to be working on it whilst still shooting his existing one, then that is of value in Hollywood. There was also added value, in that we were talking about the next *Peter Jackson* project.'

The terms of the deal on offer were, in Ken Kamins' words 'pretty severe' or, as Peter Nelson puts it, 'extremely onerous'. 'Aside from what Peter got paid,' says Ken, 'we were insisting that, as part of any deal that was made on whichever of these three movies, the studio had to put up a considerable sum towards special effects "research and development".'

More than that, as Peter Nelson explains: 'Peter was also to be what is called "a first dollar gross participant", meaning he would share in the revenues of the motion picture from the first dollar into the till to the studio and not be subject to the very considerable vagaries of studio accounting. But at the heart of these proposed deals was an agreement that Peter would have final cut of the movie, he wanted the ability to say: "This is my movie, nobody else can change it."'

In 1995, the terms seemed *too* onerous, *too* severe: there were no takers. Ask who you would have to be to get a deal like that, and Peter Nelson will tell you, 'Today you have to be Peter Jackson! At the time we gave it a try. When all three studios passed, we said to Peter, "It didn't happen on this pass but we think there is tremendous value in your next project so let's wait a beat…"'

So, they waited a beat and Universal kept seeing footage shot on *The Frighteners* and began to like what they saw. Robert Zemeckis flew down to Wellington to see an early cut of *The Frighteners*, which Universal was planning to release the following year, at Halloween 1996. However, looking at the way in which the film was coming together, Zemeckis began considering a different scenario. Universal's big summer release in '96 was to have been *Daylight*, a New York disaster movie starring Sylvester Stallone – and Viggo Mortensen. However, *Daylight* was currently running behind schedule and Zemeckis decided to suggest to Universal that they bring *The Frighteners* forward to release in its place.

Peter hastily put together a trailer-cum-showreel that showed off the digital effects in the film and Zemeckis flew back with it to Los Angeles. The footage was screened at Universal and, as Lenny Kornburg happily announced, 'People were jazzed, very, very jazzed…'

Jazzed enough to agree to *The Frighteners* being accelerated to Universal's summer release schedule.

The studio got very, very excited about what they saw: they thought the film was a lot better than they had imagined it was going to be; they saw Michael J. Fox, they saw some comedy, they saw some special effects, and they thought, 'Ooh, this shouldn't be a Halloween movie, this should be a *summer* movie!'

That decision brought with it several concerns, not least of which was the need to complete 500 special effects shots on the film against a deadline with little or no flexibility. Weta rapidly had to evolve from a one-man-and-a-computer outfit to an effects facility on which the highest levels of expectation were being placed.

Robert Zemeckis had already brought Wes Takahashi onto the project as Visual Effects Supervisor. A former director of animation with Industrial Light and Magic, Takahashi's credits included *The Abyss, Hook, Indiana Jones and the Last Crusade* and three Zemeckis productions, *Back to the Future II* and *III* and *Death Becomes Her*. Now, with the delivery on *The Frighteners* coming suddenly under even greater pressure, Zemeckis secured a US$6 million top-up to the budget and Weta's already growing staff was augmented with fifteen Americans and a new delivery of technology.

It was not three years since Weta had been established and the learning curve proved sharp and occasionally painful. There were occasional tensions to be resolved, especially since there were not inconsiderable differentials between the salaries of the New Zealand animators and those who moved down from California, and the change in dynamics impacted on the relationship between George Port and the fellow founders of Weta.

Early in 1996, George decided it was time to move on. Various factors were involved, including concerns over the initial failure to turn out effects on *The Frighteners* quickly enough to meet a difficult-to-impossible schedule on budget. Whilst George personally assumed the blame for these delays, the fact was that everyone involved in the film were – if not out of their depth – no longer swimming in the shallow end of the pool.

Another, happier factor that encouraged George to leave the Weta partnership was his decision to marry Barbara Darragh, the costume designer on *The Frighteners*. The couple moved to Auckland where George would continue creating special effects on various projects, including the New Zealand television series *Xena: Warrior Princess*, which also involved various physical effects created by Richard Taylor's Weta team and future *Rings* actors Karl Urban and Marton Csokas as well as costume designer Ngila Dickson.

As special effects work on *The Frighteners* neared completion, the word was out that the next Jackson film was going to be something special. 'There was a swirl of hype around Peter,' says Ken Kamins. 'Everyone was saying that the promise was real, that this guy, post-*Heavenly Creatures* was all that and more. "Buzz-buzz-buzz!" "Oh, my God! Zemeckis has got Universal to move *The Frighteners* to a summer release!" "Hype-hype-hype!" "Buzz-buzz-buzz…" Then we get to Monday April 1 1996 and I come home from the premiere of *Primal Fear* to find that Peter has left an urgent message on my answering machine. He'd never left an urgent anything on my machine – he doesn't use the word "urgent" – but on this occasion the message simply said, "I don't care what time you get home, you have to call me." It was eleven o'clock when called him. "Ken," he said, "I've got a problem…"'

The problem was that the buzz-buzz-buzz was exciting the interest of the American special effects houses to the extent that they were beginning to head-hunt Weta's digital animators. Peter's only hope of keeping his workforce together was to be able to offer them new contracts before those on *The Frighteners* ran out. That meant knowing what, if any, film he was going to be making next – and knowing that within a week…

'On Tuesday morning,' recalls Ken, 'I spoke first to Peter Nelson and we then made phone calls to everybody, saying, "We have to know what Peter's next movie is by Friday otherwise he loses his effects team." Peter needed to do this for self-preservation, since he thought it would be impossible to reassemble what was clearly a great team. Unwittingly, however, we created a bidding war for Peter's next movie that was predicated on the hype generated by Universal and Zemeckis over *The Frighteners*.'

The phone call with Miramax did not go well. 'Harvey was

apoplectic,' says Ken, 'he was furious that after he had been good enough to suspend and extend Peter's first-look deal we were now putting Miramax in a "bidding situation" for Peter's next picture.'

Part of Harvey Weinstein's frustration was undoubtedly due to the fact that what had seemed like a straightforward matter of negotiating the Tolkien film rights with Saul Zaentz had turned out to be more complicated than anyone had imagined. Saul Zaentz, it transpired, did not own *all* the rights to *The Hobbit*. United Artists owned the rights to theatrically distribute a film of *The Hobbit* but not the right to make one! Weinstein's attempts to buy those rights from United Artists were unsuccessful: the studio was up for sale and no one was prepared to part with any assets, however insignificant they might appear.

Harvey spoke with Ken Kamins, arguing that they should now forget *The Hobbit* and concentrate on *The Lord of the Rings* since the first 100 pages of *The Fellowship of the Ring* were effectively a review of the key incidents in *The Hobbit* concerning the One Ring. However, the deal over the rights in *The Lord of the Rings* had still to be settled.

Ken reasoned with Weinstein: 'I said, "Harvey, we started a conversation with you in October 1995; we're not saying it's anybody's fault, we're just saying it's now April 1996 and you're not even close to concluding a deal with Saul and we want to make that movie. If you are able to conclude a deal we are absolutely going to make that movie but we really need to know what Peter's next movie is and we need to know now."'

To further complicate matters, Twentieth Century Fox had got wind of the fact that Peter was in advanced discussions with both Universal over *Kong* and Miramax over the Tolkien project.

They evidently thought that they were missing out on something and decided to jump on the bandwagon with *Planet of the Apes* again. This time around, Fox were saying James Cameron and Arnold Schwarzenegger were no longer involved, and that they were happy to turn the whole thing over to us and just let us do whatever we wanted... They were very anxious to start negotiations, but when Ken and Peter told them what stage we were at in our discussions with the other two studios, the lawyers at Fox laughed and said it was crazy and that they wouldn't entertain thoughts of a deal even remotely approaching what we were being offered. So, once again the *Apes* bit the dust!

Meanwhile, Peter and Fran had gone away for a few days' break over the Easter holiday.

We hadn't had a holiday for years and there's a nice hotel in Blenheim on the South Island where we thought we'd stay for four days, go on little drives, look around the countryside and relax. As it turned out, the entire Easter holiday went into madness! Miramax, Fox and Universal all now knew what each other was doing and, suddenly, it became an absolute frenzy, with people coming at us from all directions wanting it to be *their* project that we chose. It was insane! I was constantly changing batteries in the cellphone, which never stopped ringing with calls from studio chiefs, lawyers and agents. It was totally crazy and very, very stressful.

Meanwhile, in Los Angeles, Peter's lawyer and agent, as well as a number of powerful movie people, were sitting at their telephones trying to resolve issues relating to a film-maker on the other side of the world!

The first company to break the deal was Universal. There were at least two excellent reasons for them to do so: *King Kong* was a library project for Universal; any director taking on *Kong* would have to make it at Universal, which, as far as Peter Jackson was concerned, was convenient. Says Peter Nelson: 'If there was any place in town that, arguably, had the largest appetite to have more of Peter Jackson in a hurry, it was the studio for whom who he was currently making *The Frighteners*.'

Peter Nelson recalls, 'Universal called us and said, "We've got to have Peter's next movie… we'll give you your first dollar gross… we'll give you your final cut…" So we finally had someone ready to go with our prototype deal.'

Peter and Fran heard the news that Universal were ready to go ahead and on terms that would enable them to begin work on a new project the moment *The Frighteners* was finished. It didn't take Harvey Weinstein long to hear the same news.

> We were driving along and Harvey rang us saying, 'Listen! The rights for *The Hobbit* are going to take a long time to get, but Saul has *The Lord of the Rings* rights. So forget *The Hobbit*, we'll do that some other time, and just do *The Lord of the Rings*, I can get those rights really quick!' And we said that we'd still want to do *The Lord of the Rings* as two movies not one. 'Sure,' said Harvey. 'We'll do it as two films! You can start work on it; I'll get the rights! But you're going to do *The Lord of the Rings* as your next project! We have this deal!' Harvey was angry, resentful, desperate – all of those things.
>
> I said we needed a couple of hours to decide and Harvey said that we'd to call him as soon as we'd decided or he'd call us again. So we kept driving and kept talking it over…

The situation seemed clear: Twentieth Century Fox had by now ruled themselves and *Planet of the Apes* out of the picture. Universal were ready to sign a deal that meant that Peter could start work on writing and developing *King Kong* the moment they were back in Wellington. As for Miramax, they hadn't secured the rights to *The Hobbit* and whilst they might very well get the rights to *The Lord of the Rings*, they hadn't actually *got them yet*. Arriving in Nelson, Peter rang Ken Kamins and told him that he and Fran had decided to go with Universal and *Kong*.

> I asked Ken to tell Harvey our decision and Ken said – though he'd probably deny this now! – 'I think Harvey should hear that from you. It's one thing for an agent to tell Harvey that you're passing on his project, but you've really got to pay him the respect and preserve the relationship by telling him yourself.'
>
> Ken was being very correct. He is a rare agent, who has a very strict sense of honour, and I did need to discuss this personally with Harvey – but at the time I remember thinking, 'Oh, thanks, Ken! Thank you very, very much!' I was hoping that Ken would make the calls, deal with it and leave us to enjoy what was left of our break as best we could. Now I immediately started to get stressed, waiting for this bloody cellphone to ring and what I knew was going to be a very, very bad phone call! I

knew that Harvey was already really worked up and I was going to have to break this bad news that was likely to be met by an explosively thunderous reaction! Our Easter holiday had now totally turned to custard!

Passing the time in 'a junky, second-hand antique' store in Nelson, Peter spotted an old wooden propeller from a biplane. As a lover of aviation history, he had long wanted to own a propeller that he could hang on the wall and now here was one that he could buy.

> I bought it, but I had no sort of joy at finding it because I was so tense waiting for the moment when the cellphone in my pocket would ring.
>
> I thought, 'Every time I look at this propeller I'm going to remember that I bought it when I was waiting for this bloody phone call from Harvey! It will be the Harvey Weinstein Memorial Propeller! Maybe one day, when this is all over, I'll laugh about it...' But right there and then it didn't feel like it.

Eventually, the phone rang...

> I broke the news to Harvey. I said, 'Look, we're going to do *Kong* and that's going to take us a couple of years, which should give you time to sort out the Tolkien rights and then, when we're through with *Kong*, we'll do *The Lord of the Rings*...' Harvey was furiously angry; my only memory of his side of the conversation was his just repeating, 'You don't want to tell me this... You do not want to be saying this... I am not hearing this... I am not hearing this...'

As Peter recalls it, the 'heavy hammered call' ended as badly as had been anticipated. There were recriminations, accusations of breach of contract, threats of legal action. More angry conversations followed with Peter Nelson and Ken Kamins ('Harvey was screaming, yelling, threatening; he was furious about being put in this position') It was Peter who finally brokered a compromise. Come Easter Monday, Peter and Fran were on the ferry crossing the Cook Strait between the North and South islands. As the boat made its way from Picton to Wellington, the cellphone was still ringing...

The situation had now exploded into a legal nightmare that had pretty much taken any joy away from it at all. I was walking round the decks of this crowded ferry, trying to get cellphone coverage so I could call America. I eventually managed to talk with Ken and his colleagues at the agency and made a suggestion: 'To create a situation in which everybody can feel good about themselves, why on earth don't we make a proposition that Miramax and Universal co-invest in both of these projects? Why doesn't Universal let Harvey come on board as a 50/50 investor in *King Kong* and why doesn't Miramax then give Universal a 50/50 share of *Rings*? Harvey still has to get the rights to *The Lord of the Rings* but, in the meantime, he would then be involved in our next project, as investor.'

It was an astute move and one that both companies embraced relatively quickly, on the basis that Universal would take the domestic earnings on *King Kong* and give Miramax the foreign receipts, while Miramax would take the home American box-office receipts on *The Lord of the Rings* and give foreign takings to Universal. There was one catch: whilst Harvey Weinstein was 'thrilled with the idea that he could be involved in Kong', he was quick to point out that, when *The Lord of the Rings* went ahead, Universal would be getting two films for his one! Harvey needed another movie for Miramax in order to clinch the deal.

Harvey Weinstein knew exactly which movie he wanted. In 1993, Universal Pictures were about to start filming a picture called *Shakespeare in Love*. They had bought Marc Norman's original script in 1991 and, two years later, were ready to make the film as a vehicle for Julia Roberts. Following on from her Oscar/BAFTA nominated performance in *Pretty Woman*, Roberts was to play the Elizabethan girl whose fling with the young Will Shakespeare releases him from a nasty case of writer's block and results in the Bard completing his greatest love story, *Romeo and Juliet*.

The film was to be directed by Ed Zwick, whose films included *Glory*, the American Civil war movie which had so impressed Peter Jackson a few years earlier, and who would later direct such hits as *Legends of the Fall*, *Courage Under Fire* and *The Last Samurai*. The sets had been built at Pinewood Studios in England (at a cost of US$4 million) and the crew were lined up but then *Shakespeare in Love* ran into problems: Julia Roberts' first choice for co-star, Daniel Day-Lewis, turned down the role. Then Ralph Fiennes, Colin Firth and Rufus Sewell were all rejected by Roberts who, finally, pulled out of the film altogether. The sets were dismantled, the crew disbanded and *Shakespeare in Love* descended into what is known in Hollywood as 'Production Hell'.

In 1995, Harvey Weinstein bought *Shakespeare in Love* as part of the Universal-Miramax deal on *King Kong* and *The Lord of the Rings*. Three years later, partially re-written by Tom Stoppard, directed by John Madden and starring Gwyneth Paltrow and Joseph Fiennes, *Shakespeare in Love* scooped seven Oscars including Best Actress and Best Screenplay.

Which is how Peter Jackson arrived home in Wellington in April 1996 ready to start work on *King Kong*; how *Shakespeare in Love* was rescued from Hell and sent to Oscar Heaven; and how things *really* work in Hollywood.

7

QUEST FOR THE RING

'*Drumming upon his chest, Kong began to run at a spraddling speed which ate up the intervening distance... The first bomb landed squarely on his line of advance. As it broke a thick vapour rose and enveloped the beast-god from head to foot...*'

Writing in the 1932 novelisation of the film *King Kong*, Delos W. Lovelace described the moment on Skull Island when film-maker Carl Denham uses gas-bombs to capture the great ape:

'*Kong... struggled blindly on... Both hands rose towards Ann, now almost within arm's reach. Unable to lift his heavy feet Kong groped, swung in a wide circle and crashed to the sand. Prone, his body still made a figure of incredible bulk in the moonlight...*

'*Denham squared his shoulders, cocksure and buoyant... "We've got the biggest capture in the world! There's a million in it!... Listen! A few months from now it will be up in lights on Broadway. The spectacle nobody will miss. King Kong! The Eighth Wonder!"*'

As it happened, however, it was going to take a lot longer than anyone could have imagined for Peter Jackson to put the name of 'Kong' up in lights...

The deal with Universal was finalised and Peter and Fran started work on the script, which on many plot points and character details departed significantly from the Lovelace novel and the original film.

The action opens in the skies above occupied France in 1917 with a dogfight between a handful of British Sopwith Camel fighter planes and twenty-four 'gaudily painted' Fokker tri-planes of Von

Richtoffen's Flying Circus. This opening was clearly inspired by Peter's lifelong fascination with the early days of air power.

Jack Driscoll (first mate on the *Venture* in the 1933 movie) is now a daredevil WWI flying ace, passing the time between spats with the Germans by playing mid-air baseball with his best friend 'Matt Hamon', named no doubt for Ken Hammon, Peter's school friend who shared his passion for *Kong* and such war movies as *The Blue Max*. The dogfight would be mirrored at the end of the film when Jack once again takes to the cockpit of a Sopwith Camel in an attempt to ward off the naval planes attacking Kong atop the Empire State Building.

In the post-war Thirties, Jack is running a lumber business in Sumatra where he meets Ann Darrow, no longer the waif from the streets of depression-wracked New York. In this version, Ann is the daughter of Lord Darrow, a British Museum archaeologist who stumbles across clues suggesting that the pagan mythology of the beast-god, Kong, might have a basis in fact – a discovery which catches the interest of the unscrupulous showman, explorer and film-maker, Carl Denham.

> This 1996 *Kong* script was written very much as our idea of what a 'Hollywood' movie needed to be. Reading it again, several years later, was very informative. The action scenes were still entertaining enough, but we hadn't yet learned several valuable lessons from *The Lord of the Rings* – lessons about the value of emotional truth and depth in our characters.

It was a testing time: Peter and Fran were under enormous financial pressure and driving themselves hard on *Kong*. During this period, Fran gave birth to their second child, Katie, and was still working on the *King Kong* script whilst in hospital. As Peter and Fran progressed the script, Weta started work on designing the special effects for the film: sculpting maquettes for the dinosaurs – including an impressive realisation of one of the action set-pieces in which Kong battles with three carnivorous Alosaurs (later to become three Tyrannosaurs), which was an homage to the prehistoric visions of Willis O'Brien and Ray Harryhausen and an indication of the dynamism that was clearly going to be a feature of the new Jackson interpretation of Kong's story. These maquettes were a prelude to the next stage of the film's development, which involved creating digital dinosaurs and a CG Kong.

Three months passed and the date for the American opening of *The Frighteners* approached. Describing the film, Robert Zemeckis wrote, '*The Frighteners* doesn't fall into a particular genre – it's a mixture of mystery, horror, comedy and suspense. The movie explores the folklore and mythology about psychics, ghosts and the afterlife, and is quite unlike anything ever seen before.'

The fact that the film was not easily categorised was actually to prove something of a difficulty, as was the fact that, whilst it had been expected to get a PG-13 certification, it was eventually rated R, restricting the audience to moviegoers over the age of 17 unless accompanied by an adult.

Something which might have worked to the film's advantage had it opened, as originally intended, on the last day of October, now proved a disadvantage:

> It was planned as a relatively low-budget, $26million Halloween movie. There were no great expectations of it; it simply had to go out there and do its thing at the time of the year when people were expecting to see horror films or thrillers.

As it was, the sometime-Halloween movie had become a mid-summer movie.

> Bob Zemeckis had been very enthusiastic about the idea because he had previously released summer films to great success. He said, 'There's a *risk*, but the rewards will be great if the film really, *really* hits a nerve; and, in summer, you're gonna have much bigger box office than you'd ever get at Halloween.' So Fran and I were sort of swept along with this and didn't really feel that we had the power to say that we thought it was a bad idea.

To make matters worse, the advertising campaign didn't seem to help 'place' the film or target the audience. A suitably teasing teaser poster

– a white sheet with what appeared to be a menacing skull face pushing against it from behind with the tag-line, 'Dead Yet?' – unimaginatively became the film's eventual release poster.

> The poster did nothing to sell the film when it went on release, because it didn't tell you anything *about* the picture. It felt as if Universal was only giving half-hearted support to the movie as they'd already gotten cold feet about the whole idea of opening it in summer; as if they themselves had realised it was a bad idea, but had locked into the date and couldn't really change it. And so things started to feel a bit wrong…

Just *how* wrong they were soon became clear. It was bad enough that it was to follow in the wake of the phenomenally successful opening of *Independence Day*, which crashed onto the movie screens in the week of the 4 July Independence Day holiday; what was infinitely worse, and what sounded the knell of doom for *The Frighteners*, was the fact that its opening day, 19 July 1996, was seriously upstaged by another opening – that of the twenty-sixth Olympic Games in Atlanta, Georgia.

> When we realised that our opening day was that of the opening ceremony of the Atlanta Games – and it wasn't something we were told by the studio, we discovered it for ourselves – we had suggested to Universal that it was going to have an impact on box office and that everyone was likely to be stuck to their TV watching the opening and then the games themselves. But the people at the studio had said, 'No! We don't think so; our research would indicate that's not the case…' And I just thought, *How the hell do they know?* There had only ever been three Olympic Games held in the United States in one hundred years! So where did their research come from?

Reviews proved to be mixed, with the *Hollywood Reporter* declaring it 'whiz-bang moviemaking' while the *New York Times* described it as 'a technically impressive horror-comedy-romance in desperate need of a story editor or a cold shower.' It was for Peter another valuable lesson in the ways of Hollywood.

The Frighteners went out with only a half-hearted effort from Universal and got off to a really bad start when movie-going that weekend dropped some 30 or 40 per cent across the board, because of the Olympic Games.

But I guess it taught Fran and me a real lesson about marketing films and the critical importance of release dates, posters and campaigns. It also showed us how, strategically, a film can essentially be buried, which is what we ultimately felt happened to *The Frighteners*. It was dumped on the wrong day in the middle of summer because they thought it was much more of a comedy – another *Ghostbusters* – than what it turned out to be. It was never going to make a huge amount of money because it was genre and it was quite dark and twisted. At Halloween it might have been a different story...

Reflecting on this learning process, Ken Kamins observes, 'Every time Peter would have a negative experience, he'd try to figure out how, on the next movie, he could work towards a situation where he and Fran either had actual contractual rights to be consulted or established a relationship with the studio where they would *want* them to be a part of the process. Peter's secret is that, whether or not he contractually has any rights of control or approval, he always functions "as if" on the basis that, "If I act that way then, perhaps, they will treat me that way!"'

Despite the disappointment over the critical reception and financial performance of *The Frighteners*, work continued on *King Kong*: Peter and Fran delivered a second-draft script, sets were being designed, location scouting was taking place in Sumatra and Weta were beginning the complex task of building a CGI version of New York, circa 1933.

Meanwhile, at Universal, people were getting worried...

During 1996, Universal had been working towards the completion of their volcanic disaster movie, *Dante's Peak*, only to find themselves in a race with Twentieth Century Fox's more directly named *Volcano*. There are no rules in Hollywood when two similarly themed pictures go head-to-head, but it is usually thought best to try to beat the opposition and be first to the tape – before audiences decide that two movies with one plot is too much of a good (or bad) thing. Faced with just this situation, and despite being up to their budget-limits in molten lava, Universal decided to up the ante and pour sufficient money into *Dante's Peak* in order to make sure it reached the cinemas first and that if any film were left a smoking crater it would be *Volcano*.

Universal won that race with *Dante's Peak* erupting in February 1997, two months ahead of Twentieth Century Fox's rival attraction. Then, a year later, it became clear that another battle was on its way with, in addition to *Kong*, two other marauding monster movies destined to arrive in 1998. One was Columbia–TriStar's *Godzilla*, the latest incarnation of the dinosaur-like creature that had rampaged through countless Japanese and American B-movies from the Fifties onwards; the other was RKO–Disney's *Mighty Joe Young*, a remake of the third *King Kong*-style movie to come from the Merian C. Cooper–Ernest B. Schoedsack partnership in 1949, and on which *Kong*'s stop-frame animator Willis O'Brien collaborated with, among others, the young Ray Harryhausen.

With both films racing towards a summer release in 1998, Universal were in the unenviable position of having a third monster movie on their hands that wouldn't be ready to open until several months after *Godzilla* and *Mighty Joe Young* had done their worst.

> In the first few weeks of 1997, as Universal seemed to be getting increasingly nervous about the other two creature pictures, it began to feel as if the heart of this film was fading away. Fran and I were trying to figure out some way to do *Kong* quicker or to alleviate their fears, but there was no doubting the fact that the subject matter of these three movies was very similar and, therefore, nothing we could really say.

Then Universal took a dramatic decision on the future of *Kong*. The final page of Peter and Fran's first-draft script had read:

> *For one last precious second ANN HUGS KONG'S HAND... he slowly topples back... disappearing off the side of the building.*
> *ANN SOBS with GRIEF... JACK gently takes her in his arms... she buries her face in his chest.*
> *EXT. FIFTH AVENUE – MORNING*
> *CROWDS are gathering to STARE at KONG'S BODY... we only see his HAND on the edge of frame.*

A POLICEMAN ushers people away…
POLICEMAN
Come on folks… it's all over…

Kong had plummeted to his death from the top of the Empire State Building and the latest movie to bear his name had, in the parlance of Hollywood, 'fallen over'.

> We knew things were going wrong: they weren't telling us anything yet, but we were starting to feel it. No one ever sat down and said, 'Listen, you know, we don't think that going ahead with *Kong* at this time is the best idea for us.' It didn't happen that easily, or that directly.

Universal were making monthly 'drawdown' payments to WingNut in order that they could buy materials and pay the salaries of the staff already working on the film. In early February there was a seemingly inexplicable delay on the payment from Universal. It was a critical situation: without the drawdown there was no money with which to pay anyone.

It was at this moment that Peter was required to head off for a European press junket to launch *The Frighteners* on a whistle-stop tour of London, Paris, Rome and Berlin.

> I was boarding the plane for London while the office was calling the accounting department and asking, 'Why isn't the money here? We have to have it. We've got people to pay…' There was no real response, no answers. That is the way such things happen.

'Rarely is there a perfect movie-making experience,' explains Peter Nelson. 'Rarely, even at the highest levels in the film business, do all the pieces – the financing and all the creative decisions – fall neatly into place on a movie. There is never really a moment when everybody can say with certainty: "This movie's going to go forward without a doubt." There is always *some* doubt that has to be overcome.' Nevertheless, it was a bitter lesson to learn.

Just twenty-seven hours later Peter was in London. Calls from Ken Kamins were scarcely reassuring. Lenny Kornburg, who had been the person to first approach Peter about *King Kong* and who had continued to champion the project, had been having meetings with Universal's president of production, Casey Silver. Kornburg was telling Ken Kamins, 'I think *Kong* is starting to haemorrhage!'

> I'm in a hotel in London late at night, on the day I arrived, and I'm talking with Casey Silver himself. Everything seemed to be double-speak. He didn't come out and say, 'We just don't think that we want to make *Kong* anymore...' or 'The time's not right for *Kong*...' or whatever. It was more a case of, 'Well, you know, what we really want to do is just pause for a moment, in the development of the film... We think perhaps you should do some more work on the screenplay... That would be good, and then we'll take a breath and we'll wait till the script has gone to another draft and then maybe we can start picking it up again...' But, of course, it was impossible because without any money we were going to lose everybody who was working on the film.

It was clear to Ken Kamins that Casey Silver had finally pulled the plug and he told Peter that *Kong* was dead. Peter was sitting in a London hotel about to start promoting his previous movie for Universal Pictures, which was becoming an increasingly unacceptable scenario. Ringing the WingNut offices in Wellington, Peter asked them to get him on the first plane back to New Zealand.

> I couldn't sleep, so while I was waiting to hear about the flight home, I made more calls: I rang Ken and asked him to telephone Casey Silver – I lost all respect for him by this time because I didn't think he'd been straight with us and I just couldn't bring myself to speak to him in person. I just said, 'Tell Casey I'm pulling out of the junket, I'm not going to go around Europe talking about *The Frighteners*; he'll have to understand. I've now got people that aren't going to be employed beyond the next few days and I've got to go home and try and sort out this mess that Universal have created for us.'

'Peter was devastated,' recalls Ken Kamins, 'not just for himself but for all those people who were waiting for him in New Zealand who were excited and passionate about working on *King Kong* and who were now going to be crushed. So he turned right around and went home. It was, "Oh, my God! What do we do now?"'

At eight o'clock in the morning, the day after hearing the news about *Kong*, Peter boarded a plane for New Zealand.

> I'd flown twenty-seven hours to London, straight through, in order to promote *The Frighteners*, had ended up not doing a single bit of publicity for the film, lost my next movie and, less than twenty-four hours later, was flying home again – all without having had a wink of sleep. I had a copy of *The Lord of the Rings* with me and I remember thinking I needed to take my mind off the problems we were facing and that this book might now be our only hope, so I curled up on the plane home, opened the book and started reading Tolkien's prologue, 'Concerning Hobbits'. But I'd been awake for hours and hours on end and was so totally exhausted that I only got through three or four pages before I fell fast asleep.

Meanwhile, Richard Taylor had received a tearful telephone call from Fran passing on the news, which he then broke to the crew working on *Kong*: 'We gathered the whole crew together in the area that is now our sculpting room, outside the lunch room, and we told them that the project was off. There were some tears and pretty sad people...'

Personal disappointments aside, the situation for Weta was extremely serious: 'This was a desperate state of affairs,' says Richard. 'Universal had insisted that Weta Digital engage a large number of the people on a two-year contract and now they were dropping the film. We were in the unenviable position of having all of these contracts that we had to pay out. And Weta was still a fledgling company with a very small infrastructure financially, so we were left in a real quandary.'

Over the past couple of years, Weta had kept themselves going by doing occasional work outside or between whatever films Peter was making: they had provided prosthetic make-up for the acclaimed New Zealand film, *Once Were Warriors*, as well as making props and make-up effects for various television shows and series including Stephen King's *The Tommyknockers*, *Hercules and the Lost Kingdom* and *Xena: Warrior Princess*. But the commitment to *King Kong* had prevented them from taking on any other major projects, and with that, work suddenly gone, there were now clearly going to be tough days ahead.

> I got off the plane in Wellington and went straight to Weta, and met everyone involved with *Kong*. It felt like a repeat of that lunchtime meeting when everybody had been told that *Braindead* had collapsed. Now, of course, there was no Jim Booth around, so it was down to me to explain that they were no longer going to be working on *Kong*; that we all had hopes that one day it would come back but, as of now, it wasn't going to happen. I will never forget the tears that welled up in the eyes of sculptors and designers who had given everything to the project.

'As sad as it was that *Kong* fell over,' reflects Richard Taylor, 'as with the collapse of *Braindead,* it turned out, with hindsight, to be fortuitous for Peter's career and for all our careers.'

It was now time to make a telephone call to the one other person who was a player in the game: Harvey Weinstein. Miramax had a mutual investment contract with Universal as well as a back-up deal with Peter Jackson.

'It's never a bad idea in Hollywood to make a back-up deal,' explains Peter Nelson, 'because, despite the best of intentions, movies often don't get made. We had set up a deal with Universal in order to energise the *Kong* project but since Universal had the right to say "Yea" or "Nay", we also did something that, in the test of time, served Peter well: we made a back-up deal with Miramax. Shortly after Universal had said, "Okay" to the *Kong* deal we went back to Miramax and said, "Too bad, you guys just missed out! Sorry you didn't get a chance to make Peter's next movie… We're now looking for one of the studios with which to make a back-up deal." Miramax instantly said "No, it should be us, we'll make a back-up deal with you for *The Lord of the Rings*."

'So we made a back-up deal and suddenly Peter was in the dream situation of having lined up his next two projects and would segue from one to another. And if, for any reason, Universal failed to make *King Kong* on the schedule that we'd set up, then Peter would automatically move on to making *The Lord of the Rings* for Miramax on the same kind of schedule. *Boom!* There would be "R & D" funding. *Boom!* He'd get script go-ahead and start working on it.'

'To Harvey's eternal credit,' says Ken Kamins, 'he didn't miss a beat: he saw this as the moment to jump right back in and say, "You see, I always believed in you! If I'd had *The Frighteners* I would have made $50million more at the box office, these guys didn't know what they were doing! It's a well-directed movie; it's all there, it's a little bit of this, little bit of that, but I would have helped you fix it and it would have been amazing! Now let's forget all the other nonsense and go forward with *The Lord of the Rings*." As for the Miramax agreement with Universal, the understanding was that if one side moved forward and the other didn't then the deal was null and void; so, with no *King Kong*, Harvey was off the hook with having to give half of any *Rings* earnings to Universal – *and* he'd still managed to get *Shakespeare in Love*!'

> Harvey was angry, because even though Miramax was a 50/50 investor in *King Kong*, at the point when I told him that Universal had canned *Kong*, he hadn't been consulted, hadn't heard the news, knew nothing about it. So he got very angry indeed and it's always good when Harvey gets angry, because you know he's motivated! He was immediately supportive, said he'd wrap up the rights issues with Saul Zaentz as soon as possible – the lawyers were still trying to sort all that out – and then we'd start work on *The Lord of the Rings*.

It took the lawyers another four to six weeks to get the legal situation sorted out, which for Weta was a difficult period. Richard Taylor got the workshop various prop-making jobs on *Hercules* and *Xena*: what Richard describes as 'small amounts of work for very small profit – if, at times, any profit at all.'

They took on making special make-up effects for *The Ugly*, a New Zealand film about a serial killer with an underlying plot-analogy to Hans Andersen's 'The Ugly Duckling', which kept people busy but was of little help financially since the budget for the film was small and Weta elected to do it as a non-profit job.

It was a stressful time: 'We were building *Hercules* props in the workshop; I'd be flying up to Auckland filming *Hercules* on set during the day and then filming *The Ugly* at night time. One day, I came off set at seven o'clock in the morning, flew to the States, went straight into a meeting at one o'clock that afternoon, secured quite a major job for the workshop working on miniatures for a TV drama called *Tidal Wave: No Escape*, went out to dinner with them that night, got back to my hotel room at two in the morning, got back on the plane four hours later, flew back to New Zealand, went back on to the *Hercules* set, filmed for the day, did a night shoot on *The Ugly* and then flew back down to Wellington to get started on *Tidal Wave*! It was only because of these projects that we managed to pull ourselves out of a very sticky situation.'

There was still a problem with keeping Weta's digital artists busy and it was Peter's relationship with Zemeckis which saved the day; the producer of *The Frighteners* engaged Weta to create some of the special effects for *Contact*, a film he was making at Warner Brothers starring Jodi Foster, 'It was,' says Richard, 'the project that saved our bacon.'

While waiting for the legal issues between Saul Zaentz and Miramax to be resolved, Peter and Fran asked Costa Botes to assist them by preparing a synopsis of *The Lord of the Rings*, a scene-by-scene breakdown detailing what happens when and where and to whom.

Obviously we also read the books again – but only when the project firmed up. When we first came up with the idea of doing *The Lord of the Rings*, I decided not to re-read the book because I thought to do so might jinx the project and make the film not happen! Even when we were on the cusp of making it, I *still* didn't re-read it! I knew it would be an omen of bad luck: that at the very moment I started thinking about it as a movie, I'd get a phone call saying, 'Sorry, Saul's decided he doesn't want to do it!'

I *did* re-read *The Hobbit* because we had originally thought we would be adapting that book first; but, apart from the couple of pages of the prologue which I read on the plane coming home from London, I really hadn't looked at *The Lord of the Rings* since I was a teenager. Most of my thinking about the film, therefore, was based on memories of reading it and of hearing audiotapes of the BBC's radio dramatisation made in the early Eighties that I'd listened to while I was building models in my workshop. Now, however, it was a case of getting to grips with this huge story, not as a reader but in order to adapt it as a film. So now, for the very first time since I was 18 years old, I opened the book and started reading...

Chapter 1, A Long-expected Party: When Mr. Bilbo Baggins of Bag End announced that he would shortly be celebrating his eleventy-first birthday with a party of special magnificence, there was much talk and excitement in Hobbiton...

That reading of *The Lord of the Rings* would be the first of many over the next few years and a growing, deepening relationship with Tolkien's storytelling. 'It was rather a protracted period,' says Fran, 'getting to know the true nature of the book and the job. It wasn't something you could just dive into: it was more of a slow and ongoing education.'

What makes reading *The Lord of the Rings* an incredibly interesting experience is that every time you read it, you discover new things in it. You read the book once and you think, 'Okay, so that's *The Lord of the Rings*, and then, when you are going to look at doing a scene breakdown, a treatment or a draft of the script and you read specific sections again you suddenly notice details you have missed or find yourself reading episodes as though you've never read them before.

You have to get through to the end of the book once, before things that you read at the very beginning make any sense at all. It's only then that you can start on what is really a huge exercise of 'connecting the dots', making links. It can take several reads of the book before you have fully acquired the understanding needed to put all the pieces together. The book is the story of a journey; reading it – and re-reading it – is also a journey...

'To begin with, we planned one long, epic film,' recalls Fran, 'but by the time we had got to the end, it was clear that we were talking about two films.'

The work had begun with Costa Botes' précis/breakdown of the book; this was loaded into Peter and Fran's computer so that they could start a process of 'cutting and pasting', developing and fleshing out ideas.

> We knew that we were going to represent the fundamental story – 'Hobbit goes on a journey to destroy the ring!' – in broad strokes but with reasonable accuracy: Hobbiton, Bree, Rivendell, Moria, Lothlórien, Isengard, Rohan, Gondor and Mordor are all going to be there.
>
> Once you start going to the next level of detail, below the main story points, that's when you run up against the hard decisions: which is basically a case of, 'We can't include everything, so what's our strategy? What do we want to focus on?' You think beyond what your favourite bits are and you look at it in terms of a greater strategy, which in our case was really keeping a relationship between Frodo and the Ring, keeping the events totally focussed on the forward movement of the journey. This really explains, to some degree, why Tom Bombadil, Old Man Willow and the Barrow-wights aren't there, because once Frodo left Hobbiton in the movie we wanted everything at that point to advance his journey to Rivendell and ultimately to Mordor.
>
> Every step of the way, in the movie, Frodo is encountering complications and obstacles but nonetheless it's always a forward movement; it's a story about a hobbit with a ring and the need to destroy it and, obviously, Bombadil and Old Man Willow are not really about that. Others may criticise the decisions we made, but for us they were relatively easy to make once we had identified what was to be the spine of the story in the film.

When it was eventually announced that a film of *The Lord of the Rings* was to be made, there was much speculation among fans of the book about whether Tom Bombadil and the events in the Old Forest and on the Barrow-downs were to feature in the screenplay: almost as if the inclusion or exclusion of this detour were a litmus test for the authenticity of the entire project.

> People were asking, 'Is the film going to be accurate? Is it going to be faithful? *Is Tom Bombadil going to be in it?*' But once the film was released all that debate and argument went away: nobody suggested that

it was a really bad idea to leave Bombadil out because once they've seen the film they get it, they understand why we did what we did.

In 1997, such issues were still a long way off. After two or three months of intensive work, Peter and Fran had completed drafting a treatment for the two films. The resulting ninety-two-page document, containing 266 sequences, was given (and retained throughout production) a code name – the same code name that had once been used to disguise the proposal for *Bad Taste 2* and *3* and, long before that, to mask Merian C. Cooper and Ernest B. Schoedsack's *Son of Kong – Jamboree.*

The front page of the treatment was decorated with the scout's fleur-de-lis emblem and the not inappropriate motto, 'BE PREPARED', as well as an innocuous but entirely misleading description of what was to follow: 'An affectionate coming-of-age drama set in the New Zealand Boy Scout Movement during the "years of turmoil"… 1958–63'. The writers (no prizes for guessing their true identities) were credited as being 'Fredricka Wharburton & Percy J. Judkins'!

The treatment opened with an explanatory preamble addressed to 'Dear Reader':

> *This is not a film script, but merely a treatment… a first pass at distilling Mr Tolkien's vast narrative down into a form suitable for the movies.*
>
> *Our focus has been in making whatever modifications or deletions we feel are required to tell this complex and epic story in the clearest possible way.*
>
> *We have tried to make it work for an audience who have not – and never will – read the books… but at the same time, we have tried to write something that will be satisfying for those fans of the books who cannot wait to see the movie.*

Within just the first six pages, the reader is whisked across the landscape of Middle-earth, whirled through several thousand years of history and introduced to enough characters to set the mind reeling: Sauron, Gil-galad, Elrond, Elendil, Isildur, Déagol, Sméagol (Gollum), Bilbo, Frodo, Merry, Pippin, Sam and Gandalf.

Small wonder the introduction added the caution: 'You're about to plough your way through something that is, by its nature, very dense and plot-heavy – and in that sense it does not contain the subtleties we intend to build into the finished scripts.'

The introduction concluded on a note of nervous optimism: *We hope you enjoy it…*

The opening scenes already bore the stylistic hallmarks with which the final version would be stamped:

> 'We suddenly take in a BREATHTAKING VISTA of BATTLE… mighty armies of MEN and ELVES battle SAURON'S army of ORCS – loathsome ape-like humanoids… With nearly 150,000 soldiers on screen this is probably the single most spectacular shot ever committed to film… a seething mass of SWORD and SPEAR.'

The major editorial decisions had already been taken:

> When you're making any movie, there is a real sense that too much information can be very damaging in that if you confuse the audience and they say, 'I don't quite get it,' then you've lost them and everything after that will also be confusing.
>
> It's terribly easy to lose an audience, particularly at the beginning of a film – more so in fact than at the middle or the end – because people are adjusting to the experience of seeing the film, they've just come in from the street, they've been busy all day and they decide to go to the movies; to then bombard them with a lot of names of people and places they've never heard of before is pretty risky… We were really worried that if we alienated people in the first five minutes of *The Lord of the Rings* we'd lose them for the entire film.

Many entire sequences detailed in the first treatment would survive unchanged into the final shooting script of *The Lord of the Rings*, showing that, from the beginning, Peter and Fran had grasped the story's essential elements and dramatic arc.

The differences – either from the original book or the completed film or both – are, of course, intriguing. Several additions and embellishments were already securely in place, such as the revisionist version of Denethor's demise:

'Trailing a long cloak of angry flame... DENETHOR runs across the top
of the CLIFF above MINAS TIRITH and casts himself off... he falls – a
squirming FIREBALL – 700 feet into city below.'

Quite a number of changes were still to be made: in this version, for
example, Farmer Maggot is still a key character, Bilbo attends the
Council of Elrond, Sam looks in the Mirror of Galadriel, Glorfindel
has yet to be supplanted by Arwen and there are no Elves at the battle
of Helm's Deep.

Other events were elided and several minor characters (in addition
to Tom Bombadil) were eliminated, although such is the complexity
and entirety of Tolkien's creation that even seemingly incidental
occurrences have great significance. In the book, for example, Gandalf's
ill-fated encounter with Saruman the White is told in flashback at the
Council of Elrond and part of that story concerns a meeting between
Gandalf the Grey and fellow wizard Radagast the Brown, who is
especially wise in the ways of the birds and beasts of Middle-earth.

Radagast carries a message from Saruman to Gandalf, revealing
that Sauron's emissaries are seeking for the Shire and that, if Gandalf
needs his aid, he should consult with him at Orthanc. Radagast is
unaware that Saruman is using him to set a trap for Gandalf, and that
finally proves the undoing of Saruman's plot. Before riding off to
Isengard, Gandalf asks Radagast to request the help of all friendly
creatures and to tell them that if they have any news relating to the
Enemy, they should take it to Gandalf and Saruman at Orthanc. As a
result, Gwaihir the Eagle flies to Isengard – only to discover Gandalf
imprisoned on the top of the tower.

Obviously this was another complication in an already involved plot
and, quite early on, we made the decision that Radagast wouldn't be in
the movie. We simplified the storyline by having Gandalf ride to consult
with Saruman on his own initiative, but that, in turn, presented us with
a real problem: we had Gandalf stuck at the top of the tower with no
one else knowing that he had gone to Isengard and absolutely no reason
for Gwaihir the eagle to go looking for him there. Since Radagast had
an ability to communicate with birds and animals, we transferred that
skill to Gandalf who, in our version, uses the moth to take the news of

his imprisonment to Gwaihir and bring the eagle to his rescue.

This moth also helped with the justification for a camera move that I wanted to include. Sometimes shots pop into your head and once they are there, they never go away. This was one of them.

I wanted to have the camera crane up and over the walls around Isengard – revealing the shocking image of the gardens stripped of their trees and transformed into a mass of mines and workings – before travelling on up to the very top of the tower and the imprisoned Gandalf.

The beginning of this particular shot was straightforward: craning up over the wall to reveal the desolation of Isengard; but I felt that we needed a reason to continue on up the tower. I always prefer there to be a motivation for a camera move – something to draw you in – rather than it just going from A to B simply for the sake of having a move.

Which is when we had the idea of having a moth fly into shot and to then follow it all the way up to the summit of the tower where it would eventually be caught by Gandalf.

I honestly can't quite remember which came first, the move or the moth, but out of those two ideas came the mechanism for what I think is one of the more dramatic shots in *Fellowship*.

As outlined in the treatment, the first film ended following the death of Saruman and Pippin's moment of looking into the palantír, with the Fellowship dividing once again: Gandalf and Pippin riding to Minas Tirith, Merry returning to Edoras with Théoden and Aragorn, Gimli and Legolas being delegated to ride south to gather news of Sauron's allies. The second film opened with Frodo, Sam and Gollum arriving at the Black Gates and ended on the shores of the Sundering Sea with the Elven ship sailing off into the sunset for the Undying Lands. Not until the script stage would Sam's return to Hobbiton and Tolkien's closing line, 'Well, I'm back,' become the film's final coda.

Several intriguing developments are unique to this version of the story, such as the arrival of Nazgûl in the chamber of Sammath Naur just before Gollum plunges with the Ring into the Crack of Doom, and an interesting incident following Gwaihir's rescue of Gandalf from Orthanc. The eagle carries the wizard to Edoras – alighting in the marketplace, knocking over stalls with his wide wingspan – and

Gandalf unsuccessfully attempts to reason with Théoden who is in Saruman's thrall. Wormtongue orders Gandalf's imprisonment but Éomer and Éowyn sneak Gandalf into the royal stables where he finds Shadowfax, the 'untameable' horse which no man has ever ridden, jumps on his back and gallops out of the city...

As described by Tolkien, Elrond's sons, Elladan and Elrohir, join Aragorn, Legolas and Gimli on their journey through the Paths of the Dead; so too does Erkenbrand of Rohan (as is *not* described by Tolkien), where that noble warrior meets an ignoble death falling victim to the 'spectral axe' of one of the dead. The feverish scenes beyond the portals of the Dark Door are clearly the work of the zombie-meister of *Braindead*:

> *The WALLS of the tunnel suddenly start to undulate as a FLESHY TUMOUR-LIKE texture spreads across them... Beneath their feet the tunnel floor heaves and breathes like diseased lungs!... A creepy GROUND-FOG spills down the walls and starts filling up the cavern... Suddenly GHOSTLY GHOULISH HANDS rise out of the fog and start... grabbing at clothes and equipment... ARAGORN, ELLADAN, ELROHIR, LEGOLAS and GIMLI suddenly find themselves lifted up out of the fog, held up by pyramids of groping, scrambling GHOULS! A SOLITARY FIGURE standing high on the rocky outcrop above the SQUIRMING SEA OF THE UNDEAD... their leader! He looks out through EYELESS SOCKETS, opens his decomposing jaw and utters one word... 'DIE!'*

Other intriguing developments in this proposal include a dramatically defined love-triangle:

> *ARAGORN and ÉOWYN are asleep in each other's arms. LOUD KNOCKING awakes them... ARAGORN opens the door, pulling his robes around him. He awkwardly faces ARWEN who flings her arms around his shoulders... ÉOWYN watches from the window...*

And, for Saruman, repentance and final absolution in death:

> *The expression on SARUMAN'S FACE transforms from hateful vengeance into one of CONFUSION and REGRET... GANDALF kneels down beside*

his mortally injured mentor. He forgives him, saying SAURON has used the PALANTÍR to poison his mind. With his last breath, SARUMAN warns them that SAURON is amassing a HUGE ARMY in MORDOR. He intends to march on the GONDORIAN CITY of MINAS TIRITH within two weeks. He means to continue his rampage and take Middle-earth...

By the time *The Fellowship of the Ring* was being filmed, there was no question of Gollum being seen other than for a fleeting moment in the Mines of Moria, but the original treatment contained an early, threatening encounter between Gollum and Frodo:

A LOG quietly floats down the river towards the CAMP... a SLIMY HAND appears over the log... followed by a pair of SHINING EYES... GOLLUM! GOLLUM sneaks towards the sleeping group, muttering softly to himself. He spots the RING glinting from beneath FRODO'S SHIRT! GOLLUM is beside himself with lust. He flexes his fingers and slowly wraps them around FRODO'S throat. GOLLUM suddenly tightens his grip, silently choking FRODO! FRODO'S eyes open and he looks helplessly into GOLLUM'S hateful face! Around him, the others sleep on...

GOLLUM glances up at a noise... ARAGORN is running towards him from out of the woods! GOLLUM snarls and releases his grip, snatching at THE RING...

He manages to rip THE RING away from FRODO'S neck as ARAGORN'S boot kicks him. GOLLUM flies towards the water, THE RING spilling into the mud. He reaches towards it... an arrow suddenly pins his hand to the ground! LEGOLAS has leapt to his feet, brandishing his bow!

GOLLUM screams and rips his hand away from the arrow, disappearing into the water!

THE RING slowly sinking into the mud... a hand picks it up. BOROMIR stands clutching the RING. He seems to grow in stature, as if absorbing its power. FRODO looks at BOROMIR warily... ARAGORN orders him to hand the RING back to FRODO. For a moment BOROMIR is motionless, then he quietly drops the RING into FRODO'S outstretched palm.

FRODO rubs his sore throat as he watches BOROMIR quietly wander into the woods.

The purpose of changes made to the original story are either in line with that stated aim of making the plot understood by those who have never waded through Tolkien's thousand-page epic, or they are simply a Jacksonian attempt to rack up the action and offer eye-popping amazement that would ultimately compete with that early shot of the 150,000 warriors, 'the single most spectacular shot ever committed to film.'

The siege of Gondor was, from the outset, a sequence where the director – who, as a young man, had been fascinated by movies featuring wars ancient and modern – was going to revel in the opportunity of being let loose on one of the greatest battlefields of the imagination. Snatch any few lines from the three pages outlining the scenes at, on and around the battlements of Minas Tirith and the essence of the elaborate action set-piece in *The Return of the King* is clearly already sketched in Peter's mind:

> The GREAT ORC ARMY closes in on the city. GREAT SIEGE TOWERS and CATAPULTS are hauled across the PELENNOR FIELDS …
>
> Thousands of FLAMING TORCHES light the snarling, slathering ORCS. DRUMMERS are beating the DRUMS OF WAR. The winged shadows – the NAZGÛL swoop overhead …
>
> On the battlements of MINAS TIRITH the ARMY of GONDOR waits grimly.
>
> A TRUMPETER standing on the PARAPET turns and SOUNDS a MIGHTY BLAST – the signal that the ORCS are in RANGE!
>
> THWAT! 100 CATAPULTS send their great ROCKS high into the sir, over the BATTLEMENTS! Dizzying aerial CAMERA SHOTS of huge BOULDERS flying up close to CAMERA… then falling away towards the ORCS!
>
> CRUNCH!! BOULDERS flatten ORCS. THWAT!! 100 more… THWAT!! Another 100!! The ORC front ranks are in disarray!
>
> The ORC CAPTAIN orders his catapults to fire! THWAT! THWAT! THWAT! But these CATAPULTS do not fire rocks…
>
> HORROR sweeps through the streets of GONDOR as the SEVERED HEADS of the 100 HORSEMEN land amongst the SOLDIERS!

Having completed their ninety-two-page outline, Peter and Fran flew to New York for creative meetings with Miramax, which took place in a room nicknamed 'the sweatbox' after the small airless rooms where in the early days of film, movies got shown and discussed. In the middle of summer, with no windows and no air conditioning and the obvious tensions involved in presenting a treatment for an ambitious movie project, the room lived up to its name.

It was the first time that Peter and Fran had met Harvey Weinstein's brother and business partner, Bob, whom Peter describes as 'the canny number-cruncher'. Bob was the man responsible for running Dimension Films, Miramax's sister company and genre division responsible for such horror franchises as *Hellraiser, Children of the Corn* and *Scream*. Harvey explained that, since *The Lord of the Rings* was bigger than anything Miramax had previously produced, they had decided that it was to be the first ever Miramax–Dimension Films co-production. The meetings, which were intensive and ran across two or three days, also involved Jon Gordon, Miramax's production executive, and Cary Granat, then Dimension's head of production.

> The Weinsteins were highly amusing! Harvey and Bob are very close and there's a really strong bond between them, which I admire. But there's this theatrical game that they play, where they argue and shout at one another.
>
> When Bob expressed some opinion that Harvey didn't agree with, Harvey stormed out of the room and disappeared while Bob just kept on talking as if his brother was still in the room. Then, a few minutes later, we heard the stomp, stomp of footsteps and, through the frosted glass, saw this Alfred Hitchcock-style silhouette of Harvey, marching back down the corridor.
>
> He walked into the room holding the Oscar that he had won for *The English Patient*, which he's just been to collect from his office, and he slammed it down on the table in front of Bob and screamed, 'Who knows f****** more about scriptwriting, you or me?!' We sat there watching this going on and, at first, it was pretty unnerving; then, very quickly, we realised that it is a game; there's no real aggro in these exchanges; they're just playing and having fun.

It also became clear that whilst Harvey had read *The Lord of the Rings*, or at least had a detailed knowledge of the story and characters, Bob Weinstein had not…

Bob had never read the book and was sort of proud of the fact! So it was presented to us that, because he didn't know anything about *The Lord of the Rings*, Bob was going to be 'the logic policeman'! We had to deliver a treatment and a script that was totally understandable to Bob, because if Bob didn't understand it, then it had no hope in the big wide world!

Having no allegiance to Tolkien, Bob Weinstein also felt free to offer suggestions for improving the original plot.

> At one point Bob said, 'So there's these four hobbits, right? And, you know, they go on this adventure *and none of the hobbits die*?' Well, no, we explained, Frodo, Sam, Merry and Pippin all survive... 'Well, we can't have that,' he said, 'we've got to kill a hobbit! I don't care which one; you can pick – I'm not telling you who it should be: you pick out who you want to kill, but we've really got to kill one of those hobbits!'
>
> In situations like that, you just nod and smile and say, 'Well, that's something we can consider...' It's not a very useful tactic to sit there and say, 'I don't think killing off a hobbit's a very good idea...' because you'd then get into an hour-long debate about why you should or shouldn't kill a hobbit. It's better to disengage when the silly ideas happen and say, 'Well, we'll think about that...' and then you go away and hope it will get forgotten!

There were some entertaining highlights to the meetings that Peter still recalls with amusement and affection.

> Bob Weinstein had obviously read the treatment, or skipped through it, but I remember this moment as if a light bulb had gone on and there was almost a palpable moment of sudden understanding. Bob said, 'Wait! So the Elf is like a bowman, shooting arrows, yeah? And the Dwarf has got axes and he can throw axes? And Sam, he's got this magic rope, right? And Frodo's got this light-thing?' Then he got really excited and you could see there was this moment of utter revelation and he said, 'It's like that movie where they had the explosives expert, and the code expert and the marksman and they all had their own special skill... It's the f****** *Guns of Navarone*!'

The best thing to do in these meetings is try and keep a straight face and, occasionally, kick each other under the table, which Fran and I were prone to doing from time to time!

Creative meetings in Hollywood are essentially about survival:

Fran and I like to think we have fairly strong creative instincts and we certainly have strong creative opinions. We also have a certain independent spirit: we never have liked being given edicts or mandates or being told what to do.

You have to attend these creative meetings with studio people but you would really rather just be left alone to do the job. In our experience, we've worked with great studio people whose ideas you respect, but you also can find yourself in the room with… the word 'idiot' comes to mind. In these situations, somehow you've got to create the illusion that their notes and ideas have been incredibly helpful and that they've steered you in a direction that you otherwise wouldn't have gone. With a bit of luck, their ideas will be ones that you've already had yourself, so that you can credit them back to them afterwards and quite often the next time you meet they'll have forgotten most of what was actually talked about.

So, basically, you simply play a very political game: you have the meeting, come out, and go and write exactly the same screenplay you would have written anyway!

By the end of the meetings, apart from some ideas that were clearly never going to find their way into any script, Miramax had accepted that *The Lord of the Rings* was two films, not one: 'They blanched at the prospect,' says Fran, 'but they nodded…'

Peter's recollection is that, in view of the wealth of essential story material, there was a bid – albeit unsuccessful – to push the project to an even more ambitious scenario:

Once we had started to get into the book and were working on the treatment, we realised that *three* films would obviously be the more natural way to do it. We actually shaped our treatment into three parts at one point, but Harvey said, 'No! Let's just stick with two!'

Two movies or three, it is certain that, as far as Peter and Fran were concerned – and regardless of whatever anybody else might have thought or subsequently said – that it was *never* going to be *one* movie. Later events suggest that there may have been a prevailing wish that was never truly relinquished, that this epic tale could be despatched in a more straightforward fashion with a single picture. It was an argument that would return, although not for a while…

What was a known issue from the outset was the budget. The top figure for both movies was not to exceed $75million. At the time, the maximum budget spent on a Miramax picture was in the region of $40million. The $75million was a lot of money for the company to be committing to and, in all likelihood, was a cap imposed by Harvey and Bob Weinstein's masters at Disney.

> Harvey was very adamant from the beginning that going over $75million was never an option. At that point we had no script and no budget. All we had to go on was the fact that we had just made *The Frighteners* for $27million and that had involved a lot of computer effects. Looking at it like that, we thought $27million up to $75million was certainly going to pay for a lot more production value, a lot more effects, a lot bigger film, and so we had every reason to believe that we would be able to do it for that. With hindsight, of course, we were incredibly off the mark…

Back in Wellington, Peter and Fran began work on the screenplay in order to be in a position to draw up a budget for the films:

> We started work, flogging our way through it. Writing any screenplay is hard and this was particularly exhausting because we knew that as soon as we finished the first script, we'd have to start in on the second, because they were going to be shot back to back. It was quite a burden and we began to realise that we needed help and support.

Now living in Auckland, Stephen hadn't written any screenplays since *Braindead*, but was successfully furthering his career as a theatre playwright; he also understood film and the dynamic of working with Peter and Fran. Stephen agreed to go to Wellington for several weeks to collaborate on the scripts for *The Lord of the Rings*, bringing an individual contribution to the process.

> Stephen had read the book when he was young and he read it again before he had started working with us, but he was by no means 'immersed' in Tolkien and, as a result, was reasonably cavalier with it: he felt that ultimately you had to do what was best for the film, even if it meant dramatically changing things in the book. So, some of our arguments – and you *always* have arguments during the writing process – were revolving around things that Stephen wanted to do which would deviate quite a lot from the original, and we'd be saying, 'You can't really do that!' Which was always fine with Stephen and, for us, it was really useful because having someone like that as part of the writing team is actually no bad thing, because it challenges you on your prejudices and opens up a lot of ideas and possibilities that you might easily be locked off from.

Stephen was also instrumental in introducing someone to the project who would play a pivotal role in the progress of *The Lord of the Rings*. While living in Auckland, Stephen had formed a relationship with Philippa Boyens, who was an aspiring writer and a former director of the New Zealand Writer's Guild, an organisation founded in 1975 to encourage and represent the country's script and screenwriters.

Philippa also happened to be a huge fan of Tolkien's books and during visits back to Auckland, Stephen would show Philippa parts of the script, report on the various ideas and developments, and would pick up on Philippa's fan-based reactions, which he then passed on, in conversation, to Fran and Peter.

Although it later transpired that Fran and Philippa had met at some industry events, for the most part all Peter and Fran knew about Philippa Boyens was the various thoughts and comments she had made on the scripts, which Stephen had relayed. 'At one stage, they hit a brick wall with the love story and Stephen and I actually wrote some scenes together. Some time after that, they rang me and asked me to go down and meet them.'

Recalling the moment when she was handed the ninety-two-page treatment to read, Philippa says: 'I was frankly worried, because *The Lord of the Rings* really *is* one of my favourite books. However, as I read I got very excited, because they had shaped it into an amazing journey and a great movie-story. That treatment remains the backbone of the films and shows that, from the beginning, it was a whole piece: whether two episodes or three, it is – to some extent – one movie.' Then came the moment of truth.

> Philippa showed up at our house to chat with us about her opinions on what we'd done, which was an interesting experience: someone we'd never met was now going to be telling us what she thought of our work…
>
> I remember her being rather nervous but she was really very diplomatic and started out by saying, 'Wow! You guys have done so brilliantly well! You are so fantastic! It's so great that this is actually happening! You've been so clever the way you've done this!' She gushed on like that for about ten minutes and then she said, 'But you know…' And that's when the 'buts' started to appear! And the 'buts' are the interesting part!

'I was nervous,' admits Philippa. 'Here I was offering a critique to a couple of experienced, Oscar-nominated film-makers; while as for Fran, I knew of her as this incredibly bright, gorgeous woman whom I had always thought of as "Stephen's ex-girlfriend", which felt slightly intimidating. But when we met we immediately clicked as friends.' As for her critique…

> We thought the criticism that she was giving us was smart and useful. In fact, we liked everything that she had to say – not because she liked our script, because, as the conversation wore on, it was very clear that she felt we had quite a few shortcomings! – but because her opinions and insights were good and sound, and where she'd criticise something we'd done, she always had a suggestion of how we should fix it. We very quickly gained a huge respect and affection for Philippa. In hindsight, it was a major turning point for the project.

'We really found Philippa's comments and ideas helpful,' agrees Fran, 'and we decided very quickly that we wanted to involve her in the scriptwriting process.' Philippa was initially made script editor on the project. There were initial concerns about how Stephen would react to this suggestion but he was comfortable with the situation and the work continued on the scripts with Philippa playing an increasingly important role. 'I had no idea where this was going to lead,' she says, 'which is probably just as well! I was just very open to whatever developed because I was having a great time! These guys were fantastic: the four of us got on really well and I was learning a lot: essentially it was four people in a room having a lot of fun!'

> Initially, we looked upon Philippa as really being the audience of the film; it was useful to have somebody like that on our team because if we were doing something that really irritated her, then we'd feel that we were probably going to irritate many thousands of other Tolkien fans. Whereas if she was excited and felt something was good, then hopefully that would be something the rest of the fan community would feel.
>
> Eventually, she started writing dialogue and she very quickly began to show a wonderful ability to write scenes and come up with great ideas. Philippa became a fantastic screenwriter through working on *The Lord of the Rings*. In fact, her arrival on the project was absolutely critical; the screenplays benefited enormously from her ideas, imagination and skill.

As the scriptwriting progressed to new drafts of *Rings*, Philippa observed the working relationship between Fran and Peter: 'Essentially, they are both dreamers, but I don't believe that Fran started out being in love with the story of *The Lord of the Rings*; I suspect that she had a million other stories that she would probably have done before this one, but she knew that Peter was in love with it from the very beginning. He was in love with *The Lord of the Rings* just as he loves *King Kong* – for its imaginative vastness and creative sweep: he wanted to make an epic film. Fran, I think, did it for Peter, because she believed in him and knew that this was something that he needed to do and that he could do. But then Fran also began to fall in love with the story because she always is excited by Peter's vision – and by the vision of the others, like the craftspeople at Weta – and, as a result, she becomes passionately involved and committed to the work that she does.'

How then to describe that vision? 'One of Pete's great strengths,' says Philippa, 'is writing what we call "the big print", the stuff in between the dialogue scenes, the detailed action sequences.'

Each and every version of the script, however the content may differ, contains 'big print' episodes, such as that describing the Fellowship's fight with the Cave-troll (a creature which Tolkien only mentions in passing, but which becomes a major adversary in the Mines of Moria sequence) or the graphic realisation of Frodo's struggle with Shelob:

> TWO great clusters of many-mirrored EYES protrude from her bulbous head. Her LEGS are bent, with a 12-FOOT SPAN and HAIRS that stick out like steel spines. Her HUGE SWOLLEN BODY, a vast bloated bag, sways and sags... Her age-old BLACK HIDE is knobbed and pitted, blotched with LIVID MARKS... but her belly underneath is PALE and LUMINOUS...
>
> SHELOB squats above FRODO, her EYE CLUSTERS fidgeting with hideous delight, gloating over a prey trapped beyond all hope of escape.
>
> FRODO suddenly draws STING! He slashes wildly at the GIANT SPIDER... hewing off the TIP OF A LEG! SHELOB SPASMS... a wild blur of thrashing LEGS!

'Perhaps his greatest asset,' says Philippa, 'is his original vision: his determination never to tell something in an *ordinary* way but always to tell it in an *extraordinary* way and always with immediacy. He has an innate allergy to reportage, to being told about something rather than putting you in the action so that you experience it and feel it for yourself.'

> We let Tolkien's basic narrative unfold but always from the point-of-view of the characters involved, rather than stepping back and giving too much of an 'Eye-of-God' feel. You can have all the big, impressive wide-shots of charging armies, but if you cut to somebody fighting an orc, who are people going to care more about – an anonymous soldier or Aragorn? That's just plain common sense!
>
> Also, whilst setting out to remain true to the spirit of Tolkien's story,

I was nevertheless determined to follow my personal philosophy about writing scripts and making movies, which is that you have to create a series of questions in the audience's mind – compelling questions and even *doubts* that they will wonder about – and then, strategically, as the film develops, you reveal the answers. It sounds simplistic, but if people are not asking themselves any questions then you probably have a dull, boring film!

And, in attempting to 'remain true' to what is a vast, multi-layered work, what had they most wanted to preserve? For Fran, the question is easily answered: 'The story's heart: the story of Sam and Frodo. We knew that if we failed to capture that, then it would be nothing more than an empty action-adventure yarn.'

'On one level,' observes Philippa, 'you could say that Peter is the master of filmic language and how to tell the story visually, while Fran is the master of the characters and the heart of the story. But that's deceptive because, actually, both of them can do what the other does as well. Fran has an amazing filmic sense and Pete can have an astonishing innate sense for what the heart of a scene should be, so the truth is probably that they have grown up together as film-makers and, as a result, there's no beginning or end to what they give each other and the film; there's just an inter-mingling of their talents. They also keep each other focussed, they keep each other honest, and they keep each other laughing, which, on these demanding projects, they really need to be able to do.'

So many issues had to be resolved: how to convey the weighty history that precedes the events in *The Lord of the Rings*; how to handle the story's relentlessly episodic form or cope with scenes of the Fellowship which featured, on the journey from Rivendell to Moria, no less than nine major characters – two more than in *The Magnificent Seven*!

It was one of the curses, if you like, but also, ultimately, one of the joys. It became an asset when we were dealing with the narrative in *The Two Towers* and *The Return of the King* because, as the company breaks up, you can make the most of the individual character storylines and that's quite fun. But when they're all together in *The Fellowship of the Ring* and you're trying to give them equal status in the story, it is very hard. I have huge admiration for the writers on the *Dad's Army* television series and the way in which they took their eight or nine key characters and seamlessly gave them all presence and screen time. I've now found out how hard it is to juggle that sized character list in terms of the scriptwriting.

How they responded to this challenge was in turn influenced by the decision to make the first of the then two movies 'Frodocentric'.

By 'Frodocentric' we meant that the film couldn't be split into too many diverse directions, and since Frodo is clearly the movie's protagonist we wanted to let him control moments, rather than share too much of it around. In shooting the film we tended to place the weight of the film onto Frodo's shoulders because it seemed to us that, when we were away from Frodo, we had somehow disengaged ourselves from the driving force of the narrative. That worried us so we wanted to keep it as tight as we could on Frodo's story. That was also true of the eventual editing of the film, as you will see if you compare the theatrical version with the extended edition. Look at the thirty–thirty-five minutes of extra footage in the longer cut and you'll find that most of it is of the other characters, not of Frodo.

However, maintaining audience interest in the increasingly driven and emotionally isolated Frodo was a dramatic challenge, as was attempting to balance the parallel journeys of Frodo and Aragorn as well as convincingly depicting Aragorn's relationship with Arwen – a crucial character for whom, rather thoughtlessly, Tolkien had written not a single line of dialogue until the third volume of the trilogy!

As the writers laboured under what was a Herculean task, there was the added burden of knowing that, even as they wrote, the clock was ticking and the dollars were adding up. Where previously Jackson films had virtually a shooting script and a budget based on the script by the time pre-production was due to start, that was not the case with *The Lord of the Rings.*

We felt that we were in a situation where we didn't need a script to begin thinking about the design of the film because we had Tolkien's book. I wanted to have the project as well planned as I possibly could in order to avoid finding ourselves with a huge amount of preparation to be done and not enough time to do it in, which is what happens all too often with films.

Miramax began advancing Research and Development funding and Richard Taylor began focusing Weta on beginning the complex and time-consuming challenge of designing Middle-earth for the screen. Richard recalls, 'I knew that it was going to be incredibly hard, incredibly huge, the biggest challenge that we'll ever undertake in our lives. What made it tricky was that every reader of the book had such strongly preconceived ideas of what Tolkien's world should look like and, at some time or other, we've all said that some movie was good but that the book was better! It's because the written word is as big as the human imagination; it is as expansive and colourful as whatever we imagine as we read the story. Cinema, on the other hand, is only as big as what you can encapsulate in that second of footage on the screen. So I was very aware that we had to create a world that would spread beyond the four corners of the movie screen, the feeling of the different cultures of the people and the species of Middle-earth, which are filled with thousands of years of individual integrity and creativity and involvement with one another.'

A search was begun to find possible locations for the diverse environments depicted in the book that would use the natural landscape of New Zealand to give Middle-earth a look on screen that would underpin Peter's quest for 'realistic fantasy'.

> I was determined that we wouldn't let the movie's art department take over the storytelling and that the characters wouldn't wear silly-looking costumes or get swallowed up in absurd gobbledegook dialogue!

Grant Major came on board as Production Designer with Dan Hennah as Art Director: an already trusted team which Peter wanted to enhance with two artistic talents whose work he had discovered during his researches into Tolkien's world.

While the script was beginning to be written, Peter was attempting to track down 'every piece of visual interpretation of Tolkien that had ever been done,' illustrated books, calendars, anything with images of Middle-earth that might help shape their own vision.

Two artists in particular began to fire Peter and Fran's imagination: Alan Lee, who had been responsible for the first illustrated edition of *The Lord of the Rings*. Alan's graphic interpretation in a suite of fifty exquisite watercolours had succeeded in overcoming the reservations of the Tolkien Estate, who had long resisted any depiction of the characters in the story; moreover, from its publication in 1991, the volume had established a reputation with fans as, if not the 'definitive' perspective on Middle-earth (since no two readers will ever agree about any visualisation), then at least one that was in harmony with Tolkien's sensibility.

> You look at Alan's pictures and they feel authentic, like images of a real world: as if the artist had sat down with his paints and paintbrush and had painted things from life…

As Peter began buying second-hand copies of the many Tolkien calendars published over the years, Peter discovered the work of another artist, whose style complemented that of Alan Lee whilst possessing unique qualities that clearly recommended themselves to the film-maker's eye. John Howe's paintings – depicting some of the most dramatic encounters in the book, such as Gandalf's battle with the Balrog, which he has made the subject of several pictures – were filled with an energy and dynamism and, like the pictures of Alan Lee, realism.

To begin with, Alan and John's pictures were merely a source of inspiration, pinned up around the room in which the writers were grappling with the scripts. Then Peter began to think that the perception of these two artists had such relevance to the project that they ought really to be involved in designing the film.

> We would look at Alan Lee's pictures of Orthanc, or John Howe's of Barad-dûr, and we began to realise that, one day, we were going to have to create designs for these places and how on earth would we do that

without copying what they had already done so fantastically well? Not only that, but what sort of a job was it going to be for any designer to be asked to copy Alan and John's work, and what happens if they simply can't rise to their level? More and more we came to realise that we needed to see whether we could involve these artists in the creation process…

It was a decision that Peter felt obligated to run past Miramax and, beginning with Alan Lee, suggested engaging him as a conceptual artist. The proposal was given a cool reception by one of the executives, who maintained that Alan Lee should, under no circumstances, be approached as he had strong connections with the Tolkien family and Estate, with whom the studio did not in any way want to be involved. With typical Jackson wilfulness and tenacity, Peter went ahead and made contact with Alan – itself a difficult task as, initially, no one would give him the artist's address or phone number.

Alan had worked on various film and television projects including Ridley Scott's *Legend* and the comedy-fantasy *Eric the Viking*, written and directed by *Monty Python's Flying Circus* star, Terry Jones. By a curious happenstance, another former 'Python', Michael Palin, was on a visit to New Zealand to launch his latest books at a dinner in Wellington. Peter and Fran were attending the event and managed to meet with Palin beforehand. It was an opportunity for Peter to tell one of his *Python* heroes how much his work had meant to him and, during the conversation, ask whether he could get him contact details for Alan Lee.

A couple of weeks later, thanks to Michael Palin, Peter had an address for the artist. A package containing videotapes of *Heavenly Creatures* and *Forgotten Silver* was despatched to Britain with an enquiry as to whether Alan would be interested in working on a film of *The Lord of the Rings*. Alan watched both films back to back the moment they arrived and immediately telephoned Wellington. His response was unequivocal: he liked Peter's work, he really wanted to be involved with the Tolkien film and, no, he didn't have a relationship with the family or Estate that would make his involvement an issue.

'It's really funny,' comments Alan. 'Peter spent a frantic time chasing around to find me and to get me to watch his videos and consider coming on board the project; I said "Yes," and then spent the next five years – like everyone else on this project – chasing Peter, trying to get time with him to discuss this film we were making!'

It's true! Alan's job description eventually became, 'The man trying to get five minutes with Peter to show him a drawing'!

Securing Alan Lee's commitment was a significant development for the project: on one level, it hinted at difficulties to come in the relationship with Miramax; on another, it brought to the project an artist whose vision and integrity would be of tremendous importance to shaping the look of *The Lord of the Rings*. When John Howe also agreed to join the team, bringing with him his own unique talents not just as a graphic artist but also as someone with an exceptional knowledge of medieval armour and weaponry, the styling of Middle-earth was in safe hands.

Alan and John knew of each other's work, but they met for the first time on the plane coming to New Zealand. I have this vivid memory of the day they arrived. They landed in Wellington and after going to their hotel to freshen up, they came to our house to have lunch with us.

We had spent months and months working on this script surrounded by Alan Lee and John Howe artwork: staring at it, imagining it, dreaming of their somehow being involved in the film, and then this amazing moment when the people who had created this art that we so much admired walked into our kitchen! It was really very, very exciting!

The two artists quickly caught the spirit of the project. Richard Taylor remembers: 'Alan and John were crucial to achieving one of our aims, which was to create a strong feeling of culture. They approached the different races of Middle-earth – Elves, Dwarves, men, hobbits and Orcs – and began visualising their cultures which are based in detail and are the result of generations of people building on top of past generations' work and culminating in the moment in time that is depicted in the film.'

> Normally, there would be a finished script long before anyone started designing the look of the film, but it was a joy and an inspiration to have so much imaginative visual material descending on us while we were working on the screenplay.

With the involvement of these two artists, Peter also cleverly ensured that his film would attain a look that had a visual authenticity and, for the many readers who already knew Alan and John's work, provide a familiar perspective on Tolkien's world.

When the first discussions about *The Lord of the Rings* had taken place, Richard Taylor had been adamant about one thing: 'There was absolutely no doubt in my mind that we had to look after as many of the departments at Weta as we possibly could, rather than having the various elements – prosthetics and creatures, armour and weapons, miniatures, and digital effects – being dissipated amongst a variety of companies and effects houses around the world. I didn't need to campaign with Peter because he agreed with me that, in the task of encapsulating Tolkien's vision, if we could keep all those elements under the one roof at Weta, we could create a singular, visionary, Tolkienesque brushstroke across our work. The crossover between the departments would be as simple as walking through a door into the next room and it was that cross-pollination of ideas throughout the facility that would become the backbone of our work on *The Lord of the Rings*.'

> Weta started working on developing computer graphics techniques because we knew that we had to get a head start on that work while we were still writing. We had done the Reaper for *The Frighteners*, along with a lot of special effects, but we hadn't really created a proper, lifelike, CGI creature, so we decided to build the Cave-troll as a prototype: figuring out how to convincingly create a living being with a skeleton, muscles and skin.

Among the team working on the development of CGI effects was Steve Regelous, who would make an unprecedented, groundbreaking contribution to the film's stunning action set-pieces.

We were having early conversations, and as far back as 1997 Steve pitched me this idea that he could write a software program that would enable whole battle sequences to be created almost entirely in the computer and yet which would look very realistic. I remember asking him, 'How long is it going to take you to write the software?' And Steve said that it was about a two-year job... 'Well,' I said, 'you'd better get started now!' So that was the beginning of the creation of the computer program now called 'Massive' that would eventually allow us to create those epic battle scenes I'd always envisaged between Sauron's forces and the Last Alliance, or at the assault on Helm's Deep and the siege of Minas Tirith.

By the time the writers had completed two draft scripts – running to 147 and 144 pages respectively and now carrying additional screen-writer credits for 'Faye Crutchley & Kennedy Landenburger', the aliases of Philippa Boyens and Stephen Sinclair – a change in dynamic was taking place within the group. Stephen had theatrical commitments that; would eventually draw him away from a project with which he was not, perhaps, entirely in sympathy. Philippa Boyens says: 'I don't think Stephen had a particular affinity with Tolkien, but it wasn't just that, he's a very original person who needs to be working on his own writing and I don't think he would have endured; it would have driven him insane.'

'Stephen's interest began to wane,' says Fran; 'he had plays and novels he wanted to write and he was getting fed up with being tied to this enormous task and an obligation to a project which was on-going and nowhere near being made. On the other hand, Philippa's interest grew because she was becoming more and more invested in the story and how it was being told. At one stage there were four of us, then Stephen dropped out and there were three.' Later, Stephen and Philippa's personal relationship came to an end.

In 2000, by which time *The Lord of the Rings* scripts had gone through many further transitions, an agreement was made that Stephen Sinclair would be credited as co-writer of the second film in the trilogy. It was an acknowledgement of the fact that, to what-ever extent the scripts had changed (and would go on changing up until the release of the final film), he had made a valuable and significant contribution to getting the project underway.

Stephen had also been responsible for bringing Peter and Fran together with Philippa Boyens. 'That,' says Fran, 'was another piece of serendipity.' Or, as Peter puts it: 'It was luck; it was fate, and it was a good thing...'

As the scriptwriting progressed to new drafts, the writers continually addressed the challenges inherited from Tolkien, many of which resulted from the fact that during the early stages of composing *The Lord of the Rings*, the author had still not defined the full intricacies of the plot or determined all the connections between the incidents in the narrative and people, places and events within the early history of Middle-earth.

They were also seeking ways of establishing key characters – such as the hobbits Merry and Pippin – whom Tolkien had introduced into the story without having to worry about any of the issues facing the screen dramatist. So (unlike the book or, indeed, the final film script) the four hobbits set out from Hobbiton together: Gandalf having caught not just Sam but also Merry and Pippin, eavesdropping outside the window of Bag End.

One of the chief difficulties presented by the text is that Tolkien often recounts crucial events in 'flashback'; so, for example, it is only when Gandalf addresses the Council of Elrond at Rivendell that Frodo – *and the reader* – discovers that the reason the wizard had failed to meet the hobbits at Bree was because he had been imprisoned by Saruman at Isengard. The chronological depiction of the confrontation between the wizards imposed different dramatic requirements on a scene that was no longer reportage. It also usefully interrupted the hobbits' journey across country.

Although the final edit of the film did not reflect the fact, relocating the Isengard scenes was originally seen as offering a way around the still-thorny issue of eliminating the three chapters (forty pages of incident-packed text) featuring Tom Bombadil.

The cinematic coverage of the hobbits' journey to Bree was done in such a way that when you cut back to these four hobbits scurrying through the trees and peering at the Bree gates, we figured that they could have seen Tom, spent a couple of days at his house and had their experience on the Barrow-downs.

There's nothing in the movie that says that those things didn't happen. We didn't *eradicate* Tom Bombadil from the mythology; it was simply that, in the movie, we chose to show selected aspects of the journey – anything could have happened while we were away with Gandalf in Orthanc.

Some of the approaches in the script either remained unrealised or subsequently abandoned (such as a Warg attack on the hobbits at Weathertop before the ambush by the nine Ringwraiths) or were replaced with a better solution – often involving a return to the original text.

In the early versions, for the sake of compression, Lothlórien was eliminated and the events described there were moved to Rivendell, with Galadriel attending the Council of Elrond, revealing her mirror to Frodo in the gardens at the Last Homely House and giving her gifts when the Fellowship eventually set forth on their quest.

Denethor also attended and was given a highly vocal presence at the Council, accompanied by a Boromir who is the strong, silent type, barely speaking prior to the forming of the Fellowship and, when he does, curiously referring to himself in the first person as 'Old Boromir'.

Other changes now known as part of the film trilogy scenario were put in place quite early on and survived various script changes. One such example is the substitution of Arwen for Glorfindel as the means of rescuing Frodo from the pursuing Ringwraiths and getting the Ring-bearer to Rivendell.

Our reasons for giving Glorfindel's actions to Arwen were twofold: firstly, we needed to establish the crucial relationship between Aragorn and Arwen – which Tolkien's text is singularly unhelpful in doing – and, secondly, we were faced with a problem which is peculiar to cinematic convention.

If a new character suddenly rides dramatically into a scene, grabs the hero and then gallops off with the enemy in pursuit, the signal given to the audience is, 'This person is someone important to the development of the story, someone who is going to be a major character from now on.' Since that was not the case with Glorfindel (who disappears from the narrative following the Council of Elrond), it seemed an obvious solution to have Arwen arrive in his place.

The Watcher in the Water, omitted from the original treatment, was restored and, like the Cave-troll, given far more to do than in the book; the Elves were now present at the Battle of Helm's Deep along with Arwen who, against Aragorn's better judgement, insists in fighting in the combat – an invention that would survive until after filming had begun.

There were many attempts, not all of them successful, at establishing the intensity and importance of the relationship between Aragorn and Arwen: the second film was originally going to open with the couple bathing naked in the 'crystal clear rock pools' of the Glittering Caves, where they happen to be discovered by Legolas and Gimli who are taking a sight-seeing boat trip through the caves!

Also, in the early versions of the scripts, it is Arwen – rather than Éowyn – who rides out of Dunharrow disguised as a man and later defeats the Witch-king after he has mortally wounded Théoden on the Pelennor Fields when she herself comes close to death. Whilst such a reallocation of material undoubtedly enhanced Arwen's character arc, it only did so by weakening that of Éowyn and it would be some time before the writers were able to solve that dilemma and find a way of adequately representing both women within the screenplay.

These scripts also attempted to strengthen Frodo's role in the story beyond that of being the burdened Ring-bearer. One such sequence, placed dramatically towards the end of the first film, is a good example of the many approaches that were considered but later rejected.

For the purposes of this sequence, the Seeing Seat was relocated from Amon Hen to one of the hills in the Emyn Muil. Climbing up to the seat, Frodo witnesses various things including the confrontation at Isengard between Gandalf the White and Saruman, who is despatched not by Gríma Wormtongue but an emissary of the Dark Lord:

A GREAT WINGED BEAST rises behind SARUMAN! This LIZARD-LIKE CREATURE, the NAZGÛL, has a 30-FOOT WINGSPAN… perched on the back of the NAZGÛL, in a black saddle, is a RINGWRAITH!

A TERRIFYING SHRIEK!… The RINGWRAITH wields a HUGE MACE and SWEEPS SARUMAN off the TOP OF ORTHANC!

SARUMAN'S FLAILING BODY PLUMMETS 500 FEET… IMPALING ON a piece of JAGGED STEEL MACHINERY!

The Nazgûl beast then swoops down towards Gandalf, knocking him off Shadowfax's back and causing his staff to be lost in the flood waters around Orthanc. In a bid to save Gandalf, Frodo puts on the Ring, entering the Twilight World, revealing himself to Sauron and causing the Ringwraith to abandon its attack on Gandalf and to race away toward the East…

The subsequent attack on Frodo at the Seeing Seat is a fantastical action set-piece in which Sam uses Galadriel's Elven rope to lasso one of the talons of the Nazgûl steed and hitch it to the ruined masonry. The beast and its rider flounder around, reducing the ancient structure to rubble, and are about to kill Sam, whose backpack is caught between the fallen stones making it impossible for him to move. Drawing his sword, the Ringwraith advances on the helpless Sam when Frodo, still wearing the Ring, leaps in front of the Ringwraith and raises his hand:

The RINGWRAITH halts… LUST for the RING overwhelming him. His DEAD EYES SHINE… His shrivelled, pallid LIPS TWITCH.

The RINGWRAITH extends a HAGGARD HAND towards FRODO'S FINGER. FRODO'S HAND moves CLOSER… as if by the PULL of the RING…

The RINGWRAITH'S FINGERS CLOSE AROUND THE RING!

SUDDENLY! FRODO rams the BLADE of STING into the RING-WRAITH'S HEART! THE RINGWRAITH SHRIEKS in PAIN!

The TWILIGHT WORLD turns to FLAME as the WRATH of the LIDLESS EYE ENGULFS FRODO'S VISION.

An accretion which did make the final film was the moment on the Cirith Ungol stairs when, as an antidote to the remoteness that begins to settle on Frodo as he draws nearer to Mordor, the scriptwriters injected a new sense of emotional conflict by having Frodo succumb to Gollum's mischief-making, reject Sam and send him home.

Several of Tolkien's many coincidences (or, as he viewed them, twists and turns of fate) were given a 'rational' explanation; thus, Faramir doesn't simply stumble across Frodo and Sam in the woods of Ithilien but, instead, is sent there by Denethor as a result of Faramir learning the true nature of the Fellowship's quest from the loquacious Pippin:

> PIPPIN
> Gandalf would kill me if I said anything. Look, it's not that I don't trust you... it's just that... it's big stuff: Middle-earth, the Dark Lord, the whole works!
> And I promised Gandalf that I wouldn't let anything slip: if there's one thing I'm good at its keeping secrets...

The mood-leavening gags with Merry and Pippin and Legolas and Gimli are by now a feature of the script, including one that didn't make it into the final film. On their arrival at the Moria Gate, Gimli is excited by the impressive landscape and the youthful memories that it stirs:

> GIMLI
> Will you look at this! I haven't been here since I was a toddler!
> LEGOLAS
> And you're not a toddler now?
> ARAGORN restrains GIMLI as he makes an ANGRY LUNGE at LEGOLAS!

Also established beyond doubt are those sequences of sheer visual bravado intended to lift the story into the arena of the spectacular and fantastical:

> NIGHTMARISH MONTAGE: The DEAD TREES of ISENGARD are fed into ROARING FURNACES... MOLTEN METAL pours into CASTS... LARGE SQUIRMING MAGGOT hangs from a CAVERN CEILING... RED-HOT

In the middle of our seven-year project…

During a production as long as The Lord of the Rings, *with a crew so large, it's inevitable that marriages, births and divorces will occur (not necessarily in that order). Unfortunately, we also lost some close members of our extended family. Brian Bansgrove (above), our beloved gaffer, died just one day before he was due to see* The Fellowship of the Ring *at his home in Bangkok. Carla Fry (below) was the head of production at New Line Cinema, and had to weather much of the tension between studio and film-makers. She handled it all with grace and a sensible level-headedness, and became a real friend to Fran and myself. Carla lived to see* The Fellowship of the Ring *open successfully, but died after a short illness many months before* The Two Towers *was released. She was one of the real unsung heroes in the making of the trilogy.*

Sir Edmund Hillary came to visit The Lord of the Rings *set and he attracted a large group of awestruck actors and film-makers at lunchtime.*

I'm always interested in young directors, but coming across genuinely talented kids is a rare thing. Cameron Duncan was an incredibly skilled film-maker – he was born to make movies. He had made a few stunning short films and was destined to become a leading film-maker of his generation; I had no doubt about that. However, Cameron also had a very aggressive cancer. Fran and I did what we could to help him, but his disease was unstoppable. He made his last movie, Strike Zone, a few weeks before he died. We put a little tribute to him on The Return of the King *extended DVD*. If you haven't seen it, you should borrow a copy and have a look at the work of a remarkable young man.

Viggo the day after a slight mishap with a surfboard. The day this was taken we had to shoot the section in the Balin's Tomb sequence where the Orc drums are heard after Pippin knocks the skeleton down the well. I shot Aragorn's close-ups as a right to left profile… and now you can see why!

This is the evening of the release of The Fellowship of the Ring. The main cast had each got a tattoo a year or so earlier, and now it was the turn of Richard Taylor, Barrie Osborne, Mark Ordesky and myself. Here I'm getting tormented by Orlando, who I suspect was one of the principal ring leaders.

LEFT: *An estimated 100,000 people lined Courtney Place to catch a glimpse of the stars for the premiere.*

MIDDLE LEFT: *Fran and me at the Golden Globes for* The Return of the King. *Award nights are blurry, giddy occasions after the ceremony, but in the hours leading up to it, you really wish you could watch it on TV at home. And then right at the moment the envelope is torn open, you pray it's not your name that's read out! I was really happy to see Fran win for her work on the lyrics of 'Into the West', a song directly inspired by our friendship with Cameron Duncan during his last months. Those lyrics came from the heart.*

BOTTOM LEFT: *Receiving the Best Picture Oscar from Steven Spielberg, with Bob Shaye looking on. When Steven opened the envelope, his first words were, 'It's a clean sweep', since we had won all thirteen categories we'd been nominated for. However, that threw our son Billy into a few seconds of despair. He was watching the ceremony on TV in New Zealand and thought a film called* Clean Sweep *had beaten us.*

The King Kong *premiere in New York. Actually a very cool photo – between George Lucas and myself are the 'Three Kongs': Andy Serkis, who performed Kong in our version; the 1933 armature; and Rick Baker, who played Kong in 1976. Quite historic – and a moment where self-control is quite hard to maintain. The inner geek is trying to bust out.*

Fran and I snuck out of the Golden Globes party and sought refuge with our friends, Sylvia and Rick Baker. The party was on the rooftop of a hotel, and we asked some complete strangers if we could hang out in their room for a while. I find parties – especially Hollywood ones – become very overwhelming, very quickly. People I don't know are constantly coming at me in a never-ending flood. The shy, Pukerua Bay only child wells up, and I need to escape them quickly. Must be something like a panic attack, I guess.

What I love about movie making is the research. I don't know how else I would ever get to fly in a Lancaster bomber – unless it was something to do with a movie. I'm in Canada here, researching Dambusters, *a World War Two movie about the top-secret RAF mission to bomb German dams* that we're producing for Christian Rivers to direct. I think it's one of the most astonishing true stories of the entire war and our hope is to make their heroic exploits known to a whole new generation. And by harnessing Weta's state-of-the-art visual effects, we'll be able to bring to life the events of these desperate days of 1943 in a very visceral way.

Here's Christian enjoying the flight. Christian started writing fan letters to me when he was a schoolboy; I quickly realised he was a very talented artist and asked him to do storyboards on Braindead in 1991. He has been with us ever since, designing great sequences on The Lord of the Rings and working his way up to Animation Director on King Kong – he deservedly won an Oscar for his work on that film. Christian has now reached a point where he wants to direct films himself, and I leapt at the chance to help him.

metal BEATEN by sweating URUK-HAI BLACKSMITHS... the MAGGOT
SPLITS and a SLIME-COVERED FIGURE lands on the floor in a heap...
HAMMER strikes METAL...YELLOW EYES flick open, as the newly-hatched
URUK-HAI SCREAMS... WIDE ON MAGGOT CHAMBER CEILING with
hundreds of SQUIRMING MAGGOTS... RED-HOT SWORD BLADE sizzles
in water...

The scripts now ended, as had the book, with Sam's return to Hobbiton and the line, 'Well, I'm back!'

In an attempt to better appreciate how the script would work as film, a 'storyboard' was made from the script. An aid to film-making that was initiated at the Disney animation studios in the 1920s, the storyboard presents a visualisation of the screenplay as a series of sketches, with a note of accompanying dialogue and sound effects that can be pinned up onto boards so as to be 'read' like a comic strip.

Christian Rivers (subsequently visual effects art director for Weta Digital) worked directly with Peter in drawing up a detailed storyboard for the film that showed, not just the proposed scenes and characters, but also indicated specific camera moves and angles. Once this had been completed, Peter made an 'animatic', which can best be described as a 'filmed storyboard combined with a radio play'.

An audio version of the script was recorded by a group of New Zealand actors with Frodo being played by Craig Parker (subsequently Haldir in the films) and Peter Vere-Jones from *Bad Taste*, *Meet the Feebles* and *Braindead* as Gandalf. Temporary music and effects were added to create a 'working soundtrack', and whilst the accompanying visuals were merely static pictures, the combination gave a strong indication of how the story would eventually play on screen.

It's really a sketch of the movie and, as such, is very useful, because it points up any flaws in the story. In fact, it's brutal, because instead of cutting to somebody's face, you cut to a drawing of somebody's face, so you don't have the benefit of seeing the emotion in the eyes. As a result of watching the animatic, we re-wrote the script, partly to fix a few things in the plot, but also because we felt that it was almost totally lacking in real heart and emotion.

On the face of it, the project seemed to be progressing: the script was being tightened and sharpened with characters' motivation and interrelationships being refined and strengthened; Weta were making significant strides on several fronts with Alan Lee and John Howe creating a series of evocative conceptual paintings and drawings of key settings and characters as well as their armour and weaponry; the model-makers were sculpting an impressive array of maquettes depicting the warriors and creatures of Middle-earth and an impressive scale miniature of Helm's Deep; while the digital program-writers and animators were getting to grips with new and still-developing technologies.

> It was a blessing having so much design-work in hand before the script was finalised, but it was also a curse, because without a finalised script you simply can't a budget a film. Until you know precisely how many scenes there are going to be, you aren't in a position to calculate how many months it will to take to film, how long you'll need to contract the actors for, what transportation costs are likely to be, or answers to a hundred other questions…

Lack of answers to those questions – combined with a monthly, rising figure representing the on-going expenditure being made on research and development – began to stir up concerns among the Miramax teams in New York and Los Angeles, amongst whom there were various jostlings for control over the Tolkien project.

Peter now found himself dealing with different executives from those who had been responsible for the film's development at the outset. Where his original Miramax point-of-contact had been someone with whom Peter had a good rapport, he increasingly had to deal with individuals who seemed to lack empathy with his vision for the movie. Of his relationship with one particular executive, by this time a key player in the future fate of *The Lord of the Rings*, Peter says,

> We were chalk and cheese and it was a situation of conflict from day one of his involvement. Obviously, there are two sides to every story and as I increasingly felt that he was winding me up, I started to enjoy winding

him up and wrote emails which were full of my frustration and rather rude... It was just one of those human situations: I eventually lost all respect for him and, at that stage, couldn't really hold back or disguise my frustration.

In the early months of 1998, storm clouds were beginning to loom on the horizon...

A lot of the tensions which led to my being at loggerheads with the guy from Dimension were not really to do with a creative *impasse*, because they seemed to be reasonably happy with the scripts that we were writing; the problem was really all about money.

They were indeed about money, although the scripts were a factor in that it increasingly began to look as if what was being written was unlikely to be filmed for Miramax's capped budget of $75million. When the deal had been agreed, the sum, which was greater than that of any film made by Miramax, let alone Peter Jackson, must have seemed what Peter describes as a 'do-able thing'. As the ramifications of the complex scripts hit home, it began to look increasingly less 'do-able', but Peter really expected, at that point, to find Miramax granting him some flexibility – especially as it became clear that the predicated delivery cost was woefully unrealistic.

I guess when we had embarked on the project that the fact that we were making two films meant that there would be some leeway... As the scripts developed and the project took shape, we thought, 'Okay, $75million is the limit for *one* film, sure, that's possible; but how can they really expect us to make *two* films for $75million?'

Miramax took a rather different view: it was not simply that 'a deal is a deal', the fact was they didn't have immediate means to increase the budget. Whilst movie history is full of films that, during filming, have gone hysterically over their initial budget and still been financed either to success (*Titanic*) or to near-ruination (*Waterworld*), *The Lord of the Rings* was still a long way off from shooting and was already heading towards double what they had expected to invest in the project.

Indeed, by the time aggravations began to arise, the amount already invested in the scripting process and the research and development being undertaken at Weta was approaching US$12million,

Although Tim Sanders, co-producer of *The Frighteners*, had joined the project as producer and was drawing up budgets based on the scripts, Miramax – as they were entitled to do – decided to send a representative to Wellington to 'oversee' development. To Peter, whose past experiences with Jim Booth and Robert Zemeckis had been positive and creative, the person now despatched to New Zealand was 'the executive from Hell'.

> This guy shows up and we looked him up on the IMDB. His previous credits included soft-core porn made in South Africa. Some nutter at Miramax/Dimension thought he would be a great addition to the team down here. I guess he was just doing his job, but as I saw it his attitude was one of not caring about the movie, not caring about what we were trying to achieve; it was all about the numbers, about the bottom line, about controlling expenditure, and I butted heads with him straight away and, within days of his arrival, we were actually shouting at one another.

Acknowledging what was obviously a rapidly deteriorating situation, Miramax decided that they needed to involve someone with whom Peter could establish a more productive working relationship. Bob Osher, Miramax's co-president of production, decided to approach Marty Katz, a hugely experienced independent producer with a long track record in film and television with, among other studios, Paramount, ABC and Walt Disney Productions where, as Executive Vice President, Motion Picture and Television Production, he had held responsibility for overseeing the studio's various production banners – Disney, Touchstone and Hollywood Pictures – as well as Disney feature animation and television.

Films with which Marty Katz had been involved included the feature hits *Good Morning, Vietnam, Three Men and a Baby, The Color Of Money, Dead Poets Society, Pretty Woman, The Little Mermaid* and *The Nightmare Before Christmas*.

In 1997, as 'production consultant', he had served as a trouble-shooter for Twentieth Century Fox and Paramount when James Cameron's *Titanic* drifted into decidedly dangerous waters, a role that doubtless recommended him to Bob Osher as someone who might be able to deal with what, in Hollywoodspeak, were being called 'internal Miramax issues over *The Lord of the Rings*'.

'My purpose in going to New Zealand,' says Marty, 'was to *help* Peter and to try to find some answers to what Miramax currently saw as problems. However, the answer to a problem may not be as simple as a studio envisages – or hopes! Sometimes, rather than cutting corners, it is necessary to spend more money in order to realise the full creativity of a film, although, obviously, that probably isn't what the studio wants to hear. All *I* promised to do was go and talk.'

One of the productions with which Marty had been closely involved at Disney was *Who Framed Roger Rabbit*, which had been directed by Robert Zemeckis, who, in turn, knew and had worked with Peter Jackson on *The Frighteners*. At Marty's suggestion, Zemeckis made a call to Peter intended to smooth the way by 'introducing' him as 'the new guy', who Miramax were going to be sending down to Wellington.

> I was rather surprised to hear this from Bob Zemeckis because, at this point, no one at Miramax had told us anything about Marty coming. I remember Bob saying, 'Marty is very Hollywood, but he's basically a good guy...'
>
> Marty turned up and he was *nothing* like us: he was a hyper, ramped-up guy with a California tan who chewed gum. But he was, as Bob had said, a 'good guy' – he was someone who was interested in what we were doing, someone to whom we could talk and who would listen to us.

Marty was impressed by what he saw in Wellington: 'Peter and Fran were clearly people with a remarkable vision and, for me, it was impossible not to be impressed by their vision, not to fall in love with their project, not to admire the extraordinary New Zealand ability to achieve incredible results with fewer resources but greater resource-fulness and by sticking with a work ethic that says you work till the job is done. It was also immediately evident that the problem was that there was a difference between Peter and Fran's vision for *The Lord of the Rings* and that of Miramax.'

To Marty it seemed that Miramax already knew the answer they wanted to hear: 'Peter had ostensibly agreed to deliver two films for $75million. Bob Weinstein felt that that was what he had been promised and what he, in turn, had promised to Disney and that Peter was now declining to honour that promise. Whatever the situation at the outset, it was now obvious – from the number of pages in the scripts and the number of visual effects shots that were going to be involved – that it was impossible to tell the story of *The Lord of the Rings* in two films for $75million when $12million had already been spent.'

Marty spent four months in New Zealand, becoming increasingly won over to the view that Peter's approach was the right one for the subject but, at the same time, trying to find a formula to keep the project and everyone on course. Working alongside Peter, producer Tim Sanders and first assistant director Carolynne Cunningham, Marty assessed a realistic budget for the two films as being in the region of US$130–150million. It was not what Miramax wanted to be told.

Peter Nelson remembers: 'Miramax started to tell us, "We can't do this alone, we need to solicit a partner." Peter didn't have the right to object to that and, anyway, we were open to that because we wanted to make sure the movie got made. So Miramax went to Disney. This was at a time when Disney might very well have said, "This is the next great franchise, why not do it?" But Peter had a reputation for making darker movies than the typical Disney movie, so they passed.'

The ironies are enormous since, when Tolkien was alive, he had always refused to consider Disney having any involvement with the film rights to his books; and now, with Tolkien gone, Disney were in the position of being *offered* the opportunity to become partners with Miramax on *The Lord of the Rings*, but chose to say, 'No'! It could have meant so many things: a *Rings* theme park ride, rubber hobbit feet in the shops at Disneyland... The world could have been a different place!

It is said that Miramax turned to other possible partners, including PolyGram and Steven Spielberg at Dreamworks. Peter began to feel – and he had seen this happen before – that the prospects for *Rings* were not good and were getting worse…

> The situation was becoming increasingly difficult with almost monthly cashflow problems when the money we needed to pay people was being delayed. We'd be screaming for the payment and Miramax would be saying, 'It's on its way…' It all suddenly began to feel very familiar: it was horribly like the 'cheque-is-in-the-post' days just before *King Kong* fell over. You could feel it happening: *The Lord of the Rings* was a movie that was going off the rails.

As Peter Nelson reflects, 'There are movies where every minute is filled with doubt and, deep down, you start to feel, "This is not going to happen." That's what the Miramax experience became: it went from a place where it was difficult enough to think that Miramax would make a big-budget movie like *The Lord of the Rings* to one where you started to feel that *they* didn't have the confidence to think that they should – or *could* – make a big-budget movie like *The Lord of the Rings*.'

> Harvey had never exhibited negativity towards the project or us. I believe, to this day, that if Harvey could have figured out a way to make it, he would have done so; on the other hand, I believe that Bob thought it was probably the biggest, most foolish mistake ever made in the world, and he just wanted it out of the way.

'There were no bad guys here,' says Marty Katz. 'Miramax really wanted to make the film – they already had a substantial investment in it and had not walked away from it – but they really didn't have the stomach to make the film that Peter and Fran had now envisioned. Peter wasn't willing to make a bastard version of the book; Miramax didn't feel they could afford to make the full-blown version. It was as simple as that.'

Miramax's investment had now risen to $15million and the bottom line, as far as the studio was concerned, was now painfully simple:

forget talking about budgets of $130–150million; make two films for $75million or make *one* movie for $75million.

Marty had been much impressed by the animatic, which he believed demonstrated Peter's genius, so it was suggested that the filmed storyboard be shown to Miramax as a way of winning their support for the Jackson vision.

> As we saw it, we had a budget and we needed to know whether Miramax were going to commit to making that film or not. We had to know.
>
> So, Marty went to New York and screened the animatic. I never really heard the full story but I get the strong impression the animatic screening must have gone incredibly badly. I imagine Harvey and Bob sat there watching storyboards flashing on screen for about two and a half hours and any confidence that they had left in the film wavered and collapsed. I think that was probably the final nail in the coffin…

'In the end,' says Marty, 'I think Miramax felt that the animatic *proved* what they already feared from reading the scripts: that the two-film structure contained too much information, too many characters and too many situations. However, they still thought that, maybe, it could be made as *"One Great Movie"* – the film Ralph Bakshi had failed to make – a single picture that would give a "taste" of the book for the general audience rather than the Tolkien fans… *That*, however, could only be achieved at a cost that I doubted Peter and Fran would be willing to pay.'

In mid-June 1998, Fran and Peter were 'summoned to a summit meeting' at the Miramax offices in New York.

> We knew, by that stage, that things were very, very bad: we were in a real crisis situation and the film was clearly in deep trouble.
>
> We arrived in New York and Marty, who had been involved in preliminary meetings with Miramax, warned us what was going to happen. He told us about the proposal to make just one movie and that a plan had been put together figuring out how it could be done.
>
> At first, I thought they might be suggesting spending $75million on a *first* film – ending somewhere around the Battle of Helm's Deep – and then, if it did well on release, make the second film a couple of years

later. I really didn't relish the idea of being the second guy in film history to make only half of *The Lord of the Rings*!

Then an envelope arrived at the hotel containing a memo and I realised that was not what they had in mind...

Dated 17 June 1998 and marked 'ULTRA-CONFIDENTIAL!', the memo came from a senior story editor at Miramax and boldly tackled the thorny issue of how the two-film version of *The Lord of the Rings* might become that One Great Movie.

To Peter and Fran, by now so steeped in the intricacies of Tolkien's story and the various approaches with which they had already experimented in an attempt to deal with the challenges presented by the text, the memo must have seemed unbelievably brutal, just as it must have seemed inconceivable that they could even begin to consider adopting its suggestions.

For the most avid fans of the book and the most critical critics of the film trilogy, it is salutary to consider the movie that *might* have been made of *The Lord of the Rings*.

Miramax were suggesting radical cutting and restructuring. Obviously it was not what Peter and Fran wanted to read, but the writer unerringly put his finger on what, from a film perspective, could be seen as structural weakness in Tolkien's story: there was, it was felt, no satisfactory way of concluding the first film, since Saruman was patently not Sauron and, however it was cut, it was patently obvious that the story was only half-told. Also Frodo was seen as a difficult character with too little to do and not enough moments of vulnerability with which to secure the emotional investment of the filmgoer.

Then came the suggested remedy and it proved bitter medicine: cut the Battle of Helm's Deep; cut or re-work the role of Saruman (on a 'use him or lose him' principle) making him more effectively the villain of the piece, 'Darth Vader to Sauron's Emperor'; combine the realms of Rohan and Gondor and the cities of Edoras and Minas Tirith; fuse the characters of King Théoden with Denethor and that of Faramir with Éowyn (with a preference for the female character, who would then have become Boromir's younger sister!); cut the

Ringwraiths' attack on Bree and hold them back for the assault at Weathertop; cut the events at Rivendell by half; drastically curtail the passage through the Mines of Moria (abandoning then Cave-troll on the way); have the Ents prevent the Orc-kidnap of Merry and Pippin and delay Gandalf's return as the White Wizard.

The document ended with an astute observation that, ironically, has since been proven by the eventual success of Peter Jackson's films: if the movie works as a movie, despite whatever knowledge an audience may have of Tolkien's book, any criticism from the most vociferous fan couldn't hope to damage its success. If, however, it were to fail as a movie then no degree of faithfulness to the written word could offer any protection.

Viewed from the point of view of a film studio contemplating a significant financial investment, much of what was said was common sense. Any screenwriter who had offered a script packed with so many episodes, loaded with so much back-history and introducing so many places, races, and characters with jaw-cracking names would, normally, have been laughed out of Hollywood.

> The memo itself was not really a problem. As an exercise in reducing *The Lord of the Rings* to one film, it demonstrated a lot of common sense. It was the wisdom of doing that in the first place that caused problems for us.

Peter and Fran, however, were already well aware of the challenges inherent in Tolkien's book and their aim, throughout, had been to surmount, not sidestep them. For them, the choice seemed clear: it was not about whether to make their version of the film or follow the Miramax outline, it was whether to make the film they believed in or not make it at all.

> How could we contemplate making a picture where we'd be guaranteed to disappoint every single reader of the most widely read book in the world? What would be the point? You couldn't call it *The Lord of the Rings*. We'd be defeated before we started!

It was hardly a good prelude to the meeting with Miramax. Peter and Fran were shown to 'the sweatbox', the room where they had had their creative meeting with the Weinsteins over a year before, and Marty Katz immediately left for a pre-meeting-meeting.

'Harvey wanted a magic solution,' says Marty, 'and there really wasn't one. I believe that the proposed one-movie version *could* have been made. It could even have been a *good* movie – maybe not a *great* one, but it could have been done. What I tried to make Bob and Harvey understand was that the film-maker they were working with *couldn't* make that version. I felt that it was in nobody's interests to try and force the issue, but they had reached a point where they were determined to either get Peter to see reason and meet their demands – or to go some other route.'

What that alternative route was all too soon became clear…

> Fran and me sat in the sweatbox for about an hour, waiting for something to happen. Then Harvey and Marty and others – Jon Gordon and Cary Granat – came into the room. I remember glancing up as they filed in, and noticing that Marty looked really shaken and ashen faced. He glanced at me and made a despairing gesture, like a shaking of the head. It was a look that said that whatever had happened at the previous meeting was not good.

Bob Weinstein was not present. Peter has a memory of being told, later, that Bob was 'so furiously angry' that he had refused to 'waste any more time' on them. Marty Katz's diplomatic recollection is that Bob didn't attend the meeting 'because he had said all that he had to say.'

As for Harvey, Peter remembers him striving to seek a way out of what was a painfully and expensively problematic situation.

> I think Harvey was genuinely fond of us and it wasn't a *brutal* meeting, but the atmosphere was horrible: there was a lot of anger on both sides and threats of lawsuits were hanging in the air.
>
> I asked whether, if we were to make one film, we could make just the first part and see how it worked and then, maybe, make the second film? But, no! It had to be the whole thing in *just* one film.

Then I asked whether, if we were to make one film, it could be the length of an epic like *Lawrence of Arabia*: a four-hour event. But, no! It would to have to be no more than a two-hour film.

Harvey's basic message was that the only way the project was going to happen was as one movie and if it didn't happen, then things were going to get ugly.

At the point when Peter indicated that it wasn't possible to make a single-film version of *The Lord of the Rings*, as was being proposed in their memo, Miramax made their next move. They announced that they owned everything that so far had been created for the film: models, miniatures, designs, conceptual artwork, as well as the Massive computer software, which had been developed at Weta. This was not Peter's understanding of the deal, but it was the industry norm in Hollywood and was evidently going to be an issue over which there were likely to be legal wranglings.

Harvey had a number of proposals for the eventuality of Peter proving uncooperative. The first was to announce that he was relieving Peter of any involvement in writing the screenplay.

Harvey said I was no longer writing the script, presumably because I was hostile to the one-movie version and wasn't going to trust me to compress the material. So, I was sacked from the screenplay and he then announced that Fran – whom Harvey saw as the writing talent, as, in many respects, she is – was going to work on the new version of the script with Hossein Amini.

Hossein Amini had already adapted two major literary works: Thomas Hardy's *Jude the Obscure* for a film directed by Michael Winterbottom and, for Miramax, Henry James' *The Wings of the Dove*.

So, that was Harvey's plan. It wasn't a case of our debating the merits of the idea or even expressing any opinions about the proposals; it was simply a case of Harvey saying, 'This is what is going to happen!' It was laid out for us and we were just expected to agree... Then at the end of the meeting, we asked, 'What's the scenario if we say that we don't want to do this, Harvey?' Which is when he dropped his next bombshell: he said, 'I've got John Madden lined up to direct the movie.'

John Madden had directed *Mrs Brown*, the Judi Dench film about Queen Victoria, and was about to direct *Shakespeare in Love*, the film title Harvey Weinstein had got from Universal as part of the aborted *King Kong* deal...

> Who knows whether Harvey really had this guy lined up or whether he was bullshitting names; one thing was clear: if we didn't agree to Miramax's terms, they intended to go ahead with *The Lord of the Rings* without us. Harvey said, 'I've come too far, I've spent too much money and I'm not going to see that money go down the drain. One way or another, this film is going to get made. So, you'd better go away and think it over!'
>
> We were due to be flying back to New Zealand the following day, so we promised to give it serious thought on the plane home and let him know what we decided to do.

Marty Katz observes, 'I could only commend Peter for his willingness to walk away rather than do something that didn't do justice to his vision...'

Ken Kamins remembers, 'We knew now that we were in trouble. Peter and Fran were pretty demoralised and I think, at that point, they believed that it was the end.'

> We walked out of the Miramax offices, just Fran and me, Marty didn't come with us. We walked out onto the street and we were trembling, shaking in a complete state of shock and not knowing what to do with ourselves.

Eventually, Peter and Fran took a cab to the offices of the production company, Good Machine, where former Miramax executive David Linde was now a partner. It had been David who had secured the foreign distribution rights to *Heavenly Creatures* and been involved in the decision to offer Peter and Fran a first-look deal with Miramax.

> We didn't have an appointment; we just stumbled into David's office and I asked him if he had any Scotch? I'd never drunk a whisky before – if you can believe it – but when anyone's shocked in the movies, they always seem to have a Scotch, so I thought it might help! David handed

me a glass and I knocked it back and, somehow, it seemed to calm me down a bit. That's how I came to have the first Scotch I'd ever drunk in my life – because I'd seen it in the movies!

We told David the whole story and it was a relief just to have somebody to talk to. Then we called up Ken and brought him up to speed with everything, and then, later that night, we jumped on the plane for New Zealand.

As much as they wanted to be home, the prospect of returning to Wellington was, as Fran recalls, a desperately unhappy one: 'How were we to face all these people who had put their hearts and souls into this project? It was terrible…'

Although we'd agreed to take time to consider our decision, in our hearts the decision was already made. There was never any way that we were going to make the single film version…

I mean, there really wasn't any serious debate but we had to think about it, had to think about what the repercussions would be if we *didn't* do it. It wasn't about the merits of making a one-film version of *The Lord of the Rings* or whether the fans of the book would be upset, what we were thinking about was what it would do to Weta and to all the people there: we had been going to make *King Kong*, but we didn't; then we were going to make *The Lord of the Rings*, and now we weren't going to be doing that either…

How were we going to keep people employed? How were we going to pay them? Would the company have to close? Suddenly, it was as if everything that we'd established here was under jeopardy…

The reception in Wellington was as bad, perhaps worse, than they had feared. Everyone was in despair and the project seemed all but at an end. The day eventually came on which a final decision had to be conveyed to Miramax and it was one that seemed both easy and impossibly hard.

Intellectually, we knew we didn't want to make Harvey's version of *The Lord of the Rings*, but having just seen the faces of all these people who'd been working on the film for fourteen months, we kept thinking: 'Do we owe it to them to make something?' Was it more sensible to at least do one two-hour movie than to stubbornly stand on our pride and say, 'This is a stupid idea and we're never going to do it!'?

It was the first week of July and Peter and Fran were due to take a few days' break at Wharekauhau Lodge, a remote luxury hideaway located fifty miles and a ten-minute helicopter flight from Wellington and set on a 5,000-acre sheep station overlooking Palliser Bay. The trip, which had been planned long before the summons to New York, was to cele-brate Fran's birthday on 8 July, though their feelings were now scarcely celebratory.

> On Fran's birthday we went out for a walk. The lodge is on the top of these cliffs on a stretch of isolated coast – a kind of *Wuthering Heights* setting! – and we walked and thought and talked and eventually made the decision that, come what may, we would just tell Miramax that our answer was 'No'. We were willing to continue with the two-movie version as we'd originally agreed, but that there was going to be no one-film version and no collaboration between Fran and Hossein Amini. So we rang Ken and told him to give Harvey the doomsday scenario and then we'd deal with whatever repercussions or lawsuits they decided to throw at us. Whatever would be would be. Having made the call, we felt a huge weight lift.

Burdened with breaking the bad news to Harvey, Ken duly made the call… But he was determined to keep the door open, and during the course of that conversation Ken outlined the situation at hand, and the various obstacles that would be faced by Miramax if they were to proceed with making a one-movie version. For example, a new writer would mean starting again almost from scratch, with an inevitable protracted period of further development, all of which would need to be funded at significant expense. There were also contractual complications that would inhibit Miramax from using any of the structural features that were unique to Peter and Fran's adaptation.

As Peter Nelson explains, 'Miramax knew that to make *The Lord of the Rings* in a new mould would take more years of more dollars and a better option for them might be simply to give up the project to somebody else.'

It was at this point that Ken suggested to Harvey that he allow

Peter the time to find another studio that would be willing to back his vision and reimburse Miramax for its expenditure on the project. The process, which is not uncommon in Hollywood, is known as 'turnaround'.

The difficult task, however, was negotiating that arrangement. As Ken recalls, the negotiations were tough and not pleasant: 'Miramax were not immediately moving towards letting us have a turnaround; it was much more about, "We gave these guys a chance to make this movie and they're not going to make it, so to hell with them, we're moving on!" Our response was, "Don't say 'No,' tell us what the terms would have to be if you would give it to us in turnaround. Come on! The guy's poured body and soul into this project, it's his unique vision, give us some window within which we can try and figure it out, no matter how impossible you might think it is…"'

Eventually, Harvey agreed and Ken Kamins rang Peter to break the good news; it was a lifeline they had dared not hope for, and a precious belated birthday present for Fran.

Ken then flew to New Zealand to discuss the situation further, by which time he and Peter Nelson were already deep in discussions with Bob Osher at Miramax over the proposed turnaround deal. Since Miramax were prepared to make a one-movie version of *The Lord of the Rings*, they insisted that any interested studio had to be willing to make *two* movies.

As Peter Nelson saw it at the time, 'Either Miramax really *did* plan to have someone else direct a one-film version and wanted to make it impossible for us – or it was a clever move to make everyone think that this enormous beast of a movie was actually going to be highly prized in the market. In any event, Miramax's terms were stringent and financial conditions were attached that were onerous and were going to make finding a new investor a serious challenge.'

Harvey wanted immediate repayment of the $15million that had been spent to date, the sum of which would have to be banked and cleared within seventy-two hours of a studio agreeing to take on the project. Bob Osher further suggested that Harvey and Bob Weinstein receive 5 per cent of first-dollar gross on the film when it was released and also be given Executive Producer credit to acknowledge that they had got the project started.

The most serious aspect of the offered turnaround, however, was the window in which the deal had to be accomplished. A typical turnaround period for a movie might be a year; Miramax were only prepared to give Peter four weeks – twenty-eight days to find Frodo Baggins a new home.

> We thought, 'What the hell are we going to do?' I think if you, at that point, had spoken to anybody in the film industry and asked what the chances were for us getting anyone to take on *The Lord of the Rings* on Miramax's terms, they would have said, 'Absolutely not a snowball's chance in hell!' But it was our *only* chance and we had to take it and give it our very best shot. We needed a strategy and we needed it quick. And the first thing we had to do was to get back home.

That, however, was easier said than done. The weather conditions at Wharekauhau when Peter received the news from Ken were not good: it was the middle of a typical New Zealand winter and, looking southwards along the coast, they could see a major storm raging over Wellington and heading towards them.

Having flown to Wharekauhau by helicopter, Peter and Fran didn't have a car and they knew that it would take someone two hours to drive up from Wellington to collect them and another two hours to travel back. Their only choice was to get the helicopter to fetch them, whether or not if it would be able to make the trip.

> All we knew was that we had to do whatever we could to try and save our movie: *The Lord of the Rings'* fate was being determined by a four-week clock – *and it had just started ticking!*

The chances that were taken and the decisions that were made over the next few hours would indeed decide the fate of *The Lord of the Rings* and, ultimately, secure Peter Jackson's reputation in cinema history...

8

THREE-RING CIRCUS

'**W**e fought so many battles,' reflects Peter Jackson, 'and worked through so much politics in order to get those early films made that it ultimately equipped us to take on the challenge of making *The Lord of the Rings*.'

With just four weeks to try and salvage the film project into which they had poured so much effort, Peter and Fran knew there wasn't an hour to lose. However, the word from Wellington was not encouraging: the storm was worsening and the helicopter pilot was unsure whether he would be able to make the journey to Wharekauhau. While they waited to see whether the chopper would get through, Peter and Fran began to plan their strategy.

> We didn't have a commercial success behind us; and worse, we had the stigma of having worked on this project for fourteen months with a studio which had now decided to dump – a situation that immediately gave a bad smell to the project. The question was, how do we convince another studio to write Miramax their huge cheque, pick up the project and continue on?

'We knew we had to go back to Los Angeles,' says Fran, 'and we knew that we had to take something with us to show to anyone who would see us.'

> Hollywood is a jaded town. Executives get pitched dozens of projects every day. But what they respond to best is visual imagery. You can get

somebody more excited with one drawing than an hour's talk – and we had thousands of drawings! Our greatest weapon was the huge amount of visual imagery we had created: Alan and John's conceptual art; Weta's miniatures and maquettes, and the digital tests. We had a wonderful CG Cave-troll; tests of Massive involving thousands of digital extras. The final miniature of Helm's Deep was built; so was Rivendell. It was frustrating: on one level we were convinced that if we could get any studio executive down to New Zealand, they would be blown away and pick up the project immediately. But that wasn't going to happen. So we had to think of an effective way to present this material in somebody's LA office. We knew that we had to blow people away and that the only way of doing that was to make a film!

A film that would have to be written, shot and edited in next to no time at all.

As soon as Ken told us about the four-week period, Fran and I started planning. If Harvey had to be paid in four weeks, we knew we needed to be in LA by week two.

That allowed two weeks for the deals to be done. But it also meant we had only seven days to conceive, shoot and edit our little film.

Peter made various calls and set up a meeting – more a council of war – with everyone whose help would be needed if an effective commercial for *The Lord of the Rings* were to be turned round in a matter of days.

The helicopter eventually arrived but the pilot was not encouraging about the return journey, saying that it was going to be a rough flight and questioning whether they really wanted to do it:

I really hate flying and Fran was looking absolutely sick, but I said, 'Listen, let's just get back to the city...'

It was, without doubt, the worst helicopter ride I've ever had in my life: the thing was literally bucking around the sky, swinging back and forth like a pendulum. The whole trip we were up-and-down and Fran and I were clutching each other's hands and clinging to the back seat. But we were on a mission and we weren't going to be put off by a bad flight! It felt like a *Thunderbirds* episode: International Rescue rushing to save *The Lord of the Rings*!

The analogy is revealing. Ken Kamins notes: 'There was very little time in which to get the project together and sell it on; it could easily have floundered at that point.' But Peter Jackson had no intention of letting it founder.

Reeling off the helicopter in a state of near nausea, Peter and Fran drove home and immediately launched themselves into a meeting with producer Tim Sanders; Weta's Richard Taylor and Tania Rodger; Alan Lee and John Howe; editor Jamie Selkirk; and cinematographer Alun Bollinger, who had worked on *Heavenly Creatures*, *Forgotten Silver* and *The Frighteners*. Peter and the team drew up a plan of campaign allowing themselves just one week in which to film the documentary.

Weta started assembling examples of their CGI effects; maquettes of the various races and creatures depicted in the story were placed on a turntable and shot with evocative lighting; and some of the best of Alan and John's artwork was selected and put under the camera along with examples of the many Tolkien books, calendars, maps and ephemera that indicated the extent of public interest in *The Lord of the Rings*. It was, as Peter would point out on the film's final soundtrack, a unique instance where the merchandising pre-dated the movie.

Peter and Fran drafted a script and chose a few examples of key storytelling moments from the Animatic. To link the material and deliver the selling pitch, they filmed interviews with various people involved in the project: Brian Van't Hul, Visual Effects Cinematographer, explained and demonstrated some of the film's special effects such as forced perspective technique for creating convincing scenes in which humans and hobbits would co-exist on screen while Alan and John talked about visualising Middle-earth and the philosophy of making the fantastic realistic.

> I also interviewed myself: sat in front of the camera as if I was answering questions, except I was making it all up as I went along!
>   There was a terrible sense of hopelessness: feeling that the project was slipping away from us and that we were desperately trying to save it, trying to say the right things, trying to figure out how to convince

some Hollywood guy to want to make this movie.

Despite the fact that we were all panicking inside, we were sitting there talking calmly, confidently, like it was a film that was actually happening! It looked like a 'Making of…' movie, but in reality it was a 'Saving of…' movie!

It was the greatest acting job I've ever done in my life and without doubt, the single most important film I've ever made.

That film, resulting from a desperately frenzied exercise in salesmanship, was a sophisticated promotional-video-cum-movie-trailer that, even viewed today, packs a powerful punch.

Opening with a great swell of music and the voice of Elrond – 'Power can be held in the smallest of things and be used for the greatest of evils…' – the thirty-five-minute film presents a compelling story of an ambitious dream to film another compelling story…

Passionate and committed, it highlighted many of the staggering accomplishments that had already been achieved: from hand-forged weapons to the devising of the Massive software programs and its vast armies of digital warriors. Wisely, it also tantalisingly hints at wonders and marvels yet to come.

By depicting the diversity of places found within Tolkien's story – the rural tranquillity of the Shire, the peace and beauty of Rivendell, the devastation of Mordor – and focusing on the people and beings populating Middle-earth, from hobbits and elves to orcs and trolls (plus, of course, Gollum and the Balrog), the film hits its mark with a confidence and certainty that totally belies the anxiety and panic that had caused it to be made.

In addition to the film, representing a personal investment by Peter of some $50,000, Weta Workshop mounted an impressive array of display-boards showing conceptual paintings and sketches by John, Alan and the other artists and designers who had been working on the project. The workshop also built a special metal box to transport a Gollum head, a Treebeard sculpture and a maquette of an Uruk-hai.

While this work was going on in New Zealand, Ken Kamins was already bombarding the various Hollywood studios with advance material, hoping to arouse their interest in meeting with Peter so that he could show his film and make a pitch. Ken remembers, 'We sent every studio the two screenplays and a copy of the animatic and we had to get every one of them to sign letters of confidentiality to Miramax for the material they were about to receive. We made sure that everyone knew what Harvey's terms were, up front; we made no secret of the fact because there was no point in doing so. Whoever then responded positively would be invited to meet with Peter and Fran and the thirty-five-minute film would be shown to them as an in-room presentation.'

One of those who received the two-script version of *The Lord of the Rings* was Mark Ordesky, who was now working at New Line Cinema. He knew the scripts were on their way, because Peter had put through a call to his old friend, whose couch he had been in the habit of using on his early trips to Hollywood.

'Peter called me and said, "I'm taking it to all the studios, but I'm taking it to you so you can try and bring it into New Line. There is just this window, but it's our chance, Mark! A chance for us to make a movie together!" Peter knew that I had tried, on several occasions, to get studios I was working for to finance or distribute previous Jackson films. Now he was offering me another one – not just any movie but *this* one of all things, because I'd been obsessed with *The Lord of the Rings* since I was 12 years old and had read it at least five or six times. So, I was a fanatic and Peter knew it!'

In turn, Mark was well aware that Peter's agent, International Creative Management, could have taken the project directly to New Line's founder and co-chairman, Robert Shaye, but was, instead, choosing to bring it to the studio via Mark. 'Peter is a superb strategist and a brilliant read of people; he knew Bob Shaye from his experience of working on the *Nightmare on Elm Street* script and he knew me and decided, "We'll give this to Mark – because Mark is insane! Mark will carry the water right up the hill! Mark will put in the foundations! And if we can just get into New Line, Mark will lay down covering fire like nobody's business!" Of course, he didn't say any of this to me, but he knew it. Peter knew that if he gave me this shot, I would turn myself into a pretzel to try to get it done. And he was 100 per cent right because the minute I'd hung up, I immediately felt that this was like a Holy Crusade. This now *had* to happen!'

With just three weeks left in which to clinch a deal, Peter and Fran boarded a plane for Los Angeles for what they hoped would be a series of meetings to which they would be accompanied by Ken and by Marty Katz, who they had asked to remain on the project as producer.

> We liked and got on well with Marty; he was an experienced Hollywood guy and an independent producer; he'd done a lot of budgeting work on the film and had been very supportive of us and the project.

By the time they arrived in Hollywood, however, most of the studios which had been approached had already declined any involvement: Bob Zemeckis didn't want to make a fantasy film; Centropolis, the company of Roland Emmerich who produced *Independence Day*, didn't like the scripts; Dreamworks passed, as did Sony Pictures and others. It was, after all, a daunting prospect: two films which, even before any budget was discussed, already carried a $15million ticket-price.

Twentieth Century Fox were interested but declined for political reasons: Saul Zaentz was a partner in *The Lord of the Rings* and Fox were still uncomfortably aware of their back-history with Zaentz over *The English Patient*; Universal, having only recently killed *King Kong*, were hardly ready to sign up to another Jackson film.

'Shockingly,' says Mark Ordesky, 'the other Hollywood studios showed little interest in *The Lord of the Rings*. People foolishly assumed that Peter couldn't handle a project like this, arguing that all he'd ever made were a few splatter movies and one art film. "Who's Peter Jackson? Didn't he make *The Frighteners*? Why on earth would we give him hundreds of millions of dollars?" But that's typical of Hollywood short-sightedness.'

> We flew into town, hyped up and ready to go with our film, our display boards and a box with three or four models. We got off the plane expecting a busy week – but it quickly transpired that there were only two companies really interested in meeting and talking with us: one was PolyGram and the other was New Line.

The first meeting was with Eric Fellner, co-chairman, with Tim Bevan, of PolyGram's subsidiary, Working Title Films, whose successes already included *Four Weddings and a Funeral*, *Dead Man Walking* and *Fargo*.

> We arrived at their offices in Beverly Hills, there was Fran and Ken carrying the display boards and Marty and I manhandling this big metal box of maquettes. We dragged all this stuff out of the car and hauled it up in the elevator. We talked up the project and explained why Miramax were leaving – that it was not about the project or us but about problems over the size of the budget required – and Eric Fellner and a bunch of his colleagues looked at all the materials and watched the video. At the end of the film, Eric said it was something that Working Title were really very interested in and we thought, 'Oh great!' but then he said, 'The trouble is, there's a problem...' And, immediately, our hearts sank.

The problem was that Working Title's owners, PolyGram, were on the market. No one knew how long it would be – three months, six months – before a sale might be finalised (the company was eventually bought by Universal in 1999) and there was no way that they could take on such a huge project while their parent company was up for sale.

> We explained that we needed a cheque for Miramax within a matter of days and Eric said, 'Sorry, guys, but it's impossible. We love everything we've seen, but it's just not possible.' I think he was meeting with us, hoping there might be some way in which to figure it out, but we all knew that there was no way Harvey was going to wait to see what happened with PolyGram. So that only left New Line.
>
> This was a Tuesday; we were due to fly home at the end of the week and the meeting with New Line was set for the following day. So Fran and I strategised and asked Ken to call Mark Ordesky and tell him that we were going to have to push back the meeting until later in the week because the property was so hot that everyone was in a frenzy about the project and we were so busy having meeting after meeting that we simply couldn't fit in New Line on the Wednesday but would have to postpone until Friday.

Michael Lynne and Barrie Osborne.

It was a piece of amazingly daring brinkmanship that might easily have gone horribly awry, since – unbeknownst to Peter – New Line's founder and co-chairman, Robert Shaye, had not initially warmed to the terms of the deal that Miramax had put on the table: 'When I had first heard that Miramax had got *The Lord of the Rings*, I thought it was a great coup for them. I had no idea of the magnitude of the project, but it was a smart idea. I'd just seen *Heavenly Creatures* and thought Peter did a particularly good job on that. Then, when it became available, Mark Ordesky and Mike De Luca together told me Peter and Fran were coming to Los Angeles and wanted to talk to us about *The Lord of the Rings*. I felt friendly towards Peter, but the stumbling block for me, without even talking to my partner Michael Lynne, was that we had to give a standard gross percentage to Miramax. I wasn't particularly keen on doing that. The executive producer credit for the Weinsteins didn't matter, the share of the money did. I actually said, "Forget it, we aren't going to do it!" Mark and Mike left my office and that was that.'

Mark Ordesky, however, was not easily going to take 'No,' for an answer. 'When I had arrived at New Line, I told everybody, "Some day when I'm a big mocker in this f****** business I'm going to make a Peter Jackson movie!" I told everybody. I'm so compulsive as a person that I make these contracts with the universe. If I want to do something I will run around and tell everybody. That way I shame myself into having to deliver. This is how I do things. I essentially put myself in a place where I've told 500 people that I'm going to do something and if I fail I'm humiliated. I intentionally put myself in this little corner then, by the time I'm ready to move, I will burst out with such ferocious intensity that there's no way I won't succeed. This is how I manage my professional life.'

Mark knew that there was a compelling argument to be placed before Bob Shaye and Michael Lynne: 'The story of what happened with *The Lord of the Rings* needs to be told within the context of totally separate business issues that were currently facing New Line. The studio was having trouble successfully making sequels to its previously successful hits such as *The Mask, Dumb and Dumber* and the movies featuring the characters of Freddy (*Elm Street*) Krueger and Jason (*Friday the 13th*) Voorhees. Either we couldn't put together the original talent or we simply couldn't seem to clinch the deals. In any event, the idea of making a film *with two sequels already in the can* had a certain appeal.'

As Bob Shaye puts it: 'When it came to getting sequels, our tent poles weren't holding up the tent very well. Michael and I began to think that the idea of having this trilogy available over three years could be an important and very valuable asset for the company.'

'There were many incentives,' says Mark, 'for considering *The Lord of the Rings*: apart from the sequels, there were economies of scale; and New Zealand, where Peter's muse was, offered amazing geography as well as being a very inexpensive place to shoot. You could see a million reasons why it would work. It all seemed to make perfect sense.'

Bob Shaye recalls: 'When Mark came back into my office a few weeks later to say that Peter was in town and to ask whether I wanted to meet him, I said I'd be glad to do so...'

Apart from playing the risky game of giving New Line the illusion that they had to postpone their meeting because they were getting together with other – possibly more important – studios, Peter was using the time to have other, genuine meetings with studios – although not about *The Lord of the Rings*.

> One of my first reactions when we realised that Miramax weren't going to go ahead with our version of *Rings* was to try to do something – anything – to stop Weta getting killed. I remember asking Ken, 'What's the quickest that you can get me on to another film? I'll leave New Zealand and go to Los Angeles, but you've got to get me a directing gig; something which has special effects that will keep Weta alive. After trying to make *Kong*, then *The Lord of the Rings* for the last three years, I was beaten and resigned to becoming 'a director for hire'. In actual fact, Ken unearthed several projects which were all quite interesting. Ironically, with only PolyGram and New Line meeting with us, I had time to go and visit several other studios to talk about making a film for them.

Peter had fleetingly thought about having one more attempt at getting *Planet of the Apes* up and running as a backup project, but had decided not to pursue it, and the death of Roddy McDowall, a few months later, effectively caused Peter to lose whatever remnants of interest he had left in the idea.

One possible project that had been explored some while before Peter arrived in Los Angeles on his hobbit-rescue mission would, had it happened, have been a reasonable compensation for not making *The Lord of the Rings*. Sometime in 1998, word was out that a director was being sought for the nineteenth *James Bond* feature, *The World is Not Enough*, after negotiations with Joe Dante had collapsed.

The 007 movies had made a huge impact on the young Peter Jackson and, indeed, had inspired one of his adolescent, amateur film experiments.

> As the years went by, I had remained a *Bond* fan – even when the movies rather lost their way. Basically, I think I'm a *Bond* fan for what they *could* and *should* be rather than what they sometimes actually *are*! It is one of my unrealised dreams to direct a *James Bond* film and I like to say that I came close – although, in reality, I probably didn't come anyway *near*!

When I heard that they were looking for a director for *The World is Not Enough*, I thought it might be my chance to fulfil a lifelong passion!

I think the studio view of the *Bond* franchise is that it is producer-driven, rather than director-driven. Whilst that is not necessarily a bad thing, I suspect that there is a feeling amongst those who control the copyright that they daren't ever use directors who have any degree of power or they will lose power themselves – which is why they would never consider having a Tarantino or a Spielberg direct a *Bond* film.

I wasn't in that league of course, but Ken Kamins called Barbara Broccoli, daughter of Bond's first producer, the late 'Cubby' Broccoli, who was interested in the proposal having seen and liked *Heavenly Creatures*. Ken arranged for her to see *The Frighteners*, which, unfortunately, she did *not* like! So, that was the end of *my* chances with Mr Bond!

The World is Not Enough was eventually filmed in 1999, directed by Michael Apted. If Peter Jackson's analysis of how directors of Bond films are chosen is correct, then he is now way too big a player to ever be considered. All that remains of his ambition, therefore, are a few reels of silent Super 8 film shot in 1979 – the year that saw the 'official' Bond launched into outer space in *Moonraker*.

Although there was no meeting with Barbara Broccoli, there were a number of other discussions: with Disney and Jim Henson Productions about a possible science-fiction project; with Joel Silver about a possible Matrix sequel entitled *Logose*; and with producer Kathleen Kennedy (*Back to the Future*, *Empire of the Sun* and *Who Framed Roger Rabbit*) about directing Robin Williams as the Big Friendly Giant in a movie version of Roald Dahl's *The BFG*.

There was also interest in making a film based on *Concrete*, the heavyweight superhero with rocklike epidermis from Dark Horse Comics.

When the income from Miramax dried up, Fran and I wrote a *Concrete* script for Disney. Like we'd done originally with *The Frighteners*, it was just a writing assignment – one that I wasn't necessarily going to direct. We had a lot of fun with the script. Maybe it'll get made one day.

But perhaps the most promising project was with Chris Columbus' production company, 1492, who were interested in developing a film entitled *Twenty-One*, about Frank Luke, a 21-year-old American World War I flying ace who shot down eighteen German planes and observation balloons during seventeen days in September 1918 before being brought down by ground fire and dying, pistol in hand, while resisting capture. Born in Phoenix, Luke was known as the 'Arizona Balloon Buster' and was posthumously awarded the Medal of Honor.

With Peter's lifelong fascination with aviation in the First World War, it was another filmic subject uniquely suited to his knowledge and enthusiasms.

> A copy of the script for *Twenty-One* was sent to my hotel and we had a couple of meetings with Fox about the concept. As soon as I knew about the project, I had Weta urgently courier me an old *King Kong* computer test we'd done. It featured a digital WWI dogfight, with dozens of planes wheeling around the skies. I showed up for the meeting at Fox and stuck the tape on. The executives' eyes were bulging when they saw the spectacle, and how realistic it was. The plan, if *The Lord of the Rings* didn't get picked up, was that Weta would immediately start building the period planes and Fran and I would gear up to work on the script and begin shooting. Our back-up plan was in place.

The chance to tell the story of Frank Luke was the strongest bet if the meeting with New Line failed to breathe new life into Mr Frodo Baggins.

Come the Friday 24 July, Peter, Fran, Ken Kamins and Marty Katz arrived at the offices of New Line for their meeting and were shown into the boardroom. Ken Kamins recalls: 'Mark Ordesky had warned us, very dramatically in advance, that Bob is a mercurial guy, that he doesn't care that you've flown 7,500 miles or that you've spent $50,000 out of your own pocket to produce a video: if he's five minutes into the presentation and he's not interested, he'll just say, "Thank you. I pass…"'

Mark had said that Bob might just get up and walk out of the room without saying a word. 'If he does that,' he told us, 'don't be alarmed – well, *be alarmed*, but don't be insulted or offended because it's just Bob's way and if it happens, it happens…'

Commenting on these accounts of his behaviour, Bob Shaye notes, 'I don't think I've ever been rude, but there is no reason not to be frank in a gracious way. After all, any meeting is *our* time as much as *theirs* and there are probably only some 150,000 people that want to have movies made at any given minute!'

Ken Kamins describes what happened next: 'Mark walks into the conference room, kind of white-faced, and we looked at him and said, "What's wrong?" "Bob wants to see Peter, in his office, alone," he replied. "We don't know why." So Peter dutifully gets up and leaves. He's in there for the better part of twenty-five minutes. Fran was saying, "What's going on, why is he in there?" And I said, "Well, maybe he's letting Peter down gently, letting him know he's a big fan, but that this is not something he can tackle; or maybe he's offering Peter another movie…"'

Peter went to Bob's Shaye's office (Bob's partner, Michael Lynne, was in New York at the time) and they met for the first time since Peter had worked on the prospective *Nightmare on Elm Street* script.

Bob greeted me warmly, told me that he had seen *Heavenly Creatures* and really loved it and thought that was a wonderful film, but that he hadn't liked *The Frighteners* at all – which I remember being delighted to hear – seriously! In Hollywood everybody tells you how much they love your movies, and to hear somebody say they didn't like a film was refreshing and wonderfully honest. Bob says what he thinks, and that honesty has given him something of a reputation in a town not used to people telling the truth.

Then he said, 'I understand you've got a video to show me and I'm going to look at that and I'll give this some thought; but if we don't want to do this film, I just want you to know that the door at New Line is always open to you and if you ever have a project and are looking for a studio, then you are were welcome to bring it here.'

I got the impression that he wanted to be friendly but, at the same time, was warning me that they might feel they had to pass on *The Lord of the Rings*. It certainly increased the anxiety, but at least he was being straight...

So, we went to the boardroom together and Bob met Fran and Marty and sort of grunted a greeting at Ken, because he doesn't much like agents! Then Bob said, 'Okay, let's get started...' and we made our presentation and, all the time, I was remembering Mark's warnings and waiting for Bob to leave...

Having finished his 'show-and-tell' performance on the project with the display boards and models, the videotape was finally put into the player and as Ken Kamins remembers, 'We were all of us holding our collective breath...'

I sat watching Bob watching the film. He was totally attentive; following everything closely but in absolute, stony silence and showing no reaction to anything on screen. He didn't say a single word throughout the entire thirty-five minutes; but then, thank God, nor did he get up and go!

Eventually came Peter's closing narration: 'Here we are, at a point forty-five years after the publication of this book, when, finally, the technology has caught up with the incredible images that Tolkien injected into this story of his. So, this is the time. This is the time that this movie can finally be made.'

'Peter answered two questions directly in that video,' says Ken Kamins, 'the first being, "Why was this the right time to make *The Lord of the Rings*?" The second question it answered was, "All that money – *that $15million* – that you heard I spent with Miramax: *where did it go*?" The third, more subtle question, being answered was, "Why am I, Peter Jackson, the right guy to make this movie?"

So, had it worked, they all wondered? Had they succeeded in selling the show?

Eventually, the video finished and there was this terrible silence in the room while Mark nervously took the tape out of the video player and handed it back to me...

What happened next has entered the mythology of cinema and is, like all the best myths, retold with subtle variations:

Mark Ordesky: Bob is impossible to read; completely inscrutable. The lights came up and I couldn't read the situation at all.

Marty Katz: Then Bob said, 'Why would anyone want movie-goers to pay $18 when they might pay $27?'

Fran Walsh: We just stared at him, too frightened to try and work out what he meant!

Peter Jackson: This was really perplexing... Fran and I looked at each other. Was he suggesting an increase in ticket prices and, if so, why?

Fran Walsh: Then he asked, 'Why exactly do you want to make *two* films?'

Mark Ordesky: He said, 'I thought there were *three* books... I don't understand why you're making *two* movies?'

Peter Jackson: I thought, 'Oh God, here were go again! Back to the *one-movie* discussion!'

Fran Walsh: We sat there, mutely, not knowing what to say...

Ken Kamins: Bob said, 'Tolkien did your job for you, didn't he?'

Fran Walsh: He said, 'Tolkien wrote three books – *right*?' We nodded. 'Then, if you're going to do it justice, it should be *three* movies – *right*?' We could scarcely believe what we were hearing!'

Mark Ordesky: Peter's clearly thinking, 'Dare-I-hope-that-some-one-is-really-saying-this-to-me?' and he has this look on his face of someone trying not to frighten away an animal that you want to eat out of the palm of your hand. So, Peter finally said: 'Yes, there *are* three books...' and, 'Yes, three movies would be terrific...'

And the other participant in the meeting? What is his memory of the historic occasion? Bob Shaye is characteristically frank:

'I think time blurs reality. Between them all, they've turned it into a whimsical moment of who-knows-what! When I walked into that meeting, I wasn't so sure I would like what I was going to see. I *did* like it – liked it a lot and was very impressed. We already started off with the foundation interest: an incredible piece of material that had worldwide recognition and incredible marketing momentum. In my own mind I had to be pushed over the top, have somebody suggest to me this guy could pull it off.

'The locations looked spectacular; the designs were beautiful, but not overly elaborate; and he had some really good ideas about how to achieve the special effects – we had just come off *The Mask*, on which ILM had done a fantastic, but very expensive, job. There was also the algorithm that Weta claimed to have created that could make thousands of actors out of a few, each with thirty different motions and no computer repetition. That much impressed me.

'I knew the budget Peter was proposing and was aware that our company's financial structure could handle it. I was cognisant of my discussions with Michael Lynne about our need for sequels. I knew that, after conferring with Michael – and if, one way or another, when we'd talked with Miramax, we could deal with the numbers – we were going to make *three* films. But I *didn't* say, "Aren't there three books?" or whatever I'm supposed to have said. I *did* say, "Why are we talking about two films instead of three?" Because I didn't know what Peter had in his head but I wanted to have three years of potential security and good business.'

'Timing,' says Ken Kamins, 'is everything! All those things that you don't know or can't see when you walk in the door are a factor in how your meeting will go.' What Peter and his associates didn't know was that New Line had recently spent time and money – perhaps as much as $1.5million – researching a movie project based on Isaac Asimov's celebrated sci-fi classic *The Foundation Trilogy*, only to have it fail to develop into the franchise they were hoping for. As a result, they cut their losses and let the option on Asimov's books lapse. 'At that point,' says Ken, 'in *we* walk!'

'It was,' says Marty Katz, 'the most successful meeting I've ever been at – going in to sell *two* movies and ending up selling *three*!'

'Suddenly,' says Mark Ordesky, 'everyone was getting excited: Peter is saying, "Yes, three films would be the best way to tell the story; the best way to be true to the spirit of Tolkien…' and so on. And Bob was getting pretty excited because he sees what Peter was saying, artistically, but because he's also seeing three video releases, three network television sales. It's Art! It's Commerce! It's the perfect fusion of motivation!'

Ken Kamins remembers Bob Shaye debating what the release

pattern would be if it were it be three movies: 'Would you do all three within two weeks of each other, so you basically sell series tickets, literally dominating a multiplex? Or do you go Summer–Christmas, Summer–Christmas, Summer–Christmas? Or would it be one movie a year for three years? Bob was really concerned that even though it would be three films you could not assume that everybody coming to see these movies knew these books. Nor could you assume that someone who shows up at the beginning of *Fellowship* is somebody you own all the way through to the end of *The Return of the King*. Each movie, therefore, needed to entertain in its own right and have a three-act structure with a beginning, middle and an end, so that if you went to the second movie never having seen the first movie and with no intention of seeing the third movie, it would be a satisfying movie-going experience on its own terms.'

By the end of the meeting, it was clear that Bob Shaye – pending his discussions with Michael Lynne – was committed to a three-film version of *The Lord of the Rings*. He asked to retain the videotape in order to be able to screen it for Michael.

> We weren't allowing anyone to *have* the tape, because all the studios were saying, 'Just send a copy of the tape over…' and Ken had been quite clear: 'The tape doesn't leave Peter and Fran's possession; if you want to look at it, they bring it over and they take it with them when they leave. No one gets a copy of the tape.' So Bob said, 'We gotta keep this tape, I've got to show it to Michael…' And, at that point, we decided that we weren't going to say 'No'!

'I really believe,' says Ken Kamins, 'that Bob Shaye thought that he was in a more competitive situation than he truly was, because, after all this hypothetical discussion, Bob looked at me and said something along the lines of, "I don't want to hear any bullshit; I don't want to hear any talk about other companies and other meetings; we start negotiations tomorrow morning, nine o'clock. Let's move this thing along."'

Peter and the others gathered up their display boards and their box of models and left.

Mark Ordesky recalls: 'As soon as we were on our own, Bob said, "Okay, go make the deal." I was staggered. When Bob had said, 'All right, I've heard the pitch. I buy the pitch. Let's go for it. Let's make these films.' I figured my job was done. And now he was telling *me* to make the deal...

'Shaye has this amazing kind of "authorship credo": if you bring in a deal, it's yours, because it is self-policing: if you give someone something that they've advocated, then who's going to be more disciplined and aggressive about managing it than the person who brought it in? Nevertheless, I'm thinking, "This is not my bailiwick. This is not something I know that much about..." Up until this point the only movies I had supervised from script to screen were a few straight-to-video titles and one or two low, low budget art movies; that was about it.

'But Bob put this on me anyway. He said, "Jackson's your friend and you're the one who's obsessed with Tolkien; so who else is going

---

Our New Line production executive, Mark Ordesky – he was very much the glue that held the fragile relationships together and stopped them from imploding. He was the one guy we dealt with from New Line who really knew his Tolkien.

to do it?" So I said, "All right, I'll do it then…" and that's how the process started – with my having a hell of a lot of enthusiasm but not a whole lot of knowledge!'

A good few Hollywood eyebrows would be raised over New Line's decision to commit to *The Lord of the Rings* and the sheer, mind-boggling scale of the project.

'It was risky!' admits Mark. 'It was bold! And there were people within New Line and definitely *outside* of New Line who thought we were *insane!* There was one person who, behind my back, referred to these movies within a New Line context as "Mark's Folly", which was a little mean – or maybe it was a *lot* mean! But in any case, I under-stood how that could be: after all, in the history of cinema, no one had ever made three movies simultaneously and no one has made sequels to a non-existent first-film! So, because the films were so big and so frightening and so inconceivable to so many people, I was given amazing amounts of autonomy to supervise them because I was the only one who really understood: I understood the books and I understood Peter.'

At the time, Mark made a prediction: 'I said, "One day, this will be seen to have been the most visionary business decision in modern cinema." Normally, when a film succeeds and sequels are called for, everyone's price goes up. But we are going to have two sequels in the can at prices that would never be achievable any other way. But aside from that business consideration, sequels require actors to "re-plug" into their original roles. This cast will have to live their roles for more than a year and that commitment must inevitably result in powerful and convincing performances.'

By the early months of 2002, Mark's prediction had proved true. Back in 1998, there were no guarantees…

'When I said, "Yes, we are going to do it,"' remarks Bob Shaye, 'what was implicit was "Let's see if you really can deliver!" We didn't just go ahead and sign a piece of paper the next day!'

What *did* happen the next day, as Ken Kamins recalls, was that the negotiations began: 'Nine o'clock to the minute the next morning, I got a phone call from Mark Ordesky; Peter Nelson got a call from somebody else at New Line; Miramax's lawyer got a call and Saul

Zaentz's lawyer got a call! New Line moved on three fronts at once: with us for Peter's deal, with Miramax for the turnaround and with Saul Zaentz's people because there were aspects to Saul's deal that, if Miramax sold the rights to a third party, automatically came up for review.'

> At that point, Saul could probably have stopped the whole thing in its tracks, if he had wanted. But fortunately Bob Shaye and Saul Zaentz knew each other and had a good rapport, so Bob was able to reach out to Saul who was really supportive of the project's move from Miramax to New Line.

Within a week, New Line appointed the now-late Carla Fry as executive in charge of production and she flew to New Zealand to look at Peter's facilities to see if he could do everything he said he could do.

'Basically,' explains Michael Lynne, 'we embarked on a huge vetting process: the initial numbers discussed were Peter's, not ours, and there were quite a few logistical issues, so we had a team spending close to a month in New Zealand getting their heads around whether the budget would be in the ball-park... I'm not sure they ever did!'

Although everything moved swiftly from the moment Bob Shaye committed to the film, the four-week deadline set by Miramax was soon reached without anyone having yet signed on the dotted line.

> We had taken a week to make the promotional film, we'd spent a week in Los Angeles and now the two remaining weeks were fast running out. There was a rather nervous period where we had to ask Harvey for an extension, but by then the Miramax and New Line lawyers had got fairly deeply into it, so I think Harvey saw what he had absolutely thought he was *never* going to see – the possibility of getting his $15million back, and if that wasn't going to happen at the end of the four weeks, it was going to happen pretty soon after.

The interim was a difficult time: Miramax cheques had finally dried up and the New Line cash-flow had yet to start flowing. Technically, the project was at an end and, at best, it could be considered as being at a standstill. Everyone involved had been stood down or laid-off;

Alan Lee had retuned to England, John Howe had flown home to Switzerland.

Miramax – hedging their bets in case the New Line deal failed to stick – had representatives in Wellington, making inventories of all the items of research and development, every sketch and model, and preparing to pack them into containers to be transported to Los Angeles for the use of whoever might eventually take over the project.

'The final deal', as Peter Nelson recalls, 'took a lot of negotiating. I've never worked harder in any period of my life than during those four weeks! It was a non-stop negotiation: first with Miramax to *extract* the project, then with New Line to *set up* the project.'

In what seems to have been a euphoric beginning to the relationship, New Line appeared to be going to agree to contract Peter on what is called a 'pay-or-play commitment', which would have meant that, had he been dropped from the project for any reason, they would still have paid his director's fee in full. 'Then,' says Peter Nelson, 'as New Line sobered up during the couple of weeks that were rushing by, they thought, "We don't necessarily *need* to do that…" New Line, despite our best endeavours, started to realise that it was either going to go out with them or wasn't going to go out at all, so some of the terms they originally put on the table started to leave the table, which made us a bit upset to say the least.'

Whilst Peter retained his right to make the final cut of the movie, he had to give up some of his financial participation as a result of the 5 per cent share that was one of Miramax's terms for the turnaround. 'Nevertheless,' says Peter Nelson, 'with a bit of our pride still intact, we were still able to extract a deal that propelled the movie forward. New Line calculated Peter's directing fee by multiplying it by three and dividing it by two, so that he effectively made three movies for the price of one-and-a-half, which was eventually a complete understatement of his value, but it didn't matter for a variety of reasons relating to the other parts of his financial package, as well as the fact that the movies were, at last, going to get made.'

Eventually, within about a month of the meeting with Bob Shaye, New Line wrote Miramax that cheque and *The Lord of the Rings* became a New Line film.

From the moment in August 1998 when it was announced that Peter Jackson was to be filming Tolkien's epic, the book's legions of fans, given a forum by the ever-growing community of the world-wide-web, started voicing their hopes and fears, pleading – even *demanding* – that the film-makers do this or don't do that, clutching at every scrap of hard-to-come-by information, hoovering up the dust of rumour, gossip and speculation and generally revelling in the excitement and nervous trepidation resulting from knowing that a dearly-loved friend (and often lifetime companion) was to become the subject of a Hollywood-backed movie made by a director whose apparently unlikely back-catalogue contained several gory splatter-fests!

> There was lot of nervousness at the beginning – partly because the fans didn't know who I was. If you have a beloved book that some unknown guy is going to make into a film, *fear* is really the first emotion that jumps in. You always imagine the worst-case scenario; you're not thinking that what these people are going to do might actually be *good*, you're thinking, 'How can they stuff this up? They're going to simplify it, dumb it down, change everything…'
>
> I had never felt that Miramax had any real understanding of the fans, as was borne out when they eventually presented us with the idea of how to reduce the entire story into one two-hour movie; to gut it of half the characters and half the events and still call it by its title. We knew that the only thing that was guaranteed if we had done that was that every single fan of that book would have felt let down and would have turned their back on the film.

Even though Peter was now making the film in a format that would allow him to do far greater justice to Tolkien's work than would have been possible with the Miramax one-film proposal, a palpable ripple of anxiety was still sweeping through the Tolkien/fantasy/movie web-sites. Peter cannily decided to seize the opportunity and use the internet to introduce himself to the fans and attempt to reply to some of the early concerns that were being, sometimes hysterically, expressed. Peter agreed to answer twenty questions for the *Ain't it Cool* website of the larger-than-life movie fan-boy, Harry Knowles. Within a very short time Knowles had received a staggering 14,000 questions.

I was very open and honest in answering those questions and in trying to quell people's fears, settle everybody down and say, 'I am a fan, too. I love these books as well and I am going to do my best to honour them...'

Peter's opening comments when his twenty answers appeared on 30 August 1998 were certainly not the stiff-and-starchy response of some remote Hollywood director: 'I must thank Harry for allowing me to commandeer his site. It's a bit like a scene in a war movie when a French family gets booted out of their farmhouse because the Allied Forces need to set up a command post! Using Harry's site was the only way I could imagine reaching all of you in an efficient way... After this brief warm shower together, Harry and I return to our different sides of the line – us trying to maintain secrecy... and he using his low-life methods to publish it all on the net.'

There were questions about the look of the film; Peter described it at the time as being 'something like *Braveheart*, but with a little of the visual magic of *Legend*' and without 'the meaningless fantasy mumbo-jumbo of *Willow*'; there were questions about casting (and how to get an audition!); about who would be composing the music; about how dwarves and hobbits would be depicted, what Legolas would look like and whether or not Sauron would be given any physical representation. It was early days and one or two answers were later subject to revision: asked, for example, whether 'the combat of Gandalf and the Balrog after they fall from the bridge in Moria' might be shown 'perhaps in a flashback', Peter responded: 'I don't think so.'

What Peter tried to make clear was that this was only *his* take on Tolkien's book: 'You shouldn't think of these movies as being *The Lord of the Rings... The Lord of the Rings* is, and always will be, a wonderful book – one of the greatest ever written. Any films will only ever be an INTERPRETATION of the book. In this case *my* interpretation...'

We were well aware that there were die-hard fans who held the view: 'There's no need to change a thing! The book's perfect, just give us a movie that puts the book – page-by-every-page – on film!' What *we* knew at the outset – because we'd thought long and hard about it and had already agonised over it in writing the Miramax scripts – was that it all came down to *choices.*

Eventually, people came to see that a 100 per cent faithful film version just couldn't have been made and wouldn't have worked because it would have been slow and unstructured and very pedantic. For the most part, they also came to accept what I had tried to make clear on Harry's website: that what they would be seeing was simply the interpretation of another group of fans.

Several of the *Ain't it Cool* questioners wanted to know in what ways Peter intended departing from the book. 'This,' he replied, 'is the sixty-four-thousand-dollar question I guess! Our philosophy is simple. We don't want to make any radical changes to the basic events or characters in the books. So Sam will NOT become a girl (a piece of rumour-mill bullshit that's been floating around for a year), or have

Tolkien's book was never far away – we constantly referred to it during shooting to try to make sure we didn't miss the chance to add another little bit of detail to whatever was being shoot that day.

a gay relationship with Frodo... We will have to remove certain events or characters, but they will be clean lifts...' *An advance warning to Tom Bombadil fans, if ever there was one!* 'Any changes that we do make will be centred on developing characters or events in the spirit that Tolkien created them, but maybe taking them further than he did...' *And a clue that Arwen was going to need some thinking about...*

Question 18 read: 'How open will this project be? Meaning what types of things will you be showing us fans in the years leading up to this film?' Peter replied that it would probably similar to the *Star Wars* movies: 'Expect the same level of secrecy/revelations. I will try and kept a steady stream of information flowing. I know how frustrating it is.'

As a movie fan since a kid, Peter knew all about waiting for a movie that you are desperate to see and grasping at anything and everything that will tell you *something* of what is to come. He can hardly have imaged the extent to which *The Lord of the Rings* would be followed – and in a sense chronicled by the websites of the internet.

Only a few months after Peter's appearance on *Ain't it Cool*, TheOneRing.net ('forged by and for fans of J.R.R. Tolkien') was up and running and establishing itself as the pre-eminent *Rings* film site, feeding a global fan-frenzy with news, inside stories, gossip and conjecture. Before long, this or that 'Ringer Spy' would be fuelling the fire with daily reports and covert photographs.

As he had demonstrated in going public on the Knowles site, Peter eventually found ways of harnessing the fan interest and minimising the kind of bad rapport that inevitably resulted from fans with a wilful determination to find things out that a studio is determined not to reveal. While Peter was filming the scenes in Hobbiton, one of TORn's founders, Erica Challis (or 'Tehanu' as she was known on the net), would visit the film set and meet the director and actors – an event that heralded a new relationship between film-makers and fans.

Such would be the power of the web in promoting *Rings* that when, in April 2000, the first internet preview aired, it seized a world record of 1.67 million 'hits' in the first twenty-four hours. By that time Peter was deep into filming, grappling with some difficult scenes on the slopes of New Zealand's active volcano, Mount Ruapehu, which was doubling for Mount Doom, and the public reaction proved an enormous morale-booster at a difficult time. Within one week, the number of hits on the web preview – despite being only a couple of minutes long – had soared to 6.6 million. And that was only the beginning...

The final question addressed by Peter during his Knowles web-fan-conference was: 'When you look at the films, what are you dying to capture on film, and how will you do it?' Peter's answer, amusingly framed though it was, went to the heart of his philosophy for the pictures:

'I want to take movie-goers into Middle-earth in a way that is believable and powerful.

'Imagine this: 7,000 years has gone by. We take a film crew to Helm's Deep... It's now looking a little older, but still impresses as a mighty fortress. The Art Department set to work, patching up holes and removing tourist signs. The current owner strikes a hard bargain, but New Line money finally gets us permission to film there for six weeks. Rohan heraldry is studied and faithfully reproduced. Théoden's original saddle is in a museum – far too valuable to use in the movie, but an exact copy is made. Archaeological expeditions have unearthed an incredibly preserved mummified Uruk-hai carcass. We make exact prosthetic copies of these viscous killers [and] use CG to give us a 10,000-strong army. We have cast actors who look like Aragorn and Théoden. In an amazing casting coup, Legolas has agreed to return from Valinor with Gimli to recreate their part in this cinematic retelling of the events at the end of the Third Age. They stand on the battlements of the Deeping Wall, wind blowing in their hair, leading a group of extras proudly portraying the brave garrison of Rohan soldiers... Uruk drums roll up the valley... huge lighting rigs flash simulated lightning... rain towers send gallons of water into the air... on an assistant director's signal, twenty 35mm cameras start rolling simultaneously... the battle of Helm's Deep is about to be captured on film.

'Sure, it's not really *The Lord of the Rings*... but it could still be a pretty damn cool movie.'

Having answered their questions, Peter told the *Ain't it Cool* readers, 'I have to go to ground and do some writing...' And that was, indeed, urgently the case.

> The moment the deals were done, lots of things needed to happen at the same time. One of the most pressing was rewriting our two-film scripts as three films, which was really a throw-it-away-and-start-again scenario!

'Everything had to be re-thought,' says Philippa Boyens. 'Material that had been heavily compressed could now be allowed to breathe, entire episodes which had previously been cut – such as the Fellowship in Lothlórien – could now be restored.'

Fran Walsh reflects, 'We were constantly striving to make the new structures we were building dramatically sound and emotionally satisfying. We repeatedly asked ourselves "What is this battle *about*? What are they fighting *for*?" Every time we came back to the same answer: it was about the free people of Middle-earth, their lives, their freedom, their future...

> One thing with a film where you have multiple storylines is that it gives you every opportunity to keep people's interest up and inject a degree of tension because you follow one storyline to a dramatic moment where the audience go, 'Oh my God! What's going to happen next?' Then, while you're keeping people under a degree of suspense so that they want to go back and find out what's going to happen, you cut to another storyline and do exactly the same thing! In that way, whenever you're with one set of characters, you're still thinking and worrying about what's happening to the other guys!

There were major structural considerations. One of the daunting aspects of turning two films into three films was deciding the point of transition from *Fellowship* to *Two Towers* and what the climax would be for the first film. For a while it would be the sequence at Isengard in which Gandalf confronts Saruman and, using material from the very end of Tolkien's story, Wormtongue stabs his master. There were huge issues to be faced over the structuring of the second and third films since the books whose titles they notionally carry are not a chronological account of events, with sequences in *Towers* (like the encounter with Shelob) actually taking place concurrently with events such as the siege of Minas Tirith described in *The Return of the King*.

There was also a feeling that *The Two Towers* scenario was seriously lacking in life-threatening peril for the central characters.

> We were very confident about *Fellowship*, as we got to kill two of the main characters with the fall of Gandalf and the death of Boromir, which made very powerful scenes. In *The Two Towers*, even though the opposition of the enemy is even stronger, no major characters die. The feeling was that we needed to create more drama than the book. So we pumped up the character of Haldir, who was very much a secondary character in the book, and engineered his eventual death on the battlements of Helm's Deep to give emotional impact. We also figured that we wanted to create a moment of jeopardy with the Warg attack during the Rohan retreat from Edoras – a major new action scene resulting in Aragorn being assumed dead.

'At the same time,' says Fran, 'action all too quickly becomes meaningless if there is no emotional value attached to it and so all the dramatic moments were processed through characters dealing with problems particular to them and the story.'

Whilst working to achieve these aims, the writers were also attempting to keep yet another goal in sight: that of providing a series of entertaining films that would appeal not just to the enthusiasts who read the book every year but also to those who read it once when they were a school, maybe ten or fifteen years before, and only retained the vaguest outline of key characters and main events; not to mention those with unread copies on their bookshelves gathering dust and cinemagoers with no more knowledge of *The Lord of the Rings* than the title and who really didn't know their Saurons from their Sarumans.

> It was a plain fact that if the films were not enjoyable movies then it was going to be a waste of time and a waste of the huge amount of money that New Line were putting up. To make films that were worthy but dull

would not, ultimately, have been doing anybody a service – including the memory of Tolkien himself. So we looked always for points where we could get little twists and turns into the plot, take audiences' expectations down one way and then surprise them.

'Having to restructure the scripts,' says Mark Ordesky, 'was a really good thing. To this day, I'm convinced that I may have been the only person at New Line that actually read *all* of the original 291-page scripts before we actually committed to taking over the development of the movie and when I read them, as enthusiastic as I was, I thought, "My God, this can't work! There's no way! What have I gotten myself into?" They were unwieldy and, built that way, the story didn't flow right. But I had complete faith in Peter, Fran and Philippa and as they started to build the two movies into three, suddenly all the plot points seemed to fall into place.'

The third script carried cover material that maintained the *Jamboree* joke with a design featuring a further reference to the so-called 'affectionate coming-of-age drama set in the New Zealand Boy Scout Movement', the image of a hand raised in the three-finger scout-salute and an additional tantalizing plot revelation. 'Part III,' it was announced, 'reaches a shattering climax at the 1963 Tokyo World Jamboree'! Once named *Jamboree*, the project would remain *Jamboree* throughout production.

> We had to write these scripts very quickly because New Line were now committed and once you commit to a film everybody really wants to be pushing through to shooting it and releasing it: once the money tap has been turned on, no one is going to get any money back until the film hits the cinema. So, from the moment when things are 'go'-mode, there's always a feeling almost of impatience…

As the scripts took on their new form, those supervising the production started drawing up a three-movie budget. Mark Ordesky puts it this way: 'There were no rules. The rules got written as we went along. We made all these assumptions. The film-makers made assumptions. The studio made assumptions. We imagine it will be like this. So the budgeting, the strategy, the schedule, the way we built it, the way we went about constructing the whole scenario around the movie was informed by gut instinct and – and sort of intuitive leaps based on nothing! Inevitably, when we eventually started making the movies, one by one, a lot of the assumptions flew right out the window!'

> Although you could argue that because New Line had paid so much money to get the project from Miramax there was no way that they weren't going to go through with the movie, the fact remains that, at this stage, they still hadn't officially confirmed that we were 'making' the film. All they had done was pick up the rights and put us into development again; so they were paying us to rewrite the scripts and funding Weta to do their work, but they hadn't signed off on a final budget, they hadn't green-lit the movie. As such they were in a position to apply pressure in certain areas and particularly in relation to the casting...

Whilst Mark Ordesky claims that New Line 'had made a philosophical decision that we weren't going to go to huge stars, but were simply going to cast on merit', Peter recalls that because the studio were going to be partly funding the film from investments by foreign distributors, they were initially looking for casting that would appeal to foreign markets.

One role in particular had seemed to lend itself to star-casting:

> New Line were indicating to us that casting was going to be very critical and that really wanted somebody like Sean Connery in the role of Gandalf – thinking it was necessary to anchor the movies and keep their foreign distributors happy.
>
> As a Bond fan, working with Connery was something I would have loved to do – and would still love to do – and because he has international stardom and a huge following it was, from a marketing point of view, an attractive idea. But it wasn't one that really fitted with our mantra of keeping the films as *believable* as possible, because I felt Gandalf would take on a Sean Connery persona, with a long beard and robe.
>
> At the time, however, New Line were indicating that having a major name like Connery was necessary in order for them to green-light the film. They asked us if we would agree to send a copy of the *Fellowship* screenplay to Sean with a view to trying to entice him to play Gandalf. I couldn't imagine him wanting to spend eighteen months in New

Zealand, and I didn't think they could afford his fee, but Ordesky told me New Line were going to offer a small fee in exchange for a large slice of the gross. I've no idea what was offered to his agents at CAA, but Mark said New Line were prepared to give him between 10 per cent and 15 per cent of the films' income. Some kind of offer must have gone in because in April 1999 the script was bundled off to Spain, or wherever Sean was at the time. He read it – and declined the role.

That then is the origin of the many stories that circulated that Sean Connery was going to be cast as Gandalf and had been seen on various occasions in and around Wellington.

> There were people reporting Connery sightings in, among other places, a well-known café, The Chocolate Fish. In fact, it got so silly that The Chocolate Fish got a cardboard cut-out of Sean Connery and they sat it up in one of the chairs!
> Somebody else told us that they had spoken to a friend of theirs who was so excited because they had been to a one-day cricket match at the Basin Reserve cricket ground in Wellington and were *convinced* that they had sat next to Sean Connery throughout the eight hours of the match! The city was gripped in this hysteria that Sean Connery was in town: it was hilarious but untrue!

Meanwhile, over at Weta Workshop, they were, once more, gearing themselves up to undertake the phenomenal and truly formidable task of creating the diverse and extraordinary cultures of Middle-earth – including sequences and characters that had never, originally, been envisaged as being part of the film.

> For so long, we had been haunted by this niggling doubt as to whether it really would go ahead. The happy moment happened when Carla Fry came down to New Zealand and signed off on the logistics and production structure. For so long, Fran and I had held back from getting too excited. We had been burnt one time too often, and were feeling superstitious – as soon as we gave everything to the project, it would die. Now, at long last, we were able to fully and unreservedly throw ourselves into the task.

Richard Taylor reflects: 'New Line not only picked up the project, they embraced it at a level that really excited us. They appreciated that *The Lord of the Rings* was an important piece of literature and how entrenched the story was in English popular culture and, therefore, how important it was that it was done properly and done well.'

Alan Lee and John Howe had barely made the journey back to Europe, before they were repacking their cases and heading for New Zealand once more! Richard Taylor and Tania Rodger began grabbing back some of the Weta talents whom they had had to let go and Jamie Selkirk began gearing up the editing and post-production departments for what was going to be a marathon commitment. Peter was also re-assembling his team including production designer Grant Major; art director Dan Hennah; costume designer Ngila Dickson; and first assistant director Carolynne Cunningham.

Carolynne – or Caro – had first worked with Peter on *Heavenly Creatures* and relishes the opportunity to work for a director with inventiveness and vision: 'He just comes up with ideas off the top of his head – which is marvellous with any director, but with Peter it is generally pretty cool and sometimes pretty crazy! He can even decide that he wants to change everything, in the middle of whatever we're doing, but that is fine, because change is good – and fun! Otherwise, things can be very boring. Of course, you have to be flexi-ble to work with Peter, but that's not something unique to him. Any good film-maker will want to seize a great moment when they feel it, think it or see it; you have to be prepared for that. And it's only the boring, *non-great* film-makers who don't do that and they're the ones that are, sadly, generally doing movies of the week! As for Peter, he's a great director and *never* boring.'

Rick Porras, who had first worked with Peter as Robert Zemeckis' post-production supervisor on *The Frighteners*, and had been an associate producer on *Contact* (the Zemeckis film that had thrown Weta a lifeline following the collapse of *Kong*), joined the *Rings* project as a co-producer. He would serve the film series in myriad ways, from being an indefatigable 'fixer' of problems to an occasional second- or third-unit director.

Director of photography Andrew Lesnie and myself with our Elven beauties, Liv Tyler and Cate Blanchett.

Rick brought not just great post-production experience, but a cheerfulness that infected everyone around him. He has a great spirit that makes him a delight to work with.

Peter had invited Alun Bollinger to be director of photography on the project but, despite their fine collaboration on *Heavenly Creatures*, *Forgotten Silver* and *The Frighteners*, Alun had not wanted to commit to such a lengthy schedule – although he later helped out behind the camera when extra film units were required. The task of 'lensing' *The Lord of the Rings* went, instead, to Andrew Lesnie, an Australian whose previous films had included the sumptuously photographed *Babe*.

In May 1999, responding to an invitation, Andrew flew over to Wellington for a meeting: 'I was ushered into a room with the producers and a whole lot of people – *and Pete*, who had his bare, hobbit feet up on the table. I figured that how I reacted to this was my first test!'

Andrew Lesnie was given the three scripts to read and, on being taken on a tour of Weta Workshop, quickly got the measure of what was being aspired to with the project: 'I was actually one of many people who believed that it was impossible to turn *The Lord of the Rings* into a film, simply because every person who reads the book imagines Tolkien's world in their own individual way. However, looking at what was being done at Weta was very impressive and anyone could see the meticulous amount of work going into the project. Despite this, I said that I wanted to have another meeting with Peter on his own, because it's only in a one-on-one situation that you can suss whether you can work with someone. Ultimately, once you're on the studio floor and filming, the principal relationship, as far as I'm concerned, is between the cinematographer and the director. And if you don't think the same way about things then it's not going to work.'

A half-hour meeting was scheduled for the following day and Andrew went back to his hotel and read the scripts. 'I came back the next day,' he recalls, 'and expected there to be a prearranged signal – a buzzer underneath the armrest of Pete's chair or something – that would bring someone into the room to terminate the meeting after the half hour! As it was, we ended up talking for several hours and it quickly became apparent that Pete had a good sense of humour and was very measured in his emotional response. By the end of that meeting, I felt that he was someone with whom I could have a good working relationship.'

An extraordinary level of preparation was begun on the films that would span the entire pre-production period and run throughout filming. Numerous miniature environments would be designed and constructed, each presenting its own unique challenges to Weta's model-makers, whether it was Minas Tirith, the ancient, seven-levelled city of Gondor; Lothlórien, the tree-slung kingdom of the Elves; or Barad-dûr, the towering fortress of the Dark Lord of Mordor.

On a far larger scale, Hobbiton – the hobbit village of the Shire that is the haven of rural peace which Frodo is obliged to desert in setting out on his perilous quest – was designed and constructed on farmland in Matamata, south of Auckland, a full year ahead of filming, so that the broad sweep of the landscaping and the individual detailing in the gardens of the hobbits' homes would have the realistic appearance of a long-established community by the time shooting was due to begin in autumn 1999.

> A huge amount of effort went into creating this one location and what still surprises me is that all this work was done for what, eventually, would be just nine days shooting with the First Unit and a few extra weeks with the Second Unit.
>
> There is, however, no question that it was to prove well worth all the time and trouble, because, when we came to film there, it had the look of an established, lived-in community as opposed to a movie set; this helped us present Middle-earth as a real, rather than fantastical, place. That was very important to me: I was determined that I didn't want anyone sitting through the opening twenty-minutes of *Fellowship* thinking that they were watching anything *other* than a real world.

The logistics that were being tackled on a daily basis from the moment the project got underway were staggering: exploring means of making armour and weapons using skills with the forge and anvil that were centuries old. At the same time, the Workshop was devising a method to produce authentic-looking, *lightweight* chain-mail in sufficient quantities for the hundreds of extras to be enlisted into the armies of Middle-earth, as well setting up systems for the manufacture of daily supplies of prosthetic hobbit feet, Elf ears and Orc body suits.

The boldness of Weta's ambition in taking on so many aspects of the production would be realised with incredible commitment and with a bravado that characterises the Workshop's rigorous ethic of excellence.

Under Grant Major's supervision, the film's style – so much of which had already been established during the Miramax period of production – was consolidated and began moving towards three-dimensional realisation. As Alan Lee and John Howe sketched designs

Standing around between takes on our Edoras set.

for every conceivable artefact from ancient tapestries and banners to fire-irons and door furniture, Dan Hennah and colleagues were scouring the country for such artisans as rug-weavers, candle-makers, boat-builders, glass-blowers and saddlers, as well as potters capable of producing hand-thrown pottery in small and large sizes depending on whether it was to be used by a hobbit or a wizard.

The breathtaking locations, which had made such an impression on Bob Shaye, had each to be transformed into a place that combined nature with structures that looked as if they belonged in that environment and which were constructed to serve the needs of the filmmaker. The creation of Edoras, alone – with its ornately decorated buildings of wood and thatch – proved an astonishing artistic vision realised by an unparalleled exercise in set building. The hilltop city of Rohan was both a visual highlight in the films and, in its creation, a metaphor for the dedication with which Tolkien's world was to be brought to the screen.

People often think of Middle-earth as being a completely mythical place – a different world or another planet – but Tolkien thought of it as being our world in a historical period that predates ancient history. We wanted landscapes that felt *real* but slightly heightened: an English landscape that hasn't really existed for thousands of years and New Zealand really fulfils that brief because we have the rolling hills, forests, mountains, rivers, waterfalls and lakes so that it actually feels like a slightly skewed version of Europe.

There were numerous legal and environmental issues to be settled, since many of these locations were situated on tracts of National Parkland that are subject to rigorous controls; and statistic-crunching schedules had to be drawn up in order to facilitate the moving of large numbers of people about the country – often to remote areas – and provide necessary catering, accommodation and sanitation.

Dozens of specific disciplines were required from horse-trainers to sword-masters and stunt-coordinators; while Ngila Dickson was busily sourcing unusual fabrics from fine silks and rich velvets to sturdy corduroy and rough broadcloth with which to create the robes, gowns, embroidered waistcoats, Elven cloaks and tattered Orc rags for which no historical references existed.

In terms of artistry, craftsmanship, planning and organisation, *The Lord of the Rings* was to prove, in every aspect of its visualisation and realisation, one of the most challenging productions in movie history.

A choice also needed to be made about the music for the film. When creating the Animatic from the storyboard, various pieces of music had been carefully selected in order to enhance the telling of the story. Several of the films from which the temporary music track was constructed had been scored by one composer – Howard Shore.

Even though films like *Silence of the Lambs*, *Crash*, *Naked Lunch* and *The Fly* seemed unlikely sources for music to accompany *The Lord of the Rings*, they worked incredibly well. Some of the more obvious choices, such as James Horner's score for *Braveheart*, seemed predictable and clichéd whereas once you added Howard's music to our pictures, they immediately became atmospheric, dark and evocative.

We eventually decided to call him up and he was really nice and warmed to our project.

'We talked at length,' Howard remembers, 'about music and film-making in general and, finally, they asked if I was interested – and, of course, I *was*!

> It sounds mercenary but we were looking for a composer who would give us a bit more than usual. The normal film industry arrangement is that you engage a composer, talk about the film and they then don't start working till they get a cut of the movie. You pay them a fee for about six weeks and some composers do as many as four or five scores a year. We wanted to find the right person – somebody who was willing to commit to the project for a significant period of time – and Howard turned out to be perfect. He devoted himself to it slavishly and apart from *Panic Room* and *Spider*, which he scored for friends David Fincher and David Cronenberg, he worked virtually full time on *The Lord of the Rings* for three years. Unbelievable. He was as obsessed as we were!

Howard recalls, 'I went down and visited Edoras, Rivendell and Lothlórien, saw some digital animation being done. It was obviously going to be a challenging project but for me it was irresistible: I could see that Middle-earth would be a wonderful world in which to work.'

An overriding key decision that had yet to be made was the appointment of a producer. Peter had wanted Marty Katz to continue with the project: he was hugely experienced and, during the difficult passage from Miramax to New Line, he had shown himself to be a loyal advocate of the project. Whilst wanting to be involved with a film that he had come to love, Marty had a number of personal family considerations that eventually made the prospect of being away from home on the other side of the world for five years an impossible option.

New Line approached Barrie M. Osborne who had worked with Francis Ford Coppola on *The Cotton Club* and had been a producer on the John Travolta/Nicholas Cage thriller *Face/Off*. Marty Katz had known Barrie from his days at the Disney studio when he had acted as executive producer on *Dick Tracy*: 'Barrie Osborne had been my Senior Vice President of Production at Disney for several years and I really respected his abilities. I was thrilled when he committed to *The Lord of the Rings*, because I felt he was very talented and would be a great ally to Peter and Fran. Barrie loved working out of the country and particularly in New Zealand, so it was a winning combination.'

At the time, Barrie was in Sydney, Australia, completing his work as executive producer on the 1999 hit *The Matrix*, featuring the future 'Elrond', Hugo Weaving, as Agent Smith.

Barrie recalls his first visit to the workshop and studios and being 'overwhelmed by the quality of the production.' He also has vivid memories of his first encounter with Peter at The Chocolate Fish:

'It was a beautiful, bright sunny Sunday in January, and I had breakfast with Peter and Fran. Peter, of course, was in his uniform of shorts and bare feet, and when we'd finished breakfast he said that he was going to go into town to see Nick Moran in *Lock, Stock and Two Smoking Barrels*, who was being considered as a possible hobbit – Merry or Pippin, I think – and did I want to go? So we rode down to the Paramount Theatre, where the film was showing, Pete parked the car, walked down the street in his bare feet and into the cinema where everybody knew him: the people at the ticket office and the concessionaire... It felt very, very comfortable. Within the space of that short experience, I sized Pete up as being well-grounded, friendly, laid-back and with a sense of humour. It seemed to me that if you had someone with that kind of a personality as a partner then you'd be able to get through such a big, difficult, daunting production and, on the strength of that meeting, I committed to producing the movie, and Pete committed to my doing so.'

Looking back on Barrie Osborne's contribution to *The Lord of the Rings* five years after that first meeting, Peter reflected:

> Barrie was to prove an absolutely rock-solid power, relieving us of huge amounts of pressure. Simply put, Barrie took on the part of the job that I'd have been terrible at: dealing with the studio's anxieties and grievances and allowing us to make our film. He understood that we like to knuckle down and concentrate on the creation of the film and his role – which he embraced superbly – was to enable that to happen.
>
> Whatever the external problems – and there were to be some – it would still turn out to be one of the most straightforward shoots because Barrie would always ensure that I had everything I needed and he bore the brunt and took the grief when it came. He was the glue that

held the production together, somebody who had the respect of everyone he worked with – both film-makers and studio.

In addition to Nick Moran, a great deal of thought was going into the
question of casting, and Peter and Fran flew to Los Angeles and
London to meet with potential actors and see them read.

Today, except for anyone who has been living on the dark side of
the moon, the cast of *The Lord of the Rings* trilogy are internationally
known and, for the majority of cinemagoers, are now inseparably
associated with the roles they played. Just as for several generations
of movie fans Clark Gable *is* Rhett Butler, Julie Andrews Mary
Poppins, and Alec Guinness Obi-Wan Kenobi, so Ian McKellen now
is Gandalf, Elijah Woods *is* Frodo, and Viggo Mortensen and Liv Tyler
are Aragorn and Arwen.

Similarly, most *Rings* fans have heard the stories of how the various actors acquired the roles they played: how Elijah, anxious to be
considered for the part of Frodo Baggins, donned a hobbit-style
costume and shot an audition videotape in a woodland setting in the
Hollywood Hills, performing dialogue from the books; how Sir Ian
Holm was cast as Bilbo, partly as a result of Peter Jackson having
heard his portrayal of Frodo in the BBC's classic radio dramatisation
of the book; how Christopher Lee auditioned for Gandalf and was
offered Saruman, while Orlando Bloom tried out for Faramir and
was given Legolas, and Dominic Monaghan went up for the part of
Frodo and was cast as Merry.

Sir Ian McKellen recalls meeting with Peter and Fran in London:
'They visited me at my house and showed me some designs. Peter
said that he was concerned that everything on screen should be real:
it would not be a stylised production, but illustrative and that the
acting had to fit in with that. He was adamant that he wasn't going to
interfere with J.R.R. Tolkien and that the film wouldn't be the stuff of
fairytale or have anything of pantomime about it; above all, the wizards had to be believable people. The image he wanted for Gandalf
was very clear in his mind and was inspired by the illustrations of
John Howe. Peter seemed convinced that I could act it and hoped to
be convinced by the make-up department that I could also *look* like

Sir Ian Holm and Sir Ian McKellen with Bob Shaye.

their Gandalf. What convinced me to take the part was the enthusiasm of the director, a sense that the project was worth doing – and was not a "Hollywood" movie – and the chance to play an icon of the twentieth century!'

The decision to cast Ian brought with it certain problems as filming approached, since the actor was also committed to *X-Men*, the schedule of which was being impacted by the fact that Dougray Scott – who at the time was slated to play Wolverine, a role which later went to Hugh Jackman – was stuck in an overrunning shoot for *Mission Impossible 2*.

'We re-jigged our entire schedule,' recalls Mark Ordesky, 'in order to try to push Gandalf as far along into the shoot as possible. Even so, it eventually got to the point where we weren't sure that Ian would be able to show up on the day he was supposed to start work on set. Hold-ups on *MI2* and, as a consequence, *X-Men* continued and I remember someone asking the question, "But what happens if there's another delay?" We all looked at one another and started doing the sums! Some insane number like a million dollars a day was thrown out as being the negative impact of Ian not being able to arrive on the right day. It was a complete nail-biter and we actually looked into the possibility of getting an insurance policy in case Ian couldn't get away from *X-Men* on schedule.'

In the event, Ian arrived in Wellington in time to shoot his first scenes in Hobbiton, although by that time the character had already appeared in a shot of the Fellowship trekking across country with Gandalf's double, Michael Ellsworth, in the role. By a bizarre coincidence, it transpired that Michael had worked in repertory theatre in England with Ian McKellen, some thirty years earlier!

Despite the anxieties over timing, Peter has no regrets about the casting for Gandalf and as for the question: 'What would the wizard have been like if he had been played by Mr Connery… ?'

> Ian McKellen has defined that role so much that I can't quite imagine anyone else being as effective in the part. What I found interesting was what Ian McKellen did with the role because he is basically a chameleon with the ability to get under the skin of a character, to cease to exist as Ian McKellen and, instead, to *become* Gandalf.

In 2005, six years after turning down the role, Sean Connery talked about his decision to the *New Zealand Herald*: 'Yeah, well, I never understood it. I read the book. I read the script. I saw the movie. I still don't understand it… I would be interested in doing something that I didn't fully understand, but not for eighteen months.'

> As it transpired, I think that we were lucky to end up with an entire cast of actors who embodied their roles and bring the characters in the books to life without ever dominating the movie.

There was, however, a time when any number of actors might have been cast in *The Lord of the Rings*.

> The studio occasionally had strong opinions about casting, there were certain actors they wouldn't even entertain the *thought* of being in the

film and there were names that we weren't even allowed to have *read* for a part. For example, Richard Harris had been one of our early thoughts for Gandalf, but we were told: 'Richard Harris will *not* be in this movie.'

Billy Connolly was talked about as a possible Gimli – and, had he been cast, would have been by far the tallest dwarf on Middle-earth – while the agents for Richard (*Rocky Horror Show*) O'Brien declined the role of Wormtongue, believing the film to be a potential disaster.

Two names were, at various times, in the offing for the role of Boromir: Bruce Willis, allegedly a fan of *The Lord of the Rings,* was mentioned but never approached; while Liam Neeson *was* sent the script to read but passed. New Line initially wanted Stephen Dorff to play Faramir but there were then later conversations with Ethan Hawke about the role and, simultaneous, discussions with Uma Thurman (then married to Hawke), about playing Éowyn.

> Ethan was a huge fan of the books and was very keen to be involved. Uma was less sure and rightly so, because we were revising how we saw Éowyn's character literally as we went. In the end, Ethan let it go – with some reluctance – and since, at that point, there was no word from the studio about whom we should talk to next, we went our own way and cast David Wenham.

That dealt with Faramir; Arwen was another, altogether trickier, matter. Viewing the eighteenth-century romp, *Plunkett & Macleane,* Peter and Fran began wondering whether Liv Tyler might be their Arwen.

> We were trying to think of someone who was very ethereal and other-worldly to play the role and while Liv didn't have much to do in that film we liked what she did with it. We mentioned the idea to New Line and they got very excited and suddenly, from being an idea, it became very important to have Liv Tyler in the film! The Sean Connery idea had failed to happen and they were still worried about having 'star names' on the posters; so, when Liv Tyler's name came up, they felt that it would go some way towards putting a name in there that would appeal to some of their foreign markets.

Whoever was to be cast, the role had proved – and, for some time, would go on being – a challenge to the writers.

> We were feeling very vulnerable because there was a big unknown about how much or how little you had to do with Arwen. We were going into three movies that didn't have a really strong female role or a significant romantic theme until Éowyn appears – which is not until the second film.
>
> We weren't sure whether we had to push Arwen into a stronger role or whether we could get away with her being as relatively minor as she is in the books and therefore not have a love story. That set us wondering about whether or not the films might then be seen as a male-driven story with no appeal to female moviegoers. The alternative approach was also anxious-making, because anything we did with Arwen's character would have to be a departure from what Tolkien wrote. It was a thorny situation and one about which we were very uncertain what to do…

Part of the argument had to do with the relationship between Aragorn and Arwen and the nature of Aragorn's character as the 'king in waiting'. 'The biggest challenge,' says Fran, 'is that he is a lead character and has to engage with the audience on a psychological level in some way. You have to connect and identify with him and have a degree of hope that he will achieve what his story demands that he will become. Yet in the books he is an icon, a warrior from a saga and we felt that, in terms of a movie character, he lacked emotional and psychological depth.'

> I wanted him to be more of a hero and we had the added problem of not just having to deal with a character's journey through *one* film but across *three* movies. We had to make his character development work over a long time span, so we decided that Aragorn should be more of a 'reluctant hero'. In the book he carries the broken sword around with him and seems to be waiting for the moment when he is finally to become king – a bit like Prince Charles, being heir to the throne without having much to do!
>
> In our films Aragorn doesn't really *want* to be king, he knows it's his destiny but it's not one that he particularly embraces and we felt that

worked quite well because we were taking Tolkien's ingredients but were mixing them up to produce a slightly differently flavoured cake! So, whilst our Aragorn was raised by the Elves at Rivendell, as per the book, we felt that the end result of that might be that he would feel a little alienated from the human race and would admire the Elves a lot more than his fellow men. The idea, therefore, of becoming a leader of what is, basically, a flawed race really doesn't interest him that much, even though he understands it as being his inheritance.

In fact, our Aragorn is not sure whether men are even worthy of inheriting Middle-earth, he would much rather the Elves stayed and ran the place; but, since they're not going to, he comes to see that the only salvation for Middle-earth is for men to seize control and, at that point, he realises that he must do what he has been destined to do and takes control.

Like Elijah Wood, Vin Diesel – at the time a virtually unknown actor – produced and submitted his own audition tape for the role of Aragorn: another fan of the book, he gave what Peter describes as 'a very compelling' performance but one which, ultimately did not 'feel like Aragorn'. New Line mentioned the name of Brad Pitt, but, in the event, the role of Aragorn went to Irish actor Stuart Townsend who had appeared in a couple of successful pictures including a drama based on the Northern Ireland troubles, *Resurrection Man*, and the romantic comedy, *Shooting Fish*. It was to be a piece of casting that would result in agonising difficulties that would eventually burden the first few weeks of filming.

> We liked Stuart as an actor and as a person; we were drawn to him by his looks and his energy, by the fact that he had a gentle, slightly mystical side to him and, since he was a fan of *The Lord of the Rings*, his initial enthusiasm for the project.
>
> People at New Line, however, were convinced that *we* were wrong and that *Stuart* was wrong for the part. As a result, I became increasingly determined that I wasn't going to let the studio dictate to me; after all, I argued, it was essential for the film-maker to have control over casting. Even Fran and Philippa were probably not as cast-iron certain as I was but, having got the bit between my teeth, I was not letting go without a struggle.

To be honest, we knew that Stuart was too young for the role – by at least ten years – but we thought that it would give us an interesting take on the character and that we could figure out ways in which to play him older.

The studio insisted that Peter shoot a screen test on film – not video, but 35mm film – with full make-up and wardrobe. Stuart flew to New Zealand and rehearsed various Aragorn scenes: rallying the troops on the ramparts at Helm's Deep; in conversation with Éowyn; confronting the King of the Dead and one of the character's earliest appearances in the story when, as Strider, he talks to the hobbits in The Prancing Pony.

Pieces of set were constructed, local actors were engaged to play opposite Stuart and a film-crew was put together with Andrew Lesnie as Director of Photography – the first time he and Peter worked together on set. Stuart was kitted out in a generic costume and various experimentations were carried out to make him look older: adding stipple make-up around the eyes and grey streaks in his hair.

We did our very best to sell Stuart to New Line. The test footage was couriered to Los Angeles where the studio gave it a reluctant, 'Well, if you really think so,' response. The test didn't actually change their minds and, clearly, there were still reservations, but New Line agreed to support our judgement and Stuart was cast.

During the immediate pre-production period, Orlando Bloom and the four hobbits – Elijah Wood, Sean Astin, Billy Boyd and Dominic Monaghan – arrived in Wellington, as did Stuart who was very much a part of the group and was well liked by the others. However, as preparations intensified and the actors started having costume fittings and began sword training, various issues emerged.

Getting a grip on any character in a movie script is never easy and for Stuart the iconic, yet enigmatic Aragorn was proving a challenge. What made the situation more difficult was that I didn't have the time to devote to finding a solution to that challenge.

After leaving the production, Stuart – obviously and understandably angry – railed off in the press, saying that he had rarely seen me, that I had given him hardly any time, but the truth was that that was the case for all of the actors because my attention was being pulled in a million different directions at once in those last couple of weeks of prep.

When you're making a movie, the first week becomes critical: there is a huge amount of pressure and anxiety about schedules: if you happen to fall behind on day two or three, then the studio will immediately start to extrapolate a situation where you are going to be *six weeks* behind by the end of the shoot and everything will be a disaster.

As a result I was determined that our first week would, if at all possible, go like clockwork…

Whilst everyone – perhaps even Stuart himself – was anxious, they hung on to that old theatrical adage that 'Everything will be alright on the night'; that things would come together when shooting began – that it would, in fact, be 'alright on the *day*'.

Rather as he had done on *Heavenly Creatures*, but for different reasons, Peter decided that we would simulate 'the day' – in advance. Shortly before shooting was due to begin, he planned a full dress rehearsal with Stuart and Elijah of the 'Are you frightened? Not nearly frightened enough!' scene. The results, unfortunately, did not allay everyone's concerns. Peter was still agonising over what to do when Monday 11 October 1999 arrived: *The Lord of the Rings*, Shoot Day #1…

On that first day, I was feeling pretty pumped up. Normally, I have first-day nerves, but on this movie I didn't feel that at all. I remember thinking that not only had we been developing this project for three years, but also that I hadn't actually been on a film set directing a movie for *four* years.

There had been so much preparation for this moment and yet nothing could have ever fully prepared me for what lay ahead during the looming schedule of 274 days of filming…

But on that October morning we were, at long last, beginning filming and I was relieved and excited. I was in good shape and ready to go. *I couldn't wait!*

I directed my first shot of *The Lord of the Rings* on Mount Victoria, a big area of wild parkland not far from the studios and overlooking

Wellington city and harbour – we thought we might as well start close to home! We had found a really good, spooky-looking road for the scene where the four hobbits run and hide under the tree roots as the Black Rider approaches.

We'd already taken the actors up to the location for a couple of days and had done a lot of rehearsal for the camera. I wanted to be absolutely sure that we knew exactly what we were going to be doing during those first few days and, hopefully, avoid any nasty surprises – *at least in the first week!*

So that is where it all began, rather famously in a glare of publicity, and to the great frustration of journalists and local residents who couldn't get close enough to find out exactly what was going on.

Security was tight and we were paranoid about people taking photographs. I remember, on that first day, an alert suddenly went out about a photographer being spotted sneaking in the bushes and security guards went racing up the hill to try to get him!

The problem, all the way through filming, was that normally, when you are making a movie, your *story* is your surprise. In our case, we were filming one of the most widely read books in the world, so we really had *no* surprise in terms of our story. The only thing we had left to protect was our visual interpretation. We didn't want people to know what the hobbits or the Ringwraiths looked like.

Initially, there were two film units working on *The Lord of the Rings*: the first unit was divided into two sub-units, 1A and 1B, which for the most part were directed by Peter, while a second unit began filming a week later, working under John Mahaffie. John had worked with Peter on *Heavenly Creatures* and as cinematographer and director on the *Hercules* television series. Later, when the pressure of keeping on schedule seriously began to threaten the project, Geoff Murphy, veteran director of such well-known New Zealand films as *Goodbye Pork Pie* and *UTU* joined the team and, at various times, other freelance directors were pulled in to direct a few scenes – as indeed, on occasion, were Fran and the producers!

On most movies, second units are given small, fiddly, not-too-

Second Unit 1st AD, Dave Norris, with the huge 1/3 scale Helm's Deep set behind him. It was filmed in a quarry just down the road from central Wellington.

complicated shots; on this film, the Second Unit – overseen by Peter who, where possible, reviewed what they were shooting via video-relay – was responsible for many major sequences. As filming progressed, the number of units working grew and more people were drafted in to 'direct' under Peter's supervision until, at one point, no less than seven film crews would be shooting scenes for *The Lord of the Rings* at the same time.

The mind-boggling complexities of these arrangements have been widely reported and commented on, with particular reference to Peter's staggering ability to hold so many diverse scenes – from one, two or even three films – in his head simultaneously and to be able to direct members of the cast in one scene on one set and, between takes, to switch his focus to a bank of television monitors and give notes to other directors and actors filming other scenes on other sets or even miles away on location. On the first day, however, all that was still as far off as Mordor is from Hobbiton…

The first shot of the first day turned out to be a memorable image in the first film. I'm told tourists still try to find the tree on Mount Victoria, but they never will because it *isn't* there. Like so many of the trees in our Middle-earth, we *built* it!

'The first day of filming,' recalls Elijah Wood, 'we were all nervous, and I know Peter was nervous too. There was also a tangible sense of excitement amongst the actors, the crew – *everyone*. This was the *beginning*. The beginning of a journey that seemed like it was going to go on for ever. The end was so far away that it didn't exist. The idea of beginning this journey with the four hobbits was fun for us because we'd already become quite close – but it also seemed really appropriate. It's in the hobbit's nature to be excited and full of life. So to start with that atmosphere was really cool.'

There was still the unresolved Aragorn situation but once shooting had begun Peter had no choice but to focus on directing this huge and daunting project. Meanwhile, Fran and Philippa continued working with Stuart, but relationships were becoming increasingly strained and, on the afternoon of Wednesday 13 October, Peter reached a decision:

During the course of shooting the shot of the spider crawling down the lapel of Merry's jacket, I debated with myself about what to do. Half an hour later, I had decided that casting Stuart had been a mistake – *my mistake* – and that, painful as it would be, he would have to be replaced. I take full responsibility – I made a casting error. It was no fault of Stuart's – he's a great actor, who's gone on to have a successful career – but he was not Aragorn. It was a mistake to put him in that position, and the only remedy for the movie was to replace him. It was a horrible situation for him foremost, and not the best thing for the movie. At the end of the day, the movie has to come first – there's simply too much at stake. It took me far too long to realise that.

I discussed the situation with Barrie Osborne and we were in agreement. Barrie went to break the news to Stuart and the rest of us went into Aragorn-panic. Apart from the obvious personal issues between us all, we were now facing a major crisis: we were only a few days away from filming with a central character and we had no one to play the part.

Fran remembers a mood of general disbelief: 'No one could quite accept that an actor had been let go with no one to replace him, but that was the case. We had to do it before Stuart started shooting. There was no alternative agenda, no alternative Aragorn.'

For the other members of the cast, as Fran recalls, the news came as a terrible shock: 'The hobbits and Orlando were devastated: it was like, "Who's next?"'

> Interestingly, Sean Astin *wasn't* devastated; he just nodded, and told me later that I'd made a very wise decision. Dominic and Billy were saying, "Oh my God!", but Sean wasn't; he wasn't shocked at all.

Allaying the immediate concerns of the core cast members was not easy: 'It was,' says Fran, 'impossible really. They all liked Stuart and felt it as a painful thing. They were very professional but we felt that we had to prove ourselves to them, prove that we weren't bloody-minded and fickle. It was only time that healed it.'

> There was also the question of how New Line would react: here I was, getting rid of the one person that the studio hadn't wanted in the film in the first place. I had asked for their trust in casting Stuart and now I was seemingly derailing the film by replacing him at the eleventh hour. They were amazingly supportive, but I knew they were thinking, 'What the hell is Peter *doing*?'

The decision made, everyone set to work on two fronts simultaneously: figuring out what to shoot that didn't involve Aragorn – itself hampered by the fact that other members of the cast (including Gandalf) were not available to use – and trying to recast the role.

> One name – an American – kept cropping-up on all the lists: Viggo Mortensen. Fran and Philippa watched a mass of his movies in one day: *GI Jane*, *The Portrait of a Lady*, *The Indian Runner*, the remakes of *Psycho* and *Dial 'M' for Murder* (re-titled *The Perfect Murder*) with Michael Douglas. Within two days of releasing Stuart, Viggo was on the top of our list. I remember Fran commenting that there was nothing English about Viggo and yet he seemed completely right for the part. In

actual fact, Viggo has a Scandinavian heritage, and Tolkien based so much of his story on the Norse sagas.

The second Viggo's name came up, Mark Ordesky, our executive producer at New Line, said that from the studio's point of view he would be perfect, which cemented our decision to approach Viggo and offer him the role.

Fortunately, the production's US casting director, Victoria Burrows, was a good friend of Viggo's manager and was able to facilitate quick communication. A script was sent and studio and director waited to see whether the actor would even contemplate committing to a fifteen-month project on the other side of the world...

Mark Ordesky recalls, 'We were all agreed that Viggo would be perfect, but in case he said "No," we kept coming up with other options. There were only two other people that we were really considering if Viggo hadn't worked out: Jason Patric (*Sleepers, Speed 2, Incognito*) and Russell Crowe. I called Russell Crowe's agent, explained that there was a situation with Aragorn in *The Lord of the Rings* and we'd like to talk to Russell about it – but that we had to talk *right now... Like, how about today?* We sent him a script and he did read it and was fascinated. I remember getting the phone call from his agent and being told that he had just finished *another* film which involved him having to have a sword and armour – *Gladiator!* Russell was flattered by the approach, but he had other films he was committed to and it obviously wasn't going to work out.'

In Wellington, tensions rose as the day approached on which they were to film the scenes in *The Prancing Pony*, the inn at Bree where the hobbits first meet Aragorn, then still in his 'Strider' persona. The next few days' shooting was rescheduled in order to delay that encounter as long as possible.

We were due to start shooting Aragorn scenes on the fourth day of the shoot. We released Stuart on Day Three. That meant pulling in as many Hobbit-only sequences as we could until we could find a new Aragorn – but we were running out of time. There was now little or no leeway if we were to avoid screwing up the entire schedule; yet here we were, starting to film scenes on *The Prancing Pony* set without being entirely sure if Aragorn would ever show up.

We had at least succeeded in making contact with Viggo: he had read the script, we were told, but was unfamiliar with Tolkien's book and needed to discuss the role. It was, however, still far from certain that he would accept, since word had come through that Viggo always took his time in choosing projects and liked to thoroughly immerse himself in any role before beginning filming – two requirements which time simply didn't permit.

There was one factor that, at the time, no one was aware of: Viggo's 11-year-old son, Henry, who was an enthusiastic Tolkien fan. His advice was simple and direct: 'Aragorn? You've got do it. You've *got* to play Aragorn!' Viggo read the scripts and started on the book: 'I recognized a lot of archetypes and storylines and even several names from the Nordic sagas I had first read as a boy. This is not completely unfamiliar, I thought, and it might even be fun to revisit that boyhood fantasy of fighting monsters, but instead of standing there with a wooden sword in your back yard, you'd actually be in a forest, wearing all that heavy duty stuff, and have a real, real sword – and have real monsters coming at you, instead of just the washing on the clothesline!'

Perhaps the final clincher was the fact that, as Mark Ordesky notes, 'Viggo is only *really* happy as an actor when he's frightened!' And, for an actor stepping into the breech at the final moment, there was plenty to be frightened about! It was agreed that Fran and Philippa would have a telephone conversation with Viggo and, if it went well, that Peter would interrupt the shoot and talk with him personally.

Viggo was in a phone-box in the middle of Iowa and Fran and Philippa spoke with him for over an hour. Their overriding memory of that exploratory call was that they were conscious of doing all the talking and had no real sense of whether or not Viggo was interested. Then came a glimmer of hope. Fran recalls, 'The first time we got an indication he was possibly considering accepting the role was when he asked, at the end of the call, "How old was I when I was taken to the Elves?" Philippa and I were thrilled by that.'

The call had evidently gone well enough for Viggo to agree to talk with me and I spoke with him on a phone in the bar of *The Prancing Pony*. I talked a bit about what we were doing, the style of the film, how long we were planning to shoot, and what the commitment involved. Viggo asked one or two questions but there were long silences from his end. Awkwardly long. I'd be wondering whether the phone had cut off and would start talking about something else, hoping he was still there. Then Viggo would ask another question, which I'd answer, which would be followed by another long silence!

I really felt that the conversation wasn't going well and that Viggo was reluctant to commit. Just at the point when the call was winding down and I had convinced myself that we were going to have to keep looking for our Aragorn, he said, 'Well, I guess I see you on Thursday,' and laughed. That was how he did it. I was so happy.

New Line's legal department must have moved at incredible speed, because they had tied up the deal in twenty-four hours and Viggo was on a plane heading for New Zealand.

'We banged out a deal in forty-eight hours,' remembers Mark Ordesky who was in London at the time. 'I was up all night. I worked my London day and then spent all night having a Los Angeles day hammering out the deal with Viggo and getting him on an airplane!'

The recasting presented one concern to New Line: one of the factors in accepting Stuart Townsend as a more youthful Aragorn than might have been expected was the belief that his character would play well opposite Liv Tyler's Arwen, since Liv was young – and Arwen ageless!

'In the back of our minds,' says Mark, 'this would be a double win. In the end, Stuart and Liv never interacted on film and I had to make a call to explain that Viggo was now going to be playing Aragorn. At the time, all Liv knew about Viggo was that he was this very intense, very driven, very focused borderline-method-actor and that he had worked on *The Perfect Murder* with her friend, Gwyneth Paltrow. So already there was this kind of potentially interesting dynamic: Liv was heading off for New Zealand to deal with an actor who was totally different to the one she *thought* she was going to be dealing with!'

Any anxieties were allayed when the two actors eventually met in

New Zealand. 'I remember being extremely nervous,' recalls Mark. 'I was in Los Angeles and I kept calling Wellington and asking: "Have they met yet? How's it going?" Because the ship had sailed; the deals were done; this was now our Aragorn and Arwen – *we hoped!* Happily, it was instantly and perfectly clear that chemistry-wise and otherwise it was going to work.'

Nevertheless the opening days were full of concerns and tensions...

When we started out on *Rings*, a lot of people had a perception that this was going to turn out to be a bit of a Mickey Mouse project. For example, we had originally hired a very experienced Englishman as chief lighting technician, or 'gaffer', right-hand man to director of photography Andrew Lesnie. Despite a string of credits on big films, he was only with us for two weeks prior to filming and then quit – we didn't seem to live up to his high standards.

Suddenly, we were frantically trying to find a new gaffer. The only one we could locate at a moment's notice was Brian Bansgrove, a New Zealander who'd lived in Australia most of his life and worked on a slew of interesting Aussie pictures including *Mad Dog Morgan*, *My Brilliant Career*, *Gallipoli*, *The Year of Living Dangerously* and the *Crocodile Dundee* movies.

The only trouble was that Brian had something of a reputation as a roistering, hard drinker. We were also told that age had caught up with him somewhat – he was in his late fifties – and that he was far from being the fittest guy in the world. But we had a disastrous situation on our hands and didn't have much choice; so, literally within days of the start of the film, Brian showed up.

The lighting department was in a state of disorganisation, but this loud, tough-talking, no-nonsense – *but very funny* – character stepped into the midst of the chaos and, with quite a lot of sergeant-major-type swearing, had the crew whipped into shape in pretty much no time!

I was on the Weathertop set rehearsing when Brian arrived; I shook his hand and thanked him for coming. He'd been given a bit of a tour and I remember him saying: 'Well, this job's going to sort the men from the boys – and *I* intend to finish a *man!*' Brian's comment spread and immediately became a mantra for the entire crew. We all intended to 'finish like men' – even the girls!

Viggo with our ace focus puller, Colin Deane. With a shoot spanning nearly four years, the cast and crew bonded in a way that we will probably never experience again.

And so he did, seeing the crew through principal photography and endearing himself to everyone, despite his gruff manner. In spite of predictions that Brian was past his prime and wouldn't stay the course, he worked tirelessly and, say those who grew to know and love him, came off the project like an invigorated young man.

> He was a real rough diamond – *as rough as guts* – but he was also a very sweet person and as funny as hell! He never observed the usual protocols in dealing with actors and wasn't very interested in the names of the various characters. I remember we were on Mount Victoria filming the scene where Sam is cooking and Frodo is sitting, smoking, in the crook of a tree. Brain was bawling out orders at the guys setting the lights on Frodo: 'Right!' he bellowed, 'I reckon you'd better poke another light at the little bloke in the tree!'

Brian died at the end of 2001, the day before going to see *Fellowship* and was much missed during the pick-ups over the next two years. Fran's favourite Bansgrove line was: 'We'll use available light for this scene…' Beat. '*Every* ****ing available light!!'

By the end of the second week, I'd shot parts of the scenes at Weather-top and Bree all of which were fine but not really great. I was concerned that I really hadn't got into my stride. Then on Friday the 22 October we took a two-hour drive to a lakeside location and shot the scenes with the hobbits racing to the Bucklebury Ferry and, for the first time, I really felt I had go the hang of what I was doing! I still remember the enormous sense of relief... after four years away from a set, I had captured the spirit of what these movies needed to be.

The following week Viggo arrived and was pitched straight into costume fittings, make-up tests and sword training.

The first thing we filmed with Viggo was a low-angle shot after he has finished fighting the Ringwraiths and comes running over to tend to the wounded Frodo. The next day, we moved on to film the fight and Viggo was superb, battling with the Ringwraiths, setting them on fire. You'd never have believed he'd only been sword-training for a couple of days. I remember thinking, 'This is one cool guy!' Looking back on it now, Viggo's last-minute addition to the *Lord of the Rings* team was a turning point. It feels like fate steered us there, since he has come to embody the heart, soul and spirit of the production. He was the perfect Aragorn, and although the path was fraught with anxiety and emotion, he eventually walked onto our set – and that was a great day for us.

We'd been told to send over a 35mm print of that day's shoot to New Line, because they wanted to see Viggo on film. Maybe they weren't 100 per cent sure about him, because normally they viewed the 'dailies' (the footage we had shot the day before) on videotape, rather than 35mm film footage; or maybe, having lost one Aragorn, they felt the need to be doubly sure about his replacement. Anyway, when they saw him fighting with all those burning Ringwraiths, they thought he was great and were really happy. By then, of course, he was already under contract, so I don't know what would have happened if they *hadn't* liked him!

So much had happened; it was only Shoot Day #12; there were still 262 more days to go.

9

RING-MASTER

This book began with a question posed by Peter Jackson: 'How on earth did this guy ever come to be making *The Lord of the Rings*?'

Hopefully, the preceding pages have provided something of an answer to that question. Essentially, it has been the story of a film-maker's journey from his origins and youthful passion for film through to the point at which he began work on the biggest, most ambitious movie project in the history of cinema.

'Nothing ever turns out the way you think,' reflects Mark Ordesky. 'Getting New Line to take on *The Lord of the Rings* was challenging, but it was nowhere near as hard to get Bob Shaye to buy the idea of making these films as it was to actually *make* them!'

That is an accurate assessment and much of what followed over the next four years has already been recounted by various voices in sundry forms. It has been reported in the pages of various 'Making of' books as well several dozen issues of *The Lord of the Rings Official Fan Club Magazine,* crammed with in-depth articles on every facet of the film-making from armoury and jewellery to prosthetic make-up and digital computing techniques.

Peter himself and many of those most intimately involved in the films have been seen reflecting on and reminiscing about their achievement in several hours of DVD 'extras' (or 'appendices') that accompany the theatrical and extended versions of the trilogy.

There have been, in addition, legions of articles in national and international newspapers and periodicals from film journals to celebrity magazines as well as publications catering to every conceivable specialist interest, from film effects, music and screenwriting to art and design, fantasy gaming and even fashion and philately.

Aspects of the story have also been ceaselessly catalogued and commented on by the internet spies and scribes on TheOneRing.net and numerous other websites.

All in all, *The Lord of the Rings* became a breathtaking cinematic coup staggeringly realised and exhaustively – and often *exhaustingly* – chronicled!

During more than thirty hours of conversation, Peter Jackson reviewed the daily call-sheets that are a record of what was shot where, when and with whom during the 274 days of principal photography on *The Lord of the Rings*.

It is a saga filled with elation and the exhaustion: the moments of creating inspired movie-making and the desperate frustrations when things went awry; the endless struggling with a gruelling schedule that was repeatedly hampered by mishaps, accidents, crises and disasters – actual, near and averted.

Obviously, the daily call-sheets for a film are not intended as a historical record; rather they are an essential means of communicating vital information to everyone involved on the project: names of personnel and cell-phone contacts; useful addresses, telephone- and fax-numbers, as well as information on emergency services; details of where filming is to take place (together with maps if locations are involved); times when everyone is required – or 'called' – on set; a list of all the actors, principal characters, doubles and extras, including details of their transportation arrangements; and a breakdown of every scene to be filmed that day, the number of shots involved and estimated timings, which are usually – and perhaps surprisingly – only seconds long.

Looking back at these call-sheets, remembering all the effort, frequent agony and occasional despair that they represent, it's not too hard to think to yourself: 'Thank God we don't have to wind the clock back and start all over again!'

To tell that story day by day – sometimes hour by hour – would take a book as long or longer than this one. But in chronicling even a fraction of the highlights and the low-spots, the reader will get a feel for the extremes of experience, physical and emotional, that director, cast and crew went through over the fifteen months of intensely concentrated creativity that resulted in *The Lord of the Rings*.

There are thousands of memories connected with all those months of filming. There are the trivial things like recalling the day we filmed Frodo, Sam and Gollum travelling through a pine forest with the crew being required to wear hardhats due to the hazard of falling pinecones – something that alarmed the safety-conscious Sean Astin who obviously *couldn't* wear a hardhat! But there were moments when one disaster followed another, like the final days before our first break at Christmas 1999 when, having crushed the schedule for filming the scene at the Grey Havens into fewer days than we had intended, we got fabulous material with the hobbits acting their hearts out – real tears, not fake ones – and creating a mood that was intensely emotional, only

We originally shot for 279 days, and no two were ever the same. After shooting a lot of drama, I'd always relish a day or two with Orc armies!

to find that, due to a technical complication with one of the cameras, all the shots were out of focus. The set was about to be demolished, the cast were only hours away from flying home for the holiday and we had to film the sequence over again from scratch…

Hardly any movie is ever filmed chronologically, but in the case of *Rings* the shoot often leapt back and forth across a story that, in the original book, spans ten months of accelerating intensity with pre-figuring events dating back thousands of years. This led to extraordinary juxtapositions such as shooting the Battle of the Last Alliance for the prologue only a few hundred yards away from where Frodo and Sam were beginning their final ascent of Mount Doom; or moving from scenes in Hobbiton before Frodo sets out on his quest and, on the same shoot day, filming the final shot in the film as Sam returns home from the Grey Havens.

Inevitably in all accounts of the *Rings* shoot, various crises have loomed largest – particularly those caused by the forces of nature: the acts of God that repeatedly impacted on the schedule. There were through-the-night drives with storms closing in, petrol tanks running on empty and no town or villages in sight; and there were landslides that famously left Sean Bean and Orlando Bloom marooned miles from anywhere for days culminating with a white-knuckle helicopter rescue!

Queenstown, on the South Island, was hit by floods, unprecedented in a hundred years or more of local history, which apart from reducing the town to a state of civil emergency also left a *Rings* construction crew cut off at a remote location and swept away an entire set – effectively ensuring that an elaborately planned Orc attack on the Fellowship as they navigated the Sarn Gebir rapids on the River Anduin was washed right out of the film.

We had all kinds of action planned with boats flipping over and Sam ending up in the water and Gimli struggling to keep his and Legolas' boat afloat as it bucks and tosses, while the Elf – standing with a foot on each of the gunwales – would be firing arrows at the attackers. It was going to be pretty cool stuff…

The sets were now gone and would have had to have been rebuilt, and the river was still a raging a torrent and too dangerous to film on. So, that was the end of the Sarn Gebir ambush: a sequence that only exists in storyboards and photographs of the set before it disappeared down the river!

Fran reminded me about the *Star Wars* set that blew away in a sandstorm in Tunisia and we tried to see it as a good omen. Whether or not the film would have been significantly improved by it, who knows? It certainly wasn't missed.

One of the greatest fears to assail any director is that of falling behind schedule: seeing the planned number of shots mounting up and the available days for shooting trickling away and knowing that there could come a point where your movie runs off the track. It was, for Peter, a recurrent nightmare as they battled with rain, gales and several unseasonable snowfalls.

Drawing on experience borne out of 'making do' and 'fixing things' during his early years of film-making, Peter invariably soldiered on, doing his best to adapt to situations even as they changed. The crew was on location at Bog Pine Paddock near Te Anau, about a three-hour drive from Queenstown, where they were to be shooting Strider and the hobbits crossing the Midgewater Marshes with Pippin talking about 'second breakfasts'.

It started raining, but I thought, 'We can't stop because of rain and, anyway, if they're journeying from Bree towards Weathertop and it's raining, well that will help give it a nice earthy feel!'

Then the raindrops begin getting heavier and *thicker* and, suddenly, the biggest snowflakes in the world are coming down. So *now* I think, 'In the book, Tolkien never mentions anything about snow during this part of the journey, but I suppose it *could* have been snowing... Okay, we'll shoot in the snow!' So, we keep filming and get one master shot done, by which time the place is *covered* in snow, the actors are getting cold and everyone was pretty fed up, except for Viggo who thought it was *fantastic*!

In fact, even when the police advised us to evacuate the site and we all went back to our hotel, Viggo was so upset because we hadn't finished the scene that he refused to change out of his costume in the

There was unseasonable snow wherever we went, including Edoras, which had a surprise fall that we could not work into the script of the film – I don't think it snows in Rohan.

hope that, at some point, the danger would pass and we'd be able to get back out there and complete the scene in the snow. I remember him walking around the hotel in his Aragorn wig and full costume and – much to the bemusement of a party of Japanese tourists – still carrying his sword!

On another occasion, filming on Mount Ruapehu, filming looked as if it was going to have to stop when mist began rolling in.

> Before long we were in a pea-souper and you couldn't see a thing. Rather than abandon the day's shoot, I knew that I wanted some montage shots of Frodo and Sam wandering around lost in the Emyn Muil, so I got Andrew to discard the tripod, put the camera on his shoulder, and told everyone to stay where they were as they'd slow us down – I didn't want to be dragging fifty people around with me! Sean and Elijah ran up the hill with me and we found interesting places to have Sam and Frodo looking as if they were lost. The trouble was, we needed a wide shot, but for the rest of the shoot the weather was sunny and fine! We ended up waiting for more fog, which never came, tried shooting it with a smoke machine and finally ended up having to add CG fog in post-production!

Adaptability became the touchstone for survival. When the Queens-town floods made all other shooting impossible, the search was on for a space in which to shoot some interior scenes. The options were few and narrowed down to a squash court in the Coronet Plaza Hotel. The size of the squash court dictated what could be built; while what could be shot was dictated by which actors were available – so whilst eight members of the Fellowship were on site, Gandalf was still being Magneto on *X-Men*.

> The only sequences in the entire trilogy that we thought we might manage to film were those in *The Return of the King* where Sam and Frodo have their argument on the Cirith Ungol stairs that eventually lead up to Shelob's Lair.
>
> A floor was laid over the squash court to protect it and the set was constructed...

Elijah Wood and Sean Astin were appalled! They had only been working on this film for four weeks and here we were already talking about moving on to these major dramatic scenes taking place well on into the development of the characters of Frodo and Sam. I understood how they felt. *I* was appalled – shooting climactic scenes from *The Return of the King* was not where my head was at!

We hadn't filmed a single shot of Sam and Frodo from *The Two Towers*, let alone *The Return of the King* and yet we were suddenly having to figure out what they would look like in terms of make-up and costume at this stage of their journey: the Wardrobe department were asking, 'Just how worn and ripped *are* their clothes? How *dirty* are they?'

We needed two days to shoot the scene: on one day we would shoot with the camera on Frodo and, the next day, with the camera facing in the opposite direction towards Sam. So, I said to the boys, 'Well, guys, who wants to go first?'

What an impossible decision for them to have to make! Both actors know the options. The one who is not on camera is going to have the easier time of it, because the camera operator will simply be shooting over his shoulder. The actor being filmed, however, has really got to be 'up' – in character, giving it everything he's got, 100 per cent – because the camera will be on him for the entire scene: not just filming him saying his own lines but also catching every reaction he makes to what the other character is saying.

In the end, they flipped a coin and Sean won – or maybe lost! We shot the entire scene looking at Sam: from the moment when Sam wakes up after Gollum has sprinkled the lembas crumbs over him, through to his confused and tearful reaction to Frodo dismissing him.

Shooting scenes like that with so little preparation is the stuff I have nightmares about. In the end, you just have to rely on your instincts, and if that fails you... guess! You get your head down and get on with it. Sean was fabulous and at the end of that day's shoot we had every angle on Sam in the can and were expecting to be shooting the Frodo side of the scene on the following day.

It was not to be: the next day dawned sunny, the floods had abated, roads that had been closed were reopened and the crew had to get back to location filming. The other angle on the scene was not filmed until twelve months later. 'During the whole of that time,' recalls Fran

Walsh, 'the Cirith Ungol set occupied the hotel's squash court – which is probably one reason why our budget went up!'

> A year later, we were back in the squash court, and this time the heat was on Elijah. He had to get his head back into a scene that had been half-filmed so long ago. He knew that he had to deliver a performance that matched the emotion of Sean's takes, and that he did to perfection. What is amazing, when you look at the finished scene in *The Return of the King*, is to think that every time we cut to and fro between Frodo and Sam we are actually jumping back and forth across a year-long gap.

Although there were a good many of them over the fifteen months' shoot, few, if any, of these setbacks were ever granted the status of 'dramas'.

> There is always a way round things, and Caro Cunningham, the first assistant director on *Rings,* is an absolute genius at figuring out how to get the movies shot. She and I have a similar attitude to problem solving.

'Nothing is really ever a drama,' says Carolynne. 'Occasionally, there are slight bumps in the road – the odd gale, snowstorm, landslip and freak flood – but life is too short to take those too seriously, because they're awfully easy to fix, generally. Anything's fixable. Peter and I are great believers in anything being fixable. I don't think there was a problem that we weren't able to solve. That's all they are: they might be large, expensive problems, with a lot of people involved, but in the end, they're just problems. And you sit down, you think about it and you solve it. And some of the problems were really very exciting!'

Again and again during the filming of *The Lord of the Rings*, problems – exciting or mundane – needed solving. Most of the time, Peter's optimistic nature and his Kiwi determination to make a difficult situation work, whatever the odds, carried him through. Although, now and again, there were moments when it seemed as if making the biggest motion picture project ever ought to have had a few more Hollywood-style resources.

There was a period when we were getting up while it was still dark and setting off on the one-and-a-half-hours' drive from Queenstown to Closeburn near Paradise, where we were filming the scenes at Amon Hen that form the climax to *The Fellowship of the Ring*. The road had only just been re-opened after the floods; we'd lost days of filming and were desperate to try and get back on schedule. Every day we would film for as long as the light held and then drive back again in the dark.

All the time we were fighting to keep our expenses down because this was a tightly budgeted film and I've never forgotten how, on that daily drive to and from Paradise, we used to pass the base camp for *another* film crew who were down there shooting Columbia Pictures' *Vertical Limit*. In contrast to us, they had stacks of equipment, vast catering tents, trailers for the cast: everything, it seemed, they could possibly need... I always thought that they looked rather pityingly at us as we drove past – like we were the poor relations. And, to be honest, I was really pretty envious of them and would be thinking to myself, 'Yeah! That's what it's like making a *real* film!'

There were a variety of scary moments when people or property were endangered, such as the night when a fire caused by combustible foam polystyrene broke out in one of the studios and partially damaged the Minas Morgul set; or the day when they were filming the approach to the Black Gates on a tract of Ministry of Defence land that had been cleared of unexploded mines and shells, but suddenly realised that Aragorn, Legolas and Gimli seemed to be galloping beyond the rigorously defined bomb-free area...

For the director personally, there was the plane trip from hell!

We had chartered an aircraft to fly us down to Nelson but when we arrived at Wellington airport, we looked at what was waiting for us on the tarmac and froze. There was a terrible silence and then Orlando said, 'You've gotta be f***ing kidding!' Sitting there was an old, Second World War DC-3 Douglas Dakota transport plane – still with its WWII markings! I guess someone must have decided that it was cheaper than a regular plane – a piece of madness resulting, no doubt, from what are called 'budgetary considerations'!

We had a mountain of boxes and equipment and there was no one to help us load it, so we formed a human chain and began passing all

This picture says a thousand words. The sight of Dom, Eiljah and Orly helping to load our WWII transport plane neatly sums up the wonderful, slightly chaotic, family atmosphere of The Lord of the Rings *production.*

the stuff on board. Elijah, Orlando – all of us were pitching in to load all the gear. While this was going on, the pilot came out to meet us and began looking more and more concerned at the number of boxes that were going into his aircraft and the increasing number of people who seemed to be getting out of cars. Eventually he said, 'This plane is only meant to hold 12,000lbs as a safe weight – do you know how much all this gear weighs?' No one did, of course.

We made some rapid decisions about what might get us to 12,000lbs and what could be sent down the next day on the ferry, and then started pulling everything except absolutely essential gear back off the plane. Then we all piled on board and the pilot started taxiing this thing out.

Being a nervous flyer, I asked a couple of questions about the aircraft and took a look at the logbook, which revealed that its first flight had been taking American troops to the Philippines in 1943! By then, it was too late to do anything about it, because we were heading for the runway...

The plane turns around, the guy throttles the engine and the tail lifts off the ground, the actors are yelling, 'Come on! *Come on!*' Meanwhile, I'm thinking, 'We're in a life-and-death situation and these guys are treating it like it's a rollercoaster ride!'

The plane feels heavy, but we begin to get up speed and the pilot pulls back on the stick. Then, like something out of an old comedy film, the plane lifts into the air and immediately bounces back down again! By now, I'm a nervous wreck, but Elijah and the others are screaming, '*Yeah!!*' The pilot has another go and the same thing happens; all I can see is the end of the runway coming up and, beyond that, the waters of Evans Bay with, at that point, absolutely no certainty of our getting airborne.

Somehow the pilot gets up enough speed and we finally lurch up into the air and – with twenty-odd people hooting and cheering – this old, heavily-laden plane swings out over Wellington harbour and lumbers off down towards the South Island with me wondering if we'll ever reach our destination!

Remarkably for such a big production, relatively few accidents were sustained during the shoot. Orlando Bloom got unhorsed and cracked his ribs; Bruce Hopkins as Gamling, to his great distress, accidentally sliced Théoden's ear during the fray at Helm's Deep, resulting in Bernard Hill having to have stitches; in another fight, Viggo Mortensen lost a tooth and, as is immortalised on film in *The Two Towers*, broke his toe while kicking an orc helmet in the scene where the three hunters find the smouldering remains of the Uruk band that adducted Merry and Pippin.

As everyone is aware who has viewed the DVD extras on *The Fellowship of the Ring*, Sean Astin sustained a deeply unpleasant injury when, running into the River Anduin in pursuit of the departing Frodo, he stepped on a shard of glass that pierced right through his stick-on hobbit foot and into his own. Costa Botes' documentary team, who happened to be filming the film-makers at the time, captured the whole bloody episode for posterity, from the cutting off of the prosthetic foot to Sean's departure for hospital by helicopter. There was a lot of blood, a good deal of genuine stiff-upper-lip bravery on Mister Astin's part and a morbidly amusing interest in examining the wound by Elijah and the other hobbits.

Rather surprisingly, Sean was also subject of an accident on the not-especially-dangerous Rivendell set.

Sean had gone off to read a book on part of the set. Standing behind him was an Elven loom with a half-woven rug on it. A gust of wind came along, picked up the loom, and it toppled over and hit Sean on the head. On one level, it was deeply funny, but he was really anxious about possible damage to his brain and he insisted on having a CAT scan to see if there was any internal damage. Fortunately everything was fine, but the most safety-conscious one amongst us did rather seem to attract the accidents! He's undoubtedly the only person ever to get brained by an Elven loom!

Apart from physical accidents there were occasional mishaps in filming which only became painfully obvious when the rushes were viewed the following day. As with all film-making, the process is one of setting high expectations and hoping that the realisations don't fall too far short, and Peter and Fran, particularly in the early days of filming, had to endure watching a number of 'Not Quite How I Saw It' moments.

There was the first attempt to show Frodo and Sam watching the Elves departing Middle-earth when, instead of a procession of exquisite beings, the parading Elves were notable for having bad teeth, ears that didn't look right and beard stubble showing through their make-up. Or when shooting the Ringwraiths' arrival at Weathertop, an attempt to choreograph the tall, gangly actors swathed in black resulted in them shimmying over the ridge doing what Peter describes as 'a bizarre Hawaiian hula-dance'!

I remember, during the first week of *Rings*, we were worried about all kinds of things: the make-up on the Wraith-horse – there was so much pus around the eye that it made the creature look more sick than scary – and a really curious problem with Pippin's ears. It was Fran who spotted it during one of the dailies: the wind machines were blowing so hard that Pippin's prosthetic ears started filling up with air until they looked like a couple of little kites. So those had to be redesigned straight away and, in editing, we had to cut around those shots where Billy had too much of a 'wing nut' look about him!

Naughty Sir Ian.

Despite whatever moments of depression clouded the brows and the horizons, there were also light-hearted moments that allowed a laugh or two: the Middle-earth equivalent of an urban legend sprang up about a monster eel, which had allegedly been sighted in the lake where Thomas Robbins was going to have to film the scene where Déagol is pulled out of the boat into the water while fishing. The eel got longer and longer in the telling until it was the size of a crocodile and Tom was totally terrified.

There was Ian McKellen's playful quip during Christopher Lee's first day of filming in the Isengard gardens. In a scene later dropped from the film, Gandalf spots a couple of orcs scuttling amongst the trees. 'Orcs?' Gandalf was to have asked in astonishment. 'Servants of the Enemy in Isengard?' To which Saruman replied, 'Not his servants – *mine*,' a first indication that Saruman the White was not all that he seemed… On one take, Ian revised his line to '*Orcs? – And so far from Auckland!*'

Also memorable was the day when it came to shoot the dead Saruman impaled on the machinery in flooded Isengard:

We laid Christopher on top of this great barbed wheel and attached the end of a spike, covered in blood, as though it was sticking out of his chest. I then tracked the camera over the top of him to simulate the turning of the wheel.

Christopher was in a good mood: I don't think, at that stage, he'd dwelt much on the ramifications being shown in such an obvious a stake-through-the-heart pose, because we had an amusing exchange: I said, 'This is an historic occasion, your lying here like this.' And he replied, 'Yes, I've been here before!'

I thought it would be fun to capture the moment for posterity, so I rolled the 35mm camera, and asked him to give me his thoughts on his moment of death. He opened his eyes and said, 'Twenty-eight years ago I was in this position, I looked up and I saw Peter Cushing standing over me, and now here I am in New Zealand all these years later and I look up and Peter *Jackson* standing over me!' Later, Christopher would get quite anxious about Saruman's Dracula-style death and then about the fact that we decided to cut his death altogether! But on the day it was a funny, cute moment and he was in excellent spirits about it all.

There were many bizarre moments, such as standing on a remote mountain location and watching the approach, suspended on a line beneath a helicopter, of the La-Z-Boy reclining armchair used by John Rhys-Davies when in full costume and prosthetics. Then there were shooting days at Mount Ruapehu when conservation concerns about damage to 300-year-old moss growing in the area dictated that the ground had to be covered and rolls of second-hand carpet were bought and transported to the location.

The whole area was covered with shag-pile carpeting. It looked really very weird and we had to keep stopping to make sure we didn't get any carpet shots! Whilst I was only too happy to do everything to make sure we didn't harm the National Park, what was really strange was that while the cast and crew were only allowed to walk on the carpet, there were masses of members of the public clambering about all over the place! Anyway, the moss didn't get damaged and everyone was happy – including some second-hand carpet dealer!

Things could be as fraught with unexpected complications in what might be expected to be the 'controlled' environment of the studio, as the day of filming Bilbo's Birthday Party demonstrated.

Standing on a table behind Bilbo was his birthday cake with its lighted candles; a great many candles – in fact all 111 representing Bilbo's age.

During one take, the cake, which was made out of polystyrene, caught fire and started to burn!

As the fire took hold, the hobbit extras were all staring at it and Ian, who was trying to deliver Bilbo's speech, realised that they were being distracted by something. He glanced back and saw what was happening, but remained totally in character as Bilbo and integrated the blazing cake into his performance: making a gesture towards it, raising his eyebrows and carrying on with the speech! There's no way we could use the shot, but it *was* a triumph of professionalism!

On the subject of actors continuing against overwhelming odds, Peter recalls the day on which they filmed the scene of the parley with The Mouth of Sauron, Mordor's Black Lieutenant. The shoot became near farcical as Bruce Spence bravely attempted to control a skittish horse that had not taken kindly to being encased in armour. Since Bruce was wearing a helmet that showed only his mouth and left him totally unable to see or hear, the actor had absolutely no idea where he was meant to be going or where the horse was trying to go!

None of the several equine challenges – including having to use rubber horseshoes to prevent the horses slipping on the steep slopes within Minas Tirith – can compare with the problems posed by Bill the Pony:

For a long time we left Bill out of drafts of the script because we knew how difficult – even impossible – it was going to be to physically get a pony into the middle of a marsh or halfway up a mountain.

The obvious answer was to forget the pony, but that was easier said than done because I knew that, for every reader of the book, the key image of the Fellowship on their journey from Rivendell to Moria was of the Nine Walkers – *and a pony*!

That's when I rashly suggested building a 'panto pony'! Of course, the Americans didn't have the faintest idea what I was talking about, because they don't have pantomimes. So I had to explain that it was actually two guys in a costume: one playing the head and front legs and the other poor bugger having to bend over and play the back legs!

You can imagine how this proposal went down with the studio: a high-tech movie full of CG effects and a pantomime pony! Anyway, Richard Taylor got Weta to construct this creature and it made its first

Bill the Pony came very close to being written out. We had so much to film on location, it soon became clear that transporting a real pony by helicopter, along with the difficulties of taking a foreign animal into national parks, would make it virtually impossible to film him. However, we resolved it at the eleventh hour by falling back on the oldest trick in the book – the pantomime pony!

appearance on film in the Midgewater Marshes.

Playing the pony were two people, young and very enthusiastic: a girl in the front and a chap at the back; they may have been a couple but, if they weren't, then they certainly came close to it after spending days together in that costume! We had a terrible struggle to get the pony to walk through the marshes because the performers were completely blind, buried in this costume and up to their waists in a real swamp. Bill would try to walk and then would start to wobble and everyone would have to rush in and catch him before he fell over! There was one hilarious moment when the front legs moved without the back legs and Bill got stretched into a sort of long sausage dog!

One of Peter's favourite scenes is that of Gimli sitting on the body of an Orc, with the dwarf's axe still embedded in its central nervous system. He acknowledges that the occupants of Middle-earth were probably not aware of the concept of a central nervous system but enjoys the anachronism. However the scene – for actor and director – is more memorable because of a problem over John Rhys-Davies' make-up.

John's prosthetic make-up was made from silicone, which is excellent
and much better than foam latex because it has a translucent quality.
Unfortunately, it is difficult to glue on and if the actor gets hot it lifts off
much more easily than foam latex. On this particularly day the prosthetic came unglued from John's forehead, from his eyebrows up, and
as a result he was sitting there with big folds in his face. In the end we
had to go with a ridiculous solution to the problem. Our prosthetic
make-up artist, Gino Acevedo, ended up gluing a piece of string to the
top of John's forehead so as to pull the make-up back into place. In
every shot of John sitting on the orc body, Gino was laying behind him,
out of sight, tugging on the string to keep Gimli's forehead tight!

Of the many ludicrous moments that occurred, one that has
remained firmly in Peter's mind took place while filming the battle
before the Black Gates. The New Zealand army were assisting the
production by supplying military personnel to act as Orc and
Gondorian extras. The 'squaddies' were cast as rank and file troops
with lieutenants and sergeant majors, in make-up and costume, acting as Assistant Directors in the marshalling and deploying of troops.
At the end of one shoot day, Peter spotted a curious altercation:

We'd wrapped and we were making our way back to base camp when I
heard this terrible army barracks-type voice shouting his head off. The
behaviour of one of the privates had obviously annoyed the sergeant
major, who had waited until filming was over for the day before giving
the offender a dressing down. There was the soldier standing rigidly to
attention, bolt upright while the sergeant major was just screaming and
yelling full in his face – like something out of *Full Metal Jacket*. 'How
dare you! *You horrible, hopeless piece of s***!*' Obviously this was a very
serious moment, but what made it so bizarre was that were both dressed
as Orcs and seemed totally unaware of how totally ridiculous they
looked!

Talk to anyone on set and they speak of Peter's astonishing awareness
of everything that is going on, his legendary ability to retain and act
upon vast quantities of data and as a director who has a particular
knack for encouraging actors towards memorable performances.

The cast was diverse in its background, experience and approaches to acting, ranging from Orlando Bloom, making only his second appearance in a feature film, to Christopher Lee, who had well over 200 movie titles already to his credit; from two British theatrical knights to a 'hot' Hollywood star in Liv Tyler.

Andrew Lesnie reflects, 'It was apparent to me, within a matter of days of starting filming, that we were on a project that could work because I felt that the conviction of the cast, and the relationship between them and Peter, was rock solid. From the outset, Peter exercised 'actor direction' – which a lot of directors don't do – and was forthright about the characterisations. Peter very quickly developed individual patterns of direction to suit the individual actors and pull the best performance from them: he'd work with Elijah in a different way to Sean Astin, Viggo or Orlando. That's one of Peter's gifts: to roll with the punches and be flexible. Whereas, during pre-production, I suppose I had given the project the benefit of the doubt, very shortly after we started filming I became a true believer!'

There were, for Peter, many satisfying moments: bringing together the hobbit actors and helping them give both rounded individual characterisations as well as a meaningful and moving sense of shared identity; and working with Liv Tyler and Hugo Weaving in order to create the 'look' and the 'feel' for the Elves that made one of the most precarious elements in the story – the concept of a race of immortal, all-wise beings – real and believable.

There was the obvious frisson of directing one of his childhood screen heroes, Christopher Lee, and of having the opportunity to make use of Andy Serkis' physical acting talents, Viggo Mortensen's 'method' approach of inhabiting a role and Ian Holm's vigorously free-wheeling approach in which he will give a dozen different takes with a dozen different subtle variations, which can be both a director's delight (particularly with as open a director as Peter) as well as, occasionally, a fellow actor's worst nightmare!

During one of my early conversations with Ian Holm he had said to me, 'I ought to warn you that I like to try different things on each take, so if you let me do three or four takes, I'll give you a variety of different read-

This was how Andy Serkis spent most of his four years with us.

ings; and then, if I haven't given you something that you like, just let me know what it is you're looking for and I'll try and give it to you.'

It was very interesting: he would look at every possible interpretation and, on each take, he'd come at it from a different place: he might give a quiet, introspective reading of a line on one take and then, on the next, play it animated and angry. He literally threw at you as many interpretations of a line as he could come up with.

I think Ian McKellen was rather in awe of Ian Holm's ability, as well as being slightly fazed by playing opposite a character who, on the face of it, seemed to be quite erratic, giving a whole new range of responses on every performance. Eventually, he pulled me to one side and asked, 'Do you like what Ian does?' I told him that I thought it was great and Ian just said, 'I could never do it that way. I have to decide what the scene is about and then try to achieve that to the very best of my ability.'

Which, indeed, Ian McKellen consistently did; taking the classic storybook characterisation of the wizard in the long beard and pointed hat, and infusing it with so many traits, tics and emotions – irascibility, forgetfulness, tiredness – that make him human (if a Tolkien wizard can ever be so called) and vulnerable.

There are many scenes of Ian's that I treasure, such as one of the first that we filmed in the Bag End set with Ian and Elijah in which Frodo rushes in through the door, calling 'Bilbo!' and then realizes that he has gone. It was a wonderfully moody scene with which to begin: shadows and flickering candles; Gandalf gazing into the fire, smoking his pipe and muttering Gollum's word 'Precious'; and the Ring lying on the floor in the hallway.

I also really loved the scene where Frodo looks at the letters glowing on the Ring and asks what it means and Gandalf recites the Ring-rhyme – wonderful Gothic, creepy stuff from Ian, who was now really nailing Gandalf and bringing great strength to the character.

Prior to these scenes, he'd only done Gandalf's arrival at Bag End, which was a very different tone and mood. Now he had progressed Gandalf from the amiable eccentric with his fireworks to a point where we could reveal much more of the 'essence' of Gandalf: the powerful wizard; the tactician; the Grandmaster chess-player of Middle-earth.

I know that Ian liked Gandalf the Grey much more than Gandalf the White, and I feel the same way. What I love most about the earlier version of Gandalf is his easygoing, tramp-like quality: when he's riding around Middle-earth, you can easily imagine that he sleeps under a hedgerow at night and then rides on the next day. He has this wonderful, earthy quality to him. Whereas, even in your wildest dreams, you really can't visualize Gandalf the White dossing down under a hedge!

Ian McKellen reflects, 'Peter always made sure we understood the direction in which we were going and why. He's a bit of a performer himself and understands about acting. Many directors are more interested in the technicalities of acting and find it hard to empathise with the dilemmas of the actor, but not Peter!'

Not that there weren't stressful times – as, for example, when the actor was struggling with finding a way to portray Gandalf's response to the elemental confrontation with the Balrog.

Ian got very frustrated. In interviews later, he was very amusing about filming this scene: if anyone asked, 'Can you tell us what the Balrog looks like?' he'd say, 'Yes, it's a furry rubber ball!' referring to the tennis ball on a stick that we had set up to give him an eye-line. At the time,

Saruman to Gandalf: 'And who is this irritating little fellow that's been following us around all day?'

however, he got a bit crotchety about having to do this powerhouse performance to absolutely nothing. The Balrog existed as conceptual art, so Ian had an idea of what it looked like, but it was incredibly tough on him.

'There were never any tantrums,' recalls Ian. 'That's not the Kiwi way. You discuss your point and you come to an agreement; you are doing it together. What impressed me about Peter was that the talents and gifts were there right from the beginning, fully formed – he never seems to have doubted the style of the photography and acting... On top of which, there's his wonderful sense of humour; his ability to be involved in so many different things all the time; his seemingly inexhaustible energy; his patience, his modesty, his total lack of pretension and his optimism: he was constantly good-natured and welcoming and expecting to enjoy the day ahead...'

Apart from imagining the presence of non-existent monsters, what was sometimes challenging for the cast was the fact that, to an extent, the script remained in a state of becoming throughout filming.

On one level there were the very real problems inherent in having had to launch into full-on production without the time to finalise all details relating to the three-script structure. Once filming commenced – often with scenes from the second and third movies being shot concurrently with those in the first film – it was an unrelenting race.

> Fran and Philippa were often only able to keep just ahead of the shooting. There were times when it felt like we were trying to lay the railway track in front of a fast on-coming train!

On at least one occasion, in the immensely problematical Council of Elrond sequence where the fate of the One Ring is determined, the script was literally 'hot off the press'.

> The Council at Rivendell was a laborious shoot, and quite different to anything else in any of the films. It was very static – just people sitting in chairs, talking. The seven or eight pages of script took us *five* days to shoot because of the number of characters and amount of shots. We shot the entire sequence twice: firstly as one continuous take with the camera on Gandalf so that even if Ian wasn't talking we would be seeing his reaction; then we shot it again as a series of takes, seen from Gandalf's point of view. It was really very monotonous and we were all sick to death of the scene!
>
> Then came Sean Bean's big moment! We weren't filming Boromir on the first day or two and Sean simply delivered his dialogue off-screen. About three days in, Fran, Philippa and I had rewritten Boromir's speech and handed him a brand new script! He was very happy with it, but hadn't had time to learn it. So we taped the script onto his knee and if you look at the scene, you'll see that he occasionally lowers his eyes, which is when he's glancing down at his lines!

Bernard Hill, on his first day on set as King Théoden, found himself arriving at Helm's Deep and being given the news that following the Warg attack, Aragorn was missing. When the actor asked how he was to play his response – was he supposed to think that Aragorn was dead?; was he feeling a sense of guilt? – he was startled to discover that, at that precise moment, nobody quite knew what was going to happen during the Warg attack (which was still a long way off in the shooting schedule) or in what kind of jeopardy Aragorn would have been placed. Fortunately, the emotions of confusion and concern that flashed across his face and that of Miranda Otto as Éowyn were suitably in character for the circumstances!

In the early stages of production, some characters – particularly Éowyn and Arwen – went through various transmogrifications as Peter, Fran and Philippa sought to make them meaningful to the drama and yet still maintain an integrity to Tolkien's writing.

There were rumours, at one time, that Arwen was being considered as a tenth member of the Fellowship. 'That was never an option,' says Fran. 'It was a question of to what extent do we take liberties with the story and introduce her into places where she never turned up?'

What *was*, for a while, an option was the notion of what might be described (in the country that birthed Xena) as an 'Arwen, Warrior-Princess' characterisation. It certainly became a possibility at the point when, contrary to the original text, the Elves of Lothlórien join with the race of Men in fighting the battle of Helm's Deep. 'Pete wanted to use the Elves in a dynamic way,' says Philippa Boyens, 'so we took our licence to adapt the book by going back to Tolkien's own concept of the Last Alliance between Men and Elves in the Second Age of Middle-earth.'

'It was plain to Aragorn's story,' says Fran, 'that he has to rally the diverse and disparate races of Middle-earth. They have to come to him and there has to be a unity in that. For us, Helm's Deep has to have significance beyond the world of Men. The Elves coming to join in that struggle fulfilled the myth of the Last Alliance that was part of the cultural memory of both races. I also felt that, dramatically, without having the Elves there the notion of a relatively small group of people defeating 10,000 Uruk-hai was difficult to believe. It lent credibility to the situation… Looking back on the decision, it feels probably rather more outrageous than it did at the time, although many fans of the book understood and accepted this digression from Tolkien.'

Within the context of having the Elves at Helm's Deep, it seemed natural to have Arwen fighting alongside Aragorn and her people. 'Even though we never made Arwen into a warrior like Xena, it placed her character too close to that of Éowyn.' Fran adds: 'After contemplation, it felt wrong. To change the story to that extent was actually defeating the purpose.'

A solution that was more in keeping with the original text was devised through the device of having Arwen give Aragorn the Evenstar, a jewel that symbolised her immortal nature and her willingness to sacrifice it for her love of Aragorn. That, along with scenes of Arwen and her father, Elrond, in Rivendell, together with various flashbacks, dreams and nightmare visions as the lovers think of one another and imagine the best and the worst of their future lives, holds Arwen in the story and adds an intensely human dimension to Aragorn's persona of the remote hero-figure.

At many junctures in the story, the writers sought to give veracity to their plot enhancements by drawing generally on Tolkien's prose. So, for example, the words of comfort that Gandalf shares with Pippin as the assault on Minas Tirith moves towards its climax were inspired by the author's description of Frodo's first glimpse of the Undying Lands: '…the grey rain-curtain turned all to silver glass and was rolled back, and he beheld white shores and beyond them a far green country under a swift sunrise.'

> In order to preserve Tolkien's voice, if a scene didn't exist in the book we'd filch lines from elsewhere. Philippa was the goldmine! Fran and I would say, 'There was a good bit about such-and-such somewhere, but we can't remember where it was…' and Philippa could always pinpoint material! She was our invaluable encyclopedia!

Repeatedly, in approaching the script and in interpreting it in shooting, crucial issues had to be resolved about aspects of Tolkien's narrative. One such instance related to the seeing-stones, or palantíri, by means of which Sauron bends Saruman's mind to his dark will.

Working with your heroes is one of the perks of the job. Christopher Lee was continually fascinating, with a photographic memory and an endless supply of interesting stories.

The palantír was one of those things I was always a little stressed about, because for me it was about stepping across that threshold of magic, which I didn't really like. We knew from the book what the palantír *did*, but I wasn't sure how to represent the way in which it worked and I found it particularly difficult to imagine how anyone would look when they were using it.

Was there a correct method for communicating by these seeing-stones? Was it all done by thought? Do you touch it? Do you hold it in your hand or sit with it in your lap? These were all questions that needed answering and Tolkien hadn't provided any answers in the book.

So, working with Christopher Lee, we began figuring out an appropriate palantír-handling technique! The idea was that the user would stand holding out their hand about four or five inches above the palantír. This gave us the opportunity to visually show when Sauron was drilling into Saruman's mind by having Christopher's outstretched hand quivering as he sought to resist the Dark Lord's will and then involuntarily clamping onto the stone and getting his mind reamed out at the same time.

Even so, it remained a challenge to try to get interesting shots because, just looking at Christopher standing there with his hand over what is essentially a crystal ball looked a little too fairytale-like, so I decided to heighten the camera angles and try to inject a feeling of creepiness into the shots in order to make them more interesting.

What I ended up doing with the palantír was looking for more and more inventive camera moves, craning up with a wide-angle lens and then dropping the camera low so that it distorted the room.

Whenever I'm faced with something that I find boring, I usually, after a moment of panic, try to use the camera in a way that's sufficiently different as to disguise the boring aspect!

Following what for Peter and Fran had now become an established pattern of writing, the process of taking the story from script to screen remained incredibly flexible. Even when they weren't committed to having to write against the clock, they still tried to give themselves the leeway to rethink and then freedom to rewrite.

It's part of a philosophy that's based on always trying to improve things. It encompasses all the characters and any aspect of the story and is to do with asking, 'Is this the best idea? Can we do something better?' It's not really based on anything else. We come up with ideas all the time; write scenes as we're shooting.

We found ourselves in the fortunate – and, in the case of most film productions, rare – position of being able to do this; normally it's so buttoned down and so tightly organised that if you suddenly said you wanted to shoot a new scene you'd be lengthening the shoot, but because we had three or four crews and second unit directors who quite often had free days, we were always able to absorb new ideas within our scheduled structure. This sometimes meant that Fran would direct a scene that we wanted to 'squeeze in'. The key 'Gollum talks to himself' sequence from *The Two Towers* was conceived and shot this way.

For Andrew Lesnie, Peter and Fran's approach to the script is simply a reflection of the entire film-making process: 'Making movies is an organic process. On any conventional film, the script undergoes changes and in actually filming a picture the project undergoes more

Sir Ian McKellen learning lines that might possibly have been slid under his door the night before.

changes, just as it will do in post-production. What happens is that the film develops a personality of its own: a personality affected by everything from the casting to the weather. Additionally, on any film today there are dozens of people coming aboard a production with their suggestions and demands. In the midst of that, the director has, somehow, to try and maintain a singular vision, to bring the project through to something close to how they saw it in their mind's eye. I can definitely say Peter is a control freak in terms of pushing through his vision in spite of various obstructions. At the same time, being a smart director, he will capitalise on a happy accident, find a way of turning an obstacle into an improvement on the original vision.

'For me, working with Peter as Director of Photography was about finding a way of making a contribution to Peter's vision. During the shoot that involved a certain amount of sparring: he would throw up an idea or say, you know, we could do this or we could do that, and then I would think about it and if I could come up with some way to enhance that idea, I would toss that back at him. Sometimes he'd run things by me days or weeks ahead, other times when we were on set and filming the shot.'

A number of sequences – often quite elaborate and now thought of as key sequences in the completed movies – were literally devised and developed on set. One of these was the wizard's duel between Saruman and Gandalf.

This sequence was one of the opportunities we had to indulge our own storytelling. Tolkien ends his description of Gandalf's visit to Isengard with Saruman saying that his fellow wizard is to be imprisoned on the pinnacle of Orthanc without providing any details of what exactly happened next! The idea of Gandalf being Saruman's prisoner was interesting and we wanted to create a scene demonstrating how the senior and more powerful of the two wizards succeeds in overpowering his lesser adversary. Essentially, we took something that Tolkien left off the page and developed it as part of the movie story.

However, we were actually feeling under a bit of pressure over our so-called 'wizards' duel' because, in one of the pre-production meetings with New Line, Bob Shaye had made a comment that we hadn't quite expected. At the time, *The Matrix* had just been released and was the hot new thing in the cinema and Bob said that he hoped the battle between Gandalf and Saruman would be presented in as inventive, original and dynamic a way as the fights in *The Matrix*.

That throwaway comment from a year earlier had stayed in the back of our minds, and the nearer we got to production, the more it began to generate a degree of stress. The difficulty was that, unlike *The Matrix*, we were dealing with two old guys who didn't have any weapons other than their staffs!

One of the things that bothered me about the idea of the confrontation was that it was essentially a magical fight and I really didn't want to resort to those fantasy clichés of the wizards' staffs emitting lightning bolts or having flashes or sparks and smoke coming out of their fingertips! Even though there would obviously be a magical quality to the fight, I essentially wanted to do it 'dry', rather than relying on pyrotechnics.

Because I didn't really know what could be achieved, I left the 'choreography' to the stunt team and it was, more or less, made up as we went along. They came up with ideas for two old guys hurling each other around the room and smashing into the architecture, then they would try them out and we'd see what worked.

For first assistant director Carolynne Cunningham, working with Peter is, above all, about being adaptable: 'I'm so used to working with Peter – and everybody who works around him now knows him so well – that we're generally prepared for anything to happen. He might turn up in the morning and we'll be talking about what we're doing that day and he will say, "I need forty Gondorian soldiers for that scene…" and I'll look at the call-sheet and see that we've only allowed for *ten*! I'll just say, "Oh, really… Okay…" and get on the phone. No one panics. There's forty suits of Gondorian armour hanging out the back and the extras casting people ring up thirty people and in they come and off they go.

'If, on the other hand, I say to him, "Look, Pete, I'm sorry, we just can't do that," he'll say, "Oh, okay… We'll make it work another way." Forty Gondorians would be better, but if there's only ten he'll use the ten in an imaginative way. That's what I love about him: he can think in so many different ways, and will always make things work for him.'

> There's always a way around any difficulty. When we filmed the retreat into the Hornburg, we really didn't have sufficient extras, so we filmed those that we had as charging Uruk-hai and then they went off and changed costumes and we filmed them again as fleeing Rohan soldiers! There was another day where we had people playing Ringwraiths in one scene and, later in the day, playing Elves. A Wraith in the morning, an Elf in the afternoon – typical day for an extra on *The Lord of the Rings*!

'Peter knows what he wants,' says second unit director of photography Richard Bluck, 'but will always listen to ideas. In the end, you trust to the knowledge that he'll know when you've got it right – and that he will keep on till you do!'

He has been described as 'an ideas sponge' and miniatures unit director of photography Chuck Schuman, sums it in the following analogy: 'Peter doesn't feel as if you are painting on his canvas – he welcomes and encourages it!'

'Peter is extremely demanding,' says Alex Funke, visual effects director of photography. 'He can keep in his head just about everything he's said or seen and remember what he told you a year ago in incredible detail. He is a perfectionist with a fantastic vision and knows exactly what he wants to see on the screen, but he also absolutely understands the nature of compromise in film-making. A lot of directors say, "I'm a perfectionist, that's what I want – keep going!" Peter will say, "I see what the problem is here, we'll fix it another way..." He knows where he's going, but also realistic about how to get there. He has made so much of this stuff himself – hands-on – that he knows where you can bend the rules, and how to look for solutions.'

So what makes people do what they do for Peter? 'He's immensely inspirational,' says Ken Kamins. 'He is fond of talking about the Kiwi way, which is, "We have no choice but to work ten times harder in order to show that we are capable of producing great results." That has lived and breathed within Peter as long as I've known him.'

Peter also had to cope with a great many political situations that were taking place off set and behind the scenes. Inevitably, once the first flush of marriage had worn off, New Line looked at the project they had picked up without the benefit of rose-tinted spectacles...

Peter has described the story of how he came to make *The Lord of the Rings* as being, in part, a political story; and the ups and downs and ins and outs of Hollywood politics did not cease from the moment that New Line came on board the project, particularly since the budget – posited on those 'intuitive leaps based on nothing' – inevitably began to rise. Four months into filming, Shoot Day #67 Friday 4 February 2000, came a day that is forever wedded in Peter's mind to a memorably dramatic shot in *The Fellowship of the Ring*. Taking the envelope from Frodo containing the Ring, Gandalf throws it into the fire at Bag End.

I was shooting the shot with a camera behind the fire; Gandalf and Frodo were there, leaning over with the tongs. I'd lined up the lens and then had to go and take a telephone call. Bob and Michael were calling from the States and they really laid into me on the phone about the latest budget increase, yelling at me: 'This is terrible... You're betraying us... What the hell do you think you're doing?' They had every right to feel that way. Everyone was under different pressures – theirs as potent as ours. There was nothing that could really be done. Nobody, in the history of cinema, had attempted to do what we were doing. They calmed down – we just had to get the movies made. Looking back on it, I was able to make the films I thought we needed to make – which was obviously a wonderful – and *unusual* – freedom!

But the problem did not go away. Three months later, Mark Ordesky was on the case, telling Peter that the number of effects shots was now increasing beyond an acceptable tolerance level.

It was a conversation that sent me into a tailspin towards depression. He said, 'We have to cut back on shots and obviously you're able to select exactly what shots you want to cut and how you want to do that, but I've gone through the script and looked at everything and the Watcher in the Water sequence outside the gate to the Mines of Moria... We haven't started work on the monster yet, so if we cut that out it would save us a bit of shooting time and it would save us having to build and animate the creature...' So I said, 'Yeah? And don't you think that would disappoint the fans? Isn't the Watcher important because he ultimately causes the landslide that traps the Fellowship inside the mines?' By the time I got off the call I was in a pretty bad way, because I guess I just don't respond very well to that sort of thing, having somebody telling me what to do – even if it was done in the politest possible way. Of course, from that day on, I was determined that the Watcher wasn't going to get chopped out!

As he so often does, Peter found a way around the problem, striking a deal with the studio that he could shoot the Watcher on the under-standing that it didn't take up any of Peter's directing-time. The solu-tion was that second unit director Guy Norris directed the Watcher scenes while Peter ploughed on with other sequences in order to keep to the schedule and, somehow, the monster stayed in the picture!

There were initial concerns not simply about the budget being expended on special effects, but about whether the effects would be good enough. Despite Bob Shaye's comments on how impressed he had been by the tests he had seen of the Massive software, and an appreciation of the fact that Weta promised to be considerably cheaper than ILM, there was a clear level anxiety as to whether the key CG figures would be able to match the standards set by the American special effects studios.

> Bob Shaye told me that he considered Gollum to be way beyond Weta's capabilities. So I instigated Gollum development a long time before we needed him. Weta started doing tests so that we could prove ourselves. The shot we tested was the long crane shot from *The Two Towers*, when Gollum sneaks out and takes the lembas bread and throws it over the ledge.
>
> I screened the shot for Bob and he agreed that it was fine, although, looking at it today, it's embarrassing to realise just how crude it seems and that it's really nothing like the finished Gollum. Still, it was the first ever attempt to create what we all knew was going to be a key CG figure and it at least proved that we were able to deliver.

Nevertheless, for quite a time, there existed a mood of mutual mistrust that was simply waiting for a situation to trigger a clash. Another such explosive moment came during the unending and unrelentingly exhausting night-shoot for the Battle of Helm's Deep.

> I was shooting at Helm's Deep. I remember it was a shot of a soldier that didn't end up in the movie. The shots stick in my mind because they were linked to these horrible moments. Weta had had another budget increase. New Line was not acknowledging that the primary reason the budget was going up was because the film was now being enhanced – we were doing more and more spectacular things – but New Line was operating on the basis that whilst the budget was going up, they hadn't seen any effects yet.
>
> It was something like a $15million increase that really drove them over the edge. There were accusations and recriminations and, for a while, legal threats were in the air...
>
> Because there was no cell-phone reception in the quarry where we'd built the Helm's Deep set, Barrie Osborne had been ordered to get me

On most days during the shoot Alan Lee would drop by with his conceptual art for future scenes. It never failed to lift my spirits and get me excited about the films we were making.

on a satellite phone. I turned round and saw Barrie standing there with a huge contraption with a great, long aerial, saying that Michael Lynne wanted to talk to me. I said in a loud enough voice for Michael (or his assistant) to hear, 'If Michael Lynne wants to sue me, tell him to call my lawyer! Tell him I'm trying to shoot his f****** film!'

'New Line had done this extraordinary thing,' says Ken Kamins. 'They had put up a huge amount of money to make these movies and because they had so much money at stake, I think they felt it was their duty and responsibility to be concerned and to make sure they were protecting their investment on behalf of themselves and their international buyers. That could have been interpreted by Peter, at times, as a lack of confidence in his ability to achieve them.'

Following the Helm's Deep telephone spat, the lawyers talked and that particular situation was diffused. But these run-ins were made all the more difficult and stressful by the fact that the parties involved were separated by several thousand miles and working at a different time on the world clock. There was also, perhaps, a tendency to underestimate the Jackson temperament.

'He's tough, brave and strong-willed,' observes Philippa Boyens, 'and the thing about Peter that anybody working with him had better know and understand is that he will walk away. He doesn't bluff. If he sticks himself out there and says, 'Listen, this is going to happen unless that happens...' then *it will happen*! You don't play cards with Peter.'

> There really were no villains... It wasn't a situation where 'New Line are bastards!' The budget *was* going up and they *hadn't* seen any footage. I have some horrific memories from that year of principal photography, but don't hold resentment towards the studio at all. Michael Lynne was trying to do his job and I was trying to do mine, wanting to concentrate on finishing the film.
>
> Maybe New Line seriously believed we were trying to mislead them. Perhaps there was a suspicion that it might have been in my best interests for the budget to go higher and higher since I owned the company creating those effects... but the reality is that Weta Digital earned no profit at all. Every cent went up on screen.
>
> In the end, I dealt with the pressure by thinking that my No.1 responsibility was to make the best films I could. Only by doing that could New Line's risk be protected. I would battle for what I felt was best for the film, but it was also protecting their investment as well. I'm sure they get this argument from film-makers all the time. I don't know how these studio executives do it! It would drive me nuts dealing with film-makers like me!

New Line, like Miramax before them, may well have felt that when Peter got them to commit to *The Lord of the Rings*, he didn't tell them about the *entire vision* he had for the project and that it was only when they were on board that he started to reveal the full reality of that vision. The truth is simpler – or, depending on how you look at it, more complex – in that Peter's vision for any project is constantly developing and expanding. His knack has been to hitch others to that vision and keep them there when it flies into orbit.

'Peter's got a great ability to get everyone really locked in,' notes

Jamie Selkirk. 'He brings people into the fold and then starts branching out and getting broader so that people come in with certain ideas and end up with something three times bigger than what was originally planned but, by then, they are suckered in... On *Rings*, the number of special-effects got bigger and bigger and people began to realise that one line in the script was now a whole page – not 100 horses, but 200 horses; not a hundred orcs, but a thousand...'

The concerns over the number and complexity of those special effects shots had surfaced very early on – by the second week of shooting – in particular over Peter's planned shot following the moth as it flutters up over the walls of ruined Isengard and on up the height of Orthanc to be caught by Gandalf.

> The studio seemed to think that my moth-shot was going to be way too hard and far too expensive, and in order to try and keep them and me happy and reduce costs, someone suggested that we just pick up the shot as the moth flew past the top of Orthanc and Gandalf grabs it. I thought, 'But that's not what's cool about that shot; and it's not how I'm going to do it.' I guess that was when I began to realise just how much pressure I was going to be under – and it was still early days...
>
> It was a very difficult situation to deal with: there were more effects shots than were ever planned and they were more complicated. There is no person to blame... If anything, I am to blame because, when I am under pressure, I refuse to be reined in and get very defensive of the film. The simple truth is that we never had a locked script, and therefore never could arrive at a locked budget. Script and budget have to always reflect each other. One can't keep changing and the other be locked.

'With hindsight,' reflects Richard Taylor, 'the only issue was that we didn't build a department that was flexible enough to accommodate Peter's working style. You can't force Peter to lock down to a tight schedule and a "deliverables list" because it doesn't allow him to have what is his greatest inspiration – his on-set vision. You've got to treat the work as if it is a ball of clay to be melded and moved around, and that requires a flexible environment.'

Fran Walsh says: 'If we learnt anything, it was that you have to have people with real experience in every key role.' People with good intentions, doing their best, simply wasn't enough.

The truth was that no one was completely prepared for all that had to be achieved and for the exacting demands that would be made on everyone. As a result there were various changes in staff during the first few months of filming with producer Tim Sanders leaving the project and key personnel at Weta Digital being replaced at the cost of several friendships and with certain individuals feeling saddened and bitter...

'It wasn't that they weren't doing great work,' reflects Richard Taylor, 'it wasn't that their hearts weren't in it – these people were working like maniacs to do a lovely job – but for whatever reason, the studio lost confidence in them and put great pressure on us to replace them. It's taken many years to repair some of the damaged relationships.'

> It's painful... It's a small industry. Healing has to happen over a period of time. When things like this happen you are only ever doing it for the good of the film, but what's good for the film can be very hurtful and disastrous for the individual...

Jamie Selkirk concurs: 'These were stressful times and some painful decisions were made, but we battled our way through it and kept going.'

The realisation had dawned that *The Lord of the Rings* was a juggernaut, thundering along and taking everybody's best endeavours to keep it up to speed, on time and to ensure that it didn't come off the road...

Playing out in the background was another drama that might easily have had disastrous knock-on effects on the way in which *The Lord of the Rings* was completed and marketed, and most certainly affected the way in which New Line attempted to manage the project. In January 2000, the largest business merger in history took place when America Online (AOL) bought New Line's parent company, Time-Warner. Among the many questions being asked when the new $350billion company emerged from the wedding ceremony was whether any of the children in the marriage might suffer. Certainly, a number of what Peter describes as 'AOL watchdogs' were now on the case and keeping a close eye on all expenditure. It became increasingly clear that *The Lord of the Rings* now *had* to succeed.

It was around this time that Bob Shaye and Michael Lynne paid their first visit to the Jackson studios in Wellington, accompanied by representatives from their foreign distributors. The purpose of the visit was for New Line's partners to be given a tour of the studio, but Peter had decided to produce a showreel of footage that had been shot to date to give Bob and Michael an indication of what they were getting for their ever-rising budget!

Working with editor John Gilbert over the Christmas break, Peter had cut together an impressive series of scenes: Gandalf in Bag End, banging his head on the beam; Sam and Frodo in the cornfield; the four hobbits hiding from the Black Rider under the tree-roots, and concluding with the death of Boromir and Aragorn's grieving. With an added music score, it was an impressive twenty minutes of footage.

> It wasn't required of me; it was something I didn't have to do especially since I felt that they had been so very negative towards me the last time I'd spoken with them. But we were really proud of what we'd shot and I decided that it might be strategically smart to screen something for Bob and Michael.
>
> I didn't want to meet and socialise beforehand, so we arranged for them to go to their hotel and then come out to our cinema.

There has been a much-told story about this first visit, which describes Bob Shaye walking down a corridor lined with posters for *Bad Taste*, *Meet the Feebles* and *Braindead* and wondering what on earth he had got New Line into…

'I absolutely believe that story,' says Ken Kamins. 'What Bob did in taking this gamble no one will truly understand; what drives somebody to take a risk, to speculate, at any moment in time is chemical – it's within their DNA! And the urge to do something bold and dramatic comes quickly; how you feel about it after you've done it takes some time to process and I have no doubt that coming down to New Zealand and seeing Peter's facilities and seeing those posters on the wall probably gave Bob the horrors!'

Ask Bob Shaye if the story is accurate or mythic and the answer snaps back: 'That's not mythic; that's absolutely true. I was the source of that story... We'd already committed and we were going to see the first footage. I was aware of Peter's previous movies, had seen several; I knew what the boy had in him. Those early movies demonstrated creative vision and were made for very little money, all good stuff – *but this was a whole new ball game!* So it was a little chilling to see all these posters were taped on the wall *crooked*! I mean, *come on!* We didn't need to have fancy offices, but I said to myself, "I hope what we see is going to be good..."

> Minutes later, fortunately, he was seeing the film... I remember as Bob came towards me; I did a playful boxing thing, raising my guard saying, 'Please, don't hit me!' He laughed and gave me a hug and I told them that I realised they were unhappy that we were over budget, but that I thought they would like to see some of the footage and let the film speak for itself.
>
> When the lights came up I could see that Bob had been crying. There was silence, and then Michael said, 'It's a drama!' I found that interesting and realised that certain sections of the picture were *Hercules*, *Sinbad* and pure brainless sorcery; but that the scenes they had just watched were dramatic and emotional. I honestly think they were surprised by the tone of film.

Peter had intended the film solely to be shown to Bob and Michael, but over dinner that night they asked Peter if they could screen it for their foreign partners. The footage was shown to the distributors, who were as impressed as the New Line bosses had been.

> Basically it created an uplifting mood and was a real turning point. We'd resisted micromanagement and, as much as they hated the budget going up, they knew that it was all going on screen to make the films better than we ever thought they'd be. I guess, in the end, they thought, 'We can either ride it or we leave them to it...' and I think at that moment

they made a conscious decision to let me just get on with it. I really believe it was the first time they felt that they could trust me, beyond bankrolling the film in the first place.

I love it when people trust me. I don't respond well to micromanagement. Two things drive me: one is fear, putting your neck on the line, terrified it's going to be a disaster; the other is knowing that people have put their trust in me. I've always made a point of thanking New Line for their trust.

Trust is one of the most powerful creative tools – it makes me utterly determined not to let people down.

At last, some of the early tensions began to ease. 'While the budget increased way beyond what we contemplated,' says Michael Lynne, 'we did it in a measured step way. As we saw things, became more involved in the picture and realised that Peter was delivering the goods, Bob and I made the decision that this was worth continuing with. We always had the option of pulling the plug or cutting back.'

'The truth is,' adds Bob Shaye, 'the enthusiasm level became so exciting and filled with potential that it became easier to say, "Okay, in the scheme of things, another $10million across the three films is worth that investment." It was always hard to know, when people said it would cost an extra $10million more, where to cut it back to, what it would mean if we were to say, "No, we'll only give you $5million…" There were a couple of times when that happened and Peter said, "Fine, I'll do it with what you give me." It was a give and take situation. We're not just rubber-stamp producers, we argued long and hard about some things.'

'I still believe,' says Shaye, 'that Peter made this film for less than somebody else who had more experience with big-budget films. We could have been talking about *a lot more*! I won't reference on the movies!'

Nevertheless, a huge part of New Line's expenditure was committed to *The Lord of the Rings*: 'Some of the stress that was hardest to bear,' recalls Fran, 'came in little insights. People who were close to the studio would say, "You realise all their jobs are going to go, they'll be out of work; they are so hostile as they can't green-light any other movies: you've taken all the money." It was all or nothing; it was all on us; if the film failed it wasn't just us who were going down, it was everybody. It was an awful feeling.'

'There was a lot of pressure,' recalls Ken Kamins. 'Mark Ordesky would send me the occasional off-the-record e-mail telling me about issues that were of concern to New Line and, now and again, expressing great concern about us being headed into a gigantic problem. I would never concern myself with those e-mails unless and until Peter sent me his own e-mail on the same subject, which was maybe 15 per cent of the time. But at no time did New Line call me directly and say, "If your client doesn't do X we will do Y..." That never happened.'

Throughout the rollercoaster ride, people – as companies and individuals – committed themselves to Peter. Richard Taylor remarks, 'We've never questioned the fact that Peter is a genius and is going to make exceptionally good films. We've gone along with his every wish and have had our company taken to the brink because we have always known that Pete would pull it off and that the results would be beautiful and successful.'

'What we've always said,' adds Tania Rodger, 'is that if it all fell over tomorrow, we'll simply pick up what's left and start again. Our attitude has been to go along with Pete that way and not panic about the risks that are taken, because we trust where Pete's leading us; sometimes, it might not be the most pleasant of journeys but, ultimately, you will reach wherever he's aiming to get everybody.'

For the majority of people working on a Jackson movie, the trials and tribulations being weathered by Peter, Fran and their business colleagues Richard, Tania and Jamie Selkirk, are unknown: the angst and the anxiety is never passed on.

'One of the many things that I like about Pete,' says Philippa Boyens, 'is that he takes responsibility. This is his passion; his joy; his thing that he got everybody involved in, and he's going to work to *make* it work.'

'Peter has tremendous staying power,' says Peter Nelson. 'God knows, I've seen other film-makers who *haven't* had it; despite considerable talent they have not been able to stay in this milieu. It takes a consummate level of many skills to survive and prosper as a film-maker but one also needs to be a leader, to keep motivating people, even when the chips are down, confirming them in the belief that this is going to happen and it's going to happen well, and to communicate that fact not just through your actions but by who you are.'

'What Pete understands,' says Andrew Lesnie, 'is that when anxiety starts flowing downhill on a project it begins compromising everybody's work. The further downhill it goes, the more it begins impacting on people who can't handle that sort of stress. Sharing too many anxieties in an effort to seek a solution inevitably becomes the actual crisis itself and the further it spreads round the production the more crises it generates. I admit to often being blissfully unaware of some of the things that go on because all I want to do is to put all my energy into making the movie; I don't really want to put it into the *politics* of making a movie.'

Peter Nelson reflects on his client's attributes: 'He has many of the positive traits of his fellow countrymen, but he has achieved something that nobody even from New Zealand, with their "Can-do" Kiwi belief, has been able to do before.'

Realising that achievement involved the exercise of many skills and abilities – not the least of which was Peter's willingness to get on his bike: cycling from one studio where the scene was being filmed of the hobbits having their cook-up in the hollow at Weathertop to the another studio where, in Orthanc Chamber, Ian McKellen and Christopher Lee were creating screen electricity with the face-off between Gandalf the Grey and Saruman the White.

> We tried to get an alternating pattern set up so that I could keep both sets functioning at a reasonable speed; the whole thing was mathematically worked out. I would normally expect to shoot perhaps eight shots in a day, but on these particular days we scheduled five shots in Orthanc and five at Weathertop because the rest of the time I would be pedalling to and fro, which was tough, and sometimes when I began to get tired towards the end of the day, felt like a bit of a nightmare.

Ian McKellen recalls, 'There was never a sense that time was running out or that the schedule or financial constraints might restrict the number of times you could shoot a scene. It was always: "We'll get it

Sir Ian McKellen enjoying a little South Island rainfall.

right and not move on till we have…" Always reassuring.'

That is the Jackson way. Observe him directing on set and one quickly picks up on the mantra: 'Good… Good… Let's go again… Good… Let's try another one… Good… One more… Yes, good… One more… *Just one more for luck…*'

Critics may say – *have* said of Peter – that there are maybe too many 'One more for luck' shots on a Jackson shoot and that, in fact, he *overshoots*.

We've come to be strong believers that overshooting is your friend! With hindsight, you look back and there were days where you'd done a lot of hard work and the scenes didn't end up in the film and you think about the fact that perhaps you could have shot the film in two or three weeks less. It costs $1million a week on a film like this, so that's two or three million dollars less. But there are times when you need a scene – or a moment for a scene, need to plug a hole, stop up a gap – and then you are very glad that a bit of overshooting has given you a few more options in the cutting room.

Sometimes, footage would eventually be used in a completely different way to what had been envisaged. When, for example, Peter had originally filmed the final struggle against the forces of Mordor in the final moments before the Ring is destroyed, the script had called for Aragorn to do battle with Sauron in physical form. Whilst Tolkien never represents the Dark Lord during the narrative of *The Lord of the Rings* as anything other than a malevolent all-seeing Eye, there are references to earlier times when Sauron had a corporeal presence on Middle-earth.

The designs created for Sauron at the point when he is finally drawn out of Barad-dûr to face the returning king were a 'supercharged' version of his appearance during his fight with Elendil as depicted in the film's prologue. The fight between Aragorn and the Dark Lord was filmed, but became a less enticing – and increasingly unnecessary – option.

> When this final, one-on-one battle was conceived – long before we started shooting anything – one of our perceived problems stemming from our 'Reluctant Hero' image of Aragorn was that in building him up to a point where he was finally prepared to take on his kingly mantle and yet not have a showdown with the ultimate villain, who we'd also been building up, felt to us like a mistake.
>
> By the time we had got to post-production on *The Return of the King*, which was where we reviewed the decision, it simply no longer felt right. Obviously, it wasn't in the book but, at that stage, we were also brave enough – having had two successful films on our hands – that the success of *The Return of the King* no longer hinged on having an Aragorn/Sauron showdown at the end.
>
> Also, with hindsight, it would have been an immensely disappointing climax because it would have been Aragorn re-fighting exactly the same battle as the one that we had seen in the prologue to *Fellowship* – it would have felt like we'd come all this way and yet hadn't actually gone anywhere.
>
> What ultimately became obvious to us – forty years after it was obvious to Tolkien – is that the heroism of Aragorn is really not something 'one-on-one': the heroic Aragorn versus the big bad guy, Sauron. The true heroism of Aragorn and his companions is the fact that they

are prepared to give up their lives to buy seconds of time for Frodo to fulfil his quest; and it is all the more courageous because they don't know where Frodo is or even if he's alive. And yet they still make that choice. So, that is the ultimate heroism and it's pretty obvious really; it just took us a while to get there.

Even so, the sequence was not entirely wasted: during the mêlée in the hiatus before the Ring goes into the Crack of Doom, Aragorn is seen fighting with a huge cave troll. Why a troll? Well, trolls had featured in all three movies, but they are also *large*.

> We went through hours and hours of film, culled out the best bits and basically we used the Sauron fight, except that we digitally pasted a huge cave-troll over the top of Sauron! That footage ultimately came in handy and some of it ended up in the movie even if it was in a way that we didn't conceive at the time.

Ian McKellen says, 'I never once saw Peter flag,' but inevitably on such a relentlessly demanding shoot, tiredness finally began to set in…

> Each night, in theory, you are supposed to be watching the dailies but with three units shooting this was no easy task. We'd wrap on set at around 6.30 in the evening and, an hour later, we'd be in our cinema at Weta Workshop, running up to three hours of footage. So every night, before we could go home to sleep, we'd be watching something that ran for the equivalent length of *Ben-Hur* or *Gone with the Wind* – or, come to that, one of *The Lord of the Rings* movies!
>
> It was exhausting! Brian Bansgrove, the gaffer, was usually the first to go: I'd hear him start to snore about forty-five minutes into the screening and Barrie Osborne would usually go next! Though I couldn't have imagined it at the beginning of the shoot, a time would come when I became so tired that I had to give up watching dailies on screen and would watch them at home, on videotape – for as long as I could manage to keep awake.

Even when Peter finally got home, the day's work was still not yet done.

One of the things I regard as being the responsibility of a director is to make sure that the day kicks off well; to be fully prepared, to hit the floor running, to show up on set knowing what you want and then be able to convey that to people.

The moment I got in at night, I ought to have started thinking about the next day's filming, but often my mind was so full of the vivid images I'd been looking at for hour upon hour through the camera lens or on the screen, that I couldn't think of anything other than what I've shot that day. The memory was so fresh that I'd find myself making a mental notes: 'Take six was best take of that line, but the next line was better in take eight...' or 'Take three, on the wide-shot, was the best because the smoke was just right...' That's when I'd start editing the film in my head, piecing it all together as I'm lying in bed until, eventually, I'd fall asleep...

Whenever I'm shooting, I have a recurring dream: I'm lying there, incredibly tired and sleepy, and I drowsily wake up – in my dream – and find that the film crew have come in to my bedroom and are standing around the bed, demanding instructions about what to shoot and how to shoot it. That's when I always realise with horror that I don't know what to say to them – that I don't actually know what scene we are filming!

So, after the stress of being on set all day, my nights were also full of stress. On almost every film I've made, this dream has afflicted me virtually every single night and I become incredibly disturbed at confronting the realisation that I'm shooting a movie but don't have a clue what it is that I'm filming.

As the shoot wore on and we got into the final months of the year I was running on very low reserves, finding it harder and harder to come up with inventive ideas and realising that my imagination was literally seizing up. It is very scary how tiredness begins to shrink your imagination.

Sleep deprivation eventually took its toll: one day, on the Rivendell set, while waiting for the lights to be set up, Peter decided to have a lie down on Frodo's bed and fell into a deep sleep for a couple of hours.

Philippa Boyens recalls: 'Sometimes, Pete would be so drained that he would get depressed. Nothing depresses him more than when he cannot bring to a scene his normal energy and vision and he just shoots it in the most conventional way. That makes him feel really down, and really depressed. On these occasions he can get quite dark. I don't know how he copes. I think sometimes he doesn't and he just quietly goes off and de-rails somewhere… He never burdens other people with it. If he burdens anybody then it will be Fran. She's got broad shoulders and he's got the same for her stuff; they've got broad shoulders for each other's baggage.'

> I think if I had a partner who wasn't involved or didn't understand then I really would de-rail and very quickly. You'd have all this tiredness and exhaustion and the other person wouldn't understand. It's only because Fran and I know the pressures we're both under that we're able to keep on top of them.

'It's about understanding,' says Fran, 'and it's about problem solving, if we weren't in it together it would be that much harder to help. I remember it becoming obvious we weren't going to get through everything and I started lobbying to bring in extra help to direct the other units.'

> The sheer volume just kept mounting. I'd be thinking that somehow we'd figure it all out but Fran was saying, 'We need somebody else; you need help…' She was the advocate. And she was right.

'Arguably,' says Peter Nelson, 'he's the director, she's the co-writer and producer, but, like many partnerships, it's a seamless line between the two.' As Philippa Boyens puts it: 'Theirs is pretty much a single, co-mingled, unified vision. There's no beginning and no end to the individual abilities or the way those two work together.' Or in the view of Carolynne Cunningham: 'It's not just "Pete" and it's not just "Fran"; it's actually always "Pete-and-Fran" to me – they're a little like a liquorice allsort – a stripey one with different colours.'

At long last, on Friday 22 December 2000, after fifteen months of filming, they arrived at Shoot Day #274, the final day of principal photography on The Lord of the Rings.

Fifteen months crowded with memories: the anxieties and tensions, the lost days and the missed opportunities, but also the many moments when cinema magic was being created.

> I remember filming the scene inside Mount Doom at the Crack of Doom: Elijah and Sean delivered amazing performances. We were running out of spaces in which to film and were renting anything we could find. This scene was filmed in a tin-roofed shed used for storing apples near the runway at Wellington airport, with aircraft taking off about 100 feet away!
>
> It was impossible to build the entire Crack of Doom set, so we built a kind of rock gantry, filmed against a green screen, and used a lot of smoke. I was thinking, 'I can't believe it! *This is the Crack of Doom?!'*
>
> You feel so far removed from what you are hoping for in the finished film. When we got to the point where Elijah was having his final dramatic moment with the Ring, the whole crew was mesmerised. At the end of the take, the crew gave him a huge round of applause, something that doesn't happen very often. It is a reminder that, as a film-maker, you rely totally on the power of the actors... This was their moment.

Unit production manager Zane Weiner's schedule for the final day's filming (now in the WingNut files) is scrawled over with thank-you messages from the cast and crew. One from Fran reads, 'We have rewrites for Saturday!' and another from Peter, 'Zane, find me a crew; we're shooting through Christmas!' It was, as Peter recalls, not far from the truth...

> On the morning of that last day I shot the Council of War scene: the debate between Gandalf and Aragorn which, in the book, takes place in a tent, but which we staged in the hall at Minas Tirith. In the afternoon, I shot Aragorn in the hall putting on his armour and strapping on his sword before going out to confront Sauron – a scene that isn't in any version of the movie – which means that, actually, we could all have gone home a bit earlier that day!
>
> We were shooting some really serious dramatic scenes but it was a fun day: everybody was in a good mood. Someone had brought in a feather boa and, all day long, we had guest clapper-boarder operators –

the only proviso being that they had to wear the feather boa while doing it… I remember Harry Knowles doing one!

Unit 1B were shooting across town with Fran directing the scene at Dunharrow where Théoden and Éowyn have a cheerful little conversation about what should happen if he didn't return from battle. Viggo was in my scenes and Fran's and was rushing back and forth across town between the two units all day.

We wrapped about five o'clock, but word came through that Fran was still shooting, so we drove across to her, snuck onto the set and the champagne finally came out about six o'clock!

Peter was too tired to go to that evening's dailies, but he had no choice about being anywhere other than at the wrap party, which was held in Shed 21, one of the original wharf buildings on Wellington harbour. There were limousines; there was a red carpet and two thousand invited guests including the cast and crew, the mayor and other dignitaries, and a phalanx of press and television reporters.

I would have been perfectly happy to have gone home to bed! To me, it felt like a symbolic event – I knew that we were still a long way from finishing the film.

That was, indeed, the case. The New Year arrived and brought with it a new exhausting schedule that would establish the pattern for the next three years: editing *The Fellowship of the Ring*, filming 'pick-ups' – additional footage or re-shot scenes – followed by more editing and, in London, working with Howard Shore on the scoring of the first film. Not to mention having to review a veritable department-store-load of merchandise and begin the seemingly unending task of talking about and promoting a project that was still anything but complete.

In January 2001, the promotion began: the official website was launched and – as fans had done for *Star Wars I* – lines formed outside cinemas days before the trailer was screened on Friday 12 January before *Thirteen Days*. It was the first glimpse!

New Line had made the decision to launch *The Lord of the Rings* with a special promotional event at the fifty-fourth Cannes Film

Festival to be held in May in the south of France. The plan was to screen an extended teaser for the films and host an elaborate party for the festival's media hounds.

Peter's response was to propose screening a twenty-minute sequence from the film that would give a feel and a flavour of how the finished picture would look without giving too many glimpses of other sequences, characters and creatures. It was decided that part of the Fellowship's journey through the Mines of Moria conveyed the excitement of the adventure and the look of the interpretation.

> I felt we should screen more than just a trailer. The tone and style of a film can only be accurately conveyed in something longer than four or five minutes. Looking at the way the movie was shaped, we felt the Moria journey would form an entertaining, continuous twenty-minute sequence.

Bob Shaye and Michael Lynne viewed the footage and were, it is said, unimpressed, giving it a tepid reaction, which suggested that they might be losing confidence in the product.

Bob Shaye recalls the event differently: 'Something I don't think people know,' he says, 'is that Michael Lynne and I and our head of marketing, Rolf Mittweg, went down to New Zealand as this reel was being prepared. Peter appropriately – I guess there was professional grace involved – said, "Listen, I don't do these things; I don't make selling material for films…" He showed us what he'd done and we didn't agree with what he had chosen. It was so dark, it was all interior, it didn't reflect enough of the rest of the film in order to give a context to the scale and the drama. Our complaint was with what Peter was suggesting showing, not with his skills as a director. So Peter's reaction was, "Sit with the editor, do what you want to do and we'll agree together…" As a result, that particular reel – a signal moment in the process of the film – got shaped into a marketing tool as opposed to a directorial sample.'

> Bob and Michael's lukewarm response to the material led to us adding a three-minute trailer-like prologue to the front, and an epilogue featur-

ing more footage from *Two Towers* and *Return of the King* – they were concerned that Moria was a dark, grim sequence and they wanted something that would feature more brightness and colour. It was a good instinctive reaction on their part, and the reel was definitely better with the new opening and closing sequences – almost mini-trailers of their own.

The fourteen-minute sequence from the Mines of Moria, stopping short at the point when the Balrog looms out of the fiery darkness, was 'topped-and-tailed' with a prologue and epilogue that captured something of the other moods in *The Fellowship of the Ring* – Hobbiton, Rivendell, Isengard and Lothlórien – together with glimpses of the continuing adventure in the subsequent two films accompanied by the orchestral sweep and operatic voice of Howard Shore's evocative score. The twenty-six minute reel was to prove the most talked-about footage at Cannes and threatened to eclipse even the starry gala mounted for *Moulin Rouge*.

The quoted 'estimated budget' of $90million a movie was, cumu-latively, already more than double the sum that had seemed too much for Miramax, three years earlier. As a result the press described the teaser footage as a $270million film running for less than half an hour.

The screenings took place on 12 May 2001 at the Olympia theatre where, nine years earlier, the press had got their first glimpse of a film which sported such tag-lines as 'The rot has set in' and 'You'll laugh yourself sick!' – *Braindead*…

'There was a great deal of anxiety that day,' recalls Ken Kamins. 'Right before the first screening for the press at the Olympia I remember Bob Shaye and Michael Lynne were really very tense; everybody knew that they'd bet their houses on this strategy of going to Cannes with the huge party and a twenty-six-minute preview. It was a strategy that had not gone terribly well once before when Disney had previewed *Armageddon* to a less than rapturous response. The question being asked was, 'Is this New Line's folly?'

'There were,' admits Bob Shaye, 'a *lot* of fears. Not only had New Line never taken on anything of this scale before but nobody else had either; there was no road map as to how you go about this kind of undertaking. There were fears on the part of our team, whether they'd be able to stand up to the test, which they did with flying colours, and fears on the part of Peter and his team, whether they could stand up to the test, which *they* did with flying colours! But to say there weren't any fears wouldn't be true.'

'We were very excited about what we were showing,' adds Michael Lynne, 'but we couldn't help but be anxious about the undertaking. Never had so much press been gathered in one place to see just twenty-six minutes of this supposed epic trilogy. Bob and I were very confident about the footage, but we were rolling dice. If for one reason or another there was something the press didn't respond to and the word came out negatively, that would be a burden… You can't help but have anxieties.'

'You have to remember,' continues Bob Shaye, 'that we had also enlisted the support of many international partners; it was as big a commitment for them as it was for us in a commensurate way. A lot of these people had bet their own farms with certain trepidation. Michael and I felt very responsible, not only to our own company but to the twenty different companies throughout the world that had risked more than they had ever risked for a motion picture. Even though the movie business is redolent with risk, it was a big responsibility that we had to shoulder; for me personally this was one of the major things I thought about. We'd recently lost an unfortunate amount of money with two or three other movies; I knew *we* could shoulder what we'd undertaken on this but wasn't sure everybody else could. I was really concerned.'

The lights in the Olympia went down, the film rolled and for those now-famous twenty-six minutes the audience was enraptured: they gasped, they clapped, they jumped in union at the moments of suspense. When it reached its conclusion, they leapt to their feet applauding and cheering. The response both in the theatre and as the crowd spilled out into the blazing sunlight was one of appreciation and delight and, more importantly, *of expectation.*

Ken Kamins recalls: 'The relief after that first press screening was huge! It was as if they'd seen the whole movie. It was indescribable!

And it was incredible how word spread across the Plaza like wildfire: "Oh my God, these guys are really on their way to something!"'

For Bob Shaye and Michael Lynne, who were accompanied by many of their foreign investors, the reception came like an answer to a prayer. 'It was actually overwhelming,' remembers Bob Shaye. 'Many of these people had literally mortgaged their companies; they didn't know what they were going to be seeing. This was not like a bunch of people who had walked in without commitment; there was an emotional component of relief and excitement.'

Rolf Mittweg confided to *Variety*: 'My Japanese distributor said he had a knot in his stomach for a whole year, and now it has dissolved…'

> It was a gutsy thing to do. If I was marketing the film, I probably wouldn't have done it – but New Line decided to take the chance, and everyone in New Zealand worked around the clock to complete the best reel we could. It was such a dangerous gamble. However, in hindsight it was smart. If we hadn't screened anything at Cannes, we'd have been facing another seven months of 'New Line's Folly'-style mutterings. This was a do or die attempt to shut those people up and begin a tide of goodwill towards the project. It worked. I'm full of admiration for New Line's sheer courage in doing that.

Even before *Variety* ('Three "Ring" circus commands attention') and the rest of the movie media correspondents were overwhelmingly prophesying success for Jackson's vision of Middle-earth, Cannes was crackling with the word-of-mouth and the internet sizzling with word-of-web.

Empire magazine's French website declared, 'Right from the beginning we feel it is going to be huge. *Star Wars* looks like a pale TV series compared to that.' While the indefatigable Harry Knowles was in full flight on his *Ain't it Cool* site: '…The bridge sequence is ungodly cool… the sort of ungodly cool that… well… I CANNOT EVEN BEGIN TO DESCRIBE HOW COOL THIS SEQUENCE WAS!! I've never seen anything like it… This is Cinema, big and showing me things my imagination has never conceived of. I was giggly-happy and dumbstruck all at once. Then I saw the Balrog. No s***! I've seen the Thing of Shadow and Fire as it breaks through a wall. My God. The thing is enormous, horns like a black ram from the pit of Hell itself. Old cracked horns. Fire 'coming out of the cracked skin. Glowing mean-as-f*** eyes...' And so on in an excited state of euphoria...

The biggest anxiety, it now seemed, was realising the hype and meeting everyone's expectations in seven months' time.

The party the following night at the hilltop Château Castellaras was a justifiable cause for celebration presented with flair and élan. The inspired concept of taking Middle-earth to the south of France was the work of Dan Hennah and his wife, Chris, and triumphed over the difficulties of transcontinental transportation and the French workforces!

Gondorian banners and pennants fluttered in the courtyard of the château and the hall was decked out with horse-head beam-ends, tapestries, braziers and Théoden's throne from the Golden Hall at Edoras; Galadriel's swan boat shimmered on the swimming pool, the Doors of Durin revealed and concealed their Elvish inscription and a Stone-troll loomed out of the trees.

The three hundred guests were served food by hobbit-footed extras from gaily coloured tents on a re-creation of Hobbiton's Party Field, and had a chance to be reduced to the size of Merry and Pippin in order to get their drinks from a giant of a barman in a replica of the large-scale set from *The Prancing Pony* before visiting the small-scale set for Bag End where, like Gandalf, they banged their heads on beams, and negotiated Hobbit-sized doorways and protruding tree roots.

The cast were there in force and demonstrating for the first of many times what an indefatigable team of advocates they were for the film and its director. John Rhys-Davies told the world that *The Lord of the Rings* was going to be bigger than *Star Wars*, Ian McKellen and Christopher Lee traded wizard-lore and the four Hobbit actors ran around like kids let out to play.

'It was a reunion,' says Elijah Wood. 'For us, it was like *The Lord of the Rings* vacation! It was quite bizarre to have invaded France like we did, with our set pieces and memorabilia, but it was an incredible experience for everyone involved with the film because the reception from those who'd seen the footage was so exciting. It felt like the party was our own celebration of how far we'd come and what we'd accomplished.'

Among the guests was Harvey Weinstein...

I hold no bitterness towards Harvey because, in his heart of hearts, he *wanted* to do it but he couldn't... The proposal for a chopped-down, one-film version that he had concocted was really the action of somebody who was desperately trying to justify the $15million that he'd spent to that date and trying to make a film out of it. I actually believe that if he'd been able to get the money then Harvey would have made *The Lord of the Rings.*

At the party, I gave Harvey a hug and he was very gracious and said that we had ended up at the right place. He was right, however unworkable the relationship may have looked at times...

'Peter and Fran' and New Line are very strange bedfellows. When you think of the cultural differences, it was a very odd thing to have happened: New Line with its American sensibilities and Fran and I with our more English, New Zealand sensibilities making a movie based on a cult British classic in a country half a world away from Hollywood. But somehow it happened.

I was with Bob Shaye when Harvey came over and said to him, 'You guys have done the films exactly as they should be done!' It was a cool thing for Harvey to do.

Indeed, *Variety* quoted the Miramax chief as saying, 'I think Mark Ordesky and the whole New Line team deserve to be applauded. They were willing to bet their house...'

For Mark it was the justification of his wild promise upon joining New Line that he would make a Peter Jackson movie, and a testament to his work on the project.

'Mark was our mentor and guiding light,' says Fran, adding with a laugh, 'and I think it's either a reward or a punishment for his having spent most of his teenage years closeted in his bedroom reading Tolkien!'

Mark Ordesky and me with our agent, Ken Kamins, at the Oscars. It was Ken's phone call to Harvey Weinstein back in November 1995 that had started us on the road to the 2004 Academy Awards.

A passionate Tolkien fan, Mark was very protective of the property, understanding what these films should and shouldn't be. Whenever we've been asked whether American audiences would understand certain things, Mark's always been the sounding board. He has strong creative instincts, was always very respectful of our process – apologising if ever he felt he was getting in too deep – and terribly anxious to make sure we didn't feel pressurised.

Quite simply, our relationship with New Line would not have stayed the distance if it hadn't been for Mark's presence.

Michael Lynne describes Mark as being an 'emissary and go-between'; Bob Shaye calls him 'a firewall'! Cannes was a moment of personal triumph, though there were still several years of 'firewalling' ahead, beginning with the complex post-production process…

Over the next few months, many tasks had to be achieved: producing a great many sophisticated effects shots; supervising the colour-grading of the film in order to create or enhance the mood of a scene; re-recording the actors' vocal tracks; recording the score that would sometimes drive, sometimes under-pin the drama and the emotion; devising sound effects to help generate a series of vibrant soundscapes, such as the snarl of a Warg, the grunt of a troll or the menacing sound of an approaching Balrog. And, before any of those things could be done, the editing of what would eventually become the 178 minutes of *The Fellowship of the Ring*.

> Fran and I were in the position of having the final cut on the film and we were a bit too strong-willed to allow the studio to dictate what should be in the movie and what shouldn't be there – we felt we knew the movie and the characters better than the studio did. You got feedback from all sorts of people, from the producer, the editorial team and from other crewmembers, and you listened to it, filtering out the good ideas – but, ultimately, you had to make your own decisions.
>
> The studio's attitude was that they would advocate cuts and explain it through Mark, and we would either agree or disagree. Mark would gauge the temperature with Fran and I and explain our decisions to the studio and, when necessary, fight those battles on our behalf, which took any direct conflict out of the situation. New Line always let us have final say, but you have to be fair-minded and use your instincts; it's easy to be defensive and stubborn. When the studio had a good note, I'd want us to be smart enough to recognise it – not get lost in some stubborn-headed nonsense.

'If Peter digs his heels in,' comments Marty Walsh, 'you need a lot of facts and logic to get him to *un-dig* them!'

'Sometimes, Peter seems to like to push things to the very brink,' says Barrie Osborne, 'but I've also observed him pushing things to the brink and then pulling back and compromising when he knew he had to, when it was absolutely clear.'

Philippa Boyens observes, 'Yes, Peter is incredibly wilful! He can be immovable and then suddenly he'll surprise you and change his mind. So, what everybody wants to know is *how* do you change his mind? *You leave him alone.* You cannot rush him. He either comes to agree with you, either understands what you're saying, sees it and embraces it – or else he doesn't. Peter may change his mind. *You* don't ever change Peter's mind.'

For Peter, the editing process is, like the writing, organic.

> You experiment; things come and go – you look at things again – you change your mind – sometimes you go back to what you tried the first time – it continually transforms and develops.

In the process, many shots – even entire scenes and sequences – would be left on the cutting-room floor, sometimes because the pace of the storytelling now required a different rhythm or possibly because the footage had subsequently been overtaken by later changes in structure, script or characterisation. This happened with Arwen's presence at Helm's Deep and an elaborate episode set in the Glittering Caves, in which Éowyn delivers a child born to Morwen, the mother of the two refugee children who carry the news of the Uruk-hai attack on Rohan to Edoras.

Shortly after the birth of Morwen's baby, the Uruks invade the caves, marauding and killing, while Éowyn – swiftly changing role from midwife to swordswoman – singlehandedly fights off the enemy with much slaughtering. As one of the Uruk-hai is about to seize, and presumably eat, the newborn child, Éowyn wields her sword and deftly decapitates the assailant!

It was what Peter describes as 'a hangover from us thinking that *The Two Towers* was the weakest story in the trilogy and attempting to compensate for the lack of any heroic deaths!'

> There was the love triangle between Arwen, Aragorn and Éowyn; and, at one point, we were to have had Arwen rescuing Morwen's children from an attack by a pack of Wargs during their journey to Edoras as well as having Éowyn saving babies and chopping the heads of Uruks in the Glittering Caves. We didn't use any of this as we realised that it was cheap and cheesy: Hollywood spewing itself over Tolkien's book, via us!

There was another of what Peter now calls their 'often misguided Hollywood moments' that originally provided an action-packed conclusion to *The Fellowship of the Ring.* The sequence had Frodo and Sam paddling down the River Anduin in the Elven boat when an Uruk bursts up from under the water, lurches into the boat, grabbing at Frodo, who vainly tries to defend himself with the paddle. Seeing the Ring on the chain around Frodo's neck, the Uruk seizes it and drags the struggling Frodo overboard and down to the bottom of the riverbed. Following a terrific underwater struggle, Frodo manages to kick himself free, is helped back into the boat by Sam and the boat is carried away by the Great River towards the second film!

It was almost as if the Ring itself was trying to kill Frodo by literally drawing the Servants of the Enemy to him and, in this attack, pulling him into the water and dragging him under. This was the ending that we filmed during 2000 and had every intention of using until we re-thought the material and decided that it was another misguided Holly-wood moment. We then wrote the present ending to the film, which more closely follows the book, and shot that version while filming our pick-ups the following year.

On all three of the movies, there were a number of things that we significantly changed during the filming of the pick-ups, which completely justified the time, money and effort that went into those four to six weeks' work. We were able to focus on elements of the story – or aspects of the way in which we had told it – that, in editing, we had come to realise were either missing or needed explaining, enhancing – or totally re-shooting.

Perhaps the best example of the way in which we revisited scenes and entirely changed their dynamic is the climactic struggle between Gollum and Frodo at the Crack of Doom.

When we originally shot the scene, Gollum bit off Frodo's finger and Frodo pushed Gollum off the ledge into the fires below. It was straight-out murder, but at the time we were okay with it because we felt everyone *wanted* Frodo to kill Gollum. But, of course, it was very un-Tolkien, because it flew in the face of everything that he wanted his heroes to be. It was three years before we were able to rectify that. Eventually, during the 2003 pick-ups, we re-shot it and did it two ways: one exactly as in the book with Gollum dancing about in glee and falling off himself, which within the dramatic context of a film, seemed like a major disappointment, and as it is now presented with Frodo going for Gollum – not to push him over the cliff but to get back the Ring.

Even with the re-shoots facilitated by the pick-ups, certain things were beyond that kind of fixing and had to be dealt with by Weta's computer magicians, such as the Rohan warriors' mounted charge from the Hornburg in which Arwen's riding double was clearly visible in the midst of the company and had to be digitally 'replaced'. There was also the elaborate set-up using a crane shot to show the Elven regiment marching into Helm's Deep where – when the shot was shown on a large screen – it was noticed that one of the archers had accidentally kicked up one of the bows from the otherwise ordered ranks of Elves and weapons.

Eventually, the day came on *The Fellowship of the Ring* – as it would later do on *The Two Towers* and *The Return of the King* – when the cut was complete, when the film was locked down and finished.

> At some point there's some instinct that says, 'You know what? The film's done! There ain't no more work to be done on this!' You keep on going until that moment in time when you get that gut feeling and you know that the movie has now found its shape and it's time to leave it alone. Only then does everyone breathe a sigh of relief.

Across the months, the frenzy of anticipation built and built: New Zealand's newspapers carried almost daily reports; the world's press weren't far behind; every film and entertainment magazine ran *Rings* features, the more ambitious carried special supplements, while the totally crazed declared their periodical a 'Special Issue'. Tolkien's publishers launched an effective sales campaign suggesting those intrigued by the coming film might like to 'Read it before you see it', and the BBC released its original radio dramatisation, starring Ian Holm, on a similar aural pretext. Ralph Bakshi's animated version emerged from the shadows onto DVD with an accompanying 'Making of...' book offering a rogue alternative to New Line's raft of official tie-in books. There was, quite clearly, no excuse for anyone, firstly, not to

The actors playing the Fellowship had all got special tattoos, designed by Alan Lee to represent the Elvish number nine symbol. On the day of the New Zealand premiere of the first film, they propelled Richard Taylor (shown here), Barrie Osborne and myself into the local tattoo parlour and branded us with an Elvish ten. Actually, it was pretty cool.

know that a potentially astonishing movie project was being made, and secondly, not to have a pretty keen grasp on the original story and the plot of the film!

Websites proliferated – with every permutation on Ring and King in their address – and a personal odyssey was recorded by Ian McKellen in his online Grey Book.

Cartoonists had a field day with sundry world leaders being recast as Rings characters, while Bill Amend's *Foxtrot* comic strip featured 10-year-old Tolkien nerd, Jason Fox, who gets cast (in his imagination) in the film. He brings chaos to a cartoon Peter Jackson by constantly criticising the script ('It leaves some things out…') and the props ('This rope should be made of Elven *hithlain*, by the way…') and refusing to hand over the Ring at the end of filming – 'It's my PRECIOUS!'

There was the first teaser poster: Frodo, eyes downcast, looking at the Ring lying on his open palm; the second teaser poster: the same but with Frodo looking directly at the viewer with troubles eyes; the third showed the towering carved statues of the Argonath looming above three small Elven boats and the caption: THE LEGEND COMES TO LIFE...

And finally, it did! As a compliment to the 'Englishness' of J. R. R. Tolkien and Middle-earth, the World Premiere, on 10 December 2000, was held in London. The reviews were uniformly ecstatic, confirming both the success of *Fellowship* and the cult status of a trilogy, two films of which had still be edited and completed, let alone released!

The epic was up and running and people were desperate for more: books about the movie went straight into the bestseller lists; Tolkien's original book was selling in numbers that the author could not have imagined in his wildest dreams; while with the first storeful of toys, kits, games and models, the *Lord of the Rings* Collector was born! It was an instant phenomenon.

Eighty-one award nominations yielded seventy wins, including four BAFTAs (among them the distinctive accolade of the David Lean Award for Direction to Peter Jackson) and four Oscars – though not yet for Film or Director.

The ultimate Hollywood gong may have eluded him, but another, rather different award, came his way when he and Fran were included in the 2002 New Year's Honours List. At a ceremony at Government House, Dame Silvia Cartwright, the Governor General, invested Peter and Fran as, respectively, a Companion and a Member of the New Zealand Order of Merit.

For Peter and the team, the cycle then recommenced: filming pickups for *The Two Towers*, editing and scoring the second movie as well as editing an extended version of the *Fellowship* for DVD.

There were more trailers, posters and hype and another world premiere – this time New York – followed by more rave reviews (often surpassing those for *Fellowship*) and another seventy award nominations with two Oscars among the fifty-five winners, but still nothing for Director.

'The second film,' says Ken Kamins, 'was more daunting than the first. I remember he called me once during the cutting of *The Two Towers* and out of nowhere said "I'm utterly lost, I have no idea where I am in the story." He had been living inside it for so long he couldn't find a way out. It took him a while. He genuinely struggled, but then managed to break through. The question was, "How do you make a great three-hour movie when its primary purpose is simply to advance the storyline and provide a bridge from the newness of the introduction of the world in movie one to the dramatic conclusion in movie three?" For *The Two Towers* to have exceeded that expectation and been as successful as it was is an extraordinary achievement.'

In the early months of 2003, for the third and last time, it was back on the treadmill: more pick-ups for *The Return of the King*, editing the extended DVD version of *The Two Towers* and the long, hard haul of cutting the final film in the trilogy…

Expectations had been that the third film was going to be easier. It turned out to be way bigger and far more complicated!

The challenge was in editing everything together into something that is as good as it could be but runs for four-and-a-quarter hours and then editing that down, crafting it back to a length that moviegoers are going to accept.

The only thing New Line consistently said was that they'd love it if the movie could be about three hours long; we said that we'd do our best, but ultimately a movie finds its own length – in the case of *The Return of the King*, three hours twenty minutes. You have to create a movie that *feels* right – if it *feels* too long (whatever length it actually is) it's going to die on its feet.

The sheer enormity of the task on the third film was down to the complexity of decisions about the weight of the story – keeping it centred on Frodo and Sam but embracing the rest of the mounting drama involving the rest of the characters – and as such it was constructed differently in editing than how it had been on paper. We abandoned the script: we had *shot* the script but now Jamie Selkirk and I were working that material into the best possible film.

New Line made various suggestions along the way and we always tried to listen to everything. At one point, they suggested we cut the Grey Havens but we loved that sequence and were very proud of it, so

that was dismissed very quickly. Other notes might probably have
received more consideration.

'There were times,' reflects Peter Nelson, 'when the studio was fairly
insistent in asking Peter to re-examine his view; using any number of
ways to express how they'd really like him to reconsider, but by the
second or third time they always let it be known that if Peter felt that
was the creative way to go, then they should be deferring to him. Of
course, there are disagreements every day in the creative world –
otherwise how is great art made? – but I think Peter has earned his
right to hold a place where people will now defer to him much more
than others in the creative world.'

Some of the editing decisions that were finally taken inevitably
disappointed fans – the scenes in the Houses of Healing that resolved
Faramir and Éowyn's stories – as well as cast members, most notably
Christopher Lee, who had originally expected to die as Saruman at
the conclusion of *The Two Towers* but then seemed to have survived
into the third movie. When Christopher flew to New Zealand to film
more pick-ups in January 2003, it had seemed to confirm that *The
Return of the King* would indeed open with Saruman's postponed
confrontation with Gandalf the White and his Lucifer-like fall from
the pinnacle of Orthanc.

But then his dramatic exit was cut from the final edit and
Christopher's very public displeasure fuelled a juicy press story at a
time when it might have been thought that all that could be said
about the trilogy had been said, and this inspired a 'petition' to rein-
state Saruman into the opening moments of the third film. Ironically,
those very people who had once been imploring the film-maker to
'Let Saruman live!' until the conclusion of the third book were now
demanding his death!

It simply felt too long for the beginning of the third film and also like
we were wrapping up the previous year's film rather than jumping
straight into *The Return of the King*. We experimented with ways to trim
it down and we got to the point where we'd cut it to three minutes –
which felt perfunctory and wrong for different reasons, as if it were

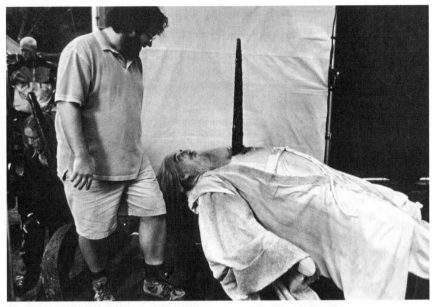

Not Christopher's favourite moment but one he endured with his customary patience and dry humour: 'There's something vaguely familiar about this situation.'

there as a 'requirement'. We asked whether it really *was* required. Put yourself in the place of an average audience member – not a Tolkien fan: what would they think about Saruman? Having seen the defeat at Helm's Deep and the Ents' destruction of Isengard wouldn't they think that Saruman had been defeated? During the last days of cutting, we reached the conclusion that taking it out would do no actual harm to the perception of most moviegoers.

Establishing the structure and cutting the material to length became a race against time, and it became increasingly clear that the film would not be edited in line with the original schedule. New Line, whose budgets were drawn up, at an additional cost of two or three million dollars funded the continued editing and the completion of all the special effects. The original concept had been for three movies with 1,000 special effects shots in all three movies; the eventual tally ended up at 500 shots in *Fellowship*; 800 in *The Two Towers* and 1,300 in *The Return of the King*, some of which – including the Mûmakil sequence – were completed only weeks before the film was due to premiere.

> New Line were fine about it; even when it became clear that we were going to be late in getting the film cut and locked, they were completely supportive. They saw a four-hour version of the film and they knew where we were at every stage and knew what was in front of us...

In a telephone conversation with Peter, two weeks before the last few cuts were made to the final edit, he told me: 'I think I'm going to feel pretty weird on the last day before we deliver the film. There's going to be a sense of relief, but because we are still working so hard there is no sense of completion yet, no light at the end of the tunnel... But I know that there will be a real mix of emotions. I'm not going to be feeling sad that there's no *fourth Lord of the Rings* movie, because I'm ready to move on to other things, but I am very conscious that I am completing work on the production that, ultimately, is going to define me for ever more – and will be unlike anything else that I will ever do in my life...'

Eventually, the day came when that work finally was complete...

> The very last thing we did on *The Return of the King* was reinstating a scene reuniting Merry and Pippin on the battlefield of Pelennor Fields. It was in, then it was deleted (because we felt that the audience would assume that's what had happened and didn't need to see it) and then, on the very last day of cutting, we changed our minds and put it back!

It was close to the wire, and it is said that there were those – some close to the production – who were anxious about whether or not the final 'drop-dead' deadline would be met; whether at this point on the final, homeward straight, Peter Jackson would find himself in trouble. Ken Kamins was not one of them: 'I was never concerned about whether or not Peter was going to make delivery. This is not a normal film-making situation and there isn't one that I can point to, save for Lucas or perhaps, on a different level, Kubrick, where literally the film-maker's hands were on every lever of the machine.'

So, was New Line Cinema anxious as the day grew closer and closer and they still didn't have the final version of the final part of *The Lord of the Rings*? Ken Kamins offers a way of looking at the situation:

'When you are a division of a multinational conglomerate like New Line Cinema is to AOL–Time Warner, the definition of success is not just about how many hundred-million dollars a movie makes worldwide, it is based on answers which the studio gave, months before the movie comes out, to the questions: "What do you *think* the movie's going to do in terms of gross revenue and what do you *think* it's going to return to us in net profit?" New Line would then be judged by AOL–Time Warner on the basis of meeting expectations; so, if a movie does US$910million worldwide, but you promised it was going to do a *billion* dollars, then the fact that it only did $910million would make it a failure!

'Bob Shaye and Michael Lynne live under a whole different set of criteria to Peter Jackson. Peter is living in the world of the artist who has consummate respect for the work and his audience. New Line has a need to earn profit and a corporate master to satisfy. If the two can coincide, great; but if they can't, then everyone's going to fight for their constituency.

'So, yes, the studio was incredibly anxious, but in reality they were no *more* anxious about delivery of the film than they were on the previous two movies!'

'Would Peter finally deliver the film?' asks Michael Lynne, rhetorically. 'I didn't have any doubt. Peter is a very careful guy, but he does take advantage of every second he's got.'

Bob Shaye agrees: 'No, we didn't doubt he would do it, but it sometimes got a bit aggravating! More than anything else, it was his reputation as far as he was concerned. He was driving everybody crazy! That seems to be his professional *modus operandi* – and, one has to say, it's out of that pressure-cooker that comes some of his best stuff!'

We could have just given *The Return of the King* a quick once-over on the assumption that it's the third movie and that everyone is going to go and see it anyway, but that is not how we work. We take a pride in what we do. Our view was, 'We want it to be the film we're ultimately most proud of…' so we just worked round the clock. And I said to those who were worrying, 'Stop stressing about not having a movie to release! I take complete responsibility and I ensure that I keep my word…'

And so he did. 'Every film ends in much the same way,' observes Bob Shaye; 'it's never a picnic, there is always the sadness or remorse of the family breaking up and people moving on. There is also, on the other hand, memories of "How many days do we have to get through?!" There's a lot of regret and a lot of relief.'

To ask Peter, or any director, to select his favourite shots or sequences is invidious, like asking a father to choose which of his children means the most to him. But there are, nevertheless, a number of candidates for special affection!

Probably one of my favourite sequences from all three films is the journey through the Mines of Moria. It was that material that blew people away at Cannes and confirmed New Line's trust in what we were doing. But I also always think of it as one of the sequences that Miramax was never going to allow us to shoot! During one of the last script meetings we had with them, when they were proposing their single film version, they suggested that we have Frodo, as an old hobbit at the end of his life, reminiscing about his adventures and covering the whole of this episode by saying something like, 'So then we went on a dangerous journey through the Mines of Moria and lost Gandalf.' Unbelievable really! So, that's why I will always regard Moria as being a special blessing.

I also get real goose bumps when Théoden and the troops arrive at Minas Tirith and they charge into the Orcs. From that point on, the final forty-five minutes: cutting from shots of Frodo's fingers clawing at the rock as, unable to walk anymore, he crawls on hands and knees up the side of Mount Doom; to shots of 100,000 Orcs surrounding Aragorn's troops as they desperately try to buy Frodo as much time as they can by putting their own lives on the line…

That was always my ambition for these movies – the dramatic contrast of the epic and the intimate…

Five years of recollections would take a good deal of processing, ranging from small, lingering, intimate pleasures such as the moment when John Rhys-Davies as Gimli looks up at Galadriel and falls in love, or the afternoon on location, filming Bilbo talking to Frodo in the gardens at Rivendell, when the sun broke through and gave a golden halo-effect to Bilbo's white wig. Sometimes it was moments of elation on a grand scale.

I remember arriving at Mt Potts where the Edoras set was located. The helicopter dropped through a tiny hole in the cloud cover and we were suddenly confronted by the incredibly spectacular sight of this great hill with the city of Edoras and the Golden Hall right there in front of us. The helicopter pilot couldn't believe it. He said, 'Holy s***! Is that *real?*' We said, 'It sure is!'

Walking around Edoras you were suddenly *in* Tolkien's books, *in* Middle-earth. This was totally unlike being in the studios in Wellington, where we were always surrounded by blue screens and with aeroplanes flying overhead! In those situations you always felt a good few degrees removed from the book, but here… Here you were literally thrust into Tolkien's imagination. It was the real thing; it was great; it was fantastic!

But, for all the ephemeral grandeur of the Edoras location, perhaps the strongest feelings for Peter were evoked by the set designed and built to represent Bag End, Bilbo Baggins' homely hobbit-hole in the Shire.

I loved its atmosphere: the roundness of it, the intriguing angles, the intricate detailing. It was wonderfully romantic.

It was just about the most profound experience I've ever had on a movie set. We were filming, yet again, in a grotty old tin building and the set itself didn't look anything very special from the outside, but the moment you stepped inside you just felt that you were in this totally magical place.

I remember sitting in there and I'd look around and think to myself, 'Most people will only ever see this at the movies, but I'm one of the incredibly lucky ones to have been *inside Bag End*!'

When the time finally came for it to be broken up, I simply couldn't bear the idea. So I asked New Line whether – so long as I stored it somewhere at my own expense – I could dismantle the set and keep it for myself.

They were happy with the proposal providing it didn't take up storage space needed for the shoot, so I hired a warehouse – it was a *big* set – and we carefully took it all apart and put it into store.

The ironic twist to this tale is that, a year later, when we had decided we were going to film pick-ups, we needed some shots inside Bag End. My refusal to part with the set meant that we were able to pull it out of storage and put it all back together again – without, I might add, any additional expense to New Line!

I've now installed it as a kind of guesthouse. I find its round corridors to be peaceful and relaxing. If anybody comes to our house to stay, they all want to sleep in Bag End!

At long last, the day that the world – but specifically Wellington, New Zealand – had been waiting for finally dawned: Monday 1 December 2003.

The city with a population of 178,000 saw its streets seething with an estimated 100,000 fans – a good few of whom, obviously, were Wellingtonians enjoying their undisputed moment of vicariously sharing in the triumph of their favourite son.

Over five hundred yards of red carpeting ribboned through the heart of town; a giant Fell Beast with a Nazgûl rider (an astonishing example of triumphal art from Weta) perched on the top of the Embassy cinema. The sun shone on a citywide street party and a parade made its way from a parliamentary reception hosted by Prime Minister Helen Clark to the cinema, where those fortunate to have tickets would get first sight of a film that the world was waiting for – and which, in its final finished form, even the director had yet to see!

Most of the media hounds who picked up on that particular admission during the previously days' press conferences doubtless filed it as a cute comment that was unlikely to be true. Ken Kamins knew better: 'It may seem extraordinary, but given the enormity of the task and Peter's need to have it be just so, he really pressed the schedule up to the limit. As a result, I think he must have been nervous about showing a movie to a world audience that he hadn't yet seen finished – except that it's not like the average film-maker saying, "I haven't really seen it…" because, truth be told, he was totally intimate with every foot of film that he shot!'

This was a photo we took for posterity. Ken Kamins and his wife, Judy, with Fran and me, seconds before we left our hotel room to head to the 2004 Oscars. Ken had been guiding us on our The Lord of the Rings *adventure since that first phone call in 1995. We were terribly nervous, but one way or another it was going to be over in a few hours – as it turned out, it was a pretty good night!*

Outriders of Gondorians and Ringwraiths followed by gangs of Orcs and troops of hobbit folk preceded an open-top motorcade carrying the stars and the film-makers past the cheering throngs and through a tickertape blizzard! Peter described the experience as feeling as if they had been 'the first people to land on the moon or something,' and indeed he looked, as Reuters told the world, 'like a victorious general at the front of his army.' What the reporter overlooked was that, with video camera in hand, Peter – ever the film-maker – was making his own director's-eye-record of the event.

The day is a blur. One day, I'll look at my home movies and remember. My main recollection of the day was being popped into a hotel suite for the two hours leading up to the parade and left alone there. It was the loneliest two hours of my life. I just lay on the bed and watched a telemovie. Once everything started... I can only conjure up fleeting memories now.

Everyone made speeches... Everyone was thanked... Everyone was cheered...

'We made the movie,' Peter told the crowd, 'but you guys have given us the party. These movies are made for people to enjoy them and it makes us incredibly humble and proud that so many of you have turned up today, so thank you very much...'

Peter commented on the fact that 23,000 New Zealanders had, in some way, shape or form, been involved, a reminder of the director's fierce loyalty to his homeland and home town; his determination to produce and direct films there and to invest in the country's movie-making industry. No wonder he is nationally admired, respected, loved...

'To Peter and all of the talent of *The Lord of the Rings,*' said Prime Minister Clark, 'the movie has done New Zealand very proud and we're really proud of you. May this premiere and this film launch you to more fame and more rewards.'

As indeed it did: 161 award nominations, including eleven Oscars (only two short of the thirteen previously received by *Ben-Hur* and *Titanic*), and this time the nominees included Best Film and Best Director.

Sunday 29 February 2004: the seventy-sixth Academy Awards ceremony. The crowds gathered outside the Kodak Theater on Hollywood and Highland; the stars modelled the latest designer gowns and glinted with borrowed gems as those hoping to carry off Gold took their seats for another Oscar-night marathon.

As it turned out, anyone nominated in a category featuring *The Return of the King* might just as well have left their tuxedo or frock in the closet, stayed at home and had an early night! For, as everybody now knows, it was Peter Jackson and *The Lord of the Rings'* night of nights: the grand slam; the clean sweep! 'Best' everything: art direction, costume design, make-up, film editing, sound-mixing, original score, original song, visual effects; adapted screenplay... *And* Best Film... *And Best Director!*

It was the final acknowledgement by the movie industry of a staggering achievement, and the night when they went against every precedent and prediction and declared a fantasy film the film of the year...

No wonder Peter Jackson began his Best Director acceptance speech with the one word, '*Wow!*'

'Thank you so much to the Academy,' he went on, 'you're giving us an incredibly overwhelming night. We just appreciate it so much. Bob Shaye and Michael Lynne, you did the most risky thing that I think anyone has ever done in this industry, and I'm so happy for you that it paid off. Your collaboration and your partnership and your support just gave me the most incredible working experience of my life. To Barrie Osborne, our producer, thank you so much, Barrie, for just being there every day and supporting us. To a wonderful cast, and a wonderful crew in New Zealand, everybody that made my working days so enjoyable. It was just there when I needed it to be there. And the actors were just doing such a wonderful job...'

Peter then added an intensely personal remark. In the arena of the Oscars, where everybody tearfully thanks more or less everyone except their plastic surgeons, it doubtless passed over most of the audience without remark. But anyone who knew of Peter Jackson as the kid from Pukerua Bay, New Zealand, who had grown up wanting to make movies, it was a poignantly emotional moment: 'And I just want to thank two very special people that, when I was 8 years old, I made films at home on a Super 8 camera that my mum and dad had bought for me. And they supported me all through the years. And they died in the last few years. They didn't see these films made. So for Bill and Joan, thank you. Thank you...'

I look back on it now and I can't really connect with the night. It felt amazing, fantastic... I was so nervous. I remember badly wanting Fran to win the Best Song award for 'Into the West'... I really wanted her to win more than any other, and I was so incredibly proud and happy when she won that. And then, from that point on, it sort of just became a blur! I feel unconnected with it, in a strange kind of way: I don't really feel like someone who's won an Academy Award. I don't think about it very much, although they are sitting on a shelf in our office so they're a

Whilst The Lord of the Rings *was destined to be made by New Line Cinema, not Miramax as first planned, Harvey Weinstein had a vital role to play in the journey of the book to the screen. As we would cross paths at various industry events during those years, he was unfailingly gracious.* (Image courtesy of Dave Hogan/Getty Images)

bit hard to miss! Occasionally I look at them and get a sort of buzzy feeling: 'Oh, that's mine! Gosh! I won an Academy Award...'

It's something that's happened now, something I've achieved and, as such, it actually takes the pressure off. It does. There have been lots of wonderful, wonderful film-makers who never ever won an Academy Award – incredible directors like Hitchcock and Kubrick – and I think what it must be like to have had their careers and to have had that body of work behind you and not to have won an Oscar. So, *having* now won means I never have to do it again! Or I never have to worry about it again in the future and I'm very relieved about that!

Long before that victorious Oscar night – in fact long before even *The Fellowship of the Ring* had been released – Peter had spoken to me of his passion for the project he was embarking on: 'I guess,' he said, 'it's a certain form of madness, but I'm a real believer in trying to push yourself and if you're a film-maker then I don't think there could be anything more amazing to be involved with than *The Lord of the Rings:* it's a once-in-a-lifetime experience and if we do it and do it in a way we can be proud of, then I feel that I would probably want to retire when it's all over because there'd be nothing else left to do!'

On 30 March 2003, eight months before the premiere of *The Return of the King,* news broke that suggested that Peter Jackson would not be retiring after *The Lord of the Rings.* A press release from Universal Pictures announced that, following the release of the final instalment of *Rings,* Peter was going to be making a new version of the tale that had inspired his film-making career; the tale of a creature described as the Eighth Wonder of the World…

A long-held ambition was finally about to be realised – it was time for *the return of the Kong!*

10

RETURN TO SKULL ISLAND

A SPOTLIGHT SWINGS across the CLOSED CURTAIN… The LARGE CROWD APPLAUDS as DENHAM strides onto the stage in the GLARE of THE SINGLE SPOTLIGHT. He waves enthusiastically… basking in the acclaim he has waited for for so long.

DENHAM
  Thank you! Thank you!… Ladies and gentlemen, I'm going to show you the greatest thing your eyes have ever beheld.
  He was a King in the world he knew but he comes to you now… a captive…
  Ladies and gentlemen: I give you Kong – the Eighth Wonder of the World!!

When Universal Pictures announced that Peter Jackson was going to make a new version of a film that the National Film Registry of United States Library of Congress had designated being among the 1,200 Greatest Films chosen for preservation as a national treasure, it was the occasion for fanfares!

'Peter Jackson,' noted Stacey Snider, Chairman, Universal Pictures, 'is a film-maker uniquely capable of capturing the core appeal of enduring classics and in expanding the visual language of motion pictures, as inarguably evidenced in his landmark achievement with *The Lord of the Rings* films. We are thrilled to be working with Peter and Fran, and we are confident that their execution of *King Kong* will amaze moviegoers… Peter will bring Kong to life as a real character.

His vision for the tragic tale of the misunderstood creature, with its poignant character development and technological wonder, will make *King Kong* compulsory viewing for any real movie lover.'

For Peter, of course, it was a return to a place he had been before, literally four years earlier, and before that, countless times in his imagination. He was quoted in the press release as saying: 'No film has captivated my imagination more than *King Kong*. I'm making movies today because I saw this film when I was 9 years old. It has been my sustained dream to reinterpret this classic story for a new age.'

Ken Kamins comments, 'Peter had said on several occasions as *The Lord of the Rings* was drawing to a close that he wanted to move on to making a smaller movie next, but when *Kong* became a possibility I think he thought about what would happen if the appetite of audiences for these big-budget extravaganzas was to wane in a few years' time. He was clearly at the height of his ability to generate the sort of creative environment he would need to make that movie in the way he wanted to make it. So, the confluence of events dictated that *now* was the best time to make *Kong*, wrestle old demons to the ground and realise a fantasy that he's harboured for ever.'

'Peter really wanted to remake *Kong*,' says Philippa Boyens, 'in order to be able to *see* that movie; to be able to sit down in a cinema, get blown away, and know that *he* made it. It's what makes him tick.'

'The story of *Kong*,' continued Peter's press release statement, 'offers everything that any storyteller could hope for: an archetypal narrative, thrilling action, resonating emotion and memorable characters. It has endured for precisely these reasons and I am honoured to be a part of its continuing legacy.'

Two years on, having played his part in the continuance of that legacy, Peter reflects:

When I first saw the original *King Kong*, on TV back in 1970, it *thrilled* me and I am still thrilled by it.

What I most like about the original film – and I think it's an important part of the way in which the story is structured – is that it plays itself out as a fairly straight, romantic drama in which Ann Darrow and

Jack Driscoll are thrown together by circumstances on a boat-trip heading off on some sort of adventurous expedition.

For the first thirty minutes of *Kong*, you could be watching a typical Hollywood romance that's ultimately going to lead to these two people getting together… Then, suddenly, the movie takes you by surprise and switches genre and you land on a mysterious island with its great high walls – to keep something out – and the film's become a monster movie.

Through repeated viewings across the years, Peter came to realise that, whilst his enthusiasm for the film remained undimmed, appreciation for the original *King Kong* was becoming increasingly limited to aficionados of early cinema in much the same way as the first versions of *Frankenstein*, *Dracula*, *The Mummy* and *The Hunchback of Notre Dame*, all of which had been re-made in various shapes and forms to suit new and more sophisticated audiences and to take advantage of technical advances in cinematography.

The truth is that, despite being a wonderful story filled with excitement, heart and emotion, all the technical aspects of the original version now seem very dated: the dialogue, the acting, the directing, the special effects.

When I was a kid, living in an era when colour television was a dream of the future, *King Kong* seemed an extraordinarily rich and vibrant film. But that was then, and I feel very strongly that no matter how much we devotees may treasure and revere the original picture, there is now a generation of youngsters who would never sit down and watch a black and white film with jerky animation and creaky, old-fashioned dialogue – no matter how good you tell them it is!

The younger generation have switched off their tolerance for things that are old and, in doing so, miss out on a lot; the truth is that if today's kids were channel-hopping on TV and happened to flick onto a channel that was showing *Kong*, they'd be flicking onto something else in a flash. I honestly can't imagine many teenagers buying or watching a DVD of the first *Kong*, or standing in line at a film festival to watch a retrospective screening of this old movie that I love so much.

Peter's motivation for making *King Kong*, therefore, springs not only from his abiding passion for the film that excited him as a child, but

Ray Harryhausen had mentioned a couple of times how much he and his wife wanted to come down to New Zealand. At the end of The Lord of the Rings, *we were figuring out how to thank the Weta crew for all their hard work – so we decided to combine the two ideas, and we flew Ray and Diana down for a couple of weeks' vacation. We arranged a helicopter tour of our South Island locations; then Ray spent a few days visiting Weta, and meeting our crew – most of whom had grown up with his films – and he hosted a great Q&A session that went on for five hours! And I finally got to show him some of my child-hood stop-motion models, and thank him for having such a powerful influence on my life.*

from a belief that today's generation – and future generations – of youngsters will probably never ever see that film and experience that sense of excitement and wonder.

I thought, 'Maybe if we can recapture the wonderful escapism of the original movie, it could mean as much to a 9-year-old kid who sees it in 2005 as the original version meant to me when I saw it.'

Because the original film is so good, the one thing I *didn't* want to be doing was just making a colourised version of the 1933 film. My intention was always to do something that feels like a modern remake of *King Kong* – not updated, but presenting the original story in a way that is familiar to modern cinema audiences and yet still manages to capture the magic of the original.

Describing Peter's ambition for *Kong*, Philippa Boyens says, 'He wants to inspire that level of love and excitement and getting lost in the story that he was privileged to go through when he was a child. He wanted that for his kids, for a new generation of cinemagoers, so *Kong* isn't just a theme park ride at Universal studios, but a real story that you engage with and which stays with you, the way it stayed with him.'

The response of the 9-year-old boy watching the original movie on TV, one Friday night in Pukerua Bay, had been immediate and intuitive. What he could not have known as he marvelled at scenes like Kong's battle with the dinosaurs or his rampage through New York, was that the film would continue to be a touchstone and an ambition that would endure into his forty-fourth year.

> What is fascinating is the way in which *Kong* has spanned almost my entire life: seeing it when I was 9; wanting to do a remake of it when I was in my teens – *and trying to do so*; putting in a very serious effort to make a new version in '95–'96; and finally, *finally* making it now!
>
> Even though all these 'versions' (imagined, semi-realised or achieved) were based on the original *Kong*, each of them was conceived as a very different film. As a result, I've never had a precise or particular vision in my head for a remake of *Kong* – it has always been a product of who I am at a particular time.
>
> Any movie reflects who you are at the time you make it, I guess, and it's very interesting that the film we've finally ended up making now is very different to the one that we *would* have made a decade earlier. Interestingly, it is like a lab experiment – the same story, firstly conceived pre-*The Lord of the Rings* films, and then again straight after. They are completely different films!

The 2005 version of *Kong* is a far more technically complex film than Peter would have been able to make a decade earlier – however much he might have wanted otherwise – because Weta Digital now has a streamlined system that was still being established during the making of the *Rings* trilogy, by which they can efficiently produce the many hundreds of complicated visual effects shots. The chief difference, however, between Peter's Nineties vision of *Kong* and the way in

Following the experience of The Lord of the Rings, *we had another terrific cast to work with on* Kong. *Boy, it makes it much more enjoyable if there's no tension on set – just a bunch of good people, doing their best for the movie.*

which it has finally been realised is in the way in which the story is told.

Peter describes his and Fran's original script as being written as 'a very *Indiana Jones*-ish, slam-bang, Hollywood-style movie, which at the time we thought was the way to go.' But as he told the press shortly after the Universal project was announced: 'We can do a complete rewrite. Now that Philippa Boyens has joined the team, it's a chance to start over. The basic storyline will be very similar but the scenes, the sequences and the detail will be very different to the flip, smart-arsed tone of our old script. We are better writers now... This movie will be so much better than the 1996 film would have been. In hindsight, fate has been kind to us!'

Not only had Peter and Fran matured as writers and developed through their collaboration with Philippa, but they had also learnt many lessons from writing and filming *The Lord of the Rings*:

I think the most predominant lesson that came out of *Rings* was to *keep it real.* Unless you make a film that feels fundamentally *real* then you've immediately entered the world of artifice and you're operating at a very shallow level. You're simply saying to your audience: 'Hey, we don't believe in this ourselves, so we're not really expecting you to believe in it; let's just indulge ourselves for an hour or two and have some fun...' And I think it's better to try and treat your subject matter with more respect than that...

Despite the often 'hammy' dialogue and the stiff stereotypical characterisations, the 1933 *Kong* was, in its day, more 'realistic' than modern audiences appreciate. The expedition in search of Skull Island is presented in a believable, naturalistic way that would have seemed convincing to a member of the moviegoing public at a time for whom foreign travel – other than war service overseas – was a largely unknown experience. The depiction of the island's natives and their rituals, which any modern anthropologist would find deeply offensive, seemed 'realistic' to audiences at a time when – outside occasional cinema documentaries and the pages of *The National Geographic* – most Americans and Europeans had no windows on to the people and places of their world.

There is also the very realistic representation of the city of New York and in particular the 102-storey building that then dominated its skyline.

It's no coincidence that the Empire State Building was featured. Kong was used to living in the top of the mountain on Skull Island, so the top of the Empire State Building was a reminder of his lair and the natural place for him to escape to in New York. But the film-makers were also using the building to showcase an extraordinary feat in architecture and engineering – the world's tallest building which had been completed only two years before. For a depression-era audience who were going to the movies for escapism (which in a very tough time they needed to do)

The huge New York street set, built in Wellington. Everything beyond the set was created with a digital New York model – as were many of the cars and pedestrians.

it must have been incredibly inspiring to see this towering symbol of American pride and achievement.

In approaching the remake, Peter took the decision not to even consider location filming in New York. Whilst the Empire State Building and a great deal of early New York architecture is still extant, the seventy years separating the film's Thirties setting and the present day would make filming on the streets difficult and costly.

Another alternative was to use the standing New York City set on the Universal back-lot but Peter also decided against this option since the set was small, narrow and had short streets. The solution was for WingNut to build its own New York back-lot set – in New Zealand.

> I believe that our recreation of New York will really showcase what CG can now do, because we have used the computer to extend the buildings and streets on our set upwards and outwards to give an impression both of incredible height and depth, of looking up at towering skyscrapers and of looking down twenty blocks with 500 CG vintage cars and 2,000 CG people.

The attention to detailing in the completed sets would be on a par with those created for *Rings*. The look evokes one familiar to anyone who has ever seen the work of American photographers in the early years of the twentieth century: brownstone houses with stoops; elevated railways and steaming manhole covers; delis and diners; street vendors and newsstands; the breadlines and the fading glamour of the burlesque shows.

> Despite the irony of filming New York in New Zealand, I think we've created a spectacular, epic view of how the city looked in the Thirties that is real and believable. I love the mixture of the believable – and I use that word a lot – with the fantastical. The truth is, our New York is just as 'fantastic' as Skull Island, or any of the other imaginary places. However, building the fantasy on a foundation of the believable is really the trick.

The quest for what might be termed 'Jackson's fantastic-realism' is reflected not just in the authenticity with which 1930s New York has been visualised, but also in the way in which the characterisations have been drawn.

Mary Parent, Co-president of Production at Universal Pictures, comments, 'Peter, Fran and Philippa have done wonders in retaining a period-specific style to the dialogue and characters without making them seem stagey or stylised. Just as the full menagerie of characters in the *Rings* series existed believably in another time but felt familiar and immediate, the scripting of *King Kong* is able to take place in the Thirties without seeming distant or arcane.'

Peter and his colleagues began by determining that they were going to apply their credo of realism to the film's eponymous creature.

> Kong is *not* a movie-monster; he is a gorilla who happens to be twenty-five feet tall. We've tried to invest him with very real animal behaviour: to extrapolate what a gorilla would behave like if he *was* King Kong; what his personality would be like if he was the only one of his kind surviving on an island inhabited by dinosaurs.
>
> We see him as a creature that has not empathised with any other living being in his life; he has to fight for survival in one of the most extreme, dangerous environments that exists and, as a result, he has become a brute.
>
> So as soon as you take a character like that and you try to have him connect with a human being, or feel emotion for the first time, it makes for a really interesting story.

A great deal of research was carried out during the pre-production period and Andy Serkis, who was to be intimately involved in the creation of Kong's screen persona, studied gorillas at the London Zoo and in the wild in Rwanda, where the Mountain Gorilla was first discovered in 1902.

'When the original film was made,' says Andy, 'very little research had been done into gorilla behaviour, so there was a real sense in which they were seen as a feared monster. What we are trying to bring to the film Kong is a characterisation that includes as much as possible of what has been discovered in the past 100 years – especially through the work in the 1960s by the late Dian Fossey, whose life story was told in the film *Gorillas in the Mist*. We have not tried to make Kong cuter and cuddly, he is a savage beast, but he is not a monster. What is extraordinary about these creatures is that, emotionally, they are 97 per cent identical to humans; obviously they transmit certain emotions differently, but we use that fact in the story to create a believable relationship between Kong and the heroine, Ann Darrow.'

> We've taken the character of Ann Darrow made famous in the first film by Fay Wray and have tried to re-think the role.
>
> It's curious because people often talk about how the original *Kong* is known as a 'Beauty and the Beast' story and, in a funny way, we always think about it as being a kind of a love story.
>
> But when you really study and analyse it, there is hardly any connection between the Fay Wray character and Kong: she's been taken against her will, she is permanently terrified of Kong – not just in the jungle sequences but also in the scenes set in New York – and she never really comes to understand him. We ultimately sympathise with Kong in spite of the way in which Ann reacts to him.
>
> We thought it would be an interesting approach to the story if we tried to build a relationship between them. We asked ourselves, 'How would she behave if she was kidnapped by this huge ape? What tricks would she use in order to survive? How can we find a way for them to connect?' It creates a puzzle, which we as the film-makers need to solve. That's what makes it such a fun job.
>
> You can go many different ways with a story like *King Kong*; there is no particular right or wrong way. You just have to choose which door you want to come in at, I guess, and we thought it would be interesting to explore what would happen if Ann and Kong succeeded in connecting in some way, so that by the time the Skull Island sequences came to a close, you were really feeling that the two of them had a bond that you could then carry through to New York and basically play out the climax with that connection very much intact.

Once it had been announced that the Jackson version of *King Kong* was to be made, public interest in the project became as keen as it had when the news first broke that Peter Jackson was to make *The Lord of the Rings.*

Of particular interest – especially to journalists in the entertainment media – were details of Peter's deal for *Kong* that *Variety* reported in August 2003 under the headline 'Rings Trio Get Big Payday for King Kong!' According to the business journal, *Forbes*, 'Jackson is receiving a beastly upfront fee of $20million to direct and produce his next film and write the screenplay for it.' The fee was in fact to be shared with Fran and Philippa but the overriding fascination was in the concept of a writer/director being paid a fee that would scarcely provoke comment were the recipient an A-list movie star.

'We made a deal,' says Peter Nelson, 'that was appropriate for Peter and Fran's level of skill and accomplishment and we made it at market level although it did happen to be the biggest deal of that ilk. There is so much focus these days on the *business* of entertainment, such as theatrical box office receipts and pay scale for actors and, even though little of the information that got out was fully correct, the deal became a lightning rod of a story that created something new in that it was about the compensation of a director.'

What was clear from the publicity stories that began to circulate around *Kong* was that Peter had succeeded in carrying many of the *Rings* audience with him beyond the confines of Middle-earth.

TheOneRing.net fan site launched a companion site, KongisKing.net, which followed TORn's formula of collecting and disseminating news, gossip and speculation, combined with articles on aspects of *Kong*'s extensive pedigree. Stories ranged from the news that Howard Shore would be composing the score for *Kong* through to a delightful report that Fay Wray (*Kong*'s original leading lady) had given the new project 'the thumbs up', saying: 'I think it is excellent and honourable that Peter Jackson wants to be true to the original. I am proud that he wants to keep *King Kong* alive.'

Recalling lessons learned in the early days of *Ring*'s shooting, Peter made the canny decision to work with KongisKing to address fans, to keep them informed about the film through an on-going series of video 'Production Diaries'. These offered tantalising glimpses into different facets of the film-making, which boldly inverted the usual

Naomi with Fay Wray a couple of days after The Return of the King *Oscars in 2004. A wonderful night – I just couldn't believe I was meeting the lady I'd watched in that old black and white 1933 movie – seventy-one years after she finished working on it. Time seemed to fold in on itself that night. When I tried to explain to her how the experience of watching* King Kong *had changed my life, I burst into tears. Fay was quite alarmed!*

film studio attitude of keeping sensitive film projects under wraps and helped cultivate interest in *Kong*.

> This idea of the video diary was born of our desire to make this a very different experience to *The Lord of the Rings*. We endured years of keeping all details 'secret' until the films were released. I thought it would be fun to go the opposite way, and have a 'making of' documentary happening in real time, as we were making the movie. There's really no other agenda. The people who log in to the KongisKing site would probably come to the film anyway, so it's not a particularly clever marketing move. Fun is the prime motivator.

The first 'Production Diary' was filed on Day 1 of the shoot, 7 September 2004 and showed Peter standing beside the SS *Venture*, the vessel used to take Carl Denham and his film crew to Skull Island.

The replica ship had been built on the parking lot at Peter's Wellington studios, an area previously covered in grass for filming bluescreen shots of charging Rohan warriors on the Pelennor Field! There was also, however, a *real* ship that became the source of an early fan site story.

> We bought a rusty Fifties ship that we converted into a period tramp steamer by adding, amongst other things, a funnel and a wheelhouse. This ship was sitting alongside the Miramar wharf looking like an old tub. Then I read all about it on TORn, how we'd painted the name on the ship – something which I'd meant to tell them not to do until the very end. So, within an hour of reading the story on TORn, I drove over to where the ship was moored and asked them to paint the name out again!
>
> The internet has shrunk the world and fan sites can now have a powerful impact on a film. Sometimes, where studios know they have produced a really bad film, they turn out a trailer that makes the movie look amazing, in order to con the moviegoer out of $10. Sometimes, the 'early word' about films can actually prevent directors from getting their films to a point they are happy with.
>
> The impact of the internet is the reason why we never did a single test screening of any of *The Lord of the Rings* films and I am eternally grateful, because it would have been a disaster. And would probably have resulted in the movies being seriously dumbed down. Test screenings for a director are not good experiences: having to screen your film to a bunch of strangers whose opinion is more important than your own! That's why part of the deal with Universal over *Kong* is that we control whether or not there is a test screening.

The internet was a-buzz with guesses about who was to feature on the *Kong* cast-list, including Ian McKellen – in an unspecified role – probably because, after playing Gandalf, he had been busily mentioning the possibility of being in the next Jackson movie – perhaps in the hope of persuading the director! As for a successor to Fay Wray, the 'hot tip' on the rumour schedules had for some time been former *Heavenly Creatures* star, Kate Winslet.

In reviewing the role of Ann Darrow, the writers had developed

Billy and Katie's cameo at the beginning of King Kong.

the character to give her – albeit within the 1930s setting – a contemporary sensibility. Ann was now a singer and dancer playing in vaudeville but with dreams of being a legitimate actress. Down on her luck, she is suckered into Denham's crazy movie project, meets playwright Jack Driscoll, whose work she admires, and eventually uses some of her skills as an actress to play for Kong's sympathy and save her life…

Despite the speculation about Kate Winslet, the role went to Naomi Watts, who had made an impressive impact with her performances in *Mulholland Drive*, *The Ring* and *Le Divorce*.

> We were big fans of Naomi, and we really wanted to work with her. It was a case of us being interested in Naomi Watts before we were in a position to make *Kong*; she was someone we'd already had our sights on, and as a result she was the first and only person that we ever offered the role of Ann Darrow to.
>
> We auditioned a lot for the secondary roles in *Kong*, but for the

principal three roles we just chose the actors, met with them and cast them.

In the 1933 film, the role of Carl Denham was played by Robert Armstrong as an ambitious movie-making adventurer, not unlike Merian C. Cooper and Ernest B. Schoedsack, the men who made *King Kong*. Armstrong's Denham is determined and ambitious, but quite different to the way in which he would be portrayed in the new version of the story. Peter presents Denham as an extrovert showman, a maverick who is constantly dodging creditors and ducking and diving in order to stay just one step ahead of the authorities, a chancer and risk-taker, an amiable rogue with dubious moral standards.

In 1996, the actor being considered for the role was Robert de Niro and when the film began its second life-cycle, there was considerable speculation on the internet about who would be offered the part – including several of the usual suspects, among them the one-time-possible Aragorn, Russell Crowe…

When you're writing a movie you stop and think, 'What's the obvious thing to do here?' The discipline we've adopted is to stop and think of the *least* obvious thing – ask, 'What *wouldn't* you expect to be happening here?' We did this with casting, and thought about unlikely choices. When we write, we always like to base a character on someone we know, or at least know of – either an actor, or a public figure. It helps to get us on the same page, and means the character has qualities based on a real person. We decided to move away from a Robert Armstrong approach to the role and thought, 'Why not go younger? We started to redefine the role a bit, and thought about Orson Welles as having a lot of Denham qualities. Welles was a highly ambitious, driven film-maker in the 1930s. He was obsessive, but also had a humorous wit. We didn't want to cast someone to *play* Orson Welles, but he was to be a good guide for Denham's character traits during the writing process.

We thought of which actor we could cast to play this new interpretation of Carl Denham. Jack Black was our first choice. He had the intelligence, wit and energy we had written into Denham's character.

Apart from playing a hobbit who had used the One Ring for an

Shooting the movie is the toughest part of the process – as opposed to writing, pre-production and post-production. The day is spent racing against the clock to get what you need on film. Having people like Jack Black, Colin Hanks and Jamie Bell around sure helps to keep the stress levels down.

experiment in intimate body piercing for the MTV Awards spoof on *The Lord of the Rings*, Jack Black was best known for starring as the down-and-out rock star, Dewey Finn, in *The School of Rock*.

> The fact that Jack was known for one particular role didn't bother us. If we'd looked at the films Elijah Wood had done before *The Lord of the Rings*, you'd realise that he was an unlikely choice for Frodo, yet people now have totally accepted him and associate him with the role. If someone is a good actor – like Elijah or Jack – they will be able to play against type. I have always rejected people thinking of me as a 'splatter director', and hate the idea of typecasting actors in the same way.

In the original film, Jack Driscoll was first mate on the SS *Venture*. Played by Bruce Cabot, Driscoll is a straight-shooting 'man's man' who doesn't have any time for women – particularly not aboard a ship, but who eventually falls for Ann Darrow and becomes her gauche but gallant romantic lead...

Again Peter, Fran and Philippa decided against going for the 'action-hero image' and adopted a revisionist approach, making Driscoll into an aspiring New York playwright who gets conned by Denham into helping with his movie project and is virtually hijacked aboard the ship. To complete the transformation, the role was given to the soulful-eyed Adrien Brody, who had won an Oscar for his acclaimed performance in Roman Polanski's *The Pianist*.

> We met Adrien in London on the day of the BAFTA Awards in 2004. The actors cast for the roles of Driscoll, Denham and Ann were all our first and only choices – which is a luxury. It's always a wonderful thing when you come up with an idea of casting an actor, then meet with that person and offer them the role and it's done. We were very fortunate in that we were fans of Adrien, Jack and Naomi and had the perfect project that enabled us to bring the three of them together.

For Andy Serkis the first inkling that he might be involved in *King Kong* came during the pick-up filming for *The Return of the King*: 'It was my birthday and Pete and Fran invited me over to see them and Fran started showing me a book of photographs of an albino

Adrien spent a couple of nights under rain towers during the storm scene. Here he's going over script notes with Fran between shots.

gorilla… It suddenly dawned on me that they were showing me for a reason! They told me that they wanted me to be involved and I was absolutely thrilled and very excited… It was just talk at that point, but they said they were going to approach the creation of Kong in the same way as Gollum, although, obviously, many things would be quite different, since he wouldn't be communicating with words.'

Andy was also cast as Lumpy, the ship's cook, a character who appears in the 1932 novelisation of *King Kong*, but who was never featured in the original film. 'Lumpy,' says Andy, 'is an ex-First World War naval cook who's had to cook horrific stuff throughout the war years and, as a result, has completely lost his taste buds. Now he's a cook on a merchant ship and is suddenly exposed to all these exotic spices and foods from around the world and goes a bit crazy with his experiments! He thinks what he comes up with is fantastic, but everybody really hates his food! In addition to being a chef, he's the barber, ship's doctor, tattooist, jack-of-all-trades and is, in a way,

After enduring the gimp suit on The Lord of the Rings, *Andy Serkis got to spend another few months in a weighted, gorilla-shaped lycra leotard on* King Kong. *I think he enjoys it.*

like the mother to the crew – although they still don't like his cooking!'

Speaking of what Peter, Fran and Philippa brought to the characterisations in the film, Andy says: 'In the same way in which they drew certain things out of *The Lord of the Rings* about love and companionship, *Kong* is very much about isolation. Kong, an alpha male beyond his prime, is essentially a deeply lonely creature; but all the characters have a massive sense of loneliness and each of the various crew members and passengers on the ship represents a different aspect of the male psyche.'

A story is told of how someone tackled Peter over why he was making *King Kong*, a film, the questioner claimed, which was really just about rampant male sexuality and featured a huge, hairy beast with a woman clutched in his hand, climbing one of the largest phallic symbols in the world. Peter, it is said, listened and replied, 'Really? I just thought I was making a film about dinosaurs and a gorilla...'

> The idea of interpreting films to mean whatever you wish them to mean is a pastime in which I've never taken much interest.
>
> Our version of *Kong* obviously acknowledges the fact that a male gorilla is an incredibly dominant and macho creature; so that aspect of Kong's character is something that Ann has to confront and certainly deal with and that awareness has helped shape the plot, but not in any particular depth.
>
> Obviously I'm fully aware that the Kong story has any number of

Freudian interpretations, but it's not the point of the movie and it was not something I was aware of when I was 9 years old and saw *King Kong*. I was, quite simply, swept away by it.

Among the many subtle nuances in the writing of *Kong* are the observations on writing and movie-making, such as a line of Carl Denham's that didn't survive through to the final cut (but which might, one day, turn up as a DVD extra): 'You can't run a film like a democracy,' says the director; 'if it's not a dictatorship, it falls apart! Now let me finish this goddam picture so I can have a nervous breakdown!'

> Because we happen to be telling the story which involves a team of film-makers, *Kong* certainly gave us an opportunity to try to hint at some of the pressures involved in writing and making a film and to have some fun with it and put a few of our frustrations on screen. We optioned a book written by a wonderful ex-Vaudeville actress, June Havoc, and that gave us an authentic voice for the time period.
>
> As for Denham's thoughts on democracy... I think it is actually true: democracy is never very helpful when you're trying to make a film!

For Peter, *King Kong* also provided an opportunity to work with a new studio after a five-year sojourn with New Line. 'By the end of *The Return of the King*,' says Ken Kamins, 'I think their relationship had run its course and they had pretty much exhausted each other. I like to describe that relationship as a well-intentioned marriage that had to end in divorce, but which produced three beautiful children!'

'That is the wrong characterisation,' says New Line's Michael Lynne. 'I don't think Peter sees it like that and we certainly don't. Until Peter decided to make *King Kong* for Universal, it wasn't necessarily clear that Peter's next project would be for a studio other than New Line...' To which Bob Shaye adds, 'It's not like a marriage; nobody said, "Till death do you part!" It's *supposed* to be over when the film is over! There was an amicable and necessary separation...'

> There's truth in all of that. In fact, I wanted New Line to be given a chance to co-produce *King Kong*, but they declined. I think it's very important to honour relationships and after five years of making *The*

Lord of the Rings, we ended up in a very happy, peaceful place with New Line. Bob and Michael are two people for whom I have the greatest respect and gratitude. It's easy to highlight tensions and bad stuff – that makes for drama, and everyone loves drama – but at the end of the day, they risked everything on us, and we killed ourselves to deliver. It has defined all our lives to some degree and I look forward to working with them again.

Comparing the two studios, I think it would be fair to say that with New Line we got off to a shaky start and for quite a time things were a little combative and there was a sense of mistrust on both sides. With Universal, we're able to have a relationship without the history.

The advantage that Universal have, which New Line never had, is the knowledge that we can make a film of this size and complexity – ironically, that has only been proven by our having made *The Lord of the Rings*.

That's one reason why they felt able to sit back and allow us to do our thing, to go through our process and not feel threatened or intimidated.

Universal's Mary Parent recalls the studio's meeting with Peter and Fran on 2 March 2003 – a date that marked the seventieth anniversary, to the day, since the opening of the original *King Kong*: 'I remember this meeting vividly. When Peter noted the anniversary of the date, I immediately had a sense not only of excitement but, maybe, even destiny…'

Of the many lessons – political, technical and aesthetic – learned in making *The Lord of the Rings* that would affect the way in which the filming of *Kong* was approached, there was one fundamental difference.

The Lord of the Rings was very much about using locations. Obviously there were sets as well, but using the natural countryside created much of the look and feel of the film. With *Kong* I made the decision not to go on location.

The jungle on Skull Island is rather like Fangorn gone mad! It is huge, high and vast and really tortuous with masses of gnarled and twisted trees and there are simply no actual jungles in the world that look like this. *Kong*'s jungle is something of an experimentation with stylisation: a little Tim Burtonesque but with a sufficient sense of reality for you to believe that this place *could* be real, could exist – except that you're never actually going to find it!

Having decided that he was going to stay in the studio, Peter wanted to try to capture something of the look and feeling of the jungles in the 1933 film, which were also created on a soundstage.

As soon as the *Kong* project was announced, work began on creating the concept art for the film and in particular the styling of the Skull Island locations. Much as had been done on *The Lord of the Rings*, this art then provided the inspiration for the creation not just of the full-size sets but also of the detailed miniature models. These would be used to extend and enhance the jungle sets on which the actors would be filmed in a similar way to that in which computer graphics would enhance the city sets.

> I really wanted to create the illusion that we had gone back to the same island where they had shot the original film...
>
> The various locations on Skull Island were a composite creation of studio sets combined with rear projections, backgrounds created using glass paintings and with tabletop miniatures for the foreground. Even though those are not the techniques that we're using this time around, we're still able to replicate the feelings they had but in a more refined and realistic way.
>
> What I'm doing with *Kong* is more akin to what George Lucas has been doing with the recent *Star Wars* films; I'm wanting to show how you can create believable environments by building sets that you need but then enhancing them either with models or by computer to an extent where a lot of the frame can actually be filled with composite images that you've put in there after the actors have left the set and gone home!

As was quickly reported by the media, in creating the new film Peter was intending to expand on the sequences set in 'the mysterious and dangerous jungles of Skull Island'. No less than two thirds of the film was to take place on the island and, recalling the impact of his first experience of seeing *Kong*, Peter was as committed to creating the denizens of the jungles as the environment itself.

> What is really interesting about *King Kong* is that it is difficult to know exactly what audiences will be expecting. Apart from the devotees, a lot

DP Andrew Lesnie and his gaffer, Reg Garside. They had some huge technical hurdles to overcome, and very big sets to light.

of people really don't think of *Kong* as being anything more than clichés, either because they saw the original film a long, long time ago or because they have never seen it – which is not entirely surprising because it has only recently been released on DVD. To many individuals, therefore, it's just a story about a big gorilla that destroys the town and throws cars around – the ape on the loose; they don't actually realise, or remember, that *Kong* has other, emotional elements to its story.

Philippa Boyens recalls the first time she and Fran watched the original *King Kong* with Peter: 'I looked across at Pete, towards the end of the film – at the point where the planes are attacking Kong on the top of the Empire State Building and he carefully puts Ann down and makes sure she is safe before he is shot and killed – and I noticed that Peter was crying. That moment, when Kong demonstrates his care and concern for Ann, always makes him cry... a recollection, perhaps, of some feeling that meant something to him when he was very young and which has stayed with him across the years.'

Apart from the emotional dimension to the story, which those less familiar with the original film may find unexpected, there is another surprising fact about Kong's cinematic career.

What is fascinating is that because the 1976 Dino de Laurentiis film *King Kong* has been repeatedly screened on television, it is the version of the story that is most widely known. It's particularly interesting for us, because our film contains ingredients that were in the 1933 film but were left out of the 1976 remake, such as the dinosaurs on Skull Island and the biplanes taking on Kong on top of the Empire State Building. So our *Kong* may come as something of a surprise to kids used to seeing Dino's *Kong*.

AT THAT MOMENT: KONG CHARGES!

KONG meets the TYRANNOSAUR HEAD-ON at FULL SPEED! He swings his fist, smashing into the TYRANNOSAUR'S HEAD... ANN has to throw herself against a tree as the DINOSAUR SPRAWLS onto the ground beside her... in a flash, KONG is ON TOP of the TYRAN-NOSAUR, POUNDING HIS FIST DOWN on its body.

This is the beginning of one of the scenes that, in scope though not in detail, featured in Peter and Fran's first screenplay for *Kong*. It is a set-piece that springs from the young Peter Jackson's memory and which will be guaranteed to electrify any youngster for whom dinosaurs are an abidingly exciting wonder – which, in practice, means *every* youngster! – not to mention those of more mature years for whom prehistoric creatures provide a science-fact bridge back to a time when a belief in the dragon-lands of fairytale and folklore was permissible!

In the original 1933 film, Kong battles with an Allosaurus; in the new version, as one might expect with the Jackson imagination, the ape takes on not one but *three* carnivores – on this occasion of the more deadly species, Tyrannosaurus Rex. It was, after several years of waiting and anticipation, Peter's first opportunity to choreograph a 'monster fight'.

Our Kong *maquette is still sitting in our office, as it had been since 1996. It was made as a gift for Universal when we developed* Kong *for the first time. It was duly presented to their senior executives with much pomp and ceremony. When the studio suddenly killed that version of* Kong *the only phone call I made to them was the one where I asked for the sculpture back! A little pathetic, I know – but in a situation like that you feel so powerless that any gesture to regain some form of pride is seized upon. Besides, it's very cool!*

Whilst the working script for *Kong* contained a tightly packed page of what Philippa Boyens calls 'Big Print' (graphically described action, liberally peppered with exclamation marks) that had remained virtually unchanged since the 1996 script, its continued presence was intended merely as an indication of possible action.

At the end of the day, the script is very much a placeholder for these types of scenes. Once the script is written, you then start work on visualising such sequences; in the process, a lot of stuff happens and it usually goes places that the descriptions in the screenplay didn't!

Two of Weta's conceptual artists, Jeremy Bennett and Gus Hunter, developed a whole series of production designs and ideas: thrilling visual concepts for Kong fighting the T-Rexes: great creatures thundering through tangled junglescapes and ancient ruins; hurling themselves at one another in a frenzy of animal rage and pain that are electrifying images of a dreadful primal world.

> I would take Jeremy and Gus' art, in much the same way as I did with Alan Lee and John Howe's conceptual art for *The Lord of the Rings*, study and think about them, immersing myself in their mood. Slowly, over quite a long period of time, I would start coming up with ideas and gags, exciting and unexpected twists and turns that were needed to create the choreography for the fight which runs to a thrilling six or six-and-a-half minutes of the film – which, in film terms, is a meaty fight!

During the shoot, the *Kong* cast had to cope with the same challenges that *The Lord of the Rings* cast had faced in confronting Balrogs, Cave-trolls and fell beasts that would not be present until post-production. For Naomi Watts, in particular, the film required a convincing portrayal of Ann's mercurial relationship with Kong that had been sensitively thought through and clearly delineated within the script.

> Naomi has an incredible ability to make things truthful and real. When she acts, like any good actor, she taps into aspects of herself, a reservoir of personal experiences and feelings. Naomi is able to reach down and basically come up with the most incredibly believable, deep, emotional stuff onscreen. She is absolutely fantastic at that.

The interaction of 'the ape and the girl', in a way that audiences will relate to emotionally, was achieved through Naomi's depiction of Ann combined with Andy Serkis' performance in providing a physical and vocal inspiration for Kong. The way in which Weta Digital has managed the technical translation of Andy's portrayal into a form

This is how Naomi spent many of her shoot days – surrounded by blue-screen and strange men dressed in low-budget superhero suits! They're actually stuntmen who would pick her up whenever she was supposed to be in Kong's hand. Naomi clutched the big blue finger, and Weta Digital eventually replaced them with Kong's hand and fingers. She had so little to work with, but threw herself into every scene with a gutsy courage. Andy Serkis was always on set for Naomi, performing Kong and giving her a pair of real eyes to play against.

with which the animators can then work to give screen life to the creature and believably unite the characters.

'I'd be standing on top of the Empire State Building,' says Andy, 'swiping at imaginary bi-planes – although there was no building and no planes. I was back in the same studio where I did all my work for Gollum, but involved in bringing a very different creature to life.'

Part of the time, as Andy explains, he would be acting with and for Naomi: 'I was her eye line, on the top of ladders, going up and down on scissor-lifts, anything to create the right height. Naomi and I developed a very organic way of working at the relationship between Ann and Kong: sometimes I'd be towering above her; sometimes I'd be right next to her and playing Kong's hand and she'd be holding on to me; all the time we'd be looking at one another and communicating emotions through those looks. We also used a sound system that took my vocalisations and put them through a huge speaker to give a sense of Kong's size and scale – we called it "The Kongelizer"! The acting was remarkably uncomplicated, but the work with motion-capture was technically complicated and incredibly challenging.'

It's a quantum leap beyond the Gollum work that was done with Andy on *Rings*. Gollum was the same size as the hobbits and humanoid so we were able to take Andy's performance, translate it one-for-one to the digital puppet and arrive at Gollum.

With Kong it was much harder: he is twenty-five feet tall and has the features and the physical proportions of a gorilla, which – despite the similarities humans respond to in apes – are quite different to those of a man.

What we've eventually managed to do is to create a software programme that has allowed us to motion-capture Andy's facial performance – down to the tiniest subtleties of expression – and then translate that performance into what would be the facial responses on an ape's face. On top of that, we have great animators, able to capture the spirit of Kong, as channelled through Andy.

It's been a very sophisticated and difficult thing to achieve, but it has proven to be a remarkable development for *King Kong* and has resulted in an incredibly expressive performance.

KONG… *we see him clearly for the first time. A very old, brutish BULL GORILLA. Tears of survival have left SCARS on his face. One EYELID is mangled and his JAW is CROOKED… leaving a huge yellowed INCISOR TOOTH jutting up…*

KONG *stares at* ANN… *she dare not move; only her RAPID BREATHING belies her INNER TERROR…*

Reflecting on the eventual on-screen chemistry between the Eighth Wonder of the World and the burlesque girl from New York, Peter adds:

I think we've ended up with something pretty powerful and the relationship between Ann and Kong is obviously the heart and soul of the film.

The tragedy of it and the irony within the story is that, for the first time in his existence, he opens a door in his heart to some other creature and it proves to be his undoing.

Talking to Peter Jackson just a few days after he had completed work on *The Lord of the Rings*, he had remarked apropos of moving on to *King Kong*: 'The notion of taking on one film and one film only seems pretty luxurious to me at the moment. Of course it's never easy to make a good movie, but technically and logistically *anything* has got to be easier than doing three incredibly complicated, three-hour movies! It was an endurance test and I never want to make another three-hour movie in my life! They are really tough, way longer than films should be and ought to be and bring with them all sorts of added pressures to justify the running time: make them entertaining and stop people getting bored and feeling uncomfortable about sitting still for so long…

'Not only that, but with three hours comes a great many special effects and every aspect of the production – sound, editing, music – has to do twice what a regular hour-and-a-half-long film would be doing. The whole thing compounds into this massive, tiring, stressful event…

'So, hopefully *Kong* will be two hours long and comparatively straightforward…'

And *was* it?

In some ways it was and in some ways it wasn't! Nothing is ever easier than what went before, because you're always trying to put as much into the film as you can to make it as good as you can and we always put in 150 per cent. Nothing will ever be quite as hard as *The Return of the King* because of the sheer expectation that was resting on that film and the complexity of having to weave the different story threads together at the climax of the film. But *Kong* was technically tough and, although it's a shorter film, it has as many effects shots as *The Return of the King*, so I'd rather not use the word 'easy' in any way about *Kong*! The tunnel was shorter, so we got to see the light a little quicker – but that didn't make it any less dark and scary!

I know that when we were going to do *King Kong* ten years ago it was

Once the cameras start rolling I focus on my monitors, which show me what's being filmed. I try to imagine I'm seeing it play on a huge cinema screen – and give notes if, for whatever reason, it's not feeling quite right.

the scariest mountain to climb; way bigger than *The Frighteners,* which I had just finished and was totally intimidating. The version of *Kong* that we have finally made is far more ambitious than what we were planning then but, because we have done all these things before and now know how to do them, the project didn't feel anywhere near as daunting.

Of course, it had its moments. The shoot was no less intense. The one side of film-making that I like the least is the actual shooting of the film, because you are carrying a lot of the stress of the day: having to make the day's schedule and stay in budget, and that doesn't really get any easier the more times you make movies.

So there wasn't any less stress but there was an atmosphere of calm confidence in which we were able to take everything that we'd learned and, hopefully, have taken what we can do a step further. Just as we'll try to do in making our next film…

What sets *King Kong* apart from any film that Peter has ever made – or *will* ever make – is its unique status as the film that set him on course to *become* a film-maker. To have revisited that film, to have set out on his own search for Skull Island and once there to have sought out Kong and brought him back to our world for us to wonder and marvel at is, perhaps, the most extraordinary achievement in a career to date already crowned with achievements.

I always thought of the Cave-troll in *The Fellowship of the Ring* as being the fulfilment of my Ray Harryhausen ambitions of wanting to do a fantasy film and have humans battling with a monster.

But *Kong*, even more than *The Lord of the Rings*, is the ultimate fulfilment of what I've wanted to do since I was a kid because, in many respects, *King Kong* is the ultimate fantasy film; and because in this film more than any other I have been able to devise and develop these amazingly visual encounters with the fantastic.

I simply wanted to make a new version of the story that I would enjoy if I went to the cinema to see it!

That's the standard that I try to apply to everything I do: *I want to make movies that I'd like to watch…*

'ONE MORE FOR LUCK!'

'I'm still having the dreams!' Peter Jackson is speaking to me in August 2005, on the day after the final pick-up for *King Kong*. 'I've had lots of director nightmares recently.' It seems that the dreams that plagued his nights throughout the shoot of *The Lord of the Rings* have not gone away.

In the dreams, Peter is lying in bed surrounded by a film crew demanding to know what to do next and without his having any idea what they are supposed to be filming.

'I had them again last night,' he goes on. 'I was dreaming that I was in the middle of doing *Kong* stuff and things were going wrong. Then, on top of that, I dreamed that Cate Blanchett and Liv Tyler had shown up! And it's not what you think! I knew I had to shoot an Elven sequence for *The Lord of the Rings* – I didn't know why or what it was – just that Liv and Cate had arrived in my dreamland and were waiting for me to tell them what to do. And I simply didn't have a clue… These stress-related dreams are so strong that they stay with me for an hour or two after I wake up. I arrive at the *Kong* editing room, still feeling Elvish tension!'

I have a memory of observing Peter Jackson on another last day of pick-ups… Friday 18 July 2003, the final day of pick-ups for *The Return of the King*.

On the studio soundstage are the ruins of Osgiliath… Crumbling masonry: a ruination of once-elegant buildings; colonnades of broken arches and smashed columns; statues toppled into dust; twisted iron grilles; uprooted trees; a mass of littered debris – charred wood, empty barrels, wooden dishes and pewter tankards. Everything covered in dust; everything is spattered with blood…

An enormous fan, twenty feet in diameter, wafts drifts of smoke around the set…

Above the set: rows of lamps, gantries and shiny aluminium air-con ducts.

On set: an assistant in a baseball cap wanders by with an armful of swords. Technicians in blue hard-hats are mingling with Orcs and Gondorians, who are enjoying a truce between shots.

Peter Jackson is wearing a jerkin with the legend on the back: 'Day 133 May 23 2000'. That was the halfway point in making *The Lord of the Rings*, when the shoot was going to be 266 days before it went up to 274.

Peter is directing John Bach playing Madril, senior officer in Faramir's company of Rangers who is rushing through the ruins when he suddenly sees (though there's nothing there yet) a swooping Nazgûl…

'Alrighty!' calls Carolynne Cunningham. 'Here we go! And – roll sound. And *action*!'

John Bach runs, 'sees' the Nazgûl and reacts…

There's another take: 'Make more of ducking out of the way,' directs Peter. 'It's a dodge, a weave… Get as much nimbleness as you can… And then you see this Nazgûl and you say, like, "Holy S***!"'

Another take…

'And cut!' calls Peter. 'Good! Good! Good! Just sell it a bit more, John…'

John Bach says, 'I was trying to make it subtle!'

'*Subtle?*' laughs Peter. 'Who told you this was a subtle movie? Right! *One more for luck…*'

Later, John Bach is now bloodied up, lying amidst the Osgiliath rubble with Lawrence Makoare (formerly Lurtz) standing over him in his second *Rings* monster persona, the grotesque Gothmog. A small hawk-nosed Orc played by Robert Pollock with the look of an eagerly vicious child, hangs on Gothmog's words…

'The age of Men is over,' growls Lawrence through his *Elephant Man* prosthetic features; 'the time of the Orc has come!'

It is one of the last shots on the last day of the last film of *The Lord of the Rings*. Peter is charged up and firing on all cylinders.

'As you look up at Lawrence,' Peter tells John Bach, 'the realisation dawns that you are not going to be taken prisoner and given medical attention. The Geneva Convention does not apply! Okay... One more for luck...'

Art Director Dan Hennah watches Peter in full flight. 'That's the essence of Peter Jackson,' he says. 'If Peter had a day off, you know what he'd be doing? *Making a film!*'

* * *

Twenty-five months later, Peter is now talking about having a few days off.

> For the best part of nearly ten years the only projects we've had in our minds have been *The Lord of the Rings* and *King Kong*. It started with *Kong* and then it was *Rings*, and then it was back to *Kong* again. That's a long, long time to only be thinking about two stories. And the one thing that Fran and I are now looking forward to the most is taking some downtime – our first in ten years – and think about projects that don't involve hobbits or gorillas. We want to recharge the batteries, regenerate some brain cells and allow ourselves to dream for a while. Dreaming about possible movies is what I first started doing when I was 7 or 8. It's the nicest and most enjoyable part of the process. I still feel like a 9-year-old with a Super 8 camera.

Among the many ideas that are already in the collective Jackson – Walsh ideas bank, some date back to before the Great Ape and the One Ring took over their lives... even as far back as the original *Jamboree* with the *Bad Taste* Boys saving Wellington from alien attackers!

Whatever project they were to choose to make, whenever they choose to make it, it will undoubtedly find a huge international audience waiting in line outside the cinema...

Peter Jackson's legal representative, Peter Nelson, recalls a conversation during the height of *The Lord of the Rings*' success: 'I remember Peter saying, "It is possible that this will be the highest level of audience achievement for any movie I'll ever make…" I disagreed and told him, as I truly believe: "You are *just beginning* to acquire an audience!"'

> When I look at what I did with *Kong*, I recognise the same film-maker who made *The Lord of the Rings*. It has the same sensibilities – which is neither a good nor a bad thing necessarily, it's just an observation, really. But there would be an expectation for my next movie to be in a similar epic style, and I honestly felt that I couldn't face another big complex project – at least, not straight away. I'm sure I will do more of these sorts of films in the future, but not right now…
>
> I feel that I am in a very simliar place to when we finished *Braindead*. I had made three low-budget horror/black comedy films in a row and was just about to do a fourth one when we went off on a different tack and made *Heavenly Creatures* instead. Emotionally, I'm in a similar place right now. I recognise the feelings.

It was while looking for such an opportunity that Alice Sebold's bestselling novel, *The Lovely Bones*, caught and fired Peter and Fran's imagination.

The Lovely Bones, which has been described as 'a heartbreaking page-turner', virtually defies advances from a film-maker with its opening sentence: 'My name was Salmon, like the fish: first name, Susie. I was 14 when I was murdered on December 6, 1973…'

Sebold's story of the rape and murder of a young girl and of the repercussions which her death has on her family and friends is narrated by the dead Susie, who observes the earthly world from her own personal heaven. Therein, as Peter acknowledges, lies the challenge of the book.

> When I read *The Lovely Bones*, I thought it was a wonderfully emotional and powerful story. Like all the very best kinds of fantasy, it has a solid grounding in the real world, so I felt immediately that it would make a fascinating film, but I also thought, 'My God! This will be very hard to adapt…'

There is the daring concept of having a central character who is basically only an observer of the events unfolding in the story, as well as the daunting concept of having to create Heaven as a *real* place that is, as Peter puts it, 'ethereal and emotional but not hokey'. There have, of course, been dead narrators in movies before (*Sunset Boulevard* and *American Beauty*) as well as literally dozens of cinematic representations of Heaven, ranging from the black-and-white sanitised environment depicted in A *Matter of Life and Death* to the Technicolor landscape paintings in *What Dreams May Come*.

> Beyond the wonderful story and characters, the fact that *The Lovely Bones* is going to be very hard to make as a film is part of the appeal to me. That's what interests me now – doing something that is challenging and very different to what I've done in the past.
>
> I hoping that, after a few months of quiet preparation, a different film-maker will make *The Lovely Bones* – at least he should feel like a different film-maker! I'd like there to be no real similarity between the *Lovely Bones'* director and *The Lord of the Rings* or *Kong* film-maker. That's part of the fun, and challenge, for me.

What fascinated the press when the story broke in January 2005 that Sebold's book was to be the next Jackson film, was the fact that there was no studio involved in the deal: 'Putting his own bucks into *Bones*,' said *Variety*, who were intrigued by the fact that the film-maker was investing his own money in obtaining the rights to the book and deferring any decisions about which studio he will work with until he, Fran Walsh and Philippa Boyens have a script with which they are happy and a detailed budget.

> Fran and I got the rights to *The Lovely Bones* ourselves, rather than go to a studio and ask them to get the rights on our behalf, because the studio would then want the script tomorrow and they would want to make the film straight away and it would be more pressure.
>
> So we're looking forward to just doing things in our own time and I think it will be a better film because of that. We will develop the project: write the script we want to write, draw up a budget for it, and get very clear in our minds the film that we want to make before we go to anyone.

Our dream is to wake up on 1st January 2006, having got through the *Kong* premieres and Christmas and not have a studio on the phone asking us when the next draft is going to be ready or when we're going to start shooting!

So, how will moviegoers respond to what is clearly – within popu-lar understanding – not a typical or obvious Jackson movie. 'Peter's projects have branded themselves,' says Peter Nelson, 'and, for the rest of his career, any movie he makes will always be branded as "A Peter Jackson film" in a way that's bigger and bolder than any other won-derful director's movies. This will bring audiences to see films who might not otherwise have been attracted to a particular subject matter or genre. But, unlike any other director – with the possible exception of Spielberg – Peter, by his personal charisma, has also branded him-self. His reputation as an auteur director is not just based on his movies, but based on his image, on what we know about him.'

I have no desire for my name to become a brand. It kind of happens without you being able to control it, if you're lucky enough to make a successful film. Have a good look at the credits for any of the *Lord of the Rings* movies, or *King Kong*. The one credit you will not see is 'A Peter Jackson Film'. I refused to allow that, and never will. Movies are collab-orations, and I would never make that kind of possessive claim on such a collaborative piece of work. I regret that we live in an age where film-makers are the object of such intense scrutiny. I'd have preferred it thirty or forty years ago, when directors stayed in the shadows.

During the thousands of interviews that Peter conducted during the publicity-fest surrounding the release of *The Return of the King*, a journalist – seeking that elusive question that a much-interviewed subject has never been asked before – asked why the manufacturers of *Rings* toys hadn't marketed a Peter Jackson 'action-figure'? In response, Peter quipped, 'Yes, it's a pity they missed out on that – it would have sold better than Aragorn!'

Despite the flippancy of this riposte, it is a fact that his represen-tatives *do* get requests to license his image. While this is something that, characteristically, holds no appeal for Peter, it is an indication of the intense interest that exists in the man and his work, which is based on an international awareness of who he is – he is a 'celebrity' whose likeness is universally known in a way that one associates with *movie stars* rather than *directors*.

'Part of it is the cause and effect of being a great leader,' says Peter Nelson. 'People want more access to him. As a result of *The Lord of the Rings*, there is a non-stop flood of fans who not only want to get close to him and get an autograph, they want to engage with him and have a few words – in many cases, *many more words!* There is a desire to know him, to have a relationship with him. That desire is a testament to what he conveys.'

It is what has given him a status that, within the context of his homeland, sees him often light-heartedly referred to as 'New Zealand's national hero' but which, in a global arena, is defined by a palpable sense of both admiration and affection.

'People recognise a bit of him within themselves,' says Philippa Boyens. 'Peter is "their man"; he is the kid who loves movies – *genuinely loves movies*. His enthusiasm, excitement and passion are infectious – that's what he puts into his films.'

> For as long as I can remember, I've been imagining movies. Imagining them is the fun part – capturing those fleeting images is tough. They're aren't any aspects of the process that I don't enjoy – writing, filming, post-production, I've slowly taught myself how to savour it all. None of it's boring, it's all film-making. *It's all fun!*

That approach is certainly one that draws actors, craftspeople and technicians to work with him and, for a great many of them, keeps them working there.

'Peter gets very excited about things,' says Carolynne Cunningham, 'and he really throws himself into those things. That's what he's always like and that's what is so delightful about him. Essentially, Peter is a 40-year-old going on 9!'

Philippa Boyens responds: 'Well, he's a funny mix, because if he's nine going on 40, then he's by far the wisest, toughest 9-year-old you've ever met; but then maybe – underneath it all – he was when he was 9 as well. So yes, there is a lot of the child in him and he has a direct line through to that and can tap right into it, but he is also an extraordinarily sophisticated film-maker who completely understands how to use that knowledge.'

'He *is* a bit of kid,' agrees New Line's Bob Shaye, 'and he certainly has the fantastic imagination of a kid; but, in the same heartbeat, he has unbelievable endurance and incredible resolve, two very important things. You need creativity, vision and a bunch of other stuff, all of which he has. But he's also an amazingly dedicated, hardworking and "I'm-never-going-to-give-up kind of guy" and without any of the calculated and diabolical traits so often found in Hollywood.'

Long-time associate, Marty Walsh, puts it very simply: 'Wonderful boyish qualities, but a man of steel. Try and bully Peter and you cannot win. You cannot menace him. That is not a childlike response...'

From the beginning Peter had to fight in order to achieve what he not only *wanted* to do but what he knew that he *could* do. He had to fight to convince the New Zealand Film Commission that backing an amateur movie, made by a local photoengraver and a bunch of mates on weekends, was worth backing; he had to fight to convince international financiers and distributors that he could do films of increasing technical sophistication and, once he had become successful – and was safely categorised by genre – he had to fight to do something different.

He had to fight to convince Hollywood that he could make one of the biggest film ventures ever, based on a quintessentially English book that, for the most part, Hollywood didn't understand, and to embark on that venture in a country most people in Hollywood knew little about and to which they had never been. And even when he had found the partners who were willing to invest belief in that venture, trust him and give it their backing, he still had to fight to prove that he and his associates could achieve all, and more, than could have been achieved in the capital city of moviedom.

Ken Kamins says: 'I don't believe that Peter would be the artist that he is in Beverly Hills: his artistry is defined by his ability to function with a freedom of being outside of the system. If you're *in* the system, then you're living in the rhythms and the *mores* of how the town does business and here he is much more able to define his creative life, in part, by being physically 7,500 miles away!'

The film industry, when it suits it, is charmed and delighted in acknowledging the achievements of a man who is 'outside' the system – he has, after all, done more for the industry than many people who are resolutely in the system. But it still often demonstrates a quizzical, doubtful view about what can be achieved in New Zealand and, when Peter has fought their corner, the Hollywoodites have cried, 'Xenophobia!' with the arrogance of what is arguably one of the most xenophobic countries on the planet!

> I've got myself involved with creating companies over the years, in order to do precisely the kind of work that we knew we needed for the kind of movies we wanted to make. We created a digital effects company and it's obvious that we'd want that company to do the effects on our films, because there are so many advantages. We bought the Film Unit in order to develop into a world-class sound mixing facility and it's obvious that I'd want them to work on my pictures.
>
> There have been times when I've felt the suspicions of studios, as if the desire to use my own companies is designed to collect incredible profits (which never actually happens); and, at the same time, there has been a paranoia that what we would produce would probably be substandard, as if to say, 'How could a company in New Zealand be any good compared to a company somewhere else?'

The visitor to New Zealand can buy in any good souvenir shop 'The Kiwi Upside Down World Map', with New Zealand in the middle at the top instead of its conventional location in the bottom righthand corner. It gives a different, enlightening perspective on the world by literarily turning perceptions – and preconceptions – upside down; showing that there is no true 'down under' because when you are *down* under, it is then the rest of the world that is down under you…

Peter Jackson has done something similar within the movie industry. He has turned the map upside down, shown that Europe doesn't have the prerogative on films of high artistic endeavour and that the blockbuster does not have to emanate only from the studios of North America.

'Peter is becoming a code for a certain level of quality in film-making,' says Ken Kamins. 'He has true pride of authorship over everything from *idea* to *realisation*. An expression which he often uses in interviews is, "We have movies down here hand-made – we don't buy things off the rack." I think that's what appeals to audiences and business associates; it's what people are buying into with him and with Fran and with everything they've created and built.'

'In the past', says Fran, 'we've always felt we've had to prove ourselves in terms of our ability to deliver; that attitude is disappearing now partly, as Pete says, because we've won a few Oscars and things!'

Those Oscars and many other awards join what is an extraordinary collection of things – books, toys, games, puppets, movie memorabilia and military collectibles with which Peter surrounds himself. Like all collectors, these things are precious not necessarily because of their financial value but because they represent memories, moments from childhood, inspirations, enthusiasms and excitements. To others, however, they are just Stuff!

'He's the messiest person I've every met!' declares Philippa Boyens. 'Have you seen his workspace? I do not know how he can work. It's hysterical! He's got everything from model soldiers to budgets for multi-million dollar films, lying side by side. Nothing can ever be thrown away and all this stuff is strewn about everywhere, but what is so infuriating is that he always knows precisely where everything is! Why does he need all that stuff? He doesn't throw stuff away, partly because he's a mad collector, but he also has this sort of canny sense that this or that is going to mean something, have some value in the future. More than that, I think he needs those things because they are part of who and what he is…'

'Peter is like a magpie,' adds Costa Botes; 'he hoards things, but, as much as anything else, he hoards memories.'

Philippa agrees: 'He certainly values the past. I think he values every little bit of it and he takes the past with him, wherever he goes. It's always with him: all those memories of what was obviously a wonderful, charmed childhood, and all his hobbies and passions and the way in which they inspired and shaped his life.'

Talking to me once about his early years, Peter spoke of the workshop, which he constructed with his father at the family home in Pukerua Bay: a basement room dug out under the house. This was where he made his models and built most of the props and effects for *Bad Taste*. 'When I left home,' he said, 'I literally shut the door and it's just sitting there, exactly as it was when I was a kid. My childhood is locked away in that basement...'

Like a lot of creative artists, treasuring the past is about respecting the foundations on which the present stands and the future is built.

> I often think it's been a very curious journey. When I think back, look back at photos, occasionally see the old films I've made on TV, I have flashbacks from the past. But it is strange because when it is you, you don't really feel different.
>
> On one level, I think I'm exactly the same person who made those little Super 8 movies as a youngster but at the same time I've learnt a huge amount and gained a vast amount of experience in all manner of things: cameras, lenses, actors, studios, budgets, Hollywood politics, every conceivable part of film-making.
>
> I'm still the same guy, but I'm in a different world with all this stuff I've picked up along the way. Some people might say that all the experiences of life change you but I don't feel that. I'm more worldly wise and understand more, but my heart hasn't changed – I'm the same person, but I've learnt a lot.

'I'm constantly amazed at how little his process has changed,' says Costa Botes. 'Knowing him for a period of time and having seen him work on various films, I don't see a lot that's different other than that now he has the means at his disposal to do what he wished he could have always done: he can now do numerous takes and employ expensive technologies. Of course, he's always been *aware* of those technologies; it was just that, in the past, he wasn't able to use them, he simply used what came to hand – he improvised and adapted, made things work for him.'

Richard Taylor reflects: 'When we met him, he was actively making things for himself; making the world around him. He'd chosen that he was going to be successful and so he was generating that opportunity for himself. He wasn't waiting for others to give it to him.' And, observes Ray Battersby, one of Peter's former colleagues on the *Dominion Post*, 'Peter forged his own luck. Things came to him or he *made* them come to him. And then, equally importantly, he *secured* them; grabbing what was passing by and locking it down.'

'Pete's blessing,' says Costa, 'is that he has the kind of talent that has this straight line to an idea, which he can bring out as cleanly as possible and develop it with as determined and dogged a vision as possible. Then, because the ideas are good, they generate their own luck and create their own kind of good circumstances.'

The strength of those ideas is that they represent the quintessence of story. Philippa Boyens says, 'Peter doesn't have any pretensions to doing anything other than telling a story really well. Although he could mix it with the best if you wanted to start deconstructing theories on film-making, that's not his approach: he just wants to tell a story.'

And, in the process of telling those stories, he relies on using the collaborative nature of the film-maker's craft to its fullest potential, as Costa explains: 'He may have had an idea in his head for years; he's imagined it as best he can and then somebody else comes along who is really good at what *they* do – it might be an actor or a lead animator – and that person takes what he's got and makes it better. That's what turns him on! Pete never imposes the selfish limits a lot of directors enforce: "I've imagined it, I've drawn it up on my storyboard and there's no room for you to come in and change it, because I want it exactly how I want it!" He's not like that. He does what truly *great* directors do: no matter how well he has it worked out he always leaves room for other people to bring their imagination into the process.'

Nevertheless, throughout Peter's career there have been those who have underestimated Peter Jackson. Peter's response has always been to vindicate himself, to make the doubters reevaluate his talents and abilities. Even now, after all his achievements and successes, there is still a danger of underestimating him, of supposing that it is possible to second-guess what he will do next or how he will do it.

Talk to him tomorrow and who know what will be exciting him; but talk to him today and he's already thinking not just in terms of new projects but of new directions.

There are films, of course, but I also want to be able to explore new directions. I've all sorts of ideas: I've ideas for a TV mini-series and I've ideas for video games.

I am getting increasingly interested in games, and the potential of what games *could be*... Part of this interest comes from having a son with whom I play video games in a way that I never used to a few years ago. Also, with a new generation of powerful gaming platforms – PlayStation 3 and Xbox 2 – the technology employed in video games is expanding and I am intrigued by the way in which films are almost merging with games. I'm interested in exploring the development of a new entertainment form that is a fusion of films and games in a way that neither of them are at the moment.

I'm talking about something that is not a traditional computer game such as you can buy now, and is not a conventional film either, but is a move towards a truly interactive film, one which has all the emotional impact that a good film should have and all the characterisations and the plot twists, turns and surprises, and yet is one in which you are a participant and a character within the body of the film; an experience in which, in some way, you can control that character's destiny.

I really believe that such a form of entertainment is on the horizon and it could be something that will be a fun and interesting extension of what we currently think of as films.

Just as Spielberg, Lucas, Zemeckis and others have done, Peter – by virtue of his success and reputation – may well want to find opportunities to take on the enabling, guiding role of a producer. 'I can see Pete moving more and more into a position where he can be nurturing and shepherding along aspiring film-makers,' says Costa Botes, 'because he will be excited about and will want to *see* the kinds of movies that the next generation of film-makers are going to make.'

If he does, he will have plenty of advice – inspiring and sanguinary – to pass on.

Carl Denham, the maverick whose wild vision for bringing the marvellous and mysterious to the movie screen sends him to Skull Island, has a telling line in the script of the Jackson version of *King Kong*. 'Here's the thing you need to decide,' he says, 'are you afraid or are you a film-maker...'

Certainly, you can't allow yourself to be crippled by fear. You've just got to go for it. I mean, you've got to be afraid, because I think that fear is ultimately not a bad motivator. I think making decisions and being driven by fear is actually a healthy thing: the fear of failure, the fear of disappointment, the fear that you're going to make a film that no one wants to see.

I wouldn't necessarily put it quite like Denham, but what you must never do is to allow yourself to be paralysed by fear. You have to harness it and use it in order to get the best results that you can. Fear – or a little fear! – is ultimately a good thing; there's nothing wrong with it at all.

I still have fears. Absolutely. I'm completely terrified of making a bad film. That doesn't change at all. We all know, from seeing other people's films, that feeling of having looked forward to a movie and coming away disappointed because the picture didn't deliver, or wasn't as good as you thought it would be. I don't want people to have expectations when they go the cinema that, somehow, I don't manage to fulfil or, at least, come close to fulfilling.

I never want that to happen, and thinking that it *might* happen is the fear that keeps me striving for the best.

Assessing the man who gave New Line Cinema a trilogy of movie hits, Bob Shaye says of Peter: 'He has a very specific vision for his life and career that isn't typical in this industry. He's looked into the future and wondered what would happen "If…" He's now living that "If…" and it works really well for him.'

To some degree, I feel that everything I ever dreamed of achieving when I was young, I have now achieved.

And so, rather than that being a disappointment or a negative thing, it is actually a huge relief. I've got to where I am now, and I've won an Oscar and had films that have done really good box-office business and I've achieved a personal ambition, which was to remake *King Kong*, something I've wanted to do ever since I was 9 years old.

It feels like a great weight off my shoulders. I have absolutely no interest in trying to beat myself, in the sense of having to try to make every film bigger and better than *The Lord of the Rings*, because it probably never will be in terms of its accolades and financial rewards. I've done that. And I don't have to strive to win an Oscar any more. I've done that, too.

I don't have any interest in doing that or in striving to do anything other than make entertaining films about things that interest me and appeal to me; good movies that don't disappoint moviegoers. That will always be hard, because with any film you make, it is going to be a challenge, but it's what I will go on trying to do.

I have no wish or interest in being in competition with Peter Jackson for the second half of my life.

* * *

A final memory from the day that was the last 'official' wrap on *The Lord of the Rings*:

'Okay, let's go…'

For maybe the sixth or seventh time, the hideous Gothmog towers over the prone Madril. John Bach, waiting for the *coup de grace*, looks up at Lawrence Makoare – or what little of Lawrence is visible beneath the mountainous prosthetics.

'It's tough work,' says Peter. 'Some actors would drown under all that make-up. You really have to pump it out – and yet not overdo it! It's all in the eyes.'

Peter gives a note to Robert Pollock, the hook-nosed Orc. 'You look up to Gothmog; he's your leader; you admire and respect him… When he says, "the time of the Orc has come," try looking around at the scene: remember – *this is a proud day for Orcland!* Okay, then… *Last one for luck…*'

And it's a wrap.

It's another Jackson milestone marked by a few emotional ad hoc speeches. Sound recordist, Hammond Peek, thanks Peter on behalf of the crew for his generosity, his ability to draw out the best from people and, 'For bringing Hollywood to New Zealand – but strictly on your own terms!'

Peter responds: 'Unlike the actors who I will very possibly never see again, this is not really goodbye: because I hope we'll be working together again and we've still got some shots to get done next week!

Meanwhile, a huge "Thank you." I needed people who'd never worked on a film as vast as this... You've all risen to the challenge. You can all feel incredibly proud of yourselves! Well done! I couldn't have done this alone...'

There's a pause, and then he adds, '*I just want to do it again!*'

ACKNOWLEDGEMENTS

To write the official biography of a living subject, obviously requires the subject's approval and I have been fortunate firstly in having Peter Jackson's confidence in my ability to write his story and his full co-operation throughout the process. The pages of this book are a testimony to Peter's willingness to discuss his life and career with characteristic candour.

Peter was also insistent that I should interview others who have known and worked with him across the years and I am deeply indebted to the following who (whether or not they appear by name or are quoted in these pages) have helped shape my perception and understanding of Peter Jackson and, in turn, the telling of his story: Sean Astin, Tim Balme, Ray Battersby, Sean Bean, Orlando Bloom, Richard Bluck, Alun Bollinger, Costa Botes, Billy Boyd, Philippa Boyens, Adrien Brody, Jed Brophy, Bryce Campbell, Erica Challis, Cameron Chittock, Randy Cook, Carolynne Cunningham, Ngila Dickson, Alex Funke, David Gascoigne, Ken Hammon, Ruth Harley, Chris Hennah, Dan Hennah, Tony Hiles, Bernard Hill, Ian Holm, Mike Horton, John Howe, Mladen Ivancic, Ken Kamins, Marty Katz, Peter King, Alan Lee, Christopher Lee, Andrew Lesnie, Rob Lewis, Michael Lynne, Mary Maclachlan, Ian McKellen, Grant Major, Murray Milne, Mike Minett, Dominic Monaghan, Viggo Mortensen, Danny Mulheron, Peter Nelson, Pete O'Herne, Mark Ordesky, Barrie Osborne, Miranda Otto, Peter Owen, Mary Parent, Hammond Peek, Rick Porras, George Port, Terry Potter, Chris Prowse, John Rhys-Davies, Christian Rivers, Tania Rodger, Sue Rogers, David J. Schow, Chuck Schuman, Michelle Scullion, Jamie Selkirk, Andy Serkis, Kiran

Shah, Bob Shaye, Lindsay Shelton, Howard Shore, Chris Short, Stephen Sinclair, Craig Smith, Richard Taylor, Liv Tyler, Karl Urban, Pierre Vinet, Fran Walsh, Marty Walsh, Hugo Weaving, David Wenham and Elijah Wood.

I am also grateful for assorted assistance and kindnesses to Gino Acevedo, Dan Arden, Mark Burman, Robert Catto, Rose Dority, Joseph D'Morais, David Drummond, Colin Duriez, Lisa Farqhuar, Nick Grant of *OnFilm*, 'Hamish' of The Ultimate Bad Taste Site, Richard Holliss, Belindalee Hope, Jeff Kurtti, 'Lewman' of The Bastards Have Landed, Tracie Lorie, Ian Mackersey, Leonard Maltin, Kevin Miller, Sandra Murray, Carter Nixon, Michael Pellerin, Malcolm Prince, Gareth Shannon, Debbie Smith, John Ward and Norman Wright.

Special thanks go to Jan Blenkin, Matthew Dravitzki and Josie Leckie at WingNut Films; Sue Yates, formerly at the New Zealand Film Archive, for vigorous and determined help with research into Peter Jackson's early films; and to Linda Klein Nixon, Jill Crouch and Barbara Boyce for their painstaking transcription of interviews.

I am particularly grateful to David Brawn at HarperCollins for unstinting support and unfailing good humour throughout the three years during which this book slowly found its way to completion; to my industrious editor, Chris Smith, for his tireless attention to detail in dealing with a text that was repeatedly being passed halfway round the world and back; to my good friends, Ian Smith and Jane Johnson, for support, above and beyond the call of friendship; and, finally, to my agent, Vivien Green, and my partner, David Weeks, without whose ceaseless advice, help and encouragement, I would undoubtedly never have completed this journey.

INDEX